U. of Wisconsin 901 (Swearingen)

0.12

A PREFACE TO MODERN NIGERIA

A Preface
to Modern Nigeria

The "Sierra Leonians"
in Yoruba, 1830-1890

JEAN HERSKOVITS KOPYTOFF

The University of Wisconsin Press
Madison, Milwaukee, and London, 1965

for MJH *and* FSH

Published by
The University of Wisconsin Press
Madison and Milwaukee
Box 1379, Madison, Wisconsin 53701

Copyright © 1965 by the
Regents of the University of Wisconsin

Printed in the United States of America by
North Central Publishing Co., St. Paul, Minnesota

Library of Congress Catalog Card Number 65-24184

PREFACE

T HIS study is an attempt to clarify an episode of West African history in the nineteenth century which has played a many faceted part in shaping modern Nigeria and which, both at the time and more recently, has had oversimplified and stereotyped interpretations.

On the West African coast, the first generations of Africans with any Western education came from one of two principal sources — the captured slave ships, whose human cargoes were released to start a new life in the English colony of Sierra Leone; or the New World, from which they made their way back to their continent of origin. As the century wore on, liberated Africans, especially from Freetown, became prominent in aiding the spread of European influence — direct or indirect; political, religious, or economic — from the Gambia to the Cameroons. From this point of view, the return of liberated Africans (called "Sierra Leonians") to the region later known as Western Nigeria came to be seen as simply a part of the fanning out from Freetown. The evaluation of what these returning Africans accomplished was made in terms of the goals set for them by English ideas of the early nineteenth century. These goals were based on much publicized expectations that given an education in certain Western skills, the liberated Africans would facilitate British penetration, the routine of government, the expansion of trade, and the implantation of Christianity.

But this view, long held and built almost entirely on extrapolations from early English predictions, as opposed to the variety of motives of the emigrants themselves, overlooks the historic coincidence that a large number of these liberated Africans were Yoruba, that those of them who were returning to Western Nigeria had special ties with the peoples of the Lagos hinterland, and were to face a dilemma of conflicting loyalties. When, moreover, on their own initiative they began their migration at the end of the 1830's, they were pursuing goals of their own.

Only when this crucial dimension is left out is it possible to see these early generations of Africans, educated in the English tradition, as having but a single role, that of "Black Englishmen," but a single purpose, that of agents of European interests, and from such a perspective to dismiss them as "poor imitations" and "failures" in fulfilling this role. Such conclusions further assume a singleness of purpose among the liberated Africans at all times, and a single aim for all of them. But, as this study shows, from the 1840's, when the return to Yorubaland began, and on through the turmoil of the rest of the century, with its different landmarks for different peoples, the emigrants can sometimes be understood only as individuals, sometimes as several groups with identical interests in some cases and conflicting ones in others, and sometimes — and that least often — as a homogeneous group.

Seen in its complexities, then, this return of the liberated Africans is as much African history in Nigeria as it is a part of the history of the English presence there. The emigrants' understanding of the diverse and often divergent Yoruba goals, and their loyalties to the different Yoruba groups in fact make their role, if one must see only a single one, at the least a temporary success. And this aspect of success is significant for the very reasons that Western eyes saw it as a failure, especially at the turn of the century when such an interpretation was in consonance with the views of the day about African capabilities.

For clearly the historian who uses such terms as "success" or "failure" in his analysis must go a step beyond and ask, "success for whom?" "failure for whom?" It is this step which, for all its apparent simplicity, is fundamental to what has been called "the new African history." And in line with it, this study seeks not to redress an earlier imbalance with a view equally unbalanced, but to carry out for this period and problem in Nigerian history the modern historian's familiar task of trying to understand events as nearly as possible in their total setting.

The book is divided into parts. Each of the first three covers a major chronological period in the study: the first goes through the

emigrants' experiences in Sierra Leone and their return to Yoruba
country; the second focuses on the penetration of British influence
around Lagos through the consular period; the third spans the
years from the creation of Lagos as a colony to the last decades of
the nineteenth century. In each part, the first chapter gives the
wider context in which the emigrant roles in the succeeding chapters must be seen.

The final part is the overview of the place of the emigrants in
Lagos and its hinterland in the nineteenth century. For within the
first three parts, my analysis deals separately with broad spheres
of activity commonly differentiated in historical works as political,
economic, and religious. I have made these differentiations for
clarity, despite my awareness that they are more precise in a European than in an African cultural context. The depth of treatment
of each segment in these parts has rested, as it must, on the materials available. For example, not in written records, nor for that
matter in oral evidence, can one find the detailed information on
the attitudes and actions and positions of liberated African traders,
especially the small traders, comparable to what is available on
African mission agents.

Partly because these strands have nonetheless been considered
separately, and partly because of the numerous personalities active
in more than one of them, it has seemed more advisable to present
the biographical material in integrated sketches, in Appendix A,
than to scatter it through the text. A further reason for this choice
comes from the unevenness of the information available about
these men and women. This unevenness, like that in the sources
for other aspects of this study, is not random. There are accounts
in some detail of the lives of even minor mission agents; there are
no such accounts of the lives of many major traders. There are
records for some minor Lagos government officials; there are none
for some men of greater influence who exercised that influence
through traditional channels. To incorporate the data where full,
then, would inevitably be to stress certain men over others in a
misleading way.

The study ends in the early 1890's. This terminal date has been
chosen because it marks the end of conditions permitting special
roles for Sierra Leonians and their descendants. The end came for

diverse reasons: wider use of quinine permitted the "Europeaniza-tion" of positions previously held by Africans, and the new racist views growing in Europe encouraged it. From the African side, the British policy of annexation destroyed the context in which the emigrants had played their parts.

A few words on terminology are necessary. To eliminate confu-sion between the text and quotations from the period, contempo-raneous usage and spelling of Yoruba names have been retained. For example, the Sierra Leonians and Brazilians returning to Lagos, though technically immigrants, are called emigrants, as they were in the nineteenth century. Similarly, the term "polyg-amy" has been used instead of the technically correct "polygyny." The liberated Africans are referred to in several other ways: when discussed in Sierra Leone, as recaptives or as Aku; when back in Yoruba country, as emigrants and, occasionally, as Saro for Sierra Leonians or Amaro for Brazilians. The word "creole" does not appear, primarily because it was not applied to the liberated Afri-cans in Lagos or its hinterland. Further, use of the word would create confusion with the creoles of Sierra Leone itself who played their own role there; in addition, it might suggest connotations, wrong in this case, of the term in its New World context of mixed racial ancestry. It is further important to note that, while in the nineteenth century the term "Yoruba" was applied only to men and women from Oyo, the word is used here, when not otherwise stated, in its modern wider sense.

Finally, all the quotations from nineteenth-century documents are unchanged and *sic* has not been used in places of awkward construction or misspelling. In quotations from non-English sources, the translations are my own.

A study such as this, which examines a West African problem from the several points of view of those who took part in it, re-quires access to materials of diverse natures and in varied locations. I am, therefore, indebted to many more than I can name, in Eng-land and in West Africa, who helped me to obtain the information I have used.

I am grateful to the Keepers of the Records, and particularly to the staff of the Public Record Office in London and at the Ashridge Repository, for the assistance they have given me. I am similarly much indebted to Mr. Louis Frewer, Librarian, and his staff at Rhodes House, Oxford; to the archivists at the Church Missionary Society and the Wesleyan Methodist Missionary Society in London; and to librarian of the Royal Commonwealth Society, where I was permitted to read the papers of Sir John Hawley Glover.

West African sources consisted of both archival and oral evidence. I am deeply grateful to Professor K. O. Diké for guiding my research in Nigeria in 1958 and for permission to consult the archives there. Mr. L. Gwam and the staff of the Nigerian Record Office in Ibadan and Enugu were most helpful. Of further assistance were officials at the Lands Office and the Secretariat of the Nigerian Federal Government in Lagos. I was, in addition, enabled to consult the Ghana National Archives in Accra, and the Sierra Leone Archives at Fourah Bay College, Freetown.

The late Mrs. Jessica Otonba Payne generously made available the papers and library of her late husband, John A. Otonba Payne, and gave me much valuable information. My particular thanks are due to Mrs. Henrietta Olaitan Lawson, Chief Akin Deko, and the many others in Lagos, Abeokuta, and Ibadan, who discussed with me their recollections and interpretations of the traditional history, or who helped me to meet the men and women from whom this information could be obtained. I am indebted to Sir M. Bank-Anthony for introducing me to the late *Oba* of Lagos. I further wish to acknowledge the kindness of Dr. T. O. Elias for making available to me a personal copy of Herbert Macaulay's unpublished memoirs.

None of this research would have been possible without the financial assistance of the Lucretia Mott Fellowship Committee of Swarthmore College; the Nigerian Institute for Social and Economic Research, Ibadan, whose grant of a bursary made possible my going to West Africa in 1958; and the Ford Foundation, whose award of a Foreign Area Training Fellowship permitted the completion of this research and the writing up of its results. Mrs. E. M. Chilver, then director of the Institute of Commonwealth Studies, Oxford, provided me with facilities in which to work up my material and added to this kindness her perceptive comments in talking over West African questions with me. I am also indebted to the

Faculty Research Committee of Swarthmore College for their financial aid in the preparation of this present manuscript.

After the study's completion as a thesis, I profited greatly from the comments of Dr. J. F. Ade Ajayi, Dr. A. A. B. Aderibigbe, Dr. Jeffrey Butler, and Mr. Peter Marris, and from the suggestions and comparative material from Sierra Leone of Dr. John Peterson. I am deeply grateful to Dr. Igor Kopytoff for his critical reading of the manuscript and his advice. Professor Philip D. Curtin, my first teacher in African history, has exerted a continuing influence on my research interests and has been generous in his advice on the preparation of this volume.

To my supervisor at Oxford, Professor Kenneth Kirkwood, who showed the confidence in my projected study to allow me the freest of opportunities to plan and carry out my research, I am very grateful. Mr. Thomas Hodgkin gave of his friendship and was always willing to talk to a student about common interests. I appreciate equally the stimulation of other senior members of the University. Dr. C. J. Gertzel, then also a student at Oxford, generously gave me several pertinent quotations from papers to which she alone had access.

Finally, I wish to thank the Cartographic Laboratory of the University of Wisconsin, who are responsible for preparing the maps in this book.

JEAN HERSKOVITS KOPYTOFF

Swarthmore, Pennsylvania
May 20, 1963

CONTENTS

LIST OF MAPS

Part I

1800-1845

THE WEST AFRICAN SETTING

A T the end of the rains on a day toward the close of the year 1839, what seemed to be a slave ship sailed into the roads of Badagry, then a major port serving what would later become western Nigeria. The ship was in fact a condemned slaver, converted for legitimate coastal trade, and from it men and women disembarked into small boats, which took them to the shore from the sand bar, toward a land that had once been their home.

These men and women were liberated slaves, primarily of Yoruba origin. They had been through war, capture, sale, embarkation on slavers, interception by ships of the British fleet, and subsequent liberation at Sierra Leone, the British base of operations against the slave trade on the West African coast. They had, as we shall see, been resettled there and exposed to selected European religious, educational, and economic practices. Later, when they made their way back to Lagos and other cities in what is now Nigeria, they were joined by compatriots from Freetown and returning Yoruba from the New World — chiefly Brazil and Cuba — to become the protagonists in the closing chapters of the story of the West African slave trade and its aftermath.

BRITISH PLANS FOR THE SIERRA LEONIAN ROLE

Throughout the early years of the colony of Sierra Leone, and especially after the 1830's, a new idea, centered on the liberated Africans, began to develop in the minds of colonial officials, missionaries, and traders concerned with the West Coast of Africa. This idea, in simplest terms, called for British enterprise — governmental, religious, economic — to employ liberated Africans. Educated to understand the important aspects and values of British life, they were to carry these ideas and facilitate their introduction among the peoples related to them throughout the West African hinterland. Bringing "civilization" and Christianity to the coast

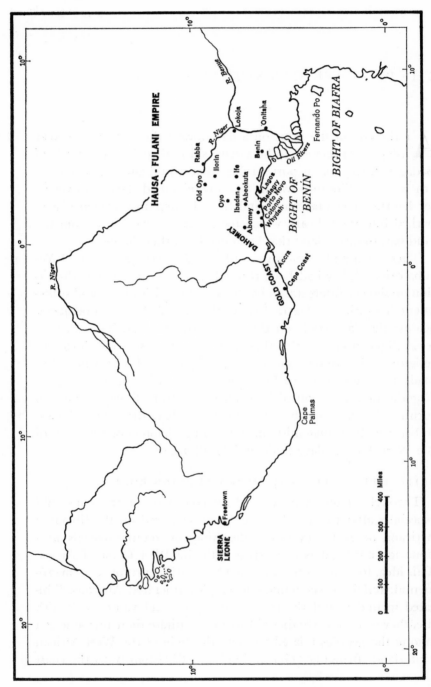

The West Coast of Africa, showing major places referred to in the text.

had always been a stated goal of those humanitarians and Evangelicals who originally conceived of the colony in Sierra Leone. Growing with and out of the Evangelical movement had been the new missionary societies, started in England and Scotland in the 1790's. The most prominent were the London Missionary Society, which concentrated its efforts in South Africa, and the Church Missionary Society, technically named "the Society for Missions to Africa and the East," founded in 1799. Among those formulating plans for the CMS were prominent members of the Sierra Leone Company, which had been responsible for the colony prior to its control by British government. And the role of the CMS in Sierra Leone and elsewhere on the coast was to be a large one.

The progress made in Sierra Leone itself through the government and the CMS in the first decades of the century was thought commendable in England, but Sierra Leone was not enough; not even its hinterland was enough. For despite the action of the Preventive Squadron, the export of slaves from western Africa was far greater than it had been at the time of the abolition of the trade.

The clear need to extend European influence and to enlist African co-operation along the coast in suppressing the traffic sent interested Englishmen in search of new answers. It was Sir Thomas Fowell Buxton who first enunciated a plan to an audience that would listen to him. *The African Slave Trade and Its Remedy*, proposing in 1839 treaties with local chiefs to end the slave trade and the encouragement of legitimate commerce to replace it, did not make startling new suggestions. Governors of Sierra Leone in the 1820's and 1830's had wanted to try the first step, usually only to be rebuffed by the Colonial Office, ever fearful of further involvements. And Liverpool traders who were making their own efforts elsewhere, especially in the Niger, did not greet Buxton's new suggestion — that legitimate trade receive active government support — with enthusiasm, though they wanted government protection.

But Buxton was sufficiently prominent a figure for both the public and the Cabinet to be willing to listen to him, and he had strong missionary support. Though his proposal was not unopposed, both within the Colonial Office and outside it, the government was convinced. New instructions were sent to governors for the making of treaties, and preparations began for the 1841 Niger Expedition, the first organized venture of "the Bible and the Plough."

This change in policy favored a mediating role for freed slaves — the idea which earlier had only tentatively been explored, first in government circles by Zachary Macaulay in 1807.[1] In his advice on measures to take when Sierra Leone became a colony, Macaulay suggested that captured slaves be landed there, where they might work as free labor, enlist in the West Indian regiments, or be returned to their original homes.[2]

The next elaboration came from the missionaries. In 1816, the CMS decided that the difficult conditions in the hinterland of Sierra Leone, combined with the continuing influx of liberated Africans into the colony itself, called for a change of emphasis in the Society's activities, until then located outside the boundaries of the colony.[3] Encouraged by the government to concentrate their efforts upon the "miserable although rescued Negroes,"[4] the CMS in 1816 sent out from England Edward Bickersteth, one of its agents, to investigate.

Bickersteth came back to England full of possibilities of Sierra Leone. The recaptured slaves, in thousands, from many tribes and nations, and of many languages, were being clothed and provided for by the Government. But Christian teaching and influence were sorely needed; and what an opening was thus presented for raising up . . . Native Christians who should themselves in after years carry the Gospel to the interior, it might be to the very countries from which they had been stolen![5]

At the same time that Bickersteth's report was being considered in London, the governor of Sierra Leone was writing in a despatch that in his opinion, "a part of the Captured Negroes might be usefully disposed of both for themselves and the Mother Country in forming Settlements in our Possessions in the Gambia and on the leeward Coast."[6]

The same idea also came, though later, to those interested in trade and its "civilizing effects." A quotation from Oldfield, who had accompanied Macgregor Laird on an exploratory expedition

to the Niger[7] and joined him in publishing descriptions and proposals in 1837, is typical of this view:

I would propose, in the first place, to establish at every British station extensive schools for rearing native teachers, combining with mental and moral
cultivation, instruction in agriculture and the mechanical arts. Supposing
seven, or even ten years, spent in educating five or six thousand of these
African youths, brought from all parts of the continent, they would then
return to their homes with the habits and manners of Europeans so indelibly
impressed upon them, that they would raise the character of their friends and
relatives to their own standard, instead of sinking to theirs; at least the
children of these men would be superior in mental capacity to the children
of those who never had the advantage of education. Amongst the number,
some would, doubtless, leave their fellows far behind; these should be encouraged in every way, — finish their education in England, be brought forward as medical men, or civil and mechanical engineers, and be taken into
the British service. These men, with British habits and education grafted
upon their African constitutions, would become our pioneers throughout
Africa, and raise the emulation of their brethren by showing them that
ability, though covered with a black skin, was appreciated and rewarded.[8]

What Oldfield did not realize, though others did, was that
Sierra Leone already had the beginnings of a supply of such "pioneers." For here were the liberated Africans who had had and
were continuing to have contact with European religion, ideas,
techniques, and way of life. Grateful to their liberators for their
freedom, and, it was assumed, for showing them the way to a
better existence than they had ever known, they could be counted
on to exert the necessary influence. What better instrument could
be found to promote English goals in West Africa, in whatever
field, than these men who could return to their kinsmen both as
emissaries and as living examples of the advantages of the western
way of life? They would be the catalytic force in making contact
with the tribal people and, in time, would persuade the traditional
authorities to support English proposals and, later, to adopt English ways themselves.

In his plans for the Niger Expedition in 1841 Buxton did, in
fact, include trained liberated Africans as missionaries and
teachers, though in his book he had suggested West Indians as
the potential instructors.[9] Of those chosen, the most prominent
was Samuel Ajayi Crowther, later to become bishop of the Niger,

the CMS's earliest and foremost example of the potential to be found in the liberated Africans.

From Sierra Leone's Governor Doherty there had also come repeated praise for the liberated residents of the colony, and it helped to fan enthusiasm for the idea of their intermediary role. This enthusiasm grew throughout the 1840's and 1850's, as shown in the statements of Henry Venn, secretary of the CMS; of Macgregor Laird, prominent promoter of legitimate trade on the Niger; and of various colonial officials. A basic conservatism, however, deferred the full implementation of this scheme until the theory had already been tested. And, significantly, the test came on the initiative of the liberated Africans themselves who, from 1838 on, began their emigration to the Lagos area.

These Sierra Leonian emigrants were returning to the land of their origin. They came from the various sub-groups of the people now collectively known as the Yoruba of the western part of what has since become Nigeria. Thus the role planned for them by the British was perforce to be played by actors whose cultural past lay in the very land to which they were coming and among people who were their kinsmen. Capture, enslavement, liberation, and resettlement in Sierra Leone — these experiences were grafted on to an earlier way of life which must be considered, and which lies in the history of Yorubaland in the early decades of the nineteenth century.

THE YORUBA CULTURAL BACKGROUND OF THE EMIGRANTS

Through the eighteenth century, the various Yoruba peoples were united into the large and powerful empire of Old Oyo. There are no figures on which to base estimates of the population that this empire embraced; it must, nevertheless, have been considerable since the present-day Yoruba number close to ten million. All these groups had many cultural similarities. While their economy was based on farming, it went well beyond subsistence. Crafts were highly developed, as was trade, carried on actively by both men and women. Almost unique in West Africa was the presence of large settlements and towns, with populations in the thousands. Other features of cultural unity lay in closely related languages, in shared myths of origins, in basic religious beliefs and rituals, and in social organization.

The primary kinship group among the Yoruba was the patrilineal lineage—kinsmen bound together by common paternal descent from an ancestor several generations back. It operated as a social and economic unit, holding its farm and town land in common, often specializing in the same craft, and living together in one compound or in several clustered ones. The lineage was usually headed by the oldest man within it, that is, by the one who stood closest to the ancestors as head of the ancestral cult. Through a process of adopting members from other lineages and incorporating slaves—an aspect of what was later called "domestic slavery" by Europeans—the size of the lineage could increase. From time to time, a lineage gave rise to new ones, as when it grew too large or when internal dissensions led a segment of close kinsmen within it to leave and settle elsewhere as an independent group. Such segments sometimes founded new settlements.

Politically the Yoruba were divided into a number of states or, as they are sometimes called, kingdoms. Each had a capital town with its king (oba), the other towns, with their own chiefs, being subordinate to it. Though these kingdoms were not alike in their political structure, a certain overall pattern existed. The Yoruba lineage organization was reflected in the way towns and states were governed, but with significant modifications. A king and a council of titled chiefs ruled in the capital; a head chief and a council similarly ruled in subordinate towns. Kingship was vested in the royal lineage; the chieftaincy of a town was restricted in the same way to the lineage that founded it; and each titled chieftaincy on the councils also belonged to a particular lineage. But within this hereditary pattern there was considerable room for flexibility and political maneuver, since the occupant of each of these positions was elected from among several candidates in the appropriate lineage. When the lineage was large and composed of several segments, there could be more than one strong claimant to the position of king or titled chief. Sometimes these opposing claims were resolved by having a title rotate, but competition and clashes over succession were always potentially present.

Other titled positions further counterbalanced the modified use of the lineage principle in government. In addition to the king and lineage representatives, the councils contained other members who represented various associations, such as age-grades, trading interests, and secret societies, whose political and police powers often gave them a pivotal role in Yoruba life. In connection with their formal purposes, all these societies had religious overtones, with rituals of initiation and periodic ceremonies. These, in turn, complemented the other major force in Yoruba life—the traditional religion of great complexity, both in theology and organization, with its many cults of deities, ancestors, and nature spirits. The pervasiveness of religion in Yoruba life made separation between the secular and the religious difficult, an obvious problem for returning Christian Yoruba.

Ideally, Yoruba government, combining civil and religious functions, rested on a coalition of the several groups of Yoruba society with their many different interests. Within this overall pattern of organization, however, the relative power of these groups in the government differed from town to town and from state to state. Moreover, these systems were not immune to changes through time. Thus in some states, most notably among the Egba, associations and secret societies became the dominant political forces in the nineteenth century.

This, then, was the background from which the Sierra Leonian emigrants had come and the context to which they were returning. Here, after their new experiences and with their own goals as well as those of their British Christian sponsors, they had to find a place for themselves. Further, during their absence history had not stood still. The Yorubaland they were coming back to was not quite the Yorubaland they had left.

YORUBALAND IN THE
NINETEENTH CENTURY AND THE RISE OF LAGOS

The relatively delicate balance of interests that characterized Yoruba towns and states was also a feature of the relations among the different Yoruba states. In the eighteenth century, they were united into the Old Oyo Empire, a confederation whose members owed common allegiance to the kingdom of Oyo but were autonomous in internal matters. At the height of its power toward the end of the century, the Empire's domain reached from the Niger to western Dahomey.

By the early decades of the nineteenth century, however, the Empire was disintegrating. The break up of Old Oyo was a measure of the confederation's brittleness, for the dissolution was, at least in part, due to internal dissensions. But it was also, and more dramatically, the result of increasing pressure from the northern neighbors of the Yoruba, the Fulani, who were bent on adding to their conquests.

These pressures from the north were African, but they coincided with new pressures from the south, and in this case of European origin. Charged with putting an end to the slave trade, the British Preventive Squadron was plying the West African coast; yet its presence, paradoxically, brought not an end to European slave trading but rather more intensive slaving from the less frequented and hence less well patrolled ports. As a result, new places came into prominence: Lagos and neighboring Badagry had grown as centers of the trade, simultaneously profiting from the disruption and civil wars in the north and the supply of slaves that this generated, and from the activities elsewhere of the British fleet, which gave them new importance as suppliers for the Atlantic slave trade. Thus for the returning Sierra Leonians the position of Lagos was paramount from the beginning.

The precise relations during the eighteenth century between Lagos and the Yoruba are difficult to determine, probably because contact was slight. For Lagos, the focus of events in Yoruba country after the mid-nineteenth century, rose to importance by a series of historical accidents, and earlier was of little significance in the momentous events taking place farther to the north.

Settlement in the vicinity of Lagos can be dated approximately from the end of the sixteenth century.[10] The earliest inhabitants appear to have been Yoruba, or Yoruba who merged with an autochthonous stock. At the end of the seventeenth century, the Kingdom of Benin to the east established suzerainty over Lagos, with the likely infusion of Bini into the ruling house as well as the population of the island and the surrounding land it controlled. Whatever the composition of the people and rulers, the

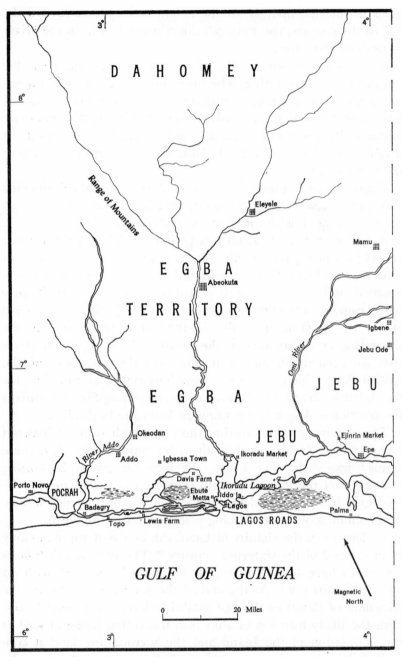

Yoruba Country in 1886, reproduced, reduced, and simplified from "Route Survey through Yoruba Country by Harbour Master William C. Speeding, who Accompanied the special commissioners H. Higgins and O. Smith from

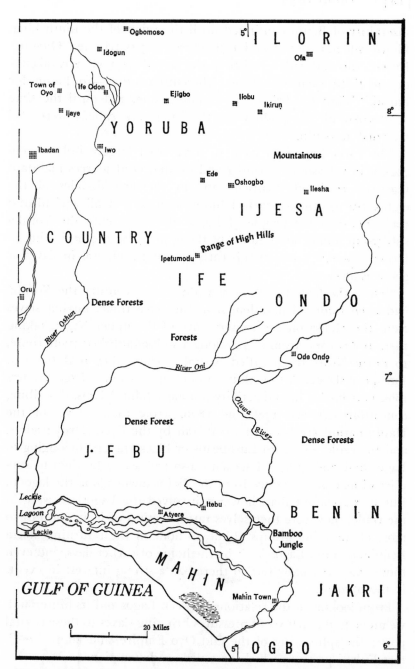

the govt. of Lagos to tribes interior of Lagos, between 17th August and 10th November 1886." PP 1887. LX (167).

suzerainty of Benin continued until the reign of the ninth king, Idewu, when, about 1830, Lagos refused to pay tribute. "Ologun" Kutere, the sixth ruler, had been the last whose body was taken — in the third quarter of the eighteenth century — to Benin for burial.[11] Thus the break was a gradual one, and until the time of Kosoko in 1845, *Obas* (as the kings are called) were still crowned at Benin.

The early Lagosians seem to have been largely isolated, engaging in subsistence farming and fishing. Oral sources maintain that the reign of Akinsemoyin — in the first decades of the eighteenth century — marked the growth of a small agricultural trade between the people of Lagos and the Ijebu, the Yoruba sub-group immediately north of them, and also the beginning of foreign trade.[12] Whether this early external trade was in slaves or goods is unknown.

Before the first decade of the nineteenth century the Yoruba had been informal middlemen in the slave trade, buying slaves from the Hausa on the western fork of the upper Niger, taking them to Oyo and from there, along a well-established trade route, to Porto Novo (then called Ardrah), where they sold them to European slavers. Although it is not clear how much Lagos traders took part in this inland activity, Captain John Adams, describing conditions between 1786 and 1800, wrote that, "slaves of the Hausa nation are brought to Ardrah by the Eyeo [Oyo] traders, and then sold, either to Europeans or black traders, belonging to Lagos and Badagry."[13] Lagosians also had access by then to supplies of men and produce from the Ijebu towns along the lagoon. But it is apparent that, however involved the Lagosians were in the trade, they were themselves rarely victims of it, in contrast to most of the other groups. Thus, to none of the returning Sierra Leonians would Lagos itself be the home of earlier days, and even those who eventually settled there had a strong interest in events in the interior.

From looking at the relations between Lagos and its hinterland, we move to the first set of pressures bringing slaves to these coastal ports: the splintering of the Old Oyo Empire, and later, the direct Fulani pressure which hastened its destruction.

Old Oyo, the capital of the Yoruba Empire located some fifty miles northwest of Ilorin, did not fall to the Fulani until 1835; [14] but the *Alafin*, that is, the ruler, had already been stripped of power and prestige through internal usurpations and distortions of delegated control. The constituent peoples of the Empire no longer had a strong common allegiance to offset their rivalries. During the unstable period before the founding about 1839 of the second Oyo, some one hundred miles south of the former capital, Yoruba groups had been invading the territory of one another and destroying each other's towns. The political center of gravity moved south, following bands of refugees who took their quarrels with them. The wars among the Oyo, Ife, Owu, Egba, and Ijebu peoples provided slaves from all these groups, led to the founding of new towns, and to alliances and persistent enmities which British naval officers, consuls, and missionaries later found hard to understand and control.

To understand later Sierra Leonian allegiances, it is useful to examine, even if in the briefest outline, this disintegration and the subsequent balance into which Yoruba country was settling at the time of the emigrant return. The first of the Yoruba states to extricate itself from Oyo rule had been the Egba. They had already in the last decades of the eighteenth century secured for themselves an independence which, though still giving them Oyo's protection and aid in their defense against the periodic raids of Dahomey, permitted them free access to trade, chiefly with Badagry, in kola nuts, and brought increased prosperity. But the towns in the Egba forest were only loosely confederated; though the *Alake* was recognized as the supreme judicial power, the towns were not bound to consult his authority, and some totally ignored it.[15] "Civil wars" broke out. The start of the collapse of the Oyo Empire thus coincided with the assertion of autonomy by the individual Egba towns and overt rivalry among them.

Beginning the series of the most disruptive encounters was the so-called Owu War, which started in 1821, and which can be taken as showing the intricate alignments in such conflicts. The *Olowu* of Owu,[16] who controlled a small area near the Egba forest, was held responsible by the authorities at Oyo for the affairs conducted at Apomu Market, an important trading center for the Owu, Oyo, Ife, and Ijebu peoples.[17] The kidnapping of Oyo people, far from home when they traded there, had been frequent. The *Onikoyi* of Ikoyi and the *Kakanfo*, who was from Ogbomosho and who had usurped what remained of the *Alafin's* power, sent word that they expected the *Olowu* to put an end to this practice. In trying to do so, the *Olowu* was forced to destroy several Ife towns; the *Oni* of Ife, incensed at the challenge to his authority and encroachment on his people's property, declared war. Victory went overwhelmingly to the Owu, who were defending their parallel claim to supremacy in the area. Five years later, a trading quarrel between the Owu and the Ijebu led to the destruction of Apomu; [18] there ensued in consequence an alliance between the Ijebu and their suppliers of slaves, the Ife, for both had grievances against Owu.

The Egba, though within a few miles of the fighting, were neutral in this conflict, partly because of animosity toward Owu, and partly, as Biobaku suggests, because of divisive Muslim infiltration instigated by the Fulani.[19] Oyo refugees, fleeing south, joined the Ife-Ijebu alliance, regardless of their common cause with the Owu. After siege and battle, the Ijebu-Ife success was decisive, primarily because of a new factor in Yoruba fighting: guns and gunpowder, to which the Ijebu, being near the coast, had access.[20]

The second major consequence of this war was the destruction of the Egba towns. During the fighting some Egba territory was ravaged; then, when the victorious Ijebu warriors returned to their homes, they took Oyo refugees with them, presumably selling Owu captives as slaves. Soon the new settlers grew restless, raiding and destroying Egba towns on one pretext or another, with the help of others of their countrymen living in a former Egba town farther north. Strife broke out everywhere, and only Ibadan, deserted like all the former Egba towns, remained a distinguishable site. There the Ife, Ijebu, and Oyo armies camped, founding, about 1830, the modern city. The new occupants admitted Egba refugees too; we may presume that those Egba who were allowed to settle were somehow considered friendly, and that those who were not were sold along with other captives by the Ijebu, and probably by the Ife and Oyo as well.

The reasons for the Egba exodus from Ibadan after only a year's

stay are not quite clear. Biobaku attributes it to the Egba realization that they were tolerated only as a ready source of supply for
slave-raids.[21] Samuel Johnson, the emigrant historian, maintains
that quarreling was rife among all the factions in the new town; that
the Egba were ill at ease; and that the specific incident which led
to their departure was the death of an Ife chief, for which the Egba
were held responsible.[22] Tradition records that, after divination,
many Egba left Ibadan under the leadership of Shodeke, the
Seriki; [23] after desultory fighting they managed to found a new
settlement, called Abeokuta, "Under-Stone," beneath an over-
hanging rock later named Olumo. Abeokuta drew in Egba refugees throughout the area; Shodeke welcomed anyone who was
homeless, including a number of Owu, who had regrouped and
were moving toward the sea. Earlier enmity was submerged in
common calamity, and the Owu, like the other groups in Abeokuta, were given a section of the town. Abeokuta became a com-
pact reconstruction of former settlements from the devastated
countryside.

Despite such resettlement, internecine clashes continued
throughout Yorubaland: Abeokuta was trying to gain control
over Egbado country; Modakeke was formed farther north as a
refuge for the increasing number of Oyo people retreating before
the Fulani; tensions grew between the Ife and Oyo people in
Ibadan, then under the rule of the Ife chief, Maye. After a re-
bellion which the combined Egba and Ife forces could not subdue,
Ibadan came under the control of its Oyo inhabitants, who welcomed more and more of their kind until the city was predominantly "Yoruba Proper," as Samuel Johnson calls it.

Simultaneously, the Fulani pressure was being felt in the north.
Confused attempts to expel the invaders failed, and Oyo fell in
1835. The inhabitants fled south and subsequently founded their
new "capital," also called Oyo, a potential rival to Ibadan. Fearing
conflict, the new *Alafin* and his principal chiefs arrived at a "state
policy": they would defend what remained of Yoruba country and
try to regain what had been lost to the Fulani. The *Alafin* was no
longer to take an active part in war; he was authorized to devote
himself to the country's religious and civil problems, entering into
external affairs only in matters of policy and in his negotiating

capacity as head of state. Ibadan was to protect Yoruba towns to the north and northeast and to have control over the Ijesha and Ekiti provinces. Ijaye was to have similar responsibilities and control over the western part of Yorubaland.[24]

But this decentralization of power was not effective in bringing new internal peace. The wars already mentioned — and others, both concurrent and later, too numerous to discuss here — had serious consequences for the region. Fulani victories brought an abundant supply of Oyo slaves, and we can conclude from the conflicts in the south, where victory was never decisive, that the Egba, Ife, Ijebu, and other smaller groups were also heavily represented on the west-bound slave ships.

Further, and of subsequent importance, was the emergence in the 1830's of tentative alliances and rivalries among the new Yoruba units. Already the lines began to be drawn: clearest was the hostility between the Egba and Ibadan peoples. From that base-line were determined, according to self-interest, the positions of the other groups in the area. The Ijebu were as yet uncommitted, though they tended to support Ibadan. It was not till later that emnity between these two allies developed, and the Egba and the Ijebu joined hands. But clearly alignments were tactical and not determined, at this early disrupted stage, by abstract principles; even the tribal differences and loyalties were not constant factors, as can be seen in the case of the Owu and Oyo refugees. In the prevalent confusion, the goals seem to have been immediate safety, permanent security, and the hope for ultimate hegemony. Though the new Oyo and Ibadan could coexist peacefully, Ibadan and Abeokuta could not. Through all of this, the one constant was the steady stream of slaves to the coast.

The final pressure which converged upon the Yoruba to produce an abundance of captives available for trans-Atlantic shipment was, as we have noted, the activity of the British Preventive Squadron. The Squadron, as the ships of the Royal Navy in West African waters were called, had been sent out in 1807 under the same humanitarian impetus which outlawed the slave trade for British subjects and which forced the transfer of Sierra Leone from the authority of a chartered company to that of the British government. Instructed to intercept all slaving vessels, whether flying British, allied, or enemy flags, the men in command were under orders to return the captured ships to Sierra Leone to be dealt with there by a newly created Vice-Admiralty Court.

Britain was soon to find, however, that although during the next decade some nations of Europe were to make slave trading illegal for their own citizens and others were to agree to limit their slave trade to regions south of the Equator, she alone was to face the responsibility of enforcement. The trade was still highly profitable, and adventurers played hide and seek with an under staffed and under equipped Preventive Squadron. Until the mid-nineteenth century slavers are, in fact, estimated to have evaded the fleet on three trips out of every four even during its most active years.[25] The estimates of slaves exported annually from the West African coast rose from 80,000 in about 1807,[26] to 125,000 by 1830, and again to 135,000 by 1840.[27] Of these only some 30,000 had been diverted to Sierra Leone by 1830.[28] Others were taken to Cuba where the ships' officers stood trial. Under her treaties of reciprocal search, secured with other European powers over the years, Britain had joined in setting up a Mixed Commission in Havana, a New World counterpart to the one at Freetown.

We can see, then, that the activities of the fleet were no more than a disappointing beginning for those who sought to eradicate the slave trade. In Yoruba country they were a stimulus rather than a deterrent, having made increasingly desirable the use of slave markets little patronized until then. There began an acceleration of a circular process by which wars supplied captives to be sold as slaves, increased demand raised profit from slaving, and greater profits spurred on new wars, albeit often because of old grievances. As trade at former depots became more dangerous, Lagos and Badagry joined the list of the largest slave ports in West Africa in the third decade of the century.

ORIGINS OF THE YORUBA SIERRA LEONIANS

Evidence shows that most of the slaves from this region were taken either in battle or as a result of conquest. Koelle, in the "Aku-Igala" section of his *Polyglotta Africana*, published in 1854, gives the testimony of a number of liberated Yoruba in Freetown for whom this had been the case.[29] He also cites accounts of some who were captured while on trading journeys, and a few sold by their own people for the offense of adultery. Even on the basis of a small sample, Koelle makes clear that no particular sub-group controlled the trade and that no group was safe from kidnapping — the Ijebu sold the Egba; the "Yorubans" (Oyo) sold the Ijesha; the Fulani sold the Oyo; the Egba sold the Ijebu and the Ota. In other words, slaving transactions took place between and among all tribal combinations.

A few descriptions of the time spent between capture and em-barkation from the coast can still be found. Thomas King, a re-turned Egba in the service of the Church Missionary Society in 1850, for example, tells his tale:

On the morning of that unhappy day that I was separated from my parents about the year 1825 . . . , I left home about eight o'clock for farm, about three miles distance from home, in order to get some corn. . . . No sooner had I got to the farm and just cut sufficient corn for my load, than the repeated reports of muskets at the town gate acquainted me of my dangerous situation. All my endeavour to escape had utterly proved a failure, as I was surrounded by a number of men, who were very eager, as to whose lot my capture should fall. . . . It was a day of inexpressible sorrow to me. About the space of an hour, they had taken three gates: remaining then only was the only road for escape. . . . We left the encampment about three the next morning for Ikporo, the place of their rendezvous but formerly the town of Shodekkeh the late chief [of Abeokuta]. So it was dawning, we came to Kesi . . . destroyed about two years since. About nine o'clock we arrived at Kemta . . . [a town] destroyed two days before they came to ours. At Ikporo I stayed five days: I was sold one evening to a mahomedan trader who carried me the same evening to Ikereku . . . which was not yet destroyed by war. We went to Oko the next day when I was sold to an Ijebbu trader. To be short, before fortnight after my capture, I was sold to one of the Havannah traders in human [beings] at Lagos. . . . About three weeks after I came to Lagos, the sad intelligence that our town was reduced to ashes reached us. A few days after, with heavy hearts and countenances, we took leave of our shores without the slightest hope of visiting it any more. . . .[30]

What happened to the captives on the westward journeys has often been described.[31] Accounts of disease, death, suicide, and attempted revolt are commonplace in the literature on slaving. During these years, journeys were prolonged by attempts to dodge the naval patrol, or by the chase when evasion was unsuccessful. Slaves who were fortunate to be on ships captured by the Preventive Squadron then had the long voyage to Sierra Leone, where the Vice-Admiralty Court, or, after 1819, the Mixed Commission Court, determined their fate.

The records of the Sierra Leone Liberated African Department, which took charge of the recaptives, do not contain direct information about the origins of the freed slaves, though they do include details of place of capture, descriptions of the ships themselves, and approximations of the ages, names, and facial markings. From Koelle, we do have an idea of the geographical areas represented and the size of the group from each area; though his language classifications are not acceptable to modern linguists, his information is useful in our special context because of his careful delineation of his own categories. In addition to taking down vocabularies, Koelle questioned his informants as to their specific places of origin and charted these on an elaborate map. He also got from each an estimate of the numbers of his fellow-countrymen living in Freetown.

Koelle's estimates can be given weight only with certain reservations in mind: he was conducting his research in the late 1840's and early 1850's — he arrived in Sierra Leone in 1847 — when many liberated slaves had already died or had left Freetown; his sample may have been unrepresentative; and his informants' ideas of numbers could at best have been no more than honest guesses. All the figures appear to be underestimates. But, taking the calculations for each group, we find that of the total from the region now called West Africa, the "Aku," speakers of the "Upper-Guinea or Middle-Coast Languages,"[32] were most widely represented. Their number is shown as over 1,000.[33] The other large groups are those speaking "Niger Delta Languages," which include the Ibo and Bini; the "Niger-Dsadda Languages," or "Nupe Group"; and the "Central African Languages," including Bornu. "It is worthy of remark," writes Buxton in *The African Slave Trade and Its Remedy*, "that the Aku language has been found to be understood by the great majority of the captured negroes."[34]

"Aku" is the term applied to Yoruba-speaking peoples in Freetown, and according to various sources, its derivation is the greeting they used: "Oku."[35] Though in the twentieth century the term has come to refer only to Muslim descendants of liberated

Africans of Yoruba origin, at that time it certainly designated anyone with the Yoruba connection. Governor Doherty gave in 1841 his opinion and description of these people.

It is known to everyone who knows Sierra Leone that the Ackoos are all Liberated Africans, for they are a race attracting more attention than any other, being the most intelligent of any tribe in the liberated population, or of any native tribe in the Colony — a people fully justifying the high character of their nation in the Kingdom of Yarriba as it is given by Captain Clapperton. . . .[36]

Koelle includes in his "Aku" classification Ota, Egba, "Idsesa" (Ijesha), Yoruba (Oyo), "Yagba," Eki (Ekiti), Dsumu, Oworo, "Dsebu" (Ijebu), Ife, Ondo, "Dsekiri," and Igala. The Egba, Ijesha, Yoruba (Oyo), and Ijebu peoples had, according to his researches, the largest representation within the category.

THE SIERRA LEONIAN ROLES

The conditions we have seen, both in Sierra Leone and in Yoruba country, provide the framework for posing the four critical questions we shall be considering here: How did the Sierra Leonians, as the former captives and their children were called in Lagos, see their own role there and in the hinterland, and how did their views of it change with changing circumstances? What were the assumptions on which the British government sought to create a working political unit on the West African coast with the assistance and co-operation of these mediating groups, and what pragmatic steps were taken accordingly? To what extent was the Evangelical movement for African education and religious training successful in the catalytic goals it set itself? Finally, how did factors stemming from traditional relationships and the attitudes of the local population toward these "emigrants" influence the part they would themselves seek to play, or be permitted to play? And what was the effect of these indigenous attitudes on the expectations of the emigrant communities and of the several British groups that sponsored them?

From the answers to these questions will emerge the changing and multiple roles of the liberated Africans in Lagos and its hinterland in the second half of the nineteenth century. In seeking these answers, we shall see the continuous interplay between two sets of forces with which the Sierra Leonians dealt: the views and actions and reactions of the British in England, Sierra Leone, and Lagos on the one hand, and on the other, the attitudes, actions, and reactions of the Africans in Yoruba country.

In the early decades of the nineteenth century, their British sponsors fully expected the Sierra Leonians to shape the places they went into something "modern" — that is, western; it was not until the end of the century, and for all the reasons we shall explore, that Europeans dismissed these people as poor imitations of Englishmen and also came to believe that the journey into the "modern age," that is, contemporaneous western ways, was to be by definition a slow and even hard one for the peoples of Africa. But neither the early expectation nor the later judgment was quite right, for the Sierra Leonians did indeed make their contribution to a modern Nigeria, but to a modern country which, partly because of them, was not a plaster cast from the English mold.

THE SIERRA LEONE EXPERIENCE AND THE
BEGINNINGS OF THE EASTWARD MIGRATION

IN 1807 Sierra Leone became a Crown colony. For the roles the liberated Africans were to play in West Africa, the most important result of this change was the provision for the new colony's part in the fight against the slave trade along the coast.

In March, 1808, the governor had received an order-in-council, authorizing him to admit and protect Africans who disembarked from the slave ships condemned by the Vice-Admiralty Court until these freed slaves could be enlisted in the Royal African Corps or West Indian regiments, or apprenticed to a settler — that is, one of the earlier arrivals from the New World [1] — for a period of up to fourteen years, or "disposed of according to the true meaning of the Abolition Act." [2] The effect of this order was an immediate and continuing increase in the population of the colony. This growth, for which no one in England had planned, had a direct impact on military recruitment and on the apprenticeship system, both of which became subject to abuse. Thus serious problems affecting the very subsistence of the recaptives faced those, both in Freetown and London, concerned with their welfare. [3]

After struggling to maintain the liberated Africans in the face of great pressure on the available land, the administration gained permission for settlement in unoccupied parts of the Sierra Leone peninsula, where the recaptives were to receive government supplies for their essential needs. Leicester, the first village for liberated Africans, was formed as early as 1809 and to it were sent those recaptives who had been neither recruited nor apprenticed. But the village system itself was only begun with official approval under Governor Charles MacCarthy in 1816. [4]

When in 1817 the CMS moved their stations from the hinterland to the colony, mission activity meshed conveniently with MacCarthy's recently formulated plans for the village system, as he had indeed anticipated. Parishes were named to correspond to the villages, and where the mission had clergy to staff them, churches and schools were opened. Where mission staff was lacking, the manager of the village, the government's official in charge — from the 1840's on often an African, either settler or recaptive — took over the essential religious functions. During his tours, the governor conducted marriage ceremonies and baptised children at stations which had no mission representatives. He was thus, in effect, a quasi-bishop for the CMS as well as governor of the colony. For the liberated Africans, these measures were the start of integrated communities fostering at least formal ties with western worship and schooling, certain western skills, and, in embryonic form, western goals.

Although the colony still faced difficulties in solving recurrent problems — nearby slave trading, quarrels with peoples in the interior, and insufficient planning for dealing with the recaptives — conditions gradually improved. Between 1814 and 1824, 12,765 Africans were recorded as having passed through the Liberated African Yard in Freetown, and of those, over 11,000 were settled in the colony.[5] The chief justice had begun recruiting qualified African jurors from the villages, a precedent which would in later years be cited throughout Britain's West African possessions. Mac-Carthy had also managed to put an end, almost without exception, to the apprenticeship system, and he had developed the villages and encouraged trade with the hinterland people. When special situations called for extending government control over small neighboring enclaves, the administration at Freetown was granted discretion to take what measures were necessary.

Conditions in Sierra Leone were, however, not to be stabilized for many years. The European mortality rate was high, and changes of policy were almost as frequent as changes of governors. One annual report would claim progress and prosperity; the next would describe continuing deterioration in conditions. The government in England appointed Parliamentary commissions and committees of inquiry whose reports were invariably critical, sometimes, it is true, because of inaccuracies in the information gathered. The recommendations of these investigators often proved as impractical as the earlier solutions. Ideas such as apprenticeship were instituted, rejected, reapplied. Maladministration was a constant charge. With the recurring suggestion that the focus of work to rehabilitate liberated Africans be shifted to Fernando Po, came others to encourage "emigration" from Sierra Leone to the Gambia and MacCarthy's Island.

SIERRA LEONE IN THE 1830's

It is difficult, then, to isolate any particular set of conditions as typical of what awaited the recaptive, and thus to show dominant influences during the formative years in Sierra Leone upon the later emigrants to Lagos. We shall, therefore, concentrate on the situation in the 1830's, when an appreciable number of Yoruba-speaking people were already in Sierra Leone, with a steady accretion of new arrivals, fed to the slave trade by the continuing wars north of Lagos.

When Major H. D. Campbell[6] took charge of the Sierra Leone government in 1835, he found conditions facing the newly liberated slaves at one of their periodic low points. Following established procedure, the recaptives were sent first to the government yard — men, women, and children together — to await court action on their captured ship. Before a favorable decision led to assignment of plots of land, able-bodied men worked in gangs on public works. After three months' "location" on such plots, they went to villages, where they were supervised by managers.[7] If it were the dry season, they could begin to clear the land; if not, they were dependent on their neighbors until they could grow their own food. When government supplies and charity were not sufficient to still hunger or satisfy the less patient, some would venture into the surrounding, unprotected countryside, often to be enslaved once more.

Nonetheless, the Liberated African Department Letter Book in the early 1830's reflected a more hopeful view. The official in charge submitted his report, listing the number of liberated Africans under the jurisdiction of the general superintendent; the number employed, and how they were employed in the villages; the amount of land under cultivation; the number of liberated Africans receiving allowances. He did complain, however, of the apprenticeship system, under which over 4,000 persons were in-

dentured for periods of from three to seven years. So
tices, often reacting to mistreatment or neglect by thei.
tried to escape and were subsequently enslaved outside the co.
But the official's description of life in the villages was optimistic:

I have visited the different Villages and it is extremely gratifying to me . . .
[to report on] the improvement these people are making in the style of their
dwelling. . . . The people in general are decently Clothed, some are possessed
of a number of Cattle; a few keep horses and Asses; others have large Canoes
which they send to different Rivers to trade with the Natives. . . . In the
Western District a great number employ themselves in fishing . . . , not only
keeping up a constant communication with the Liberated African Villages
but also with the Natives adjacent to the Colony from whom they receive in
exchange for their dried fish Gum Copal Wax honey rice &c [8]

Furthermore, by 1838, procedures for handling the liberated
Africans were more efficient. After adjudication and liberation
the new residents were given clothing and released from Queen's
Yard, where three half-pence a day had been paid for their food.
Those who were still ill remained at Kissey Hospital, where they
received two-pence a day for maintenance. The women of mar-
riageable age were placed with "the most respectable married
women in the villages until married." [9] No family unit, distinguishable in European terms, was broken up, and the children
were sent to mission schools. The assistant superintendent of the
Liberated African Department or, in his absence, specified managers selected sites for the "location" of families or single men; the
allocated plots of land were to begin at four acres, and plans for
"huts" were provided. The apprenticeship system still existed, but
it was more carefully controlled, with periodic inspections, and
with security required from each person receiving an apprentice;
no child who had not been in school at least twelve months was to
be indentured. [10]

The managers were expected to assist and supervise closely the
early activities of the new arrivals, as well as make the rounds of
the schools, organize the building of roads, inspect and handle
supplies, and "attend divine service, at least once every Sunday." [11]
To be sure, these were the stipulated conditions, but, as Governor
Doherty observed in 1838, they were not beyond abuse, especially
by the managers who, he wrote, had too many unsupervised re-

sponsibilities which they often neglected, particularly in the care and education of children, and advice and assistance on the farms.[12]

In the main, the liberated Africans were settled outside Freetown itself. This is generally explained by the fact that those of the original settlers who survived — the Maroons and Nova Scotians — were hostile to the new arrivals, feeling superior because of their own contact with Europeans before their arrival in the colony years before. "[The liberated Africans] . . . have to contend with the jealousy, not certainly honourable rivalry, of the Nova Scotians and Maroons; who regard them as an inferior and degraded caste; and who haughtily oppose their admission into those parts of the town which were originally assigned to themselves." [13]

Although it was not a matter of official British policy to create tribally homogeneous villages, sections of villages did come to be known by such names as Aku Town, Egba Town, or Ibo Town, designating the common tribal origin of the residents. We can assume that in some instances this clustering was due to settling together whole cargoes from specific slave ships; in others, because new arrivals were sought out by their countrymen who were already established.[14] But by whatever circumstance the homogeneous clusters were formed, their existence is important for understanding the consolidation and retention of the traditional ways of the homeland which were to counterbalance the western influences on the liberated Africans returning to Lagos and its hinterland.

The Aku in particular seem to have retained their language and customs. Religious practices, traditional or sometimes Muslim,[15] were tenaciously held.[16] Associations, called Church Relief Companies or Burial Companies, enlisted the participation and allegiance of virtually all Aku.[17] While membership in these companies did not necessarily preclude the acceptance of Christian influence — some companies, in fact, assumed ties with one or another Christian church — it did permit continuation of earlier customs, however much these were opposed by missionaries and government officials.

Nor were such companies concerned only with burials and perpetuating religious practices. From the 1820's, when they were first founded in the villages on the model traditionally familiar to the recaptives, many associations included economic co-operation as well. The Aku were further distinctive in having not only village organizations but also "a supra-headman or 'King' to whom all Aku of the Colony owed allegiance." [18] These cultural retentions persisted through generations that had not themselves known the homelands of the original recaptives, and one cannot overemphasize their significance in fashioning the role the returning Aku were to play from 1839 on in Yoruba country.

THE RECAPTIVES AND THE ECONOMY

What was the economic position of these liberated Africans in Sierra Leone? Acting Governor Campbell, writing in 1837, was optimistic. He had, in April, 1836, concluded a peace treaty with the chiefs of the tribes surrounding the colony and tried, with temporary success, to set up channels for more contact and trade between the colony and hinterland, less with the intention of encouraging commerce than of supporting the extension of agriculture. He was pleased with the further stimulus from Freetown's "Public spirited Merchants" who bought the produce grown in the villages.[19]

However, a closer and more objective examination of conditions did not yield so sanguine a picture. Only a few months later Governor Doherty reported several vexing problems. British merchants were trading directly with inland groups, thereby diminishing the tribal interest in commerce with the Sierra Leone villagers, and the prices offered the farmers for their produce by the merchants in Freetown were far from generous.

The only exportable articles of value which the Liberated African farmer has hitherto grown are ginger, arrow-root, and pepper. These are received from him by the Merchant at the low evaluation of three . . . four . . . and five pence a pound. . . . Even at this rate they are not paid for in cash, but in goods — in goods on which the merchant admits that he charges a profit of fifty per cent . . . and goods not allowed . . . to be selected by the party receiving them, but given at the merchant's convenience: and consisting for the most part of blue bafts, common delf ware, or, as the African expresses it, white plates, and rum — the two former, in the quantities in which they are received, being commodities such as can neither be retailed nor employed for domestic purposes.[20]

Some European sources suggested that the male liberated African's distaste for agricultural pursuits was due to another factor: an opprobrium attached to cultivating the soil because traditionally it was the work of women and slaves. One expression of this view is found in a CMS publication reviewing, more than a decade after Doherty's governorship, the effects of the mission's activities in the colony.[21] However, a different interpretation appears on a copy of this article in marginal notes, presumably by John A. Otonba Payne, a Lagos Sierra Leonian who will figure prominently in these pages and in whose library the publication was found:

I never met with this feeling but in the Colony born Akus have often told me that the British Government had better let the Spaniards or Portuguese take them to their destination than settle them on a territory without sod to cultivate. These men had undoubtedly been simple agriculturalists in their own country.

Certainly the government officials, and even those Europeans who suggested the cultural factor, recognized that the explanation lay primarily in the unsuitability of the soil around Freetown for successful cultivation, for even when it was carefully worked and the crops carefully tended, productivity was low. In the first place, the soil was acid, and furthermore, since much of the land set aside for farming was on the steep hillsides which surround Freetown, erosion was unavoidable. More important still, the allotted land did not permit traditional methods of cultivation, that is, for the rotation of crops and for fallow periods.

Thus, in Payne's words, "very many who would have been agriculturalists had the soil of Sierra Leone permitted, . . . [were] compelled to turn trader."[22] Despite some danger of capture and enslavement, their first ventures were into the interior, as middlemen between the indigenous people and the Freetown merchants and often as agents for Europeans. They hoped in time to accumulate a small amount of capital and to undertake these transactions on their own account. Doherty in his despatches continually admired their drive and diligence, both in agriculture and in trade, and the way in which they were slowly bettering their economic and social position. Later some of them were actually described as having "comparative wealth,"[23] despite — or partially, perhaps, because of — employment for wages being rarely possible for them:

If . . . there be any truth in the assertion so frequently made in England, that one object of British policy in founding this Settlement, the civilizing of these Africans, remains unattained, the failure is not to be ascribed to the people themselves. I have to repeat my former assertion that they have had to labour under great discouragements, peculiar to their position or to the Colony. They have had no employment in the timber factories as labourers. They are, with rare exceptions, not even employed in Freetown as servants and messengers, by the merchants, by officers of Government, or even in Government offices themselves, where, as in the case of the Custom House and the Mixed Commissions, they are not immediately under my own control: — and I would suggest that a change of system in this particular should be recommended to both those Departments by Her Majesty's Government.[24]

THE RECAPTIVES AND CHRISTIANITY

The recaptives' social adjustment in the new environment — that is, the "civilizing" process, a prime objective in founding the colony — was seen to be the province of the missions. The missionaries were to concentrate on spreading Christianity and the benefits of education. As we have seen, from the time of the first decision by the CMS Parent Committee to focus on the liberated Africans in Sierra Leone, the growing area was divided into parishes which corresponded to villages. In theory, every village was to have a missionary, a church, and a school. With the high rate of European mortality, it is not surprising that this goal was not reached for some years. Village managers were often expected to step into the vacant missionary posts, preaching sermons and officiating at marriages and baptisms. Equally often, missionaries had for one reason or another to do the work of government officials, putting up houses as well as church and school buildings, and teaching methods of growing crops.

Ideally, all those settled in the villages were to be encouraged to attend Christian services, and the children were to go to some sort of classes which would teach them "to read the Bible, to live God-fearing lives and to give them such Agricultural and Industrial Training as to enable them to earn their living."[25] This education lasted varying lengths of time; the regulations governing apprenticeship show that the minimum was set at twelve months.

In the villages the missionaries, operating schools which most of the children were required to attend, holding services, and conducting other church activities, met with considerable success in their major work — the conversion of the liberated Africans to Christianity. For despite an exaggerated belief in the paramount importance of the break with the past, it is true that some of the diverse peoples in and around Freetown — detached from their traditional environment, grateful to their liberators, responsive to the tangible benefits coming to those who had mastered western patterns — were receptive to the teachings of the Bible and all it offered. This does not mean that "paganism" was the less reluctantly or the more completely renounced, especially, as we have seen, where peoples of similar origins managed to keep in close contact. Nor did it mean that the missionaries did not have to compete with the attraction of Islam.

The group for whom Muslim worship held the greatest appeal was the Aku. Some of them had been under its influence before their capture,[26] for though the military advance of Islam to the south had been halted before it penetrated beyond the fringes of Yorubaland, the religion was being peacefully spread by Muslim travelers and traders who, with the decline of the caravan trade across the Sahara, had infiltrated coastal West-African commerce.[27] From the early days of Sierra Leone Colony, government officials showed concern over the potentially disruptive influence which the "Foulahs and Mandingoes" from the north might have on the new arrivals. A determining factor in the Aku choice of Muslim affiliation was that the mosque provided yet another excellent focus for a common and distinct identity.[28]

According to . . . [Aku] verbal tradition, there was about this time [the 1820's] a European lawyer named Savage who lived in Fourah Bay and who had an Aku as a servant. This man used to ask his employer on Fridays for leave to go visit his friends. Savage enquired after these people, so his servant brought some of them to meet him; these men formed an association known as *arota* — the friends — who held meetings in part of Savage's property known as 'Yardee.' Some of them, it is said, were already Muslims. When visiting the prison, Savage found a number of Muslims there who had been committed for following the practices of their religion; he had them released and they took his name in gratitude. Many Yoruba settled in the neighbourhood of his house, where one of the principal streets is now named Savage Square. . . .[29]

In 1833 the government found itself in the uncomfortable position of having to deal with a group of Muslim Aku who had moved up country to a village called Cobolo, from which they were raiding surrounding villages and, it was rumored, were eventually planning to attack Freetown itself.[30] This specific threat was thought removed by a punitive expedition, but the plotting, as it was clearly regarded by the government and missions, continued quietly in and around Freetown.

The matter came to a head in 1839. Governor Doherty wrote to the Colonial Office, endorsing the views expressed in enclosed memorials from the Church Missionaries and from some African teachers who protested against Muslim influence and conduct. The objections were as follows: first, that one of the reasons for the founding of Sierra Leone had been the spread of Christianity to Africa and that Islam seriously interfered with this end; second, that the Muslims practiced polygamy and other "corrupting" habits; and third, and most to be deplored, that Muslim masters influenced the liberated African children apprenticed to them in ways contrary to the specific provision in the terms of indenture for "instruction in the truths of revelation." [31] Doherty suggested removing the Muslims from the center of Freetown — the people of Foulah Town even agreed to leave, provided those at Fourah Bay would comply as well — and the plan was approved, though with some reservations, by the Colonial Office. However, the new governor who replaced Doherty advised in 1841 against such an expulsion, and it was never carried out.[32]

From the government's point of view, the problem was serious because, while the missions had a promising number of converts, they did not have a following large enough to make Sierra Leone the Christian colony they envisaged. For out of the estimated population of 35,000 in 1836, the CMS missionaries counted an attendance of only some 6,500 at their churches and chapels.[33]

EDUCATION FOR RECAPTIVES

In Sierra Leone at this time, as throughout the period of British colonial activity in West Africa, the need to relate religion and education was stressed especially for those liberated Africans seen as potential emissaries of British influence. Governor Campbell's report that in 1836, 6,800 children were in school, an increase of 1,700 over the previous year, and that there were "but very few villages where the Children may not now obtain Instruction," was seen as encouraging.[34]

The emphasis on making education available to the recaptives had long since led the CMS to expand their efforts beyond mere village schools. In 1816 they had opened at Leicester, the new village outside Freetown, the Christian Institution, an industrial training center with separate facilities for boys and for girls. It was supported largely by gifts from England, though it received some help from Sierra Leone's government. In addition, presumably, to English and the Bible, the boys learned trades and farming; the girls, sewing and knitting.[35] The Institution progressed to the satisfaction of all, though the CMS soon began to feel its operation a financial burden.

Only a short period of uncertainty preceded the suggestion in 1816 by Governor MacCarthy that the missionary wives should instruct the girls, while those boys who after one or two years' schooling might be found "better calculated for handicrafts and labourers than for scholars" should go to jobs in and around Freetown. He offered the further idea — one which was to prove a key factor in the roles played by some returning Sierra Leonians in Lagos — that the Institution might be "converted into a College" for a select few whose studies would include "the classics, Arabic, and other languages."[36]

The Parent Committee of the CMS accepted these suggestions. The children from the Christian Institution went back to the villages; the school was rechristened a seminary; and there, with its removal to Regent's Town, a fluctuating number of students, about twenty in number, began their studies in 1820. Though industrial training was no longer central, the statement of the curriculum of the seminary gives a preview of educational theory which continued to dominate curricula in many parts of Africa: "Let us, as much as possible, combine industry with learning — otherwise we shall have a house full of Bookmen and no Workmen, when at the same time, intelligent Tradesmen would be an ornament to the Colony." [37]

Until 1824 the seminary had made good progress and had graduated teachers who were already helping in the village schools. But by 1826, for reasons of direction or lack of it, it found itself in serious trouble and finally closed toward the end of that year. The Parent Committee, however, was reluctant to give up the plan: in December, 1826, they sent out the Rev. C. L. F. Haensel, a tutor at the Basel Seminary, to "revive the Christian Institution . . . as a nursery for the College" then being built in England at Islington, where selected Sierra Leone pupils would be sent for religious training. In addition this new Christian Institution was to provide "a liberal education to any promising youths whatever their intended vocation." [38]

The curriculum of the re-established school in Freetown was to emphasize English, followed by Arabic and the study of local languages. Grammars, dictionaries, and translations of the Bible into "all the dialects of the neighbourhood" were major goals. "Music was to be taken up as relaxation, manual exercise for pleasure. All was to be grounded on the impregnable rock of Holy Scripture." [39]

By then even the buildings of the old seminary had collapsed, and the new educational center was fortunate in being able to rebuild cheaply on the estate of a late governor. Thus, in February, 1827, Fourah Bay College opened with its first student, Samuel Ajayi Crowther, an Aku who, as already mentioned, was later to be important in the 1841 Niger Expedition.

Fourah Bay became the center for the training of teachers and catechists. By 1841 its course had been completed by thirty-nine students, some of whom — such men as Samuel Crowther, Thomas King, William Marsh, and Edward Bickersteth — were shortly to figure in events in the Lagos area.[40] With the arrival of the Rev. Koelle in 1847, the college became a linguistic center as well, translating the Bible into the various African languages in order to facilitate the later work of the graduates.

The other field the CMS stressed in Sierra Leonian education was called "industrial training," in line with Henry Venn's belief in the desirability of "training an African middle class for both Church and state." [41] In 1845, Venn and his supporters had started a program with two aims: first, to bring selected Africans from Sierra Leone to England for technical training; and second, to send European artisans and mechanics to West Africa. Again European mortality on the coast interfered.

The CMS concentrated on the first goal, and here the areas of specialization were diverse. For example, two went to Thomas Clegg's factory near Manchester to learn English methods of cleaning and packing cotton. Two others were also sent to Manchester, but to learn the building trade, and how to make bricks and tiles. Two more went to Kew Gardens to find out about new varieties of plants which could be grown in West Africa. One became a printer after a stay in London. Only one, Thomas Babington Macaulay, had non-technical training: he went to Islington to the CMS Training College, and also attended a few lectures at King's College, London. Another, Samuel Crowther, Junior, also did some medical courses at King's College, after his apprenticeship to a doctor in Freetown. [42] These last two Sierra Leonians, as well as some of the others who received early training in England, were before long to put their talents to use in Yoruba country, from which they, or their parents, had come.

It is, parenthetically, interesting to notice how frequently Sierra Leonians bore surnames of governors, missionaries, and other prominent Europeans. The CMS had committed itself to naming a child at the Christian Institution after any English benefactor who contributed £5 for his or her support,[43] but most recaptives preferred to choose their own new names, as can be seen from the difficulty CMS agents were having in implementing the policy five years after it had been set forth. [44]

THE BEGINNING OF EMIGRATION

In September, 1838, Governor Doherty wrote in a despatch to the Colonial Office,

The [liberated Africans] are satisfied with their new position generally, and cherish no wish to revisit their former savage homes. On this subject I have myself repeatedly questioned them in the suburbs and villages; and not in any instance have I found that they varied in their replies or would for a moment entertain the idea of return.[45]

But scarcely over a year later, he was forwarding a petition, dated November, 1838, from a number of these same liberated Africans, stating their intention to go down the coast to Badagry.[46] These signatories (listed in Appendix B), some of whose names will recur later, asked for missionary and government support; they wrote of their realization that they had "a soul to save" and their hope that their presence would hasten the end of the slave trade. The preponderance of petitioners were Aku, though at least one was Nupe and one Hausa.[47] Doherty, in transmitting their request, recommended its support by the Colonial Office and pointed out once again that if projects to promote "civilization" and trade were on the Whitehall agenda, Freetown could provide volunteers willing to carry them out, even on their own initiative.[48]

The Colonial Office, seeing a potential danger of recapture, was not particularly receptive to the suggestion. As one official wrote succinctly, "We cannot send them without giving them protection which implies expense, but they may go if they wish." [49] Only James Stephen agreed with Doherty that "if Mr. Buxton's project is to be carried into execution, there will here be found Agents ready made to his hands." [50]

Before the Governor had received the views of the British government for transmission to the Sierra Leonians, one of them had already purchased a condemned slave ship for £383 and was preparing to sail it down the coast.[51] The ship, renamed the *Margaret*, had as its captain and owner a liberated African, William Faulkner, who carried a letter from Governor Doherty to George Maclean, the senior administrator at Cape Coast — a letter stating that the vessel was,

to be manned & navigated by other inhabitants of the Colony who are, like himself, persons of colour; and this being the first enterprise of the kind which has been undertaken by such persons, & deserving, in my opinion, of great encouragement; I shall feel obliged by any countenance or facilities which you yourself or any of the commandants of H.M. Settlements on your part of the Coast may be able to afford to Mr. Faulkner or his people.[52]

Early in 1840 Doherty reported that this first contingent had split into two groups: one, of twenty, disembarking at Accra; the other, of fourteen, continuing to Badagry.[53] And, he wrote,

At this moment not fewer than two hundred persons, belonging chiefly to the Houssa Country, and the Kingdom of Yarriba . . . , have subscribed the amount of four hundred dollars each towards the formation of a fund, have purchased with it a condemned prize vessel [the *Queen Victoria*], in which it was their intention to proceed to Badagry, and from thence to seek their native homes at a distance of some hundred miles inland.[54]

But at that point the Governor intervened. Having found that some one hundred children were to be among the passengers, he forbade their embarkation and that of their parents, allowing "passports for not more than forty-four men and seventeen women, who are all persons without children, and of an age so mature as renders them not likely to become the prey of slave dealers." [55] The Colonial Office approved his action which did not, however, indicate a complete turnabout from Doherty's earlier support of the emigration movement. The *Queen Victoria* did sail soon afterward, carrying to British officials on the Gold Coast a letter in which the governor of Sierra Leone asked that any feasible aid be given to the emigrants and expressed concern for their welfare in Badagry, requesting any information on the conditions they would meet.[56]

MOTIVES FOR EMIGRATION

Emigration down the coast continued despite the government's uneasiness and some restrictions on passports. What determined the participation in this movement of certain groups of liberated Africans from Sierra Leone? There appear to have been at this time two distinct types of ventures gaining momentum out of Freetown. One of them was initiated by men interested in commerce along the coast. They purchased condemned slavers to trade European goods and Sierra Leone's produce for palm oil and other products. As Doherty described their activity,

The hawkers or native merchants . . . turn rapidly to the best advantage opportunities as they offer [themselves] of extending and increasing their commerce.

These traders now number in Freetown and the villages not fewer than 400 persons; and they are extending their views beyond the Settlement itself. During the last 12 months they have purchased and equipped two vessels for the Coast trade, of which one has made three, and the other two voyages and in these they trade as far as Lagos in the Bight of Benin.[57]

The other group contained men and women who wished to leave Freetown to settle permanently in the Lagos area. This group, in turn, showed a range of economic interests. Some, like those who sought to extend their trading activities down the coast, had already accumulated sufficient capital to undertake such ventures on their own. Others, considerably less prosperous, were nevertheless able to obtain vessels for their journeys by the method perfected earlier by those liberated Africans, especially the Aku, who were now financially independent — the pooling of savings, however meager.[58] The original petitioners, described by Doherty for the benefit of the Colonial Office, were of "the class of the liberated population . . . known by the designation of hawkers; . . . who have realised comparative wealth; and are all of them of great respectability." [59]

It would seem, then, that a major motivation for the movement back to the Bight of Benin was economic. Presumably the "wealthy," having been successful traders in Freetown, now wished to try their talents in their new homes. But for many of the emigrants there is no record of great economic achievement in Sierra Leone. We have seen that for the majority agricultural conditions were not particularly good: employment was scarce, and while they were increasingly overcoming the competition, if not the hostility, of the earlier settlers, many found their economic position unsatisfactory.

The liberated Africans had other less tangible incentives for leaving Sierra Leone. Family traditions in Lagos even now stress the basic and self-evident desire to go home. Once the way had opened for the Aku, the wish to try to find their families was understandably strong. In the view of one contemporaneous mission observer, this reason tied in with others, some of which we have enumerated:

The love of their native land has been assigned as the reason why the Akus wish to return to their country. . . . But the fact is that there are various other reasons of importance with them, such as, for instance, as they alledge, the great *unhealthiness of this Colony* as compared with their country, where they say, but few diseases are known, such as small pox, measles, &c. whereas in the Colony they are troubled with Yaws, Dissentary, Dropsy, Elephantiatis, Lethargy (always fatal), and large indolent ulcers often lasting for years. Another evil . . . is the spirit of insubordination and the habits of idleness which the

Colony-born children embibe. . . . Add to this that concubinage, adultery, and fornication are most common sins here never taken notice of by the law . . . and it cannot be surprising that parents should look upon the future car- riers of their children with serious concern. . . . (Note: the sins above re- ferred to are severely punished in many, if not most, heathen countries in the Interior of Africa); another reason assigned by the Akus for returning to their country is the alledged Inferiority of their soil for agricultural pur- poses.[60]

Finally, the motivation for which the British theorists had hoped also emerged. In the petition sent to the governor by the first emigrants the spokesmen wrote,

you humble petitioners are Liberated Africans, and we feel with much thank- ful to Almighty God and the Queen of England who has rescued us from being in a state of slavery, and has brought us to this Colony, and set us at Liberty, and thanks be to God of all mercy who has sent his servants to de- clare unto us poor Creatures the way of Salvation, which illuminates our understanding, so we were brought to know that we have a soul to save, and when your humble petitioners look back upon their poor Country people who [are] now living in darkness, with out the light of the Gospel, so we taken upon ourselves to direct this our humble petition to your Excellency.[61]

These sentiments, considered by Doherty secondary to the eco- nomic stimulus, proved to be an expression of sincere intent. As we shall see later, it was pressure from the returned Sierra Leonians, and not missionary initiative, that brought the first Christian missionaries to Badagry and Abeokuta.

The Governor found it hard to give a reasonable explanation to the Colonial Office for the sudden change from the contentment and total lack of desire to emigrate, which he had reported the year before, to the interest in moving down the coast, especially since the new ideas implied permanent residence in the places where the liberated Africans wished to go. His suggestion of the influence of conversations with Hausa passengers on a ship en route from Trinidad to "that country"[62] seems to overemphasize the impression made by a brief encounter and to underestimate the capacity of the Sierra Leonians for a reasoned appraisal of their opportunities and prospects.

Once news of the success of the first emigrants in settling in Badagry and their hope to move on to Abeokuta had reached Freetown, the idea of emigration gained popularity. In 1842, Gov-

ernor Fergusson reported that not only was the *Queen Victoria* —
one of the ships that traveled first to Badagry — making frequent
voyages, but also that two other vessels, the *Wilberforce* and the
Free Grace, had been purchased by liberated Africans and had
begun to trade and to carry emigrants. He estimated the number
of men and women who had left the colony at 500.[63]

By 1842, another factor seems to have entered into the Aku
rationale for returning to Yorubaland. Since the emancipation of
the slaves in 1833, the Colonial Office had been faced with the need
to alleviate the labor problem in the West Indian colonies. There
were alternatives, but they required indentured laborers from
other parts of the world. If, however, the recruits could be persuaded to remain in the Caribbean after the term of indenture,
there would be substantial savings, with the expense of one-way
passage providing a permanent labor force.

Ironically, the liberated Africans living in Sierra Leone were
considered to be suitable on several grounds as a source of labor
for the West Indies. First, not being an indigenous population
and thus not being strongly attached to their present homes, they
could, the reasoning went, be the more easily uprooted a second time. Again, they were accustomed to the climatic conditions
they would find in the West Indies, and, moreover, it was argued
that their addition to a population of similar, that is African, origin would produce a homogeneous, stable community. Finally,
and in more immediate terms, passage from West Africa would
obviously strain the West Indian exchequers less than would transport from the east.

Plans were drawn up in 1841 for a direct supply line from Freetown to the Caribbean islands, the idea having been explained
earlier in despatches from the Colonial Office to the governors of
Sierra Leone. The conditions across the Atlantic were painted in
bright hues for the recaptives. But the fear was soon to spread
that this plan was only a new form of slavery in the guise of an
economic opportunity. Suspicion was first aroused when some of
the "Delegates" who were sent out had not returned at the expected time.[64] Furthermore, when they did return in April, 1842,
they reported what an official termed "serious misrepresentations"
of conditions "little better than slavery" for them in Trinidad.[65]

Whatever the claims against the accuracy of these reports, we cannot be surprised at the mounting uneasiness after reading the instructions sent to four of the village managers from the Liberated African Department in 1844:

> I am to inform you that . . . you should intimate to all the school children and other Liberated Africans on Government allowance under your care, the propriety of their emigrating to the West Indies by the opportunity now afforded them, as well as the advantages they will enjoy by doing so, and in the event of their refusing to emigrate you are authorized to locate the whole of the Scholars above twelve years of age . . . taking care clearly to make them understand that no further assistance will be given them by the Government either on food or clothes, after which you are to send in a Nominal Return of those remaining in School and in Hospital. . . .[66]

At almost the same time, Macdonald wrote of a decrease of about 3,000 in Sierra Leone's population; he also reported that the number who went to the West Indies had been counterbalanced by the number of men and women liberated by the ships of the fleet and that the decrease, therefore, came principally from the departure of many Aku, who had gone to Badagry and the country surrounding it.[67]

The government persisted in promoting the West-Indian scheme, but we can see how little it appealed to the liberated Africans by looking at later reports. In 1855, the trans-Atlantic emigration was given as 61 for the preceding year; the trans-African emigration, specifically cited as being "to the neighbourhood to Lagos," was approximately 1,500.[68] In 1860, the governor complained about an "evil" which he had, it seems, tried unsuccessfully to counteract before:

> [T]he 'Mary Ann' [a West Indian emigrant ship] arrived . . . and is now unlading her cargo. But I regret . . . that some of the idle natives and Akus have insinuated themselves into the African Yard in spite of all vigilant and active precautions I had previously taken; and have induced the Liberated Africans to change their minds, and they have been clamorous to get out and indeed many of them have absconded but have since returned after the intimation of my displeasure. . . .
>
> I visit them frequently and see that they are properly attended to. I still have hopes that I shall find sufficient volunteers for the 'Mary Ann'. . . .[69]

The emigration agents blamed the missionaries in 1842 for discouraging West-Indian emigration because it would deprive them of their newly found agents for penetrating other parts of the coast.[70] There is no doubt ground for the claim that the missions were not in favor of the scheme, but this factor is only one of many which determined the choice of the liberated Africans to go down the coast rather than across the ocean.

In essence, then, we can see that not one motive but many, acting singly or in combination, had spurred individual emigrants and their families to make the trip eastward to Yoruba country. The bases of both unity and heterogeneity of the Sierra Leonian emigrant group emerge clearly. But here, as later in Lagos and its hinterland, it is impossible to isolate one reason, one dominant loyalty, one compelling belief from which a unified emigrant position can be deduced.

THE RETURN TO YORUBA COUNTRY:
LAGOS, BADAGRY, ABEOKUTA

THERE is no record of the events immediately following the 1839 arrival in Yoruba country of the first shipload of Sierra Leonians. It is not even clear where they landed. According to the Rev. Henry Townsend's *Memoirs*, they reached Lagos — " 'This is our country; it is Eko' " [1] — and there learned of the disintegration, chaos, and reorganization of the old Oyo kingdom. Townsend added that it was in Lagos that they heard of Shodeke and of the Egba successes, and that this information made them decide to go to Abeokuta.[2] The next party to arrive in Lagos after the exploratory trip — presumably the one mentioned by Townsend — was reported to have been robbed.[3] When word of this misadventure reached Sierra Leone, along with more news of the growing prosperity of newly founded Abeokuta, the later emigrants decided to try landing at Badagry, which was reputed to be on friendly terms with, if not tributary to, the Egba.[4]

Some scattered attempts to reach Lagos itself continued to be made, but little reliable evidence about them is available before the establishment, in 1852, of the British consulate there. We may infer that the returning Sierra Leonians would have found but slight incentive to settle in a town mainly remembered as a stopping point on their way to the slave ships. It is also unlikely, as has been remarked, that native Lagosians were among the emigrants, since during the early nineteenth century Lagosians were primarily slave traders, dealing in captives from the hinterland.[5]

There was, moreover, another obstacle, and that a local political one. Lagos was embroiled at the time in a power struggle over succession to the *Oba*ship. Oluwole, the incumbent, was being challenged by Kosoko, who also had a claim to the title. Until Oluwole's death in 1841, civil strife had been a constant threat; with the succession of yet another claimant, Akitoye, and the consequent setback to Kosoko's ambition, the conflict broke out into the open. For the next four years — until the ouster of Akitoye by Kosoko and his forces — the two factions clashed sporadically. These events had, as we shall see, far-reaching consequences for the hinterland, but, more directly, they suggest that for the emigrants Lagos was then scarcely a desirable place to settle.

Records do show that the great majority of early emigrants landed in Badagry. Badagry was a loosely organized town, founded some one hundred and twenty years before the arrival of the Sierra Leonians, that is, about 1720, by refugees from Whydah and Porto Novo, which were then under attack by Agadja, King of Dahomey.[6] Its coastal location made it an outlet for one of the trade routes to the sea, and with the growing supply of war captives Badagry, like Lagos, had become an important slave port. As the trade grew the population became increasingly heterogeneous, with an influx of African and European slave traders.

The town was divided into "wards," each headed by a dominant chief. Insofar as there was a *primus inter pares*, he was the *Akran*, the head of Jegba section. The chiefs met annually to take an oath of allegiance to each other and to Badagry.[7] The sections of the town bore the names of European countries — Portuguese town, English town, French town — not because of any particular European political influence in them, but because each of the chiefs traded with specific men who were nationals of these countries and, thereafter, had undisputed rights over commerce there.

When the Sierra Leonians first came to Badagry, they made friendly contact with several ward chiefs, especially the one termed the *Wawu* who, it is not without interest to note, was chief of the "English" section, and who thus came later to be called the "English Governor of Badagry."[8] The emigrants also found that their journey to Abeokuta required permission from the Egba authorities and that their path was currently blocked by an Egba campaign against the town of Ado.

Talbot reports that the *Wawu*'s first representations on behalf of the new arrivals to the *Sagbua*, who was in charge of the Egba forces, were rebuffed. The *Sagbua* is said to have replied that, "they did not 'want to see people again whom they had sold,' and [he] invited Wowu and the Badagrians to share them out as

slaves."[9] This statement, not appearing elsewhere, seems not altogether in character, primarily because the majority of the returning Aku were Egba, and tradition did not sanction the sale of
one's own tribesmen except for serious crimes. We can only spec-
ulate why the Badagry slave traders did not take such action on
their own initiative. Was it because of their friendship with the
Egba, or because they were slave dealers as opposed to slave raiders,
or because the emigrants came with suitably attractive and valuable
gifts?

YORUBA POLITICS IN THE 1830'S AND 1840'S

Inasmuch as the emigrants themselves, or their parents, had
been captured and sold into slavery during the tribal wars dating
from the breakup of the Oyo Empire, it is important to look at
the political situation in the southern part of Yoruba country, to
which they were now returning. To what extent had conditions
stabilized? Some of the Sierra Leonians may not have known of
the new Ibadan; it is clear that many had been unaware of the
founding of Abeokuta.

Rivalry among the Ibadan, Ijebu, and Egba had been continuing throughout the 1830's. Ibadan and Ijebu were in a loose alliance; the Egba sought to consolidate their own position. The
two groups had frequent clashes, notably the Arakanga War,
about 1835, won by the Egba, and the Iperu War, about 1836, in
which victory went to Ibadan.[10] An uneasy balance of power was
emerging. The leaders of Abeokuta wanted control over an outlet
to the sea, both to have direct access to gunpowder and for trade,
which was still predominantly in slaves. This need Badagry could
eminently satisfy, and Abeokuta had worked out a special relationship with it—one of friendship, it appears, rather than of tributary dominance, as some sources suggest. But in the way of free
access to the port stood the Egbado peoples, with whom the Egba
had been having minor skirmishes.

In 1842 at the latest, an army set out from Abeokuta to lay
siege to Ota, a village some twenty-five miles northwest of Lagos,
inhabited by the Awori, another Yoruba sub-group.[11] The purpose
of the attack, it seems, was, typically, to remove interference with
Egba trade to the coast. Despite assistance from Kosoko—an as-

pirant, as we have noted, to *Oba*ship of Lagos — and the further help he had elicited from Ibadan, Ota was unable to meet the economic challenge, although it had successfully resisted the military attack. The town fell to the control of the Egba and remained under them for decades.[12]

From Ota the soldiers of Abeokuta moved on to Ado, a small Egbado village directly on the caravan route to Badagry. One motive for the attack is said to have been punishment for aid given to Ota, but the primary reason seems again to have been economic, having to do with direct access to the coast. The Egba found Ado more difficult to subdue; the siege continued even after the establishment of the consulate in Lagos, and it remained an obstacle for the returning emigrants and for the missionaries who wished to follow them to Abeokuta.[13]

EARLY SIERRA LEONIANS IN BADAGRY AND ABEOKUTA

Onto this disturbed scene came the Sierra Leonians, all wanting to resettle among their own people and some with a zeal to bring western ideas and British support to their kin. The early experiences of the emigrants are difficult to describe with accuracy. They seem to have had protection from the *Wawu* and perhaps other ward chiefs in Badagry, but with few exceptions they stayed there only as transients, their fixed goal being Abeokuta. The siege at Ado made this goal hazardous to reach and, while a new route was being devised, several shiploads of emigrants waited in Badagry.

The first known communication from them was sent to the Rev. Thomas Dove, superintendent of the Wesleyan Missions in Sierra Leone, where interested Europeans, including the governor, were wondering about their fate in a relatively unknown land of undoubted heathenism.

It was my desire to write to you this day hoping it may not offend you true by the Providence of God I was brought to Africa where the sound of the Gospel is and I have seen and tasted the blessings of Jesus, and now I asked permission by the name of the Queen to go to my native land; and it was granted so I took passage by the 'Queen Victoria' and by the goodness of the Lord I arrived there in safe which I do think as I have already seen it that the place is very good, no war is there no nothing of such kind is there, so I humble beseech you by the name of Jehovah as to send one of the Messen-

gers of God to teach us more about the way of salvation. Because I am now in
a place of darkness where no light is. I know that I was once under light
and now I am in darkness. It is to bring our fellow Citizens in the way which
is right and to tell them the goodness of Jehovah what he had done for us;
and by so doing if the Lord will have mercy to broke that stony heart from
them. . . . Hoping you must not be afraid to send us any. If anything matter
to him we will stand we will take good care of him as our Father and Mother.
. . . Sir the Governor of Badagry his compliment to you and he is very glad
to hear the word of God he understand English well.

> Yours humble poor obedient Servant
> James Fergusson and
> the Governor of Badagry by the
> name of Warrarú.[14]

It was this letter from a Methodist convert, and similar oral communications brought to the headquarters of missions in Sierra
Leone by the captains of emigrant vessels, that started a missionary
scramble for Abeokuta. The reported warmth of the Egba welcome to their returning relatives, the friendly reaction of Shodeke,
the request of the emigrants for a missionary — a request made on
their own initiative — and their apparent willingness to promote
the cause of Christianity themselves, all aroused missionary curi-
osity in the Egba center. From here on Abeokuta came to dominate first their interest and then, for the CMS, their whole view of
the hinterland.

The Wesleyans, to whom the letter had been sent, were the
first to respond to the appeal. Thomas Birch Freeman, superintendent of their mission at Cape Coast, was instructed to start a
station in Badagry. On 24 September 1842, Freeman, together
with William de Graft, an African from Cape Coast who had been
working at Winnebah, and his wife, arrived in Badagry and were
welcomed by the *Wawu*. They soon found that, notwithstanding
the arrival of additional emigrants, most of the Sierra Leonians
had already reached Abeokuta.[15] While beginning work on a mission house and chapel, Freeman sent James Fergusson, author of
the letter that had aroused Methodist interest, to Abeokuta. At
the end of October a friendly reply came from Shodeke,[16] and on
11 December Freeman and de Graft reached the Egba capital,
which they found larger than they had expected.

Freeman was impressed with the intelligence and dignity of
Shodeke; with his hospitality, both toward the emigrants and the

visiting missionaries; and particularly with the fact that he allowed the Sierra Leonians to wear European dress and exempted them from the traditional salutation, that is, from prostrating themselves before him. The missionary held several meetings with the new arrivals, from whom he learned that there were between two and three hundred of them in Abeokuta. They praised Shodeke for the way he had received them and encouraged Freeman to begin his work. They predicted what was later to surprise the missionaries and fill them with optimism for their future success, that Shodeke was not only willing to have Christianity brought to his people but that he himself wished to learn more about it, as he showed by attending the first service they held.

The economic activities of the Sierra Leonians impressed Freeman too:

Those emigrants who have some knowledge of any mechanical profession or business, have, since their arrival . . . endeavoured to work at their respective trades and callings, whenever an opportunity has offered itself; but, as such opportunities have been somewhat rare, they have chiefly employed themselves in trading, agricultural pursuits, — such as the cultivation of corn, yams, cotton &c. Coffee is not known here. . . . Cotton is in considerable demand in the native markets. . . .[17]

The Wesleyans left Abeokuta on 20 December, promising to return. On his arrival in Badagry Freeman found that the CMS was embarking on a plan similar to his. There he met Henry Townsend, a young CMS missionary who had shortly before come from Freetown on a "mission of research," and who was also staying with the *Wawu.* As Townsend told of his trip,

The vessel in which I sail is the property of three young men of Yaruba and has been, twice before, employed to convey Akus or Yarubeans to their own country. The vessel is very small, being only fifty tons . . . and [is] called . . . 'The Wilberforce.' Our little vessel is literally crowded by human beings. I believe there are fifty nine persons on board including the crew. Each person is charged twelve dollars for his passage and provides his own provisions, but my passage is given me by the owners to show their desire for the introduction of the gospel into their own country. . . .[18]

And, although his passage had been free because he was an agent of Christianity, Townsend was unsure of the religious commitment of his fellow passengers, for he continued that he had not as yet discovered "that any are truly pious, although many are professedly Christians. . . . There are four Mohammedans."[19]

Freeman left de Graft and his wife to look after Methodist interests in Badagry and on 29 December went to Whydah to explore mission prospects there, while Townsend went to Abeokuta where he was welcomed as cordially as Freeman had been, both by the emigrants and by Shodeke. The adjustment the Sierra Leonians had made impressed him, as did their use of their newly acquired skills and knowledge:

This morning I was a long time engaged in writing notes for the people of Abbeokuta to their long lost relatives in S. Leone. Two or three boys, formerly of our schools . . . I find, have occasionally been similarly engaged; by which means, I hope, the inhabitants will be led to see one of the advantages of education; one step towards the advantageous establishment of schools. . . .[20]

Shodeke offered him land for a mission, but Townsend, though giving a tentative promise to return, was not authorized to make a definite commitment. He tried instead to persuade the chief to send several of his children to school in Sierra Leone but was countered with the logical argument that if the mission were indeed to come to Abeokuta, moving the children would be unnecessary. Townsend left Andrew Wilhelm, an Aku emigrant teacher and interpreter, to promote the CMS cause in Abeokuta, just as Freeman had left de Graft in Badagry. He himself returned to Sierra Leone and then to England, to make his report and to be ordained.

In the meantime, de Graft reported progress in Badagry. *The Friend of the African* of December, 1843, gave its readers accounts from his letters in which he claimed "several" converts; an increase in the Christian Society from 20 to 45 members; growing congregations of Badagrians and Sierra Leonians every Sunday; and a successful day school, with "40 or 50" boys and girls already enrolled as pupils, some of them children of the ward chiefs, who continued to be friendly toward his work.[21] He also told of the arrival the preceding May of yet another emigrant ship, this time with 180 male passengers.

SIZE OF EMIGRATION

What was the volume of this emigration movement? Freeman's estimate of 200 to 300 Sierra Leonians in Abeokuta in 1842 has already been cited. Samuel Crowther, writing from Freetown to Sir Thomas Fowell Buxton in April, 1844, summarized the state of transport to Badagry:

The liberated Africans now own four vessels which go backward and forward to Badagry with emigrants. A fifth, *the Victoria*, was hauled on shore at Badagry, being considered unseaworthy. . . . Mr. Henry Johnson, the owner, returned here to purchase another condemned slaver to supply her place. . . . *The Maria*, owned by a company of liberated Africans, chiefly Mahomedans, sailed for Badagry . . . about the middle of March.

The *Duke of Wellington*, also owned by a company of liberated Africans . . . sailed for Badagry on the 6th instant with a party of emigrants.[22]

In addition, there are the several reports of the arrival at Badagry of new shiploads of various sizes — 59, 150, 180. One emigrant boat in particular, the *Wonderful*, owned by William Johnson — sometimes called Captain Harry Johnson, and possibly the same man as Crowther's Mr. Henry Johnson — one of the most prosperous of Sierra Leonian trading Aku,[23] made continuous return voyages between Freetown and Badagry during the mid-1840's, with additional emigrants arriving each time.[24] In 1850 Commander Forbes of the Royal Navy estimated 3,000 in the Egba capital.[25]

It would be strange if no emigrants had been displeased with what they found and returned to Sierra Leone. The only mention of its happening, however, is in an 1846 journal entry by one of the CMS missionaries:

Today the Brig 'Wonderful' left for S. Leone and in her a party of discontented Emigrants, who return partly, because they met with a less favourable reception from their relatives, than they anticipated, partly, because they could not make so much money and in so easy a manner as they had calculated. It appears that these persons never maturely deliberated on the step they were taking by leaving S. Leone, but allowed themselves to be carried along with the tide of Emigration, else they would have been as happy here or at Abbeokuta, as many of their fellow Emigrants.[26]

REACTIONS TO EMIGRATION AND THEIR REPERCUSSIONS

This continuing emigration was bringing a mixed reaction in European quarters. True, the missionaries soon changed their position from doubt about permitting their new converts to return to a "pagan wilderness" to enthusiasm for the opening wedge into Yorubaland. The government officials in Sierra Leone also came increasingly to support the emigration, taking pride in the achievement of their "wards." But there were also some skeptics. Thus, R. R. Madden, a doctor with experience in the West Indies and humanitarian inclinations, who had been sent out by the British government to inspect its West African posts, praised Governor Doherty's cautious control of departures in his report submitted to Parliament in 1842. Madden held that the need for issuing passports and for excluding children was obvious because, he as saw it, of "the fate of the unfortunate people who had imprudently gone . . . [to Badagry], and in all probability have fallen into slavery." [27] Doherty, on the other hand, cited letters from Fergusson — "whose person I perfectly recollect" — and others as proof that, in fact, the Sierra Leonians had been successful in their move and were to be supported.[28]

The Colonial Office, however, remained dubious; the movement had unfavorable implications for the West-Indian-emigration scheme, and there was also the fear of future entanglement and increased responsibilities. They were soon to have grounds for their anxiety. Possibly at the emigrants' suggestion, or inspired by the missionary visits, Shodeke wrote in 1844 to Governor Macdonald of Sierra Leone:

It is my desire to be united by ties of friendship with the British Government. The kindness of the English nation in delivering my People from Slavery and enabling them to return to their Native Country convinced me of their desire to promote our welfare.

I wish that not only my own People may return but that the English missionary and Merchant may settle among us. And if the Queen of England would assist me in building a Fort for the protection of my people she would confer a great favor upon us.[29]

The letter was evidently sent by one of the Sierra Leonian ships; there had been some delay in its receipt, but when the Colonial Office finally saw it, instructions went out to the new Governor, Fergusson, to "return a conciliatory answer in the Queen's name . . . , discouraging at the same time all idea of Military aid being granted to him." [30]

But the pressures toward eventual involvement were growing. Large parts of the Aku population in Sierra Leone were working energetically to enlist missionary support for and participation in their emigration. They wanted both British protection for their countrymen and the benefits of conversion and with it education. Throughout 1841 and 1842 the Wesleyans and the CMS reported that their Aku congregations were raising subscriptions among themselves, not alone to send missionaries to Yorubaland, but also to provide them with "elementary school books, slates, bibles, and testaments." [31]

Finally, it was Crowther who, in his letter to Buxton in April, 1844, began to build explicitly the case from which would later grow important missionary agitation for the British to protect emigrants. Noting that while the Sierra Leonians returned to their country despite the grave dangers that faced them, he described their fund of gratitude toward and confidence in the British government, saying that they felt assured that, "its anxious eye is upon us as that of a tender mother is upon her children, who are going away from her . . . . The occasional appearance of her Majesty's men-of-war in the roadstead of Badagry is an indication of this." [32]

It is also clear from Crowther's letters that while the interest in emigration was a continuing one, the motives for it were not confined, as the missionaries would have wished, to Christian evangelization. This is self-evident in the participation of Muslim Aku. And the point emerges implicitly in a later letter from Crowther to Buxton about the entire Sierra Leonian community in Badagry: they were "respected" and were "making a great stride in civilization and in a trading point of view, yet they are not pious men," and sometimes even took advantage of the local inhabitants. This behavior, by Crowther's interpretation, was further responsible for any accounts of unfavorable treatment of the emigrants at Badagry. Though such reports were few,

had not such cold water been thrown over the ardour of the people for emigration to Badagry, there would have been a general desertion of Sierra Leone for the Yarriba country, both by Pagans and Mohammedans of that nation, to the detriment of the missionary proceedings in the interior. . . . Although unintentionally done, it gives the missionaries a great influence; it is the opinion of all the people, that unless missionaries go first to 'make the country good,' they could not long remain unmolested.[33]

EMIGRANTS AND MISSIONARIES IN THE 1840'S

Both the CMS and the Wesleyans were eager to pave the way. In April, 1844, Samuel Annear and his wife came from Sierra

Leone to replace the de Grafts in Badagry. While Annear's work there went on despite attempts by slave traders to burn his house,[34] his goal was Abeokuta, and he began negotiating with the Egba chiefs outside Ado.

On the 17th of January, 1845, the CMS party arrived on the *Barque Adario,* a ship described as "American." The group, twenty-seven men, women, and children in all, included Samuel Crowther and his wife, Henry Townsend and his wife, Charles Gollmer and his wife,[35] two emigrant schoolmasters, William Marsh and Edward Phillips; Mark Willoughby, the interpreter, who had been liberated with Crowther in 1822; four carpenters, headed by Thomas Puddicomb, three communicants employed as laborers, and two servants — all Sierra Leonian emigrants.

They had letters to the *Wawu* and Shodeke from Governor Fergusson, recommending the missionaries to the chiefs' protection and including requests for the abolition of the slave trade.[36] They had instructions from the Parent Committee:

Next to your own personal piety let it be your special care to cherish and watch over the piety of the native Sierra Leone Christians. Strive to raise among them a sense of their increased responsibilities and of the obligation which lies on them to let their light shine before their countrymen. . . . They may prove such an advantage to your work as no modern Mission ever yet possessed. They may, if they backslide and relapse, prove the hindrance and ruin of your Mission. . . .[37]

The directions continued that, apart from preaching the Gospel, the missionaries were to work on translating the Scriptures and introducing "such useful arts and elementary knowledge as they may be capable of acquiring"; that the "Native Teachers" should "as far as possible conform in their houses and in the frugality of their mode of living to the native standard."[38] Further instructions stressed promoting agriculture and trade, though, of course, the missionaries "must not engage in commerce themselves, nor in agriculture, except to a limited extent." They were not, in fact, to give an "undue proportion of time" to secular matters, and under no conditions were they to have anything to do with firearms, powder, or "ardent spirits."[39]

The CMS missionaries immediately sent a messenger to Shodeke, only to find that the chief had just died; they therefore began negotiations with the Egba chiefs at Ado. The new arrivals were also trying an experiment: they took no gifts to the chiefs where they went. They were nonetheless well treated by the *Wawu*, though he "looked very sour at" them, and by "Ogubound,"the Egba war chief. Crowther attributed this friendly treatment to the intercession of the Sierra Leonians who, presumably, had previously brought presents.[40] The missionaries, particularly Gollmer, soon realized that presenting "themselves" as gifts, as they had been instructed to do, was unlikely to be very effective. The emigrants pleaded with them to conform to the customary pattern, and they finally relented, though Crowther and Townsend were firm in substituting cowries for the desired rum.[41]

The trip to Ado was as successful as it could be in view of the disruption caused by Shodeke's death. Particularly useful to the missionaries in the unsettled situation were the prominent emigrants in Badagry: "Mr. Sawyer is a relative of Ogubound; he and Messrs. Savage, Johnson, Wright, and Thompson, are influential Sierra Leone emigrants . . . . These men obtain information of the state of things, through messengers from their native correspondents, in all the neighbourhood of Badagry, as well as in Abbé-Okuta." [42] The Egba war chief advised Townsend and his friends that, although everyone was waiting to welcome them in Abeokuta, it would be unsafe for them to go there before a successor to Shodeke had been chosen, for there would be no one to protect them.

Townsend, writing to the Parent Committee, gave the reasons for their next move:

The most influential of our Sierra Leone friends . . . strongly advised our forming a station in Badagry. Their opinions in all matters connected with their own country should be respected; we have every reason to suppose that they feel personally interested in the welfare of our Mission and a desire for the spread of Christianity. They possess means of obtaining information that we do not and are respected by the Chiefs of their country and feeling a confidence in them we consulted them and are assured that our confidence is not misplaced.[43]

The missionaries were more convinced of the correctness of their decision when, on their return to Badagry from Ado, they unwittingly became involved in a quarrel arising from the resentment of one chief to whom they had neglected to pay their respects while doing so to another. Townsend concluded that, "without a rightly constituted head in the place of Sodeke it would be the better policy to remain quietly in Badagry." [44] He thought that the only possible deterrent was the already existing Wesleyan station, but when the Methodists joined in advising him and his companions to remain, he decided to stay in Badagry despite the instructions to go to Abeokuta. Thus, amid the turmoil of the surrounding countryside, the CMS agents began their work. Crowther preached every morning in Yoruba to "a congregation of from 100 to 250 persons" under a tree between two markets; [45] Townsend and Gollmer preached in the church they had built and held services through interpreters in the compounds of chiefs, rotating among them.

Shortly after settling themselves in Badagry, the missionaries learned of a new threat — Dahomey. They thought that the Dahomean army was persuaded by Kosoko, the thwarted aspirant to the *Oba*ship of Lagos, to assist the Ado people against the Egba and thus showed awareness of the alignment of these two parties in the conflict. But is it not clear whether their interpretation was, in fact, correct, or whether the Dahomeans, as enemies of the Egba, came independently to the aid of Ado which paid tribute to their allies at Porto Novo.[46]

The siege at Ado continued. The European missionaries remained on the coast, where they made what headway they could with the residents of Badagry. Both Wesleyans and Church Missionaries continued their preaching under trees and in their churches. At the end of 1845 both groups wrote to London telling of success in their educational projects.[47]

But Sierra Leonians could travel to Abeokuta if they were willing to take the risk, though the way there was still closed to the Europeans in Badagry. In June, 1845, William Marsh, a catechist who had come in January with the others of the CMS, determined to make his way to the Egba capital, which he reached after five days' travel. His description of his homecoming was typical of those recounted to the mission supporters in England, and could be relied on to move the British congregations and stimulate gifts for the extension of mission work.

I reached Abbeokuta and came upon my parents quite unprepared; They gaze upon me very earnestly, when the guide who knew that I was their son, asked them whether they knew the stranger. Then my father all at once fell upon me, calling my native name, 'Olujobi, Olujobi, Olujobi! Mo di ri 'o! Mo di ri 'o! . . . Do I see you again!' All this while my mother, was at a loss how to express her joy, was shedding tears of joy. Our house was soon crowded. Many of them were my own relations, and others came to see my strange dress.[48]

For six months Marsh remained in Abeokuta, where he helped Andrew Wilhelm who, unaided, had been carrying on officially the work of the mission.[49]

Abeokuta was unsettled. Akitoye, expelled from Lagos in August, 1845, by Kosoko who claimed to replace him as ruler, had sought asylum there. The issue of protecting him had caused some division among the chiefs, though statements that Kosoko's partisans endangered the life of the ex-king seem unfounded. However, in December, 1845, Akitoye, having asked for and received assurances of friendship and protection from the "British Subjects at Badagry," [50] transferred his headquarters there.

Events relating to Akitoye's failures to regain Lagos, and which need not concern us here in detail, led to the opening of the road between Badagry and Abeokuta, although the siege of Ado continued. Permission for all missionaries to travel the reopened road was granted in August, 1846. We may infer that the defeat of Akitoye's expedition against Lagos the previous March and the advice of respected emigrants had persuaded the Egba leaders that British support was essential for them to reach their commercial objective — direct access to Lagos — and that this support could be most effectively urged and won through missionary pressure. The original obstacle to European entry had been the delay in selecting a successor to Shodeke, but, partly perhaps as a result of the Egba appraisal of the role of the emigrants in their midst, they now gave the missionaries permission to go to Abeokuta even though no "king" had yet been chosen.

The Crowthers and Townsends received their anticipated welcome, climaxed by the reunion of Samuel Crowther with his mother. The missionaries set to work immediately — they found the Egba willing to listen, though skeptical; they met enthusiasm in some of the Sierra Leonians and apathy in others who had "backslidden."[51] In December Townsend started the first station in the Ake section of the town, on a grant of land from the *Sagbua*, the leading chief. By Christmas a year later, there were small stations in four other districts: Igbein, where Crowther preached; Owu, Itoku, and Ikija. Mrs. Crowther had begun a girls' school; there was a Sunday School for adults where English as well as the Bible was taught; and at the end of 1847 Charles Phillips, a full-time Aku teacher from Sierra Leone, arrived. The attendance at Sunday services was in the hundreds, and when the Townsends left Abeokuta in March, 1848, they could report thirty-nine Sierra Leonian communicants who formally thanked the CMS for sending them the missionaries.[52]

In Badagry, Gollmer and Martin remained at CMS and Wesleyan centers. Political intrigue made the work of proselytizing among the Popo people, who lived there and whose intransigence was proverbial among all missionaries,[53] even more difficult than it would have been in peaceful times. Economic conditions in the town grew more and more desperate as the cruisers of the Preventive Squadron became more vigilant, while trade with both Porto Novo and Abeokuta was impossible with the blockades brought by the Dahomean war. Gone were the days of Freeman's early description:

Before the disastrous wars which commenced in 1845 at Lagos . . . Badagry was famous for its markets: . . . I walked through the Badagry market . . .; my admiration was unbounded; every conceivable article of native food and produce was there exhibited; artizans laboured at their stalls with their goods and wares laid before them for sale; and all bespoke a busy, active, thriving people, as far as such a state could advance amidst the degrading horrors of the slave trade.[54]

The only British trading concern there was Thomas Hutton and Company, which concentrated on Porto Novo and Whydah; its agent at Badagry barely managed to subsist.[55]

Slaving was, of course, the constant problem, and the missionaries were particularly agitated when emigrants were involved, either as victims or as participants in the trade.[56] Missionary influence often secured the release of kidnapped Sierra Leonians, but the question of the ambiguous legal status of the returned Aku inevitably arose and caused confusion in the Colonial Office and

Admiralty. Charges of slave-raiding by the emigrants themselves brought dismay; so concerned were the missionaries with the frequent accusations made against William Johnson, captain of the brig *Wonderful*, that in 1845 they conducted a thorough investigation which, however, cleared him of the charge.[57]

In Badagry, the emigrants met covert hostility which erupted on several occasions and was principally rooted in economic competition. The first clash arose over the refusal of the Badagrians to permit Sierra Leonians to work at the factory of Hutton's agent in 1846.[58] An even more serious encounter took place in October, 1850, when the Sierra Leonians of the English quarter, provoked by attempts to burn their houses, attacked the Popo people.[59]

Both Gollmer and Martin were discouraged by what they came to see as the futility of their work in Badagry. Their attempts to penetrate the Muslim community, most of whom according to Martin were Sierra Leonians, brought gestures of friendship but no response to the Christian appeal and thus further discouraged the missionaries.[60]

Not even in Abeokuta was progress so rapid or so smooth as the missionaries had hoped. Despite their efforts and the ground they gained, there were the many Sierra Leonians who had "lapsed," particularly those who were practicing polygamy.[61] And then, in 1848, persecution of the members of the infant churches broke out and violence erupted at intervals until 1851. Both Wesleyan and CMS Egba converts were attacked:

the Sierra Leone emigrants who have turned to heathenism are the principal parties who instigate the people against the members of both societies, and ... nearly all our brethren are chained and imprisoned. ... No assault has been made on the premises of the Missions nor against the Sierra Leone people who they say have learnt European fashion.[62]

Bribes given to Egba chiefs by Kosoko to assure interference with the trading activities of converts increased the pressure.[63]

EARLY POSITION OF EMIGRANTS IN YORUBALAND

How then, against this background, did the Sierra Leonians stand in this period preceding the formal British penetration of western Nigeria? Since the arrival of the first Freetown Aku in 1839, the number of emigrants had increased annually. The ma-

jority went to Abeokuta, though several hundred stayed in Badagry, and a few were scattered in villages between the two centers.
The fact that these men and women did not act as a homogeneous
group could be foreseen from the variety of motives which had
brought them there, and from the fact that, while almost all were
of Yoruba origin, not all were Egba, and, as Fyfe has pointed out,
"only in Sierra Leone were all the children of Odudua, the Yoruba
ancestor-god, united." [64]

Some were clearly firm Christians, and it was upon them that
the missionaries leaned heavily for advice and assistance. Both
mission societies relied on the work of specially recruited emigrants: the CMS had the already famous Samuel Crowther and,
among others, Andrew Wilhelm, William Marsh, Thomas King;
Mark Willoughby, the interpreter; Charles Phillips and Morgan,
the schoolmasters. The Methodists depended at Badagry on John
Martin and at Abeokuta on the lone efforts of Edward Bickersteth,
a Sierra Leonian catechist who had replaced Morgue.

Although thirty-nine was thought to be an encouraging number
of communicants to report to the Parent Committee in London,
the CMS missionaries in Abeokuta could scarcely consider this an
impressive accomplishment if the estimate of emigrant population
at 3,000 was remotely accurate. Already some of the returned Aku
had found their traditional customs more congenial than those
newly learned. Polygamy, the adherence to certain Egba religious
practices, the assumption of traditional social responsibilities, and
the participation in such key organizations as *Ogboni* [65] — whether
these were due to insufficient cultural contact and indoctrination,
as Europeans were apt to see it, or whether they were deliberate
assertions of preference, or even direct responses to social and
psychological pressures, it is impossible to ascertain. But in these
early years, we can already glimpse the beginnings of the complex
influences which were to have profound effects on the later development of the country.

Part II

1845-1861

THE IMPOSITION OF
BRITISH CONSULAR CONTROL IN LAGOS

Two key factors, as yet only touched upon, in the return of the Aku to Lagos as it continued through the 1840's were the disturbed political situation on the island itself and the parallel increase in British concern and activity there. The struggle for power in Lagos had repercussions that were felt from Abeokuta to Abomey, from Badagry to Whydah. It created factions which demanded that the Sierra Leonians, as well as the Lagosians, make choices in allegiance even after the Lagos succession had supposedly been settled.

British intervention must be considered here because its supporters in Badagry — Sierra Leonians themselves as well as Europeans — used the presence of these liberated Africans in arguing for such a move. Local political factors, combined with the shift in official British opinion in response to concerted pressure, brought about the "reduction" of Lagos in 1851. The advocates of this step saw in the posting of a British consul there a solution to the problem of Lagos for all concerned. For the Sierra Leonians specifically, it assured protection against possible re-enslavement, opened the way for them to reach their former homes, and, as the British hoped, encouraged them to step successfully into a mediating role.

Even the barest outlines of the consular period, however, show the problems of Lagos to have been more complex and less easily solved than was anticipated. A review of this decade will give us the backdrop against which the emigrants were to play not only the part envisioned for them but many others that were not foreseen. In seeking to weigh these factors we shall consider first the conflict which was developing in Lagos in the 1840's.

[63]

LAGOS POLITICS IN THE EARLY NINETEENTH CENTURY

Three sons of "Ologun" Kutere, the sixth *Oba* of Lagos, figured in the later disputes over succession — Eshilokun, Adele, and Akitoye. Eshilokun, the eldest, was the most eligible successor. Why he was not named is unclear, though it seems to have been a matter of his own reluctance to assume power; thus, his younger brother, Adele, succeeded their father.[1] Later, however, Eshilokun's ambitions changed, and after much maneuvering, he and his faction expelled Adele, who took refuge in Badagry, where, during their explorations, the Lander brothers met him plotting to recapture his throne.[2] Despite the efforts of Adele and his supporters in Badagry, Eshilokun was followed by his son, Idewu, whose unpopularity, according to one version of the events, led the *Oba* of Benin to suggest the traditional solution — the enforced ritual suicide of the Lagos ruler.[3]

In order to keep in perspective the manipulations of the contenders for the office of *Oba*, it is necessary to outline the procedure for choosing a new ruler and note particularly the men who influenced the choices. When Ashipa came to Lagos as the first *Oloriogun*, sanctioned by the *Oba* of Benin, he received a sword and a royal drum as symbols of his authority, and he was accompanied by a group of Bini "officers" who were to preserve the interests of Benin. These men were the initial members of the *Akarigbere* class of White Cap Chiefs of Lagos, and, with the *Oba*, they were the rulers.[4]

The original number of these chiefs is unknown; there were at least ten, and gradually their number was increased to twenty-four. But the key member of the group, as far as determining succession was concerned, was the *Eletu Odibo*. Because his office was hereditary, he was always at least partially Bini. It is clear from Herbert Macaulay's description of the proceedings just how important his role was:

The Eletu Odibo, immediately he is informed by the Ashongbon (the Head War Chief) that the Seat of State is vacant through the demise of the royal occupant, hastens to the Iga Idunganran [palace] ... to personally verify the fact, after which he promptly returns to his Sanctuary ... and there he consults, according to custom, the Ifa Oracle, submitting in turn, the name of each male issue of the ruling House whose father has ruled; in order to obtain a divine announcement and prophesy that will indicate under whose rule among them, both the people and the country will prosper. . . .

. . . The Eletu Odibo arranges with the Ashongbon . . . to summon a meeting . . . of the Omo-Obas [Oba's children], male and female, the Ibigas, the White Cap Chiefs, the War Chiefs, and the representative members of the Native Community who owe traditional allegiance to the Ruling House, at which meeting the Ashongbon, by direction of the Eletu Odibo brings out from the assembled Omo-obas, the individual chosen in the Eletu's sanctuary and hands over to the Eletu Odibo who offers a short prayer, after asking the whole community whether they accept the individual chosen when all answer in the affirmative invariably.[5]

The most likely candidate to succeed Idewu was his brother, Kosoko, also the son of Eshilokun. But if Kosoko ever hoped to inhabit the Oba's "palace" — and later events show that that was his driving aim — he had made a singularly unwise move when he had alienated the Eletu Odibo, without whose consent, as Macaulay's testimony clearly shows, he could not hope for success. Exercising a prerogative of kings and, to a certain extent, of royal sons to claim as wife any woman of their choice without regard to the rights of others, he had married a woman betrothed to the Eletu.[6] It is thus no surprise, though it seemed to have taken Kosoko unawares, that the Eletu recalled Adele instead of naming the obvious candidate.

Adele ruled only three years, until his death in 1834. Oluwole, Adele's son, had a strong claim to the succession, and his father's restoration had built up popular support for this line. The deciding factor in the choice of Oluwole over Kosoko was, however, again the enmity of the Eletu. This second time Kosoko tried to press his claim by force, but he was defeated and went to Whydah where, in an exile partly enforced, partly self-imposed, he continued plotting to gain the throne.

It was during the last years of Oluwole's reign that the Sierra Leonians began to return to Badagry and to enter Lagos. They found the Lagosians apprehensive about Kosoko's intentions. After Kosoko's departure, the Eletu had further exacerbated the ill feeling between them by digging up the grave of the "pretender's" mother and throwing her remains into the lagoon.[7] Kosoko vowed revenge for this outrage, and all Lagos knew that they could expect nothing but harassment so long as this feud continued.

In 1841, Oluwole died and the *Eletu* was again called on to fulfill his primary ceremonial function. Kosoko had supporters in Lagos, but because they were unable to produce their candidate, the *Eletu* could make his selection unopposed, and the title of *Oba* went to Akitoye, the third son of Kutere and, therefore, in European terms, the uncle of Kosoko.

Akitoye, from all reports a gentle, kindly man, decided to discover the whereabouts of his brother's son and invite him to come back to Lagos. Akitoye's chiefs, especially the *Eletu*, warned him in vain of the danger of Kosoko's return. Their fears proved well grounded, for no sooner was Kosoko back in Lagos than trouble began. The *Oba* tried to mollify him by giving him a title and residence in the palace. The *Eletu*, who since Kosoko's return was in Badagry, received an urgent summons from Akitoye. Kosoko protested this move, and tension grew between the ruler and his would-be successor. On 21 July 1845, the *Eletu*, returning to Lagos with an army of supporters from Badagry, was met by Kosoko's men stationed along the waterfront to prevent the *Eletu*'s entry, and fighting broke out.

A twenty-two day siege of Lagos by Kosoko's followers began. The *Eletu* was captured and drowned — a fate which avenged the "drowning" of the remains of Kosoko's mother. Akitoye's forces could not hold out, and the king fled to Abeokuta, where he could have refuge as the son of an Owu woman, and later to Badagry.[8] Kosoko was at last to occupy the palace — "without the Emblems of Authority, and without the sanction or confirmation of the King of Benin,"[9] the long coveted title of *Oba* was his.

BRITAIN AND THE "SLAVE COAST" IN THE 1840'S

British interest in the West Coast of Africa had increased steadily during the fifty years preceding 1840, mainly because of humanitarian pressure. But this greater concern, seen in relation to involvement elsewhere in the world, was still minimal. Moreover, it gained an increasingly negative aspect. The small West-African establishments were not particularly efficient, and they were expensive to administer. One of the reasons for introducing the

West-Indian-emigration scheme had been to reduce the cost of governing Sierra Leone and maintaining the liberated Africans. Dr. Madden's report of 1842 had shown weaknesses in the existing system of administration. There was no evidence that the changes implemented since then had had beneficial effect. And, as reports of continued and in some cases increased slave-trading came to England, the suspicion grew that the activities of the Preventive Squadron produced few of the desired results; that, indeed, they made conditions on the slave ships worse because of the slavers' need for haste and elusiveness.

But those wanting to abandon West African commitments in the 1840's — commitments which deeply affected the lives of the liberated Africans in the Lagos area, as in Sierra Leone and elsewhere on the coast — were facing a new challenge. The Squadron's protection during the early years of the decade had opened the way for European trading and the beginning of missions along the Bight of Benin. Such activity had continuously increased on the Gold Coast, and despite the apparent failure of the Niger Expedition in 1841, the attempt to penetrate the interior had given the CMS and traders like Macgregor Laird a glimpse of opportunities that would reward greater effort. With vested interests already taking root and the "man on the spot" controlling the only first-hand evidence, it could be anticipated that such information would be used to support their case.

Between 1845, when opponents first pressed for review of the Squadron's activities in the hope of disbanding it, and 1850, when they were finally defeated, there were three Select Committees — two of the House of Commons and one of the Lords — charged with examining the question.[10] The missionaries and the Sierra Leonians in Badagry and Abeokuta feared the possible removal of their only protection; the legitimate traders on the coast cried out against injustice; many naval officers also protested against suspending the patrols which were, they were certain, about to be fully effective. Given the chance, the diverse interests on the coast were well able to defend their case. They were fortunate in having Henry Venn, honorary secretary of the CMS, in a sufficiently informed and powerful position to organize their efforts.

Only the missionaries approached the crisis with a singleness of purpose. The trading interests in England made varying demands and often conflicting ones, while because of high mortality, danger, and discouragement, both the Admiralty and officers of the fleet fluctuated in their positions. But Venn rallied supporters from as many and as varied quarters as possible. The testimony of these men before the Select Committees, buttressed by evidence based on first-hand experience, was unquestionably a major factor in the ultimate decision to continue enforcing, and even strengthening, the preventive measures.[11]

AFRICAN POLITICS AND BRITISH POLICIES

The events on the coast which gave force to these pressures bear closer examination. In Badagry, the position of those who styled themselves "British Residents" in their petitions was particularly precarious. When the missionaries first reached Abeokuta, they had found the political structure there less unified than they had hoped, but they had sufficient popular support, deriving in no small measure from their association with the return of the emigrants, so that the chiefs were willing to protect them. But in Badagry authority was completely decentralized; worse, a number of the chiefs were hostile both to emigrant economic competition and to mission enterprise. Even the *Wawu*'s professions of friendship were not unequivocal. After confirming his suspicion of slave-dealing among the "English chiefs," a disillusioned Annear wrote in his journal, "I now see clearly that they are only 'English' for the sake of the gain to be obtained by English vessels coming here, and the special favour of the British residents." [12]

Missionaries, traders, and liberated Africans alike soon realized that, since the British government was unwilling to take possession there, their real protection lay in the agreed set of signals to passing warships which the Badagrians came to regard with awe. The Sierra Leonians were prominent among those concerned for Badagry's safety. In May, 1845, some of them wrote to Annear,

as natives of these parts, we understand more of the manners and proceedings of the surrounding tribes, and can hear their secrets . . . than one who is not a native. . . . We have heard and believe the combination of certain slave-dealers at Lagos, or Eko, who knowing that our living here would prove pernicious to their horrid trade . . . and who knowing that they are not able themselves to come and destroy this Badagry, are now stirring up . . . a certain man at Whydah, a powerful, notorious, and a Portuguese slave dealer . . . , to come — not personally — but ordering the Dahomey to come and destroy Badagry . . . .

We wish . . . to ask . . . what way we ought to write to a *man of war*.[13]

Annear promised to present their case to the next cruiser that called at Badagry; he did so faithfully, but got no firmer commitments than those on which the petitioners already depended.

Compounding the tension brought on by the threats to Badagry and the Akitoye-Kosoko conflict in Lagos was the continued Egba siege of Ado. Townsend, already in sympathy with the position of Abeokuta, advanced his explanation of the prolonged struggle:

The intentions of the baser sort of people of the towns on the coast are to shut up the people of the interior and to keep all the markets in their own hands; but it is too late, such things were but never will be more, too much knowledge of European affairs have been disseminated by the Sierra Leone people, and by them the natives of the interior have found out the great percentage laid on all goods that are not purchased thro' the natives of the coast, this will not permit the natives of the interior quietly to submit to the old monopolies. . . .[14]

Because of these continuing conflicts, apparent to the British from the time of missionary penetration of Abeokuta, the Foreign Office and the Admiralty were under pressure, sometimes overt, sometimes subtle, to take direct action against Lagos. There were in the last years of the 1840's also counterpressures. Palmerston was pursuing the policy of negotiating anti-slave-trade treaties similar to those that had been concluded in the Niger Delta,[15] and his goal was the signature of the King of Dahomey on such an agreement. Missionaries and travelers had brought accounts of the kingdom to the west of Abeokuta as the worst of all slaving areas; Freeman, though interested in Badagry, wanted to center Wesleyan activity in Dahomean country;[16] and Thomas Hutton's agents went on frequent expeditions to Porto Novo and Whydah, seeking to establish themselves where they saw better prospects than in Badagry.[17] Since humanitarian and economic interests coalesced in these more westerly centers even more strikingly than elsewhere on the coast, it was only the CMS that gave much publicity in England to events in Abeokuta and threw its weight at this time farther to the east.

In June, 1849 Palmerston, giving added force to the defeat of those wanting to remove British influence from the coast, appointed John Beecroft as consul in the Bights of Benin and Biafra. He was to make his headquarters at Fernando Po and was instructed, as were all consuls, to "regulate the legal trade." Though his instructions named ports from the Cameroons to Dahomey for him to supervise, they did not mention either Badagry or Lagos. He was to prevent quarrels between local chiefs and agents of British firms; to persuade the Africans to farm the land; to convince the chiefs of the advantages of legitimate commerce and assure them of "Her Majesty's desire for their welfare and improvement." [18]

At the time of the appointment, the King of Dahomey seemed willing to negotiate with the British. To follow up this major interest, early in 1850 Palmerston sent Beecroft on a mission to the King — a mission which, however, was unsuccessful. Only then did the Foreign Office realize the futility of continuing to stress Dahomey. Officials began listening more carefully to the arguments of the CMS.

On their part, the trading interests on the coast, searching for alternative openings, now brought before Palmerston their new case, this time aligned with that of the missionaries. In particular the agents of the London firm of Thomas Hutton and Company, with its African base at Cape Coast, though concentrating their eastern efforts in Whydah and Porto Novo, had long been investigating the prospects of Badagry and Yoruba country. They did not abandon their factory in Badagry even when political conditions brought trade to a near standstill. By 1850 the same firm was even venturing into legitimate trade in Lagos.[19]

In January, 1851, Lagos was blockaded in an attempt to bring Kosoko and the King of Dahomey to accept the British terms; in the months that followed, all the Dahomean coastal outlets, especially Whydah, were closely watched. But surveillance over slaving activities did not prove sufficient; the conclusion was that nothing less than a total blockade would bring results.[20] Badagry alone was exempt in order to give the missionaries there and in Abeokuta a base of supply and protection, and as a result, the coastal town had a temporary economic revival.

With this new importance of Badagry the number of Europeans there increased. In January, 1851, Thomas Hutton, nephew of the director of the firm, came on another visit and, to help his agent there, he brought with him William McCoskry, later to figure prominently in Lagos affairs.[21] In May J. G. Sandeman arrived with two assistants to start a post for the London firm of Forster and Smith.[22] All these men joined in pleas to the fleet for help, adding their voices to the increasingly urgent representations being made to the Foreign Office and the Admiralty by commercial and religious interests in England.

THE CASE FOR BRITISH ACTION

In effect, for the preceding six years the missionaries, both European and Sierra Leonian, had been laying the foundation for the arguments on which the case for taking over Lagos was to be based. To the Navy, success in Lagos and the resulting acquiescence of Dahomey to the British proposals would mean accomplishing a major part of their task. To the British traders, it would mean new opportunities: with consular protection for their interests added to the advantage they already had over legitimate traders from other countries, they hoped for profitable expansion. The Foreign Office was responsive to both these aims.

The motives of the missionaries, however, were more complex. Their first concern in the affairs of Lagos had grown from their suspicion that Kosoko was inciting the persecution of the Egba Christians. In the larger view, they sought the *de facto* abolition of the slave trade and, because it would ease the Christianizing process, the introduction of legitimate trade. But they focused these aims on Abeokuta, which, with the enthusiastic support of their Sierra Leonian adherents, they were seeking to build up to show the potentialities for a "civilized" way of life in Africa. Lagos itself was important to them primarily because it was "the natural port of Abeokuta."[23] They had long envisaged some central authority lodged at Abeokuta, with the Egba in direct control of at least Badagry.[24] In their journals, in their letters to their home secretaries, in their petitions to naval officers, they were continually giving reasons for British action in Lagos as it became increas-

ingly clear that, without interference there, the government of
Abeokuta was not strong enough to gain such control.

Henry Venn again marshalled the arguments and, in December,
1849, presented them to Palmerston. Thereafter, the case rested
on a position spelled out by Townsend in a letter to the CMS
secretaries. He suggested in it that the forthcoming deputation
to the Foreign Secretary stress four points: first, the good that
would come from starting commercial relations with the Yoruba
by suppressing the slave trade at its source; second, that free navigation of the Ogun River would finally achieve the goals of the
Niger Expedition of 1841, for Niger traders could come to the
markets of Abeokuta, and Egga and Rabba might be reached;
third, that the Egba chiefs were favorably disposed toward the
English and the abolition of the slave trade, and that the Yoruba
tribes, "live under a free form of constitutional government, very
different from the tyranny of the Kingdoms of Dahomey and
Ashantee"; fourth, that there had been attempts to kidnap Sierra
Leonian emigrants who were entitled to protection and "encouragement." [25]

These representations led to the decision to send an envoy to
Abeokuta, and in February, 1850 Palmerston wrote Beecroft, "to
ascertain by enquiry on the spot, the actual wants, and wishes, and
disposition of the Yoruba People." [26] The Foreign Secretary still
hoped for a settlement with the King of Dahomey, and Beecroft
was to visit him first. This part of the Consul's mission was a failure, as mentioned earlier, in that the King remained intransigent.
But while in conference, Beecroft mentioned the growing friendship between the Egba and the English and inadvertently learned
from the King's reaction of Dahomean plans to attack Abeokuta.[27]
Beecroft's report of this impending move brought British remonstrance and warning to the King of Dahomey, with Palmerston's
full approval.[28]

Beecroft waited for the dry season and then, in January, 1851,
set out for Badagry, where he stayed five days with Gollmer, met
the chiefs, sensed the discontent and danger in the town, met and
was favorably impressed by Akitoye and asked from him a petition
setting forth his grievances and aspirations. Going from there to
Abeokuta, he received an enthusiastic welcome from the Egba

chiefs and people, and forwarded their requests, as interpreted by the Sierra Leonians, for fortifications against the Dahomean attack of which he had warned them; for abolition of the slave trade and the introduction of legitimate commerce; and for help in restoring Akitoye and protection for him until then.[29]

This eagerness for British protection is not difficult to understand. The Egba, threatened by the Dahomeans and keenly receptive to the plans of the missionaries — plans which, if effected, would give then new hegemony in the region south of Abeokuta — had good reason to enlist British aid. Akitoye in Badagry was, no doubt, similarly motivated. As we have seen, the dispute over the succession in Lagos did not revolve around the question of legitimate versus slave trade.[30] Records of slave-trading activities during the time when Akitoye was in power show that he did not eschew the practice himself. The argument that he was aided by Domingo, one of the most notorious slave dealers, is less relevant because Domingo's clear interest was in successful trade of whatever kind.[31]

What seems certain is that after his expulsion from Lagos in 1845, and especially after the failure of the attack on Kosoko some months later, Akitoye knew that to regain his position he needed stronger support than any local source on the coast could supply. Such support could come only from Britain, and Akitoye, like the other chiefs along the coast, had learned that appeals to the English had to be built around abolition of the slave trade and the introduction of legitimate commerce. Even as early as June, 1845, when it was common surmise that some move by Kosoko against Lagos was imminent, Akitoye had written to Annear in Badagry, enclosing a letter to be sent to the governor of Cape Coast asking for intervention on his behalf in exchange for conforming to British regulations on trade.[32]

And by January, 1851, Akitoye's position in Badagry was not any more secure than before. Economic conditions, though showing improvement, were still critical. Badagrian co-operation with Akitoye in blockading Lagos had brought angry retaliation from Porto Novo and from the Dahomeans, who destroyed the farms which supplied food to Badagry. The chiefs harboring Akitoye were becoming alarmed, and four of the most important, including the *Wawu*, already were showing open hostility to him.[33] Only one, Mewu, remained a dependable ally, and he, far from being an important Badagry chief, was simply an exile from Porto Novo who had been given control over the town of "Mo" — Amowo — which paid tribute to Badagry and was on the route to Abeokuta. In December, 1850, Akitoye again appealed for British aid:

My humble prayer . . . is, that you would take Lagos under your protection, that you would plant the English flag there, and that you would re-establish me on my rightful throne at Lagos, and protect me under my flag: and with your help I promise to enter into a Treaty . . . to abolish the Slave Trade . . . and to establish and carry on lawful trade, especially with English merchants.[34]

He appears to have assumed that he could continue his end of the struggle from Badagry, but Beecroft had other plans. Hoping to persuade the British government to take action against Lagos, he took Akitoye with him to Fernando Po, ostensibly for protection. True, one of the pleas made by the chiefs at Abeokuta was that Beecroft insure the personal safety of the Lagos king and there was broad latitude for interpretation; but Akitoye himself had never asked for such action. According to both Gollmer's and Beecroft's accounts, he was distressed by the proposal and very reluctant to agree to it.[35] Certainly it was not according to any tradition he knew that at the time of crisis a ruler should desert his people.

Beecroft's departure with Akitoye on 28 January only increased tension. The missionaries anticipated violence, for the town was clearly divided. Mewu, Akitoye's supporters, the missionaries, and the Sierra Leonians were on one side, while the majority of Badagry's chiefs and Kosoko's supporters were on the other.[36]

THE EMIGRANTS AND BRITISH ACTION

In the unflagging campaign for the British government to take action in Lagos, the emigrants from Sierra Leone played at times openly active, at times seemingly passive roles. Their position in Badagry and Abeokuta was not yet defined, for though there was a division between those who were under mission influence and those who were not, it is not clear that the other Africans had yet seen the distinction.

In Badagry, where the returned Aku had no family connections to draw them close to the chiefs and the people, economic competition provoked hostility. Not only were the Sierra Leonians active traders who were encroaching on local enterprises, but they had been influential in centering the attention of Abeokuta on Badagry. The involvement of Badagry in the Dahomean-Egba conflict, exacerbated by the troubles in Lagos, brought, as we have seen, disruption of Badagrians' sources of food and their supply of articles of trade from the north. All this they blamed in part at least on the emigrants, and tension mounted between the two groups, with occasional outbreaks, the most serious of which, in October, 1850, has already been mentioned.[37]

Furthermore, as the chiefs of Badagry correctly saw the situation, the Sierra Leonians were blatantly in the "enemy" camp in their support of Akitoye and Mewu: whatever the feelings of the Aku toward slaving—whether or not they participated in the trade, they did hold domestic slaves[38]—they knew that their way to Abeokuta was blocked by Kosoko and his allies. Thus, if conditions of uninhibited slave-trading were to be restored, they themselves would again be likely victims. Aware of the feelings they were arousing in the people of Badagry, they gave active assistance, always described as self-defense, to Akitoye, and as a result saw their lives, like those of the missionaries, seriously endangered.

The Aku, as we have seen, joined the Europeans at Badagry in the barrage of petitions to the officers of the Preventive Squadron and were, further, always in the foreground of any argument of the missionaries for the defense of the port.[39] The Europeans there considered the emigrants as British subjects and stressed this point to exert the desired psychological pressure upon the fleet and the government. In a typical petition written to "Any of H.M.'s Naval Officers on the West Coast of Africa," Annear, who composed the document, wrote, "Feeling that we have no power to resist so formidable a foe [Kosoko], . . . we feel it both our duty to the hundreds of British subjects in the interior (the emigrants from Sierra Leone), and expedient for ourselves, thus to make you acquainted with our state, and to solicit, most earnestly, your assistance."[40]

The validity of this assumption was less readily acknowledged by Whitehall; in fact, the members of the Colonial Office were by no means agreed on the legal status of the returned liberated Africans, a question which was not to be acceptably answered for many years.[41] But so long as no official decision was on record, feelings of guilt could be aroused among both naval officers and officials in London for the neglect of these men and women. The missionaries applied themselves with all zeal in urging this interpretation. The appeal could be made on humanitarian grounds even if the legal ones were insecure.[42]

The number of Sierra Leonians in Abeokuta was far greater than in Badagry. They were evidently accepted by the community, for, as we have seen, they were not molested during the persecution of the Egba Christians which was taking place at this time. Though the missions still viewed all the emigrants as being within the Christian sphere of influence, some were suspected of slave-trading activities. Beecroft, on his mission to Abeokuta in January, 1851, took them to task for these practices, but his words met emphatic and unanimous denials. He told them that they were expected to behave like British subjects — presumably he considered that they were — and to abide by British law. He also reported that

on their arrival there, the late Chief, Sadokee, had offered them a choice of ground to form their own town and abide by their own laws; but it is too obvious the offer was treated lightly. . . . Under all the circumstances of the case, the people are not to blame; if they had had a head, it would have been somewhat better for them at this moment.[43]

It did not occur to Beecroft that there was no contradiction in appreciating the benefits of English philanthropy or accepting certain aspects of the English way of life, and at the same time wishing to live with families or relatives, rather than as strangers forming a separate community within a community of their own kin.

From the point of view of the English missionaries, this integration was distasteful and gave rise to a suspicion that the emigrants did not fully accept the British position in the affairs of the hinterland. In a letter to Commodore Fanshawe in November, 1850, the missionaries in Abeokuta wrote,

There are a large number of Sierra Leone people residing here, but so intermixed with the native population, that we could not expect to be able to form any sort of combination for self-defence. We are afraid, also, to ac-

quaint them of your offer of ammunition, lest it should come to the knowledge of the native chiefs, who would be induced thereby to lean upon us for
assistance instead of exerting themselves, and would probably think we have
an unlimited supply of the munitions of war, and expect from us what we
could not give.[44]

The plan to organize the Sierra Leonians for defense came later,
on the proposal of the most prominent member of the group,
Samuel Crowther.[45]

Crowther was, additionally, to be the prime Sierra Leonian figure in putting direct pressure on the government in London.
Palmerston had come around to open support of the missionary
point of view, and Venn tried to extract from him an order for
direct intervention in Lagos for the sake of Abeokuta. But Palmerston was unable to persuade the Admiralty to act, for they had no
legal grounds for going into Lagos.[46]

By the middle of 1851 the British public, as a result of wide publicity given to the dangers to Abeokuta, was psychologically most
vulnerable, and Venn seized this moment to summon Crowther,
on leave in Freetown, to be the trump propaganda card against
the Admiralty. What could be more effective than persuasion
from Ajayi, the former slaveboy, whose story was being told in
parishes all over England; who had, thanks to Her Majesty's
cruisers, been set free; who, by the grace of English humanitarian-
ism, was delivered from the depths of "savagery" and carried to
the heights of civilization; who was himself now acting as one of
the foremost agents of this civilization, preaching the gospel, reducing a local language to writing, and translating the Bible into
it?

Crowther arrived in England in August, 1851, and Venn arranged a heavy schedule of preaching and lecturing, but more important, took him for interviews not only with Palmerston and the
Lords of the Admiralty, but also with Queen Victoria and Prince
Albert.[47] Crowther gave his arguments, previously transmitted to
Palmerston, for Abeokuta's special claims to direct assistance: that
the liberated Africans were entitled to British protection; that
Beecroft's visit had implied assurance of England's interest; that
although there was no damage to British property during the unsuccessful Dahomean attack on Abeokuta the preceding March,

prisoners had revealed that they had had no instructions to spare it. He went on to express gratitude for the ammunition sent by the governor of Sierra Leone, and proposed that Aku who had been trained in artillery be brought from that colony for future protection of the Egba capital. The case ended with an appeal to British commercial interests, with the argument that if Lagos were placed under Akitoye — "its lawful chief" — and were allied with England, an extensive cotton-producing area, reaching 200 to 300 miles inland, would be opened.[48]

The Sierra Leonian's account was influential in placing Palmerston firmly in the missionary camp. The Foreign Secretary wrote to Crowther, thanking him for his information, and instructing him to assure his people that the British government would "take a lively interest" in them.[49] Basing his decision largely on information received from Crowther and Beecroft, he then sent instructions to the Admiralty for a strict blockade of Dahomean territory, especially Whydah; and he asked for an evaluation of the amount of force necessary to occupy Lagos and to restore Akitoye to the *Oba*ship.[50] The Admiralty concurred and wrote Commander Bruce to investigate accordingly, though cautiously directing him "not to keep possession of Lagos, nor to remain there beyond what is absolutely necessary."[51]

THE "REDUCTION" OF LAGOS

While these interviews were going on in London and instructions were being issued, which as often as not reached the scene after the event, the situation in Badagry had grown far more desperate than in Abeokuta. The plight of Badagry received much less publicity, however, for interests in England were less directly concerned with the "Popo" than with the Egba.

In June, 1851, a minor squabble led to civil war in Badagry between the Akitoye and Kosoko factions.[52] The supporters of Akitoye, reinforced by troops under the *Bashorun* of Abeokuta but without British help, emerged victorious, and the Badagrian chiefs allied with Kosoko were expelled from the town. Conditions in Badagry nevertheless continued unstable; the repeated pleas for English intervention were not to be satisfied until Lagos had been taken.

On orders from the Admiralty, Commodore Bruce of the Preventive Squadron went first to Sierra Leone, where he loaded the £300 worth of arms and ammunition he was authorized to transport to Abeokuta.[53] Then, following Crowther's suggestion, he sought to recruit Egba Aku trained in artillery. He was astounded that they refused to volunteer when they found that they were not to be paid for their services.[54] It is unclear whether a tradition of the paid mercenary or some other constraint lay behind this refusal, for the Yoruba in Freetown were not unconcerned with the critical situation in Abeokuta and, by October, 1851, had contributed £30 worth of gunpowder and flints for use there.[55] In the meantime, another British officer, Commander F. E. Forbes, was sent to Abeokuta itself with a small force of marines. There he interviewed the emigrants and chose "thirty able-bodied men to act as gunners," after telling the assembled group of "1500 men and boys" that since they were "a great number and should be all men of some education; set an example to the Egbas; show them the advantage of the knowledge the white men have, through God's assistance, ingrafted in you." [56]

The reputation of Britain on the coast was, after an unauthorized and unsuccessful action by Beecroft against Kosoko in November, 1851,[57] inextricably bound up with the fate of Lagos. On 1 December, Commander Wilmot reported the destruction the previous night of the slave baracoons on the eastern end of the island; there had been no casualties.[58] And on Christmas Eve, Commander L. T. Jones, with 400 British officers and men, 3 large ships, the armed boats of the Squadron, and a force of Akitoye's followers from Badagry and troops from Abeokuta, appeared off Lagos ready to attack. Out of respect for Christmas, the invasion force waited until the 26th to begin battle. After two days of heavy fighting Lagos was taken, with 16 British dead and 75 wounded. Kosoko had fled with his supporters to Epe, east of Lagos in Ijebu territory, and Akitoye was reinstated.[59]

On 1 January 1852, Akitoye signed the long sought treaty with Bruce and Beecroft. He consented to end the export of slaves to foreign countries; to destroy any buildings put up in future for the slave trade; to let the British use force against any revival of this trade; to liberate any slaves then held in Lagos; and to destroy remaining baracoons. He also agreed to allow free, legitimate trade with British vessels, and to show no special privilege to those of other nations; to abolish human sacrifice, and to give "complete protection to Missionaries," helping them to build their houses, chapels, and schools, and in no way obstructing their work.[60]

A copy of this treaty, with two clauses guaranteeing unrestricted right of travel to the missionaries and the emigrants, was signed by the chiefs of Abeokuta on 5 January. In March, Mewu put his mark on a similar treaty on behalf of Badagry, as the chiefs of the Ijebu had done in February.[61] The era of British control over the events in Lagos and the hinterland had begun.

EFFECTS OF THE BRITISH CONSULATE

The return of Akitoye as King of Lagos was, however, only the most tentative beginning of the search for solutions to the problems of the area. Kosoko who, as we have seen had fled with his supporters to Epe on the eastern edge of the lagoon, was by no means reconciled to his position, while Akitoye had not sufficient strength to expel the slave traders and to restrict trade to legitimate ends.

In the early months of 1852, the population of Lagos was growing. Sierra Leone emigrants, feeling a new measure of safety and anticipating opportunities for trade, came in increasing numbers. The missionaries, both Wesleyan and CMS, moved there from Badagry. Lorenz Diederichsen, one of three brothers trading along the coast, opened a factory in March, 1852.[62] Sandeman and McCoskry moved their headquarters there and were soon joined by a Mr. Legresley of a London firm called Banner Brothers; later, a German trader named Hermann Grote took over Diederichsen's concern on behalf of William O'Swald and Company of Hamburg.[63]

This influx brought a new source of potential conflict, this time between the missionaries and the traders. In the joint effort to stabilize conditions in the newly opened port, however, and to obtain a consul specifically appointed to deal with events around Lagos, the two factions were not yet aware of the divergences in their positions. In May, one of their goals was reached with the appointment of Louis Fraser as vice-consul in Lagos. Fraser was not, in the view of the Church Missionaries, the "able man" for whom they had hoped; they suspected him of appeasing Kosoko and his followers for the sake of promoting trade, instead of using his influence to establish Akitoye more firmly.[64]

That the chaos on the island could not be cleared away by the rule of a weak *Oba* alone had become apparent. The first solution was any consul; the second, a strong consul; and only gradually did the view prevail that nothing but a complete assumption of authority by Britain, backed by gunboats, could put a final end to slave dealing and other trading maneuvers which encouraged it.

The first eighteen months of the consular period were disturbed by threats from Kosoko and his allies, who found in Epe a convenient base from which to attack Lagos. The perpetually unsettled state of the hinterland interfered with trade. The only hopeful step toward peace was the successful mediation by Townsend, Crowther, and Andrew Wilhelm in the raising of the Egba siege of Ado in August, 1853.[65] The Ijebu, who were hostile to the introduction of European influence into their country, were allied with Kosoko, for they controlled the port of Epe.

On the island itself, the Consul and Akitoye were meeting opposition from the Portuguese traders and from two of the chiefs, Ajinia and Pellu, who were working for the expulsion of the English and for Kosoko's return to the throne. The English residents and the Sierra Leonians were again grateful for the frequent, well-timed arrivals of war ships, though the missionaries were still suspicious of the naval officers who would not take responsibility for active interference, and offered such suggestions as evacuating the residents to Fernando Po.[66]

In July, 1853, Benjamin Campbell, who had spent years in trading and semi-governmental activities in Sierra Leone,[67] arrived to take over the post of consul. Gollmer, with whom he lived for the first three months of his stay, was much impressed with him, especially with the authoritative and efficient manner in which he sought to solve the potentially explosive problems. But the fire still smoldered, and the whole population waited for the outbreak of the blaze. On 5 September Kosoko entered Lagos and a battle followed, with many killed and wounded on both sides. After fighting all day, Kosoko withdrew, with victory going to neither side.[68]

Three days before, "another event took place . . . of rather more serious import, because involving more serious consequences."[69] The King, Akitoye, died. The circumstances surrounding his death are not clear, but they seem to point to poison, probably ritually administered. Such action would fit into the traditional Yoruba pattern, whereby, as we have seen, a ruler who failed to meet the expectations of his subjects was called on to put an end to his life. It is also possible that the king had at last realized that the aid enlisted to assure his re-entry into Lagos meant his replacement by British authority.

Insofar as popular support was important, a large proportion of it was aligned behind Kosoko. The explanation for this does not lie solely in pro-slave-trade sentiment, but also in the desire to follow the stronger man.[70] But it is unlikely that Kosoko, said to be singularly astute, did not realize that with the British in Lagos neither he, nor Akitoye, nor any of their successors would continue to rule in the way of their ancestors. In any event, on Akitoye's death his son, Dosunmu, of whom "great hopes were entertained by the European community," was at once installed as *Oba*.[71] Not all of the traditional authorities were consulted, but Campbell approved of the choice;[72] he would certainly not have countenanced reconsidering Kosoko's claim.

But the threat of Kosoko remained no less serious than it had been, despite the efforts of Campbell and various naval officers to persuade him to give up peacefully his designs on Lagos. Added to this problem was the clear emergence, by the beginning of 1853, of the rift between the missionary and trading interests in Lagos. Before everything, the missionaries wanted annihilation of the slave trade, and they objected to any dealings with those even suspected of an interest in it. They saw the issues and the men involved as good and bad, and for them there was no compromise with those they labeled bad.[73] The representatives of the CMS in particular were still working toward enhancing the position of Abeokuta; they identified their interests with those of the Egba, showed animosity toward the Ijebu, who had rebuffed them, and were ever wary of the plans of the King of Dahomey.

The traders, on the other hand, even those who were unsympathetic to the slave trade, soon came to realize that products shipped by the Egba down the Ogun River were only a fraction of what would be available to them were the country opened to legitimate commerce, but without extended British control such an expansion would not occur. Badagry was still in the hands of Mewu who, as an exile from Porto Novo, was not acknowledged by his neighbors and relatives to the west. Until he was removed, Porto Novo would not only refuse to encourage trade with Lagos but would interfere with boats taking goods along the lagoon. On the other side, the Ijebu country would remain closed so long as the people there were allied with Kosoko. The commercial interests, therefore, began putting pressure on the Consul to resolve these tensions by negotiation, and since Campbell's primary concern was the expansion of legitimate trade — in part as a way of putting an end to the slave trade — he changed his approach.

In the light of this new hostility between the European traders and missionaries, the accounts of the events of the 1850's must be read with the deeply felt biases of the time firmly in mind. Campbell and the traders became anathema to Gollmer and the missionaries at Abeokuta. Only Gardiner of the Methodists was in sympathy with the Consul's group,[74] for his interests focused not on Abeokuta, but on Freeman's earlier plan for extending mission activity into Dahomey. It is clear that there were errors of judgment and principle on both sides. Stated most simply, the Consul and traders were, as accused, treating with slave traders. The Church Missionaries, on their part, were supporting as ruler of Badagry a man who had no legitimate claim to office; their unceasing concern was the repercussions any contemplated action would have upon the Egba. Because of the strength of the two key personalities in the controversy — Gollmer and Campbell — the battle raged on until the Consul's death in 1859. As we shall see, the returned Aku were in both camps.

By the middle of 1854, Campbell had arranged an uneasy truce between Lagos and Kosoko's forces, with Kosoko recognized as head of Epe, Palma, and Leckie, in exchange for his promise not to molest Dosunmu in Lagos. The port of Ikorodu was to be neutral territory where representatives of both groups and the people from the hinterland could trade.[75]

Campbell had also turned his attention to Badagry. After accusing Mewu of slave-trading with the help of Domingo Martinez, the Consul arranged for the return of the banished chiefs. Mewu went to Lagos, under the protection of Dosunmu, and died there a year later. Heated controversy between Campbell and the Church Missionaries on this issue brought impassioned accusations against the Consul's betrayal of the staunch ally of the British and the Egba, and cogent arguments about the hypocrisy of replacing a chief for slave-dealing by men who had been longer and more deeply implicated in the practice.[76] Campbell won the day at the cost of deepening the rift between himself and the missionaries and between the Lagos authorities and the Egba.

The dispute became more and more bitter as conflicts arose over issue after issue, with insinuations of insufficient consular protection for the missionaries, and counter-accusations of missionary "meddling" in political affairs. One quarrel even revolved around the land assigned for the consulate, which, according to Gollmer, encroached upon land already granted to the CMS.[77] The division spread to relations with the Egba: Campbell blamed the church agents for the hostile reaction to him there; and the missionaries retorted that Campbell had betrayed Abeokuta, despite the aid he had sent when the Dahomeans threatened a second attack upon the Egba capital.[78]

The Consul's quarrels were not only with the missionaries. When he managed by 1855 to reduce the missionary conflict from the boiling point to a simmer, he found himself under heavy attack from the traders, who argued that he impeded their success by being too concerned with matters which the missionaries repeatedly accused him of disregarding and compromising.[79] That is to say, the traders accepted the protection his presence implied, and which he could make more tangible by a summons to the fleet, but they resented his supervising and sometimes restricting their practices.

But in Lagos in the 1850's protection was still the key issue. With the continuing threats of invasion from Kosoko despite agreements,[80] and his attempts to organize support in Abeokuta[81] and throughout the hinterland,[82] the European community knew that despite their differences they depended upon each other, and particularly upon the Consul, for survival in the face of crisis. And the crises continued unresolved. The questions which Campbell had to answer when he was on leave in England in 1858 — about slave-trading, threats from Dahomey, threats from Kosoko — had to do with problems which Lieutenant Lodder, acting in Campbell's place, had to face; with which Campbell had to cope on his return and until his death in May, 1859; and which Lodder again, and his successors, George Brand, Henry Hand, and Henry Foote, had to try to resolve in the two years that followed. There was no single pressing issue which dictated that the British take Lagos as a colony in 1861. Rather, it was a continuing state of affairs tantamount to anarchy which, the Foreign Office became convinced, was undermining all that the original "reduction" of the island in 1852 had been intended to achieve.

Against this background we shall now look more closely at the position the emigrant communities came to occupy and to develop for themselves in this period.

SIERRA LEONIANS AND TRADE

T HE expulsion of Kosoko and the resulting conditions of relative safety stimulated the movement of the Sierra Leonian emigrants from Badagry to Lagos. They came with the missionaries; they came with the transfer of the headquarters of European firms; they came because Lagos was emerging as the new focal point on the Bight of Benin. In the meantime, the influx from Sierra Leone continued, now directed to Lagos; in 1853 Gollmer reported from there that, "Many people leave S. Leone for this part. There were about 80 passengers in Johnson's vessel [*Wonderful*] mostly Egbas — and some come almost by every mail." [1] Many of these emigrants eventually made their way to Abeokuta, but Lagos held sufficient attraction so that in 1865 William McCoskry could estimate that they were one-fifth of the population of the town.[2]

The emigrants were called "Saro" by the Lagosians and Africans of the surrounding area. The word is said to be simply a contraction of Sierra Leonian, though through time it acquired in certain cases other connotations, some derogatory, as, for example "mingy," or stingy.[3]

BRAZILIANS IN LAGOS

There was another significant movement to Lagos contemporaneous with that of the Sierra Leonians: the return of self-emancipated slaves of Yoruba origin from Brazil.[4] On his arrival in 1853 Consul Campbell found 130 of these families already living in the town:

having had the good fortune to escape being sent to the mines, or the plantations in Brazils, [they] were enabled by their industry, frugality, and good conduct to purchase their own freedom, and, that of their wives and children. . . .

During Kosoko's reign, these people on their arrival at Lagos were plundered by him; and, in some instances when attempting to evade or resist his forcible extortions, they were unmercifully butchered.

They appear to have lived here without anyone to protect them.[5]

Because of their common experience — many of them had come from Bahia — because of their knowledge of the Portuguese language and their shared beliefs in a Roman Catholicism syncretized with Yoruba traditional worship,[6] this group of emigrants was more tightly knit and more self-contained than were the Sierra Leonians. The Brazilians were sharply separated from the European community by some of these factors, and from the Lagosians by others.

But the emigrant groups were not without some common characteristics. As the Sierra Leonians were called "Saro," the Brazilians were known as "Amaro," a word which, like "Saro," had depth through implication, for it meant commonly "those who had been away from home." The prominent Sierra Leonians referred to themselves as "daddies"; the Brazilians talked of the leaders of their group as "papae" and "mamae," the Portuguese words for "father" and "mother," both translations of the Yoruba titles of respect for seniority.[7]

Increasing numbers of Brazilians continued to arrive through and beyond the consular period. In 1855 Chapman, one of the CMS secretaries, wrote to the Rev. James Beale in Freetown,

You may probably have heard that the last mail took to Lagos a large party of Yoruba (40 in all) who had purchased their freedom in the Brazils, and paid they way to England. They report that there are two thousand of their countrymen in America who have redeemed themselves from slavery and are only waiting an opportunity to return to their own country. The influx of these men, all of whom must have something of European civilization among them (though doubtless alloyed with European vices and much error for many of them are Roman Catholics) together with the return of so many from Sierra Leone, must have a most important influence for good upon the interior of Africa.[8]

But not all the Brazilians were Yoruba. Some were from "Haussa and Nuffi [Nupe]" country. Campbell issued these men and women "passports" to facilitate their unmolested journey to their homes.[9] And another group of emigrants, a much smaller number, came from Cuba and tended to merge with the Brazilians because of similarities in religion and in language.[10]

PATTERNS OF RESIDENCE IN LAGOS

It is instructive to look at a map of Lagos, dated 1885, which indicates the areas settled by the various segments of the population.[11] In the first place, swamps covered much of the land which is now inhabited — including the northeast region and the part of the island between the palace of the *Oba* and the western point of land called "Olowogbowo" (meaning "the creditor claims his money from the debtor"). Around the palace was the quarter in which the Lagosians themselves lived, as they had since the early days of the founding of Lagos, following a traditional pattern of surrounding the *Oba* with his supporters.

The initial problem for the new Brazilian residents, therefore — as for everyone who came later — was to find unoccupied land, and conditions pointed to the central part of the island, where there was sufficient space to accommodate 130 families and others who would follow them. In that central section, southeast of the King's palace and northwest of the race track, came to be concentrated the whole Brazilian population. It was accordingly called the Brazilian Quarter, Popo Aguda (Portuguese), or Popo 'Maro,[12] and there the most striking contribution of these returned artisans, the fine examples of Brazilian colonial architecture, can still be seen.

There were, of course, no paved streets in Lagos — Richard Burton's description of the unhappy physical state of the island is eloquent as to this fact.[13] All new arrivals, Africans and Europeans, settled, as had the Brazilians, where land was available and convenient. For the handful of Europeans, sites along the water — what was later to become the Marina, running along the southwestern shore of the island — were most desirable, and particularly so were those on the high land at the western tip, where defense could be effectively mounted. From here, too, they could make contact with the ships of the fleet and, because many of them were traders, be near their wharves and the commercial vessels calling at Lagos.

For similar reasons the Sierra Leonians frequently chose to live in the same areas, for though Olowogbowo is usually spoken of

as the Sierra Leonian domain, analysis shows that the Saro lived
not only there but throughout the southwestern portion, their
homes interspersed in some parts with European factories and
residences, with mission stations and government buildings. There
was no room for them close to the palace; those who came with
missionaries were encouraged to remain near by, while those who
were interested in trade evaluated their position as the Europeans
did theirs. And in the early days of the consulate, with conditions
still unstable, defense may also have been a consideration.

For Europeans, who did not understand that local custom forbade the sale of land, and for the emigrants, who did understand
but chose to view the Lagos area, and themselves within it, as not
subject to these traditional rules, full ownership of land was important. This they obtained both by verbally authorized alienation
and by written grants from the *Oba* of Lagos to individuals, to
corporate bodies such as missions, to the consulate, and to the trading firms.[14] The system began under Dosunmu, who was in no
position to resist pressure from those who wanted it.

ROLE OF TRADE

Once settled, the new residents of Lagos set about establishing
themselves in the community. Their chief way of gaining a liveli-
hood was trade. This occupation they shared with a large part of
the former and new elements in the population. As Wood wrote
in 1877, "the real Lagosian loves above everything else to be a
trader."[15] An analysis of the role of the Sierra Leonians in the
consular period can well begin, then, by considering the state of
trade. The few Europeans who had entered the town without
either British government or mission connections came to profit
from trade, latterly from dealing in palm oil. The Sierra Leonians,
with interest and experience in commerce from their days in Freetown, were trading both in Badagry and in Abeokuta. Apart from
those attached specifically to the missions, they came to Lagos
because of its commercial prospects, since it was not "home" for
any of them. These prospects emerge in a letter written by Gollmer, shortly after his arrival there:

One thing I must hint — that we must be prepared for a greater Expense . . .
than I anticipated — as may be imagined the Portuguese Slave traders had

Plan of the Town of Lagos. See page 93 for key to numbers.

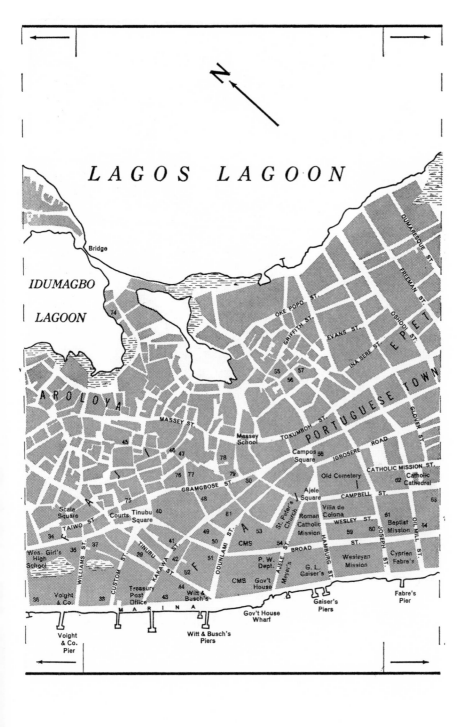

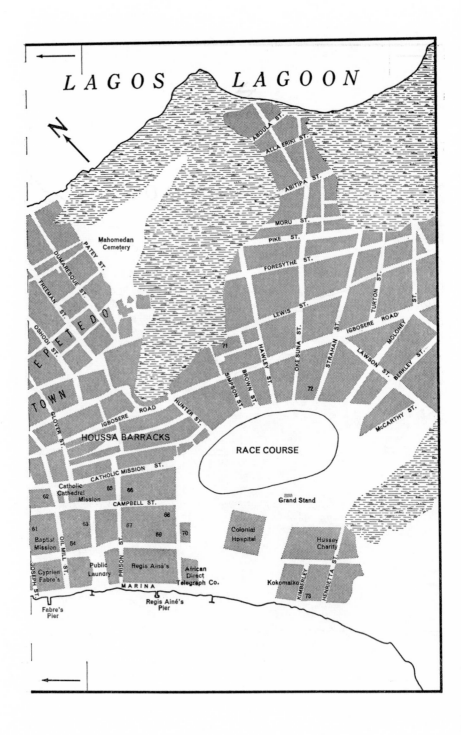

Plan of the Town of Lagos (pages 90–92), reduced and slightly simplified from a map of the same title, "prepared for the Lagos Executive Commissioners of the Col. and Indian Exhibition 1886 . . . by W. T. G. Lawson, C. E. &c. (Native of West Africa), Asst. Colonial Surveyor — Lagos. 30 December, 1885. Corrected to June 1887." The original of this map is in the Lands Office, Lagos.

1. I. H. Willoughby's
2. T. F. Cole's
3. J. S. Bucknor's
4. H. A. Wright's
5. C. J. Porter's
6. C. S. George's
7. Z. A. William's
8. T. J. Hoare's
9. A. Bailey's
10. Mrs. Berkley's
11. J. A. Savage's
 E. J. Austin's
12. J. J. Thomas'
13. C. A. Monnier's
 Ben Dawudu's
14. Chas. George's
15. Ben Dawadu's
 Bp. Crowther's
 Jas. A. Lewis'
16. J. B. Benjamin's
17. Jacob Williams'
18. M. Carr's
19. W. E. Cole's
20. Haga Mcaulay's
21. Harry Pratt's
22. R. B. Blaize's
 S. S. Davies'
23. D. A. Glouster's
24. I. W. Green's
25. W. P. Richard's
 W. P. Campbell's
26. Mr. Johnson's
27. T. A. King & Co.
 J. D. Fairley's
 Jacob Williams'
28. R. B. Blaize's
 J. S. Leigh's
29. Mrs. J. J. Williams'
30. H. Robbin's
 J. O. Turner's
 Williams Bros.

31. J. S. Bucknor's
32. Danl. Martin's
 J. Haastrup's
33. I. A. E. Ludrich (?)
 W. W. Lewis'
 T. A. Lawrence's
34. H. A. Caulrick
 D. C. Taiwo
35. Layeni's
 P. Jose's
 T. E. Williams'
36. C. B. Moore's
 Samuel Crowther's
37. W. E. Lumpkin
 R. Osborne's (?)
 J. H. Hamilton's
 N. Williams'
 Phoenix Hall
 Dr. Lumpkin's
38. H. Robbin's
 H. Campbell's
39. J. A. Payne's
40. Bataza's
 J. A. Fernande's
 M. J. Ferreira's
 N. C. King's
41. M. J. St. Anna's
42. Madme. Balbina's
43. Colonna's
44. R. B. Blaize's
45. A. C. Willoghby's
46. I. John's
47. W. R. Harding's
48. P. F. Gomez'
49. Soares'
 Juao Da Rocha's
50. late Dr. King's
51. Dr. Mayne's
 Marian Crowther's
 R. A. Coker's
52. Joaquin's
 Da Rocha's

53. Josiah Crowther's
54. Rev. Wright's
 Emal. Wright's
55. N. A. William's
56. C. J. Cole's
57. A. L. Hethersett's
58. J. A. Campos'
59. Dr. Grant
 Adolphus Pratt's
60. R. B. Blaize's
 J. L. Baptist's
61. G. Pike's
62. T. F. Palomera's
 Alex Campbell's
63. A. L. Hethersett's
64. William's
 J. S. Taylor's
65. Ramon Campos'
66. H. A. Sanu's
 R. A. Wright's
 H. A. Lawson's
 Colly Green's
67. J. W. Cole's
68. H. Joague's
69. E. T. Scott's
 G. I. Samuel's
70. B. J. Gilpin's
71. Lafiaji Compound
72. R. Z. Bailey's
 F. Dunstan Cole's
73. W. T. G. Lawson's
74. L. L. Collins'
75. Nash Villa
76. B. F. Damazio's
77. A. J. Barcellos'
78. Kijerro's
79. Walter's
80. J. George's
81. Smith Cot
 Mr. S. M. Harden's

money enough & could afford to pay high wages for everything — to this people are still accustomed. . . . Carpenter work is paid 300 per cent higher than at Badagry. The Victuals of the Natives seem to be . . . cheaper than at Badagry — but that portion Europeans make use of . . . is considerably dearer on account of the many Portuguese still here — and many other merchants . . . & many ships (there are 14–15 in the harbour) at and off Lagos.[16]

We have seen that the aim to substitute legitimate trade for the slave trade was responsible for bringing direct British influence to Lagos. European merchants, who had struggled with difficulties stemming from the absence of stable authority in the area, saw the consul's primary task as protecting and encouraging their trading interests, a position in which the Foreign Office concurred.

Nevertheless, these European traders, some of whom had experience in the Niger Delta, saw that they must to some degree work through the traditional political authority. Consequently, one of their first acts on arriving in Lagos was to draw up and sign with Akitoye and his chiefs an agreement which set forth and regularized the specific roles of all who signed it in the future trade of the island. The core of the agreement was as follows: the King promised to protect the traders and their goods and gave them virtually sole possession of the Marina area for their storehouses and piers; the merchants and the supercargoes of the vessels then in the roads agreed, for their part, to pay to the King customs duties of 3 per cent on imports and 2 per cent on exports.[17]

Although there was some trade in ivory and some in locally produced cloth, the emphasis was on palm oil. But Akitoye and, after his death, Dosunmu were unable to supply the European merchants with the amount of palm oil from the hinterland that the Delta traders could expect from the local rulers there. The reason for this lay in the fact that, unlike the Delta chiefs, the *Oba* of Lagos had no political control over any of the palm-oil producing country and, therefore, could not act as primary middleman for the palm-oil trade.[18] Thus it soon became clear both to the traders and to the consul that the "reduction" of Lagos had not been sufficient to achieve the essential stability and co-operation in the hinterland which would make possible the steady flow of oil to the port. This realization led to pressure from the traders to co-operate with Kosoko, himself the most immediate disruption; to the resulting consular concessions in the Badagry dispute; and most significantly to the agreement of January, 1854, whereby Kosoko gained autonomous control over Palma and Leckie, in return for his promise to stop hostilities against Lagos and interference with the trade to the north of the island.[19]

At this time the two emigrant communities entered into Lagos trade in several capacities. The ideal, which all strove to realize, was to control enough capital to permit competition with the European oil exporters. Such a success was barely short of impossible for the Brazilians, who came back to the Lagos area with little or no capital, while relatively few of the Sierra Leonians brought with them sufficient resources to be able to establish themselves independently. Some accumulated small amounts of capital by working for a time as assistants to the European merchants. Under the agency system established on the coast in the 1820's, almost all tried trading with the large British commission houses which sent goods to West Africa on credit in exchange for shipments of palm oil destined for the London and Liverpool firms.[20] Many of these enterprising exporters fell deeply into debt; the local court records show that from the 1860's onward, the commission houses were constantly trying to recover their losses on advances made to some of these men.

Most of the Sierra Leonians in Lagos became "petty" traders, able to sustain themselves though not to amass large profits. There were relatively few restrictions on going into trade in Lagos and its hinterland; anyone wishing to try his hand could do so and, on a small scale, could be successful. The impossibility of rigidly controlling trade worked against the interests of the Oba and his chiefs, and in some respects against those of the European trader, but was to the distinct advantage of the emigrants. Just as the missionaries had found that the Sierra Leonians had reliable contacts in the interior and were, therefore, valuable sources of information, the Lagos trading community soon saw that such contacts were being profitably used to strengthen the important position of the Saro as middlemen on the coast.

The "petty" trader thus could scarcely be dismissed by the European entrepreneurs as a negligible competitor whose share was an insignificant fraction of the island's profits. Not only was the "petty" trader a trader in his own right, he was frequently the agent who represented the European concern in the hinterland. When he was not himself an intermediary, he was often in closer touch with those who were and reached them before the European factor could do so. The competitive position of the emigrants was such that the large European commercial houses, with headquarters at the water's edge, were compelled to put up special buildings more centrally located for retail trade. O'Swald and Company, for example, opened a retail "office" of this kind early in 1860.[21]

But apart from the competition provided by Sierra Leonians because of their close association with the local people, the "petty" traders served two important economic functions for the European merchants. For one thing, the activities of these middlemen were a means of increasing the demand for the imported goods, and for transporting them into the interior without the direct participation of the European traders themselves. For another, they performed the increasingly essential task of breaking bulk for the importers. Because the African consumers, who were themselves producers of small amounts of palm oil, for example, had neither the need nor the resources to buy in quantity, the successive intermediaries reduced goods to marketable — often fractional — units. Reverse operations, with the produce coming into Lagos, meant additionally that the merchants there received the large quantities with which they were equipped to deal.[22] The trade between Lagos and the hinterland was carried out then not in three stages — exporter, middleman, producer-consumer — but involved numerous middlemen in the chain of trade to and from the coast.[23]

Not all the Saro, however, were small traders, even though in the highly competitive, growing community, only a handful had the resources to engage in large-scale trading. Those of the Sierra Leonians who did attempt larger ventures held an advantage over their European competitors because of their inland contacts, but were always at a relative disadvantage because of their limited supply of capital. Lacking the credit support of large commercial houses, they found it particularly difficult to weather such critical periods as during the embargos on goods from the interior.

In general terms, though, it can be said that in this period these Sierra Leonian entrepreneurs were seen and saw themselves as part of the group of European merchants. It was in their interest to support the demands of the Europeans, and emigrant names appear on petitions and in negotiations over trade issues throughout the consular period and afterwards. Most of them — men such as William Savage, J. M. Turner, J. P. L. Davies, James Cole, Samuel Crowther, Jr., I. H. Willoughby, Thomas F. Cole, S. B. Williams, James George — were leaders of the emigrant community.[24] Active members of either the CMS or Methodist congregations, they were often the men called upon by the consuls and later the governors to use their influence in the hinterland and in dealing with other local problems.

Consul Campbell also furthered the opportunities of some prominent Saro traders by enlisting their services in purely commercial schemes. Henry Robbin, an Egba Saro in charge of the CMS cotton concerns,[25] wrote in 1857 of an interview in which Campbell explained the Lagos government's willingness to help "anybody who wants to begin the cotton business," and offered him a £60 annual salary as a full-time agent in Abeokuta either for the consul himself or for the government, with the promise of increasing payment commensurate with success.[26]

Robbin's reaction to this proposal gives an insight into the attitudes of the emigrants toward European direction of their economic activity, and, as we shall see later, of other aspects of their lives:

I objected against being direct agent for any soul [?]. Besides I think Africans should have such business directly under our own Superintendence and for our own interest — again I have been successfully established in the oil trade and my business is such that it will be counted foolishness were I to leave it altogether for the cotton business dependantly upon another man and his interest, (the government's) for £60 a year. Then intelligent Africans will continue to be servants and the spirit for promoting our country's and our own interest with independent authority will lie dormant still. Hence I have proposed to begin the business on my own standing under the firm of W & brother.[27]

Robbin did not, in fact, trade as "W & brother," but as "H. Robbin & Co." The capital for the company also came from a Sierra Leonian, J. P. L. Davies,

who was formerly a shipmaster and was educated on Board a man of war he unfortunately lost his vessel and is now an agent and a great merchant at

Lagos he it is who commands all the capital belonging to the firm H. Robbin & Co. I have not a single farthing in the same but I transact a part of the business and receive a share in the profit. Capt. Davies deals chiefly in oil . . . but . . . the hope of turning his attention to cotton is one chief reason to myself why I accepted his kind offer as a partner and you will see that I have obtained my wish.[28]

Davies was, indeed, a prosperous merchant and evidently much interested in the cotton project for, as Robbin continued to describe him, he was "the person to whom much is owe[d] for all the Cotton shipped at Lagos, he commands several English canoes and boats and have shipped on board his vessel the 'Saltern Rocks' some hundred bales of Cotton when there was no ship to take them and then he could have shipped oil instead." [29]

In contrast to such Sierra Leonians, the Brazilians initially had less success with large ventures.[30] Aside from the fact that they had insufficient capital to establish themselves independently, they faced problems in adjusting to Lagos life that the Sierra Leonians did not. Language difficulties with the English-speaking merchants had to be overcome, for example. More important, however, was the fact that they brought from their Brazilian experience skills as artisans and craftsmen and they consequently had more, though different, possibilities than did the Saro, who relied chiefly on trade to subsist. Found among them were:

master masons, carpenters, painters, cabinet makers and master-smiths from whom the present generation of these tradesmen directly or indirectly learned their trades. On the women's side, proficiency in bakery . . . , laundery, and dressmaking distinguished the Agudas, and their Protestant rivals and Mohamedan compatriots or townsmen became apprenticed to them and carried away as much as they could learn.[31]

They did, however, enter commerce on a small scale in Lagos itself, and there is some evidence that Brazilians promoted trade between Lagos and Bahia, via Dakar.[32] It is probable, though firm documentation on this point is lacking, that trading interests in Brazil had the co-operation of the Lagos Amaro when they reached an agreement with Lorenz Diederichsen, who began managing trade in rum and tobacco between Lagos and Bahia for O'Swald and Company in the early 1850's,[33] or with the French merchants, whose "Vessels [were] trading regularly apparently between Bahia and this part of the Coast." [34]

Lagosians themselves, of course, played a key part in the commercial development of the island. Some were chiefs, some had lesser positions. Many had been trading in slaves before the British arrival. All were controlled to some extent by the *Oba*, or at least were considered to be under his patronage. The best known of these traders was Madame Tinubu, variously reported as a "niece" and as a "good friend" of Akitoye, over whom she is said to have exercised more influence than he did over her activities. Born in the Egba forest, she had been an important figure in the slave trade both in Badagry and Lagos, and with the advent of the British consulate and the signing of the agreement covering the commercial future of Lagos, she turned largely to palm oil, though keeping her hand in illicit slave dealing as well.[35] A powerful group of trading chiefs, the most prominent named Tapa, were allied with Kosoko and had left the island with him, becoming influential in commercial transactions in Palma and Leckie.[36]

STRUGGLE WITHIN THE TRADING COMMUNITY

The trading community in Lagos was by no means united; groups and individuals struggled for dominance, often with conflicting goals. At the end of 1854 and in January, 1855 the Consul and his supporters were faced with the first organized attempt to reintroduce the slave trade. In December several influential Portuguese slave dealers, who had been expelled three years before, returned; Dosunmu took no action against them, and once again it was only with the aid of a British cruiser that the new authority was successful in serving its deportation notice.[37]

Shortly thereafter Campbell reported that

for several months past there has existed, on the part of King Docemo, his chiefs and people (Domestic Slaves), and a few of the mischievous Sierra Leone people, and self-emancipated Africans from Brazil, a feeling and disposition hostile to the English residents generally, and to myself in particular. . . . This hostile feeling increased to the extent of heading a conspiracy by some of King Docemo's domestic slaves, the Woman Tinnaboo, and some others, to get rid of myself by assassination and of the English Merchants and the leading men among the Sierra Leone and Brazilian Emigrants, known to be favourable to the English, either by assassination or forcible expulsion.[38]

The expulsion of the slave traders brought a crisis. It became known that the King and Madame Tinubu were passing out ammunition to their supporters. The consul and the other targets had only a successful Brazilian trader, Antonio Martins, and his "150 well armed, devoted domestic Slaves" to defend them.[39] Once again a ship of the British fleet came to Campbell's rescue.

After the danger had passed, the Consul authorized an inquiry to be conducted by "some of the most intelligent of the Sierra Leone people." The findings showed that the opposition to the British was divided into two factions. One, headed by Madame Tinubu, plotted to assassinate the Consul, expel all those favoring the British, depose Dosunmu and replace him with a son of Adele. The second, composed of Dosunmu's own men, agreed to these ends but wished the *Oba* replaced by Kosoko. Dosunmu himself, kept in ignorance of the second half of this plan, was found to have supported the first half in all its implications.[40] Commodore Adams' arrival led to the reprimand of the King, execution of the man who had attempted to shoot Martins, and the first of several expulsions of Madame Tinubu.

With the agreement concluded with Kosoko in January, 1854; with the missionaries resigned to what they believed were injustices perpetrated to ease trade; and with the suppression of the January uprising, Campbell considered the general state of the port satisfactory. In June, 1855 he was reporting conditions of "perfect tranquillity," with "peace, security, and free navigation along the whole extent of the Lagoons." The palm-oil trade was growing; there were twelve merchant vessels, five of them English, anchored in the harbor. The value of oil in England was £40 a ton, in Lagos it was £20 a ton, and the anticipated export for the year was 12,000 tons.[41]

With this apparent calm, Campbell could give some attention to the internal problems of Lagos. Among his duties was adjudicating trading disputes, and to lighten the massive burden he was expected to carry alone, he set up in May, 1855 a "sort of Court or tribunal" to deal with these matters when they involved the emigrant communities. Campbell's high opinion of some of the Sierra Leonians and Brazilians led him to place their court in their own hands, for, as he phrased it,

There have been . . . a considerable immigration from Sierra Leone of the better class of Africans, men, who had been residing in Freetown, and, of that class who serve on juries in the Law Courts of Sierra Leone, Civil and Criminal, and, who have become advanced in civilization, and . . . attained correct notions of right and wrong.[42]

The committee unanimously elected William Savage as president and James Gooding as vice-president. These two men, with "not less than three" of the committee, were to "hear and determine all disputes and differences arising among the Emigrants from Sierra Leone and those from Brazil and Cuba." They were also empowered to hear cases concerning emigrants and Lagosians, though the final authority in the event of a disputed decision lay with the *Oba*; if a similar deadlock arose in a case involving two emigrants, the verdict was to rest with the consul.

The regulations set down by the committee elaborated on these points and, in addition, provided for giving advice to new arrivals and handling estates of members of the community who might die without heirs; also, Brazilians and Cubans were to be included in the operation of the court, and a "night patrol" was organized, on which every emigrant was to serve, find a substitute, or pay a fine. It was further stipulated that, although persons from Lagos or the hinterland could be seized and taken before the King for any criminal offense, no emigrant could similarly "arrest" a debtor without prior permission from the *Oba*. And no emigrant was to engage in subversion against the King, on threat of expulsion and return to Sierra Leone, or involuntary transportation to Fernando Po.[43] Two years later Campbell reported that, "the Court has . . . sat regularly every Saturday and has, on the whole, . . . worked well and many of the European merchants have availed themselves of its medium to obtain payment of debts due to them by the traders."[44]

TRADE AND UNREST IN THE HINTERLAND

Although for the time being trade was continuing smoothly along the lagoons, a comparable tranquility did not exist in the hinterland, and this unrest seriously affected the commercial activities of the Sierra Leonians. In August, 1855, Campbell finally reported to the Foreign Office an Egba embargo on trade which had been in effect for the preceding five months, and under which the "Sierra Leone Traders in particular" were suffering, since "they imprudently, as they now find out, gave considerable quantities of merchandise on credit to the Egba Traders."[45]

The Consul recounted the complaints from Abeokuta: that the Egba traders had been cheated by those in Lagos and, having been inadequately paid for their oil, were refusing to continue trading. He found their complaints partially justified — for instance, the measure of palm oil were found to contain from eleven to thirteen gallons and not the standard ten. He could not, however, accede to the *Alake*'s demand that the British officially regulate the price.[46]

The controversy was temporarily resolved some weeks later, when the Egba traders came to a conference with the Sierra Leonians and Brazilians who had extended them credit. The Abeokuta delegation complained of their losses in a trade that was "for women, not men." After a walk-out by some of the emigrants because of insulting criticism of the English, those who remained were given the Egba terms of settlement: a 20 per cent increase in price. After consultation with the Consul — "better to get 15/- on the pound than nothing" — these terms were accepted by all the emigrant traders.[47] The Egba had won, for the moment; the Lagos traders respected the decision. And it had become clear that, in purely economic terms, the large emigrant traders had no less a stake in peace with the hinterland than did the European merchants.

Furthermore, their counterparts in the Egba capital also shared this interest. In 1860 some of the prominent emigrants there formed the "Abbeokutan Mercantile Association," which resembled in part a traditional co-operative society and in part a European pressure group. Its general aim was to take in hand "the arrangement of the commercial affairs of the Oyibos [emigrants] residing in Abbeokuta for commercial purposes." Its officers were Henry Robbin, president, and J. C. Dewring, secretary; other prominent members, all traders, were Samuel Crowther, Junior, J. G. Hughes, Josiah Crowther, C. W. Faulkner, J. Ribeiro, C. M. Young, and N. G. Munday.

The rules of the new Association clearly stated its specific goals: to arrange an equitable tax levied on the traders and paid to the "Chief"; to keep the roads to Lagos open; to get the help of the local authorities in collecting "just debts" and detecting and punishing those responsible for robberies "by canoemen or others"; to facilitate "the general settlement of all disputes that may arise between the Chiefs and the commercial body"; and finally, "to advance the general welfare and extension of legitimate trade in this country by just means." [48]

PERSISTENCE OF SLAVE-TRADING INTERESTS

It was not only in the hinterland, however, that the Consul and both emigrant and European traders working under the British aegis met continuing difficulties. In mid-March, 1856 came the second attempt to expel forcibly those engaged in legitimate trade. Campbell had gone to evaluate trading possibilities in Benin and to Fernando Po for consultations with Beecroft. The British trader, William McCoskry, who had recently opened a factory in Badagry and acted as unpaid vice-consul there,[49] was given charge of Lagos in Campbell's absence. As McCoskry reported developments,

Tinaboo and the Caboceers were no sooner aware that you had gone to some distance ... than they commenced their intrigues to get up a disturbance; their grievance is, that Sierra Leone and other immigrants are becoming Masters of the town; that the King and Natives are thrown altogether aside; and that they would prefer being driven into the bush as they knew they would be on the arrival of a man of war, but, that in the mean time there was a good opportunity to attack and plunder the emigrants and merchants.[50]

McCoskry summoned Commander Hickley to restore order.[51] There was much commotion but little conflict, for the cruiser was an effective deterrent, and Madame Tinubu was again banished to Abeokuta.

Ten days later, when the Consul returned to what seemed a peaceful Lagos, he began his own investigation of the incident. On the basis of information from "leading Sierra Leone people and African emigrants from Brazil" he found that McCoskry's analysis of the events was acceptable. But he added that,

it is not the growing influence of the Sierra Leonians and Brazilians alone which has led the native population of Lagos headed by war captains seeking

to obtain their expulsion, there is another cause . . . , the utter prostration of
the slave trade and hopeless prospect of its being revived at Lagos. The war
captains, finding their occupation gone . . . will try to rid Lagos of those
whose presence as they think prevents a return to Slave trade. . . . Kosoko is
not mixed up in this.[52]

Nor, according to this report, had Dosunmu been implicated
initially. On the contrary, when Commander Hickley crossed the
bar to aid the *Oba* in expelling Madame Tinubu, it appeared that

Mr. McCoskry, together with Mr. Sandeman and Mr. Grote, endeavoured to
thwart the intention of King Docemo; and, the woman hid herself in the
house of a Sierra Leone man, named Turner. On the King's proclamation that
he would heavily fine any person who hid the woman, she left her hiding
place, and surrendered herself to one of the leading Sierra Leone men, and declared that she had been advised by Mr. McCoskry to conceal herself until
night; when he, with Messrs. Sandeman and Grote, would carry a large
quantity of cowries to the King's house and prevail upon him to allow her
to remain at Lagos; on the plea of her indebtedness to several persons in the
Town.[53]

Madame Tinubu had then been taken to the palace, and, according to the Consul, the traders' interpreters had pleaded for her
with Dosunmu. But the cowries did not come, whereas a message
telling of the arrival of the armed ships did, and Madame Tinubu
was banished to Abeokuta.[54]

TENSIONS AMONG EUROPEAN TRADERS

In subsequent months tensions grew among the important
traders in Lagos, tensions arising mainly over the collection of
King Dosunmu's duties, and the relative position of English and
"foreign" — that is, other European — merchants. Until this time
the dominance of the German firms had been undisputed.[55] Actually a monopoly of the cowrie supply was in the hands of William O'Swald and Company, who shipped the "currency" from
Zanzibar to various points on the Bight of Benin.[56] Their interests
were ably handled in Lagos by their agent, Hermann Grote, relieved on occasion by one or another of the Diederichsen brothers,
who had originally interested the Hamburg firm in Lagos trade,
and by other O'Swald agents. Their greatest threat came from
another German concern, Adolph Jacob Hertz and Company, also
operating in Zanzibar, but by 1856 Hertz was having to work

through O'Swald agents.[57] William O'Swald and Company were doing a flourishing business in Palma as well. They had carefully cultivated the friendship of Tapa,[58] Kosoko's ally, and had thus wanted to promote the rapprochement between the consul and the exiled former king.

Trade was booming in 1854. The agreement with Kosoko had opened Palma, and peace in the interior had brought an increasing flow of palm oil to the coast. In Europe the price of oil had risen by almost 50 per cent.[59] The French house of Régis Frères had established itself in Palma, though it had had no success in Lagos.[60] The O'Swald firm, however, was apprehensive of more determined French moves, which did, in fact, take place in 1856, when the rival company, which had earlier started trading in cowries on the east coast, determined to break the O'Swald monopoly in West Africa.

The effects of this competition were only gradually to become apparent, for not until 1858 was the market so flooded with cowries that the currency was no longer in demand.[61] But in the meantime resentment had been growing among the British merchants — and the Sierra Leonians included themselves in this category — toward the other Europeans. This ill-feeling centered on the Sardinian consul and trader, Scala, whose role in the developing difficulties must now be considered.

The arrangement for the payment of customs duties to Akitoye had been continued by his successor.[62] But soon after Dosunmu was installed as *Oba*, he complained that his own people were not collecting his duties properly. "Having great confidence in the integrity of Mr. S. B. Williams . . . the Interpreter to the Consulate, and, his Salary being small," Campbell recommended his Sierra Leonian interpreter for the post of collector of duties for the King.[63] The Consul rejected an offer from Scala to take the position at that time.

Williams' efforts to tighten controls met with protest.

The Duty in the agreement being fixed on Puncheons, *averaging 120 gallons,* and being no doubt found onerous, ways . . . were sought generally, and by the Sierra Leone people in particular, to lighten or evade it. . . . Mr. Williams, considering this to be a violation of the agreement obtained a copy of the original . . . , sent it to Sierra Leone, and had a considerable number printed;

some of which he distributed in that Colony, and others he gave to different traders here.[64]

This action led to insults and threats by the traders against Williams, who, as a result, wanted to resign. Scala renewed his offer, which the Consul rejected, persuading the interpreter to remain until the end of 1855. Finally Scala was appointed, to the dismay of the European merchants, for though Williams had watched the shipments of the Sierra Leonians with great care, he had been more lax with the Europeans, "trusting to their honor." [65] Scala demanded that notice be given of impending shipments so that he could inspect them; the merchants, led by Grote, ignored the request. The British merchants, on their part, with some of the Sierra Leonians, sought special privileges, which the Consul refused to give them.[66]

Under Campbell's watchful eye, Scala continued to supervise the collection of the King's duties; the hostility of the other traders toward him and toward the Consul did not abate. In September, 1856 ten English and Sierra Leonian traders sent a petition against Campbell to the Foreign Office. Those who signed complained that the Consul was dictating all Dosunmu's actions, and their accusations clearly referred to the question of farming the duties.[67]

The issues became even more clear in June, 1857, when a suit was brought against both the Sardinian and S. B. Williams, claiming that they were in debt to a trader in England named Gregory. Gregory, himself implicated in questionable practices on the coast, had appointed the Sierra Leonian trader, J. M. Turner, to act for him and subsequently gave Turner power of attorney, not neglecting to send a bribe to Dosunmu.[68] Campbell insisted that the dispute be settled in England. He had originally thought highly of Turner, whom he had appointed to the committee of the Sierra Leonian Court and recommended to the *Oba* to supervise a project of "slum clearance" around the palace. But after learning of such things as Turner's extortion in his work for Dosunmu, the Consul berated him for having tried to summon Scala before the emigrant court.[69]

The dispute was taken outside Lagos for settlement, but the Foreign Office reprimanded the Consul for giving insufficient attention to the Gregory-Turner claims. The officials in London thought that some machinery should be set up whereby British merchants could make successful claims against "foreign" ones.[70] They were clearly becoming concerned with the primacy of British trading interests in Lagos over those of other European nationals. The agents of William O'Swald and Company felt it necessary at this time to ask their home office to make representations for consular protection.[71]

By early 1858 the Lagos market was flooded with cowries, chiefly by the action of the French firm, Régis, which had finally succeeded in establishing itself there. Despite agreements with the representatives of O'Swald and Company, they continued their large importations in order to depress further the value of the cowrie payments.[72] Moreover, the revival of slave-trading in Whydah lessened the interest of the interior people in shipping palm oil. New conflicts were reported in the hinterland. In 1859 the war between Ibadan and Ijaye broke out; the Egba were again threatened from Dahomey; in Lagos and Abeokuta the following of Kosoko increased, and the *Awujale* of Ijebu Ode closed his roads to palm-oil trade.[73] But these difficulties, typical of those to face government and commerce in Lagos for years, were as yet thought to be only temporary.

In February, 1859, the most important merchants, of whom over half were emigrants, signed a new agreement with the *Oba*, whereby Dosunmu was to receive increased duties on palm oil, ivory, and shea butter. In return the King was to see that no "Native" be allowed to build a house "where the Merchants' stores are situated"; he was to give up trade himself; he was to see that, except for refusal to pay duties, no merchant's trade was to be interfered with; he was to collect debts from his people on behalf of the merchants and to punish thefts; he was to allow traders to build their own houses in any place they chose. The King was to receive his duties in cowries, unless individual merchants could be persuaded to agree to special arrangements for specie.[74] This agreement was renewed eight months later, when the Consul persuaded Dosunmu that it was as yet inadvisable to collect duties on cotton exports.[75]

Once again Sierra Leonians were to be customs collectors for the *Oba*. The bid of 1,800 bags of cowries, offered by W. A. Savage, was accepted for the year 1859,[76] and that of J. M. Turner, of 1,900 bags of cowries, for 1860.[77] In 1861, however, Dosunmu agreed to McCoskry's assumption of the post for a three-year period, cut short by the pensioning of the *Oba* in compensation for his loss of revenue after the cession of Lagos in August, 1861.[78]

PROBLEMS OF SLAVERY AND SLAVE-TRADING AMONG AFRICANS

Although legitimate trade looked more and more promising to those engaged in it,[79] its successful introduction did not eradicate all traces of the slave trade. The extent of emigrant participation in this trade is unclear, but Consul Foote wrote in 1861, in his attempt to persuade the officials in Whitehall to increase responsibility for Lagos, that,

So demoralizing is . . . [the] influence [of the slave trade] upon every one, whether white or black, that not only do Europeans engage indirectly in it, but the very liberated Africans who have been fostered under our protection, and for whose sake many good missionaries have died . . . , have forgotten all the teachings of the missionaries, and are now engaged in the barter and sale of their own countrymen.[80]

It is, of course, necessary to distinguish between the trans-Atlantic slave trade and that integral part of Yoruba social and economic institutions known as "domestic slavery." [81] It was difficult for Europeans on the coast to make this distinction, though it did come to be recognized, especially by some missionaries, one of whom gave this account of the system:

The slave system here is not like that of America, a great number of them obtain their freedom by their own labour, and great numbers by their relatives seeking them out, a great number run away and a great number remain contented with their lot. Many after obtaining freedom remain in the country where they were slaves. But if slave wars should cease, Domestic Slavery would die out. In this event the population are not provided with a substitute for slave labour; but as labour does not degrade a man in public estimation, necessity, whenever it happens, will find a remedy.[82]

Yet this partial understanding did not take into account traditional differentiation between the forms. The idea prevailed among the English that if they could convince the Africans that slavery in general was bad on religious or humanitarian grounds, domestic slavery would disappear as part of the whole distasteful practice.

When the Europeans, particularly the missionaries, first discovered that the returned Sierra Leonians and Brazilians, who knew at first hand the evils of slavery, were holding domestic slaves, they were much distressed. In their sermons they denounced the practice "as a heinous sin," and Samuel Crowther "in particular" was said to exhort his congregation against it "in the most earnest terms." [83] Periodically, the consul and the Foreign Office took up this problem, the issue generally arising from the wish of an owner to recapture one of his domestic slaves who had fled to another part of the country.[84] Constant warnings were posted by the consul,[85] and some of the charges against the emigrants were proven false.

In January, 1860, Brand submitted a list of domestic slaves redeemed in the preceding year, and over half had been set free by emigrants.[86] In the same year he countered accusations by the British naval officer and later governor, Lieutenant John Hawley Glover, "in his connexion with the Niger Expedition," against three Saro officials of the consulate: S. B. Williams, J. B. Pearce, and John Peter Boyle. Pearce, said the Consul, never held slaves; Williams had them, but fewer than Glover claimed and had, furthermore, redeemed a number of them; Boyle, a British subject — that is, he was born in Sierra Leone Colony — was "aware of his responsibility as such," and had even redeemed slaves not his own.[87]

Throughout this period of trading activities and emigrant association with the British role, it must be noted that the legal position of the liberated Africans was still not settled satisfactorily. In 1856 the Foreign Office stated that,

Liberated Africans . . . in the absence of any special legislation to that effect . . . cannot be . . . considered [as British subjects] when they voluntarily return to and become Residents in the Territory of the Native Chief whose subjects they were by Birth. Nevertheless, Her Majesty's Government can never cease to take a warm interest in the Welfare and safety of these Africans.[88]

This despatch did not extend the Lagos consul's authority as earlier defined: "I. . . [have] no legal control over the Sierra Leone people, unless they were born in the Colony." In effect, the position was that the emigrants could agitate for British protection when they needed it and refuse consular jurisdiction when it was less advantageous for them to have it, while the consul could also exert himself on their behalf as little or as much as he chose.

In 1861 Foote tried a novel approach, basing protection on good behavior: he refused to bring to trial any case in which "the Plaintiff being a British Subject or under British Protection, may be either a slave holder or directly or indirectly connected with the trade," thus placing "colored British subjects" who violated these terms "completely under the rule of the King." [89] The Consul hoped that such a step would lead to the eventual extinction of slavery in all its forms. But the legal position of the emigrants as a whole was yet to be unequivocally defined.

6

SIERRA LEONIANS IN ADMINISTRATION, POLITICS, AND MISSIONS

SOON after his arrival in Lagos in July, 1853, Consul Campbell saw the complexity of the task he was expected to perform. This realization grew as the conflicting forces with which he had to deal multiplied. He was aware of Foreign Office reluctance to subject yet another Englishman to the "pestilential" conditions of the island, or, more significant tactically, to increase emphasis on Lagos by sending the consul a British assistant. He also knew of the unwillingness to add to the administrative costs of the consulate. He needed, at the very least, the services of an official interpreter and messenger, and he availed himself of the talent at hand — the Sierra Leonians, with whom he had particular rapport because of his earlier service in the Liberated African Department in Freetown.

The interpreter's post was at first filled by James White, a CMS catechist, and that of messenger by J. B. Pearce, who was also employed by the mission, though in a lesser capacity. "Both these persons . . . [had] hitherto given their services cheerfully and gratuitously to the Commanders of Her Majesty's Ships of War stationed off Lagos, in their intercourse with the Chiefs." [1] Campbell reported that he could no longer impose on these men and interfere with their religious duties, but, convinced as he was that he still needed their services, he requested and was granted salaries for them of £20 and £10 per annum, respectively.

When White returned to mission work six months later, the Consul insisted that the post of interpreter be filled by "a native person that has received an education at one of the Schools in Sierra Leone," [2] and S. B. Williams, prominent in the emigrant community, was duly appointed. These men, with the later addition of another Saro named John Peter Boyle as clerk, [3] made up the consular staff during the rest of the decade.

In 1852, just after the "reduction" of Lagos, Commander Bruce pressed the Admiralty to continue efforts to end slave-trading. He advised, among other measures, decreasing the size of the squadron and installing "Consuls and Agents" along the coast in the interest of economy. "The persons best adapted for these situations," he wrote, "would be intelligent and fairly educated Creoles of the West Indies, or natives of Sierra Leone, as they alone are capable of withstanding the effects of the climate." [4]

Almost ten years later Consul Foote, complaining of inadequate staff, made a similar recommendation to the Foreign Office, specifically for Abeokuta and Badagry, and possibly for Benin. For Badagry he suggested Pearse, the CMS agent who had worked at the consulate; for Abeokuta, the consular clerk, Boyle.[5] But the officials in Whitehall, still showing greater caution toward liberated Africans than did their agents on the coast, were dubious about such a policy, and since the African rulers received the proposal with something less than enthusiasm, it was discarded.[6]

Whether directly employed by the consular authority or not, emigrants gave Campbell and his successors much information unobtainable elsewhere. As the missionaries had explained to their home committees, the emigrants in and around Lagos, as in Badagry, could tap local opinion and knowledge as the Europeans could not. Sometimes their reports contained word of impending surprise attacks;[7] sometimes they merely confirmed rumors of happenings which the consul suspected, as in the case of the revival of slave-trading in 1856.[8] It may have been the expectation of a new fund of information, as well as confidence in the abilities of a junior government officer, that led Campbell to recommend S. B. Williams for the post of Dosunmu's collector of customs in 1856.[9]

EMIGRANT PRESSURE ON BRITISH AND AFRICAN POLICIES

Working in the political sphere as well as the administrative, the emigrants put what pressure they could on the British government. They sent their own petitions to be forwarded by the consul to officers of the Preventive Squadron or to the Foreign Secretary. But in these instances it is clear that the emigrants were not a cohesive unit. Divergent economic interests or questions of conflicting loyalties did arise among them and precluded their acting as an effective pressure group.

For example, one petition was filed against Campbell in September, 1856—signed by John Macaulay, J. M. Turner, J. P. L. Davies, Thomas F. Cole, and William Edwin Cole as the emigrant representatives;[10] another, a rejoinder sent to Commodore Adams of H.M.S. *Scourge,* was signed by William Savage, S. B. Williams, James Thompson, and "68 others"—all were Sierra Leonian, Brazilian, or Cuban.[11] Turner, Davies, and Cole were among the few large, successful Saro traders in Lagos. With the European merchants, they had opposed both Williams' and Scala's farming of Dosunmu's duties; they resented Campbell's support of these men. Williams, in the other camp, appreciated the Consul's efforts on his behalf and rose to defend him; Savage, prominent in the mission community as well as being interested in trade, had obvious reason to support the Consul in his siding with the missionaries against the merchants.

Toward the end of the 1850's, the emigrants in Lagos and Abeokuta began to form organizations having philanthropic aims —groups which were to gain importance in later years. They worked with the British and local authorities, often asking for sponsorship by either or both. In Lagos the first of these seems to have been the "Young Men's Benevolent Association," which had seven Sierra Leonian "directors." When Brand arrived to take over the consular post at the end of 1859, he was invited to become its "patron," and at the same time he was informed of the existence of the "Abbeokuta Road Improving Society."[12]

The members of these societies were traders who, following a traditional co-operative pattern carried from early experience to Sierra Leone and back, engaged in good works for the welfare of the community, but also to facilitate their own trade. The consul and the African rulers looked with favor on such activities. Another such organization, the "Abbeokutan Mercantile Association," negotiated the opening of the roads to Lagos with the chiefs of the Igbein district of the Egba capital by agreeing to pay fifty bags of cowries quarterly, to be collected through a duty of 1 per cent on all produce exported from Abeokuta.[13]

Acting through their societies and as private individuals, the emigrants came to play yet another role — one of their most important — which was of direct interest to the government. Apart from their frequent services as official messengers,[14] they were the vehicle for opening negotiations between the consul and the people of the hinterland. But since they performed this function for the missionaries as well, discussion of it may be deferred until the role of the emigrants in mission work has been examined.

EMIGRANTS AND MISSION WORK

The missions were the oldest European establishments in Yoruba territory, but even for them, and particularly for the CMS, the decade of consular authority was a formative period. The Wesleyans continued understaffed because of their emphasis on the Gold Coast and Dahomey; after the death of John Martin, Gardiner at Lagos and Bickersteth in Abeokuta were their only agents. Gardiner was replaced in 1857 by Timothy Laing, and not until 1859 did Bickersteth get his long sought European colleague in the person of Thomas Champness.[15]

From the beginning the concern of the CMS had been to extend its influence to the north rather than, as with the Wesleyans, concentrating on Dahomey to the west. What had not been reached by the 1841 Niger Expedition could, according to CMS reasoning in London, perhaps be reached overland; gradually the idea grew of a series of links from Badagry — and later Lagos — and Abeokuta to the confluence of the Niger and Benue Rivers at Rabba. As early as January, 1849, the CMS sent out another graduate of the Basel seminary, David Hinderer, to the Yoruba. His instructions were to learn Hausa with a view to eventual missionary influence in Hausa country.[16] At his first station in Abeokuta, Hinderer had initiated the idea of a "chain" of outposts reaching north to the "Tschad," where forces could be joined with those making their way up the Niger.[17]

The CMS was badly understaffed in relation to the scope of its projects, and although Townsend began to express doubt about placing much responsibility in the hands of Africans (the term then meant Sierra Leonians) he and his associates, no less than the administration, had to face the problem of high European mortality.[18] Thus, of the approximately forty men employed by the CMS during the consular period, fifteen were emigrants.[19]

The major European figures in mission activity — Townsend, Gollmer, and Hinderer — were placed at Abeokuta, Lagos, and Ibadan, respectively; in 1853 Adolphus Mann started a mission at Ijaye. But to the smaller stations in Abeokuta and to the villages between the centers went Sierra Leonian catechists, where possible, men with local kinship ties. Charles Phillips accompanied Mann to Ijaye in 1853; James White, who preached the first sermon in Lagos in 1852, went two years later to Otta to take over the station opened there by William Morgan, another Saro, in 1852. Catechists were later sent to Ikorodu, Offin (Shagamu), and Igbessa.

The ordained Sierra Leonians held more important posts, though they were not yet given, like Bickersteth of the Methodists, sole control of any key station.[20] Crowther stayed in Abeokuta until his departure for the Niger Expedition in 1854; Thomas King worked there throughout the consular period. In 1852 the CMS brought from Freetown Thomas Babington Macaulay, an Aku of Oyo parents, to run the Christian Institution in Abeoukuta; after two years in that position, he headed the Igbein and then the Owu stations until, in 1859, he was sent to Lagos to found the CMS Grammar School. Samuel Pearse began his career helping Gollmer in Lagos and in 1859 took sole responsibility for the Badagry station which had tenuously reopened in 1854, when it was administered by two Saro agents named John and Lawson.[21]

In general, mission operations in both Lagos and Abeokuta were going well in the view of those directing them. The high attendance at the churches and schools testified to continuing interest, if not conversion.[22] However, the relations of the European missionaries with the consul and with the traders, both European and emigrant, were still strained except when there was a threat of attack. Criticism was being leveled at the European bearers of the Christian message for being too much concerned with matters of politics and trade. In 1855, when Gollmer and Townsend were in England, the Foreign Office received a petition through Campbell asking that pressure be put on the CMS to prevent the return of the two men, and to substitute for them others who would confine their activities to the religious sphere. Again some large emigrant traders joined the European merchants in the demand.[23]

Henry Venn did not submit to this pressure, although it was not until September, 1860, that he formulated specifically the stand on missionary participation in political activity which was to guide the CMS agents for many years:

> "Political affairs" is a wide term. There are worldly politicians who would desire to include in their exclusive province national education, the State support of idolatry, the social institution (as it is called) of slavery, the treatment of the aborigenes, the private religious action of Government officers. As soon as a minister of religious action touches these questions, an outcry is apt to be raised, as if he were meddling with politics. But such subjects as these are not simply "political affairs"! . . .
>
> However earnestly, therefore, the faithful missionary may strive to confine himself to his one great work, the ministry of the Gospel of salvation, he is liable to be involved in many questions of a social and political kind. . . .[24]

Though the controversy over Badagry and relations with Kosoko had destroyed much of Gollmer's political influence in Lagos, Townsend remained the main adviser to the Egba leaders in Abeokuta. But even he began to despair of the evolution of a strong, centralized government there. In 1852 the Egba had agreed to install the *Alake* as a kind of paramount chief, fulfilling, as the British saw it, the function of king. The strong missionary candidate for this office was rejected as disloyal, and after additional complications the *Sagbua*, Okukenu, was elected in 1854.[25] But, contrary to Townsend's plan, this change was only in name and brought no increase in power. Throughout the period the *Alake* was but a figurehead, and both the missionaries and the consul were frustrated in their dealings with a ruler who was co-operative in theory but helpless in practice.[26]

Abeokuta was still in danger from Dahomean attack, though how real this threat was continued to be a point of controversy between the consul and the CMS agents. When, however, in 1855 a request for aid reached Lagos through CMS channels, Campbell and the Sierra Leonians and the Brazilians all sent ammunition.[27]

Townsend's emphasis on the central importance of Abeokuta in the Yoruba Mission was being tempered by acquiescence in

Hinderer's plan for a chain of stations to the north. Throughout the years of the consular period in Lagos, the missionary files are full of accounts of one exploratory trip after another. Of the ordained Sierra Leonians, only Samuel Crowther was charged with leading one of these probing expeditions. In January, 1853, accompanied by another Saro, James Barber, he set out for Ketu to discuss with the king, who had issued Crowther several previous invitations, the possibilities of beginning CMS work there.[28]

Meanwhile, the Church Missionaries in Abeokuta were starting another project in which the emigrants played an important part. Henry Venn, the men at the stations, and Campbell all realized that the agreement with the *Oba* of Lagos, and even the presence of the British consul, could not counteract the preoccupation of the people with slave-trading until legitimate trade was made sufficiently lucrative. Venn called on his missionaries to send him samples of all the commodities produced locally, had these tested in England, and decided that the cultivation of cotton, to supplement the export of palm oil, offered a particularly promising return. The project was begun on a small scale early in the decade, with Venn sending out the first cotton gins to Samuel Crowther, who was to be in charge.

Venn knew the importance of keeping mission activities separate from trading ventures, but he also knew that to bring about tangible action from Manchester it was essential to maintain the support of some merchants whose interest could initially be aroused by a religious plea.[29] This assistance came first, and spontaneously, from a cotton merchant, Thomas Clegg, to whose factory the CMS had earlier sent Sierra Leonians for training. Clegg had heard Venn preach in Manchester and agreed with the view that the successful promotion of "Christian civilization in Africa" required teaching "the Natives not to waste the products of their country."[30]

The CMS gave its lay agent, Dr. Edward Irving, full charge of the Abeokuta part of the cotton plan in 1854. Irving reported that Samuel Crowther was pleased to be free of responsibility for it, although his wife, "a shrewder trader," was making good profits already.[31] As another aspect of this project, Venn had selected Henry Robbin, an Egba Sierra Leonian, to be trained at Clegg's factory near Manchester in the techniques of processing cotton. Robbin returned early in 1856 to Freetown, where he set up cotton presses for the Wesleyan missions as well as for the CMS. He then went to Lagos, where he was to take charge of the cotton interests, and arrived there in May.[32]

By then plans had already gone ahead for setting up an Industrial Institution in Abeokuta, and in Lagos premises were acquired from which cotton could be shipped. Robbin had been told to supervise both the growing in Abeokuta and the shipping in Lagos, but on his arrival in the Egba capital he found opposition from the Rev. J. A. Maser, who told him that, "business at Lagos will be as much as will keep a person regularly busy."[33] Robbin was distressed, for he had looked forward to teaching the techniques of growing cotton and of installing and repairing machinery; working solely in Lagos would entail only "the shipping of cotton, keep[ing] the Society's Store, the buying of provisions for Missionaries in the Interior, as well as buying them Cowries: but as no Cotton of any kind is to be had at Lagos, it is just denying me of the express purpose for which I have been trained in England and for which I am here."[34]

Nonetheless, Robbin remained temporarily stationed in Lagos, though he frequently visited Abeokuta and was by 1858 virtually in charge of the CMS commercial enterprises there, as well as the Industrial Institution.[35] In the interval, Samuel Crowther, Junior, managed the cotton store in Abeokuta, while being fully responsible for the dispensary there.

Campbell encouraged the plans for growing cotton. Scala, the Sardinian trader, was also interested. Intent on outwitting the merchants who had opposed him in Lagos, he went to Abeokuta with recommendations to the *Alake* from the Consul and the elder Samuel Crowther. There, in September, 1856, he concluded an agreement allowing him to open a factory for trade in palm oil, cotton, and ivory.[36] The missionaries were pleased with the arrangement, which would make European goods more easily accessible to them, increase the revenue of the *Alake*, and set the precedent of a direct European trading link with the Egba, thus eliminating, they thought, the ubiquitous Saro middlemen of Lagos.[37]

The Consul had suggested that as an assistant Scala should have Charles Macaulay, brother of the CMS Aku missionary, Thomas Babington Macaulay, then running the Christian Institution in Abeokuta. Within a year, however, Macaulay was dismissed by Scala for, according to missionary sources, setting the *Parakoyi* — the society of Egba trade chiefs — against the Sardinian because of friction between himself and Scala's European clerk. A disturbing situation had thus arisen in Abeokuta: the *Parakoyi* claimed that because he traded indiscriminately, Scala interfered with their traditional right to control commerce; the *Alake* maintained that he opposed Macaulay but was powerless in the face of opposition from the *Parakoyi*. Wrote Townsend, "The Parakoyis are wise in their way[;] their aim has been to destroy Mr. Scala's trade and they are backed by the Sierra Leone people of Lagos. They want to keep the trade as a monopoly as it was in the slave trade days, which [would] effectually destroy or at least check the advance we desire to see." [38]

Townsend feared that the dispute would affect the CMS cotton interests, and he told Henry Robbin to keep the Egba — individual "Chiefs, Parakoyis and common people" — in the position of creditors by having them give Robbin cotton to send for them to England, and to encourage "as many influential Chiefs" as possible to become exporters through him.[39]

The CMS, however, was rapidly becoming interested in transferring its share of the cotton production to other hands. Campbell, who had been receiving technical advice about varieties of cotton and their cultivation from the Rev. Crowther,[40] repeatedly wrote to the Foreign Office asking for pressure upon Manchester interests to relieve the CMS of financial responsibility for promoting this new commercially promising venture.[41]

Three months later, the Foreign Office told the Consul that the contact he had suggested with the Cotton Supply Association of Manchester had brought an optimistic, though noncommittal, reply. It was in connection with promoting this project that the Consul was to return to England in 1858.[42]

Before leaving, Campbell sought to extend interest in growing cotton to the south of Abeokuta. Already Saro farming on the mainland across the lagoon from Lagos had added the potential

cash crop to the corn and yams they raised on their "plantations." [43]
Furthermore the Consul reported,

I am . . . through a Mr. Davis, an intelligent African born in Sierra Leone,
making an effort to induce the people of Jaboo who possess a fruitful soil to
extend their cultivation of cotton, and at the request of the Chiefs four cotton
Gins have been sent to Icorrodoo, which, being a market Town attended by
several thousands of people every eighth day, the working of these machines
there will be the means of making many acquainted with the ingenious means
employed by the White man to separate the seed from the cotton; and which
I have given them to understand they can purchase for the first cost and
expences. [44]

The CMS began to dispose of its equipment for the cotton
scheme, not only because its agents were becoming too involved
in trade, but because they were losing money which they felt they
could ill afford. [45] In August, 1858, they sold their cotton boat
through the Consul to J. P. L. Davies; [46] and despite protests that
the cotton warehouse in Lagos would be useful as living quarters
for the future catechist and schoolmaster of the newly completed
Breadfruit Chapel, the premises were rented to Thomas Clegg for
the year 1860. [47]

Townsend thought that the prospects for cotton continued
good, though he expressed his usual disillusionment with the participation of the mission in the project and his distaste for this
role. [48] It was not, however, until 1863 that the CMS managed to
detach commerce completely from training in the cotton-growing
scheme. Then Henry Robbin was instructed to "give up the
Institution to the Church Missionary Society [in Abeokuta] . . .
but to remove all such machinery and other articles [that] formerly
belonged to Mr. Clegg." [49]

EMIGRANTS AND MISSIONARY EDUCATION

Industrial training was only one part of the education which
the CMS had planned to introduce in Yoruba country. From the
start of their activities there, the missionaries had in mind starting
schools — a persistent request of the emigrants. Where they could
recruit sufficient staff, the missions gave primary schooling with
its stress on the teaching of English and Bible studies. More advanced education began with the founding of a Christian Institu-

tion in Abeokuta in 1852. The Rev. Thomas Babington Macaulay, who had taught from 1849 to 1851 at the grammar school in Freetown, came from pastoral work in a mountain district of Sierra Leone to be in charge of it.[50] After his ordination in 1854, he married Abigail Crowther, second daughter of Samuel Crowther, and took over first the Igbein and then the Owu stations in Abeokuta. In 1859 arrangements were at last made for a grammar school in Lagos, and he was sent there to direct it.

I am . . . commencing the Grammar School . . . on the 6th of June ensuing according to a notice that I have put forth about the same. I am in the mean time trying to get a few Form Writing Desks and Stools made ready for the use of the Pupils. Capt. Davies has kindly projected a Contribution scheme now going round the town successfully defraying the expenses of these necessary preliminaries. . . . And I am thankful to be able to inform you that I have a fair prospect of half a dozen boys already to begin . . . and these will be Day Scholars at the same charges as in Sierra Leone, i.e. *one guinea* per quarter, each pupil.[51]

The school opened with five students. A year later Macaulay could boast of twenty-four.[52] Their ages ranged from eight and a half to nineteen; sixteen of them were over fourteen. Almost all the parents or guardians were Sierra Leonians; of the others one was Brazilian, one was Walter Hansen, the trader from Cape Coast, and the third was Otto Diederichsen of O'Swald and Company who was financing the education of one of Tapa's sons. Except for one clergyman, one scripture reader, and one carpenter, the parents were all described as "merchants" or "traders" (see Appendix C). The following year Macaulay reported that nine of the pupils had finished their schooling: four were apprenticed to carpenters, and the others were employed as clerks or shopkeepers.[53]

In 1860 in the interest of furthering education — "to spread general information among the native inhabitants of this Country and to induce them to obtain knowledge by reading" — the CMS started in Abeokuta the first newspaper in the area, *Iwe Irohin*.[54] It was to appear bi-weekly and was to cost 1 penny or 120 cowries per issue. The experiment proved a success, and soon there was an English supplement to the Yoruba edition.[55] The paper was printed by Egba under the supervision of the European missionaries in Abeokuta; very few African contributions seem to have been elicited or included.

EMIGRANTS AS INTERMEDIARIES IN THE HINTERLAND

In the Lagos hinterland conditions during the consular period remained unstable, with traditional tensions heightened in some instances by the events on the coast. Two major issues were the friction between Dahomey and the Egba, and the Ijaye War, which began in 1859. These conflicts will be discussed when the diplomacy of the later period is considered.[56] But the most immediately irritating problem which faced the European elements — government, missionary, and trading — was that of the Ijebu in the country immediately to the north of Lagos. Throughout the decade of Foreign Office responsibility for the affairs of the island, the Ijebu showed a determined resistance to penetration which was to be an obstacle to British interests until 1892, and which no other group exhibited with such tenacity. Though the Egba were to draw the line at political interference, they accepted, or at least tolerated, religious proselytizing. Lagos was obliged to accept both. But those Ijebu who looked on the *Awujale* of Ijebu Ode as their ruler accepted neither.

It is beyond the scope of this study to analyze the reasons for this intransigence. It can be said simply that the Ijebu had a strong, tightly knit political organization which owed allegiance neither to the north nor to the south. As middlemen in the slave traffic that found its outlet at Lagos, a traffic highly profitable to them, they encouraged its revival at every opportunity, whether by supporting Kosoko at Epe, or by blockading the routes by which palm oil came from the north. They wanted no part of the new influences which would destroy their favorable position and were unwilling to permit any loophole for the infiltration of persons, ideas, or techniques. In their relations with the rest of the Yoruba, they worked to undermine the power of any group whose strength threatened to exceed theirs, though they did not seek to augment their own by overt aggression. Thus, when the power of Ibadan grew to dangerous proportions, the Ijebu severed their alliance with them. Acting on the same premises, they were willing to aid anyone opposing penetration from the coast, as can be seen in their later co-operation with the Egba.

The Europeans who entered the Lagos scene in the early 1850's had, of course, no way of discerning this pattern and foreseeing its development. Both the consuls and the missionaries made repeated overtures to the Ijebu leaders. In 1852 Gollmer wrote,

I should very much like at once to gain a footing in the Ijebu country . . . as through this country our direct road lays from Lagos into the Interior. It is almost nearer from Lagos through Jebu to Ibadan than to Abeokuta. The great enmity that exists between Abbeokuta and Jebu is a great drawback on this account — I cannot employ an Egba at present in Jebu . . . . I am looking for a Yoruba man to send to Jebu — I hope soon to go myself.[57]

This statement makes it clear that the missionaries were aware of the more obvious African alignments; it also shows that they planned to use Sierra Leonians of acceptable origin — for it is Saro that Gollmer meant when he wrote here of Egba or Yoruba — to facilitate entry of the missions. As he soon discovered, however, emigrants were going to have to do more than the initial work there, if work were to be done at all. Four months later he reported that Ijebu was "still unoccupied"; there had been correspondence between the *Awujale* and Capt. Foote of H.M.S. *Prometheus* which brought the declaration that "the King of Jebu will not receive '*White Men*' because their ancestors never did"; the letters were carried and translated, on Gollmer's instructions, by James White, accompanied by "a Jebu Sierra Leone and a Lagos Jebu man."[58]

Continued attempts by the CMS to win the *Awujale's* hospitality were unsuccessful; incidents, such as the detention of missionary messengers on their way to Ibadan, were frequent. The only encouraging gesture from Ijebu Ode was a letter to David Hinderer in September, 1854, indicating a desire for "free communication with Ibadan."[59] Hinderer, hoping that at last he had found an opening, set off for Ijebu country with Dr. Irving and James Barber as interpreter only to meet the usual rebuff.[60]

In Offin, it is true, the party received a comparatively warm welcome from the King of Ijebu Remo. They tried to clarify the confusions about the white man "who sharpens the iron and slackens the iron again" by explaining that only the Portuguese who had left were slave traders; that the English, who were then in Lagos, were not. The *Oluwo*, the head of the elders, spoke for the *Akarigbo*, the leading chief of Ijebu Remo, and made one request:

namely "that his country people might be allowed to return from S. Leone as the Egbas and Yorubas did" to which our answer was that as soon as we should be able to report he had opened the road for us and received teachers of the word of God into his country, they could come, it was only the risk of danger in their country that kept them back.[61]

The Consul and the traders fared no better with Ijebu Ode. The blockaded roads and the resulting stoppages of trade, especially toward the end of the decade, created serious problems for Lagos. But Campbell discovered that, although none of his pleas and threats produced the results he wanted, he could keep channels of communication open if he sent S. B. Williams or another of the emigrants to the *Awujale*.[62] His European delegations, such as the one sent in March, 1858, heard only repeated refusals to admit any white man; the European emissaries faced alarm and insults — they were allowed neither to see the King, nor to walk about the town, nor to have protection from the sun.[63] But even with his great suspicion of European influence, the *Awujale* wrote to the British consul in 1860 that, "he begs the Queen, he hears that all the Yorubas and Egbas [are] coming to their country; he sees none of his people, and [he wishes that] she will be pleased to proclaim through her territories if any Jebu intends to come let them come." [64]

Not until 1861, though, did the *Awujale* consent to see a European — the Rev. Thomas Champness, whom the Methodists had as last sent to assist Edward Bickersteth at Abeokuta. Accompanied by Bickersteth and the Saro trader, J. M. Turner, Champness obtained permission for Wesleyan missionary work.[65] This victory was a brief one, and only after the death of this ruler in 1885 did his successor permit a brief attempt at conciliation, although even then the policy of exclusion of Europeans was again instituted.[66]

Nevertheless, in certain parallel cases elsewhere the missionaries had more success. They often found that reluctance to admit them could be overcome by persuasion from a Sierra Leonian, a trained Christian belonging by birth or descent to the group being approached. Thus in 1854 Gollmer wrote,

Some 14 months ago two Chiefs from Igbessa were here when I expressed a desire to come and visit them. . . . Since I have sent Mr. Morgan of Otta three times to remind them of my desire to come but they were undecided til a short time ago H. a communicant from Waterloo S. Leone a truly christian man — belonging to Igbessa — came — and laid the case before them. After considerable hesitation and consideration they agreed to receive the White man — for said they surely such a thing — viz our own children come back alive after we thought them dead long since and we have never seen and surely our own child meaning H. cannot deceive us.[67]

We find a comparable political effect in the central Sierra Leonian role in solving the Badagry problem of 1854 and 1855. The emigrant traders in Lagos actively supported the position of the Consul, and he sought to use their influence as Egba men on the rulers in Abeokuta to counteract what he felt was Townsend's biased advice. Campbell explained the position of the emigrants in a way that justified his own:

the Sierra Leone people of all shades of opinion, who saw clearly that if the Abbeokutans interfered [on the side of Mewu] it would bring on an interminable War with the surrounding tribes, and, be the means of paralysing commerce, . . . took the matter up and wrote a letter to the Chiefs of Abbeokuta dissuading them from carrying hostilities to Badagry; this letter they wished me to support by one from myself . . . which I agreed to do, on condition, that some of their number would carry the letters to Abbeokuta, have an interview with the Chiefs, and see that the letters were interpreted by some other person than Mr. Townsend. Three intelligent persons were selected, a Mr. Thomas, a Mr. Smith, and, a Mr. Turner, the two latter relations of Chiefs, and, I agreed to defray the expenses of the Mission.[68]

This delegation brought back to Lagos a positive answer, written for the *Alake* and with his consent by Edward Bickersteth; it stated that so long as restored chiefs were not hostile to Abeokuta there would be no aggression against them.[69] With such results, even if only temporarily effective, it is not surprising that Campbell saw advantages in using Saro intermediaries.

The Consul also based his case in the Badagry conflict on the evidence of the two Sierra Leonian CMS agents there, Coker and Thomas Wright.[70] The missionaries obviously could denigrate this testimony only with difficulty; they blamed the misinformation, as they regarded it, on the influence of the Methodist schoolmaster there, John Moses — "married to the daughter of one of the expelled chiefs and consequently leaning that side." [71] But it became apparent that allegiances were not determined solely by affiliation or identification with certain segments of the European community. Just as some prominent names in CMS circles appeared on the Sierra Leonian letter to the *Alake*,[72] others were signed at the end of an emigrant testimonial to the integrity of Charles Gollmer.[73]

In effect, Sierra Leonian allegiance was not restricted to the European authorities, nor was it for the Europeans alone that the emigrants performed services. The relation between them and the ruler in Lagos in this period is not documented, but in the hinterland there is both explicit and implicit evidence that they had gained the confidence of some chiefs. For just as the Saro were the means whereby the Europeans could communicate with the African rulers, they were, once mistrust was overcome, the most effective link from the other side between these rulers and the new consular and missionary authorities. An early example is reported by Hinderer: when, in 1854, the Ilesha king sent word of his friendly disposition toward the British in Lagos and Abeokuta and implied that missionaries might be welcome, his messengers were headed by a Sierra Leonian who was described as a trader in Ilesha.[74]

The activities of the emigrants in this period, particularly in Abeokuta, foreshadowed the more important involvements in indigenous politics that were to grow in later years. According to Biobaku, the "real rulers" of the town were the members of the *Ogboni* Society.

Briefly, it is a society of wealthy and influential men and a few old women who could be relied upon to place duty before sentiment and maintain secrecy. It was at once the civil court, the town council, and the electoral college for the selection of the sacred chief from candidates nominated by the ruling houses. By keeping their proceedings secret and binding their members by blood oaths, the *Ogboni* ensured solidarity for their decisions.[75]

In 1861 the European missionaries in Abeokuta made a discovery which disconcerted them: J. King, the schoolmaster attached to Gollmer's station — Gollmer had been transferred over his protests from Lagos to avoid his further political immersion there —

had joined *Ogboni*. Upon further enquiry it developed that "nearly all" the schoolmasters were members, and that "all the young men at Ake . . . [had] been admitted to Ogboni secrets."[76] Gollmer was shocked and proposed that such membership should not only mean dismissal from the service of the missionary society but removal from church membership as well.

The issues at stake were relayed to the Parent Committee in London by the Rev. Thomas King, himself a Sierra Leonian, as well as by Gollmer; King defended his countrymen who were participants on two counts, stating that Gollmer had been misinformed, and that membership in *Ogboni* did not necessarily imply the practice of idolatry:

All what I could gather is, that there is no object there presented to be adored or worshipped. The bases of their maxims may be justly said to have been intended to maintain truth and justice, though connected with many errors and injustice through the imperfection of human wisdom. Now Ogboni in this country, and chiefly among the Egbas is nothing but Civil Constitution or Political Community; or in other words, African Freemason[ry]. They have secrets to keep very close from others, consisting I believe in signs and words, which none dare reveal on pains of death. They strictly enforce some rules of morality and severely inflict punishment upon atrocious deeds and other acts of injury to any individual, as theft, murder &c when detected.[77]

King went on to explain that it was reasonable for converts to join, since they thus avoided "inconveniences" which arose from not being a member, in addition to the fact that, "at any time that one happens to fall unwittingly into their hands, he must necessarily be admitted into the secrets, whether he likes it or not."[78] King also added that it was not essential to continue participation once admitted, and he pointed out that *Ogboni* had not "molested" the missionaries nor destroyed the power of the church over the converts.

This matter of participation in local politics, as practiced within a traditional framework, aroused controversy and took time to settle. But mission pressure[79] does not seem to have brought the renunciation of *Ogboni* activity by the Saro initiates; this would seem to be an early manifestation by the Sierra Leonians of a continuing refusal to look upon the new and the old cultural practices as mutually exclusive alternatives.

EMIGRANTS IN PERSPECTIVE: THE 1850'S

How were the returned liberated Africans regarded by the other members of the community in Lagos and its hinterland? The views of the Africans who had not been out of their own country are, of course, difficult to establish. In Lagos itself, a heterogeneously populated coastal town, the infusion of new African elements was less conspicuous than in some of the inland areas. There appears to have been little disabling stigma attached to these returning men and women because they had once been sold as slaves.[80] Because of the Yoruba wars, the slave trade had affected no particular stratum of society; that any member of any family could have found himself on a slave ship is demonstrated by the number of emigrants who could trace direct connections with African ruling houses.[81]

On the other hand, control of certain manifestly useful aspects of European culture enabled the emigrants, as those who theorized earlier had predicted, to draw the same prestige as could the European residents. The following account, written in 1860 by Robert Campbell who, with Dr. Martin Delaney, had come to Abeokuta to plan a resettlement scheme for their fellow American and Canadian Negro countrymen, shows a similarity of treatment accorded to the most westernized emigrants and the Europeans, though, through its oversimplification of attitudes, it may not be an accurate interpretation of the reaction itself:

It has been asserted that the native African does not manifest under any circumstances the same deference for colored men, as he does for white men; ... It is indeed true that more respect has been accorded to white men, on account of their superior learning and intelligence, than to the generality of semi-civilized black men from the Brazils and other places, who now live in the Aku country; but it is a great mistake to think that the same is withheld from colored men similarly endowed with their white brethren. Let any disinterested person visiting Abeokuta, place himself in a position to notice the manner in which such a person, for instance, as the Reverend Samuel Crowther, or even his sons of the same name, each a pure Negro, is treated, and he would soon perceive the profound respect with which Africans treat those of their own race worthy of it. The white man who supposes himself respected in Africa, merely because he is white, is grievously mistaken.[82]

The differentiation between deference and trust, overlooked by or unimportant to Robert Campbell, meant that the "native African" reaction was not unqualified, nor was it inherently lasting. It was the result, first, of interest in new methods of communication — reading and writing — and in technology. Secondly, the prominent position of the emigrants was granted them because of expediency again as predicted. If the African rulers were to accept British authority of whatever variety, even its simple presence, they were obliged to use the only agency at hand to deal with it, in communication, negotiation, or ultimatum, and the emigrants were uniquely suited for this role.

But even where their good offices were appreciated, the emigrants had still to convince any faction of their allegiance. When and where they seemed to take the part of the indigenous Africans, to aid them in trade or politics, they were popular; when their own interests and those of the local population conflicted, they were not. Neither as a group nor as individuals were they completely trusted in the hinterland until they demonstrated that they subordinated their own interests to those of the indigenous group. And though in some instances the signs of such allegiances were already appearing, there was much evidence that the Sierra Leonians, in particular, still looked on themselves essentially as *Oyinbo* — white men.

This suspicion of alliance with the Europeans, reinforced by the key position in trade held by the emigrants, aroused more hostility in Lagos than in the interior and resulted in the outbreaks, directed against them as well as against British authority, in 1855 and 1856, although even here we must notice that at least one Sierra Leonian — J. M.[?] Turner — took part in the Tinubu plot.[83] In Lagos itself, where much of the population supported the return of Kosoko, association with King Dosunmu could scarcely bring confidence or acceptance.

In 1857 Consul Campbell made a careful analysis of the position as he saw it:

For some time past there has existed a deep feeling of jealousy on the part of the Native inhabitants . . . [in Lagos] towards the Sierra Leone emigrants, created, no doubt, by their superior intelligence and the higher social position attained by them over the Natives, who do not hesitate openly to express their aversion to men, who they state were sold from this place only a few years since, and who have now returned so much their superiors, occupying a considerable portion of the best part of the town and enjoying so large a portion of its trade.[84]

But the Sierra Leonians and Brazilians seem to have been differentiated in the attitudes of the Lagosians, and the Consul examined the reasons:

Although the self-emancipated Africans from Brazil and Cuba . . . are as numerous as the Sierra Leone people, there does not exist the same antipathy on the part of the Natives towards them; which . . . may be accounted for from the difference . . . of the education of the same people in two different schools. — The Brazilian and Spanish . . . Africans have been trained in a servile state in the school where slavery exists, and have acquired a habit and demeanour of deference and submissiveness towards their equals and superiors; while the Sierra Leone people having from their first arrival in a land of freedom not had to pass through a course of long servitude . . . their bearing and demeanour rather border on Republican equality. It is this which the Native inhabitants feel offensively.[85]

Campbell also attributed the irritation of the local people to the actions of some of the younger emigrants born in Sierra Leone. He thought that those who were themselves from the Lagos area gave no offense. It is possible that the reactions to these groups of emigrants were colored largely by the relative economic threat of each. They were certainly influenced by the close association of the Sierra Leonians with British authority.

In this early period there is no evidence of the emigrants' weighing their own loyalties. Their emulation of and identification with the British at this point appears little in question. They co-operated with the Europeans and enjoyed and profited from the resulting position of prominence. It is important to note that the attitude of the local rulers remained sufficiently reserved toward the Sierra Leonians so that in 1861 Foote could write to Russell that, "On reference to . . . appointing coloured men as Vice Consuls, I find that Your Lordship's doubts are well founded. The Kings and Chiefs unanimously object to the appointment of Coloured men." [86]

European attitudes toward the emigrants differed with time, circumstances, and the personalities involved. At one extreme were the mission officials in England and the consular agents on the coast who wanted to continue training programs to extend emigrant influence by qualifying them for important positions. In 1852 Hector Straith, secretary of the CMS, wrote to the Rev. Koelle in Sierra Leone, encouraging him to trace the origins of new converts so that they might be sent as mission agents to their own areas.[87] By 1855 the Secretary, on behalf of the CMS Parent Committee in London, was investigating the progress of the self-supporting system of education at the Bathurst mission, Sierra Leone, and looked to the introduction into Yoruba country of this system. Writing to Charles Macaulay, a Sierra Leonian then in the Yoruba Mission, he said:

it is high time for your Countrymen of Africa to shake off dependence and to put forth Christian efforts to build their own Churches, maintain their own Ministers and Schools — and especially to send their own Native Missionaries into the regions beyond. . . . We think here that the time is come for Africa — we mean your part of it and the Yoruba Christians — to . . . engage more fully in Missionary work.[88]

Samuel Crowther wrote to Henry Venn in 1854, encouraging the use of Sierra Leonian Ibo agents on the banks of the Niger.[89] MacGregor Laird wrote shortly thereafter to Lord Clarendon, with a similar request, this time in connection with exploration: "the advantage we possess is having in the educated African youth of the Colonies of the Gambia, Sierra Leone, and the Gold Coast, most efficient Native agents; by their means new energy and a higher standard of living may be introduced naturally, unobtrusively, and rapidly, into the remotest regions of the interior." [90]

Similarly, Consul Campbell was favoring in 1854 the extension of the plan whereby students from the CMS schools could go through a kind of apprenticeship aboard vessels of the Preventive Squadron, in the same way as James P. L. Davies and his brother, Samuel, had done three years before.[91] Campbell, as has been shown, had a high regard for a number of the Sierra Leonians, and he showed no hesitation in employing them. However, he did discover that, as in all groups of people, some were more reliable than others.[92]

The Church Missionaries in Yoruba country were toward the center of the continuum of attitudes toward the liberated Africans. Their reactions show ambivalence. Except in instances — usually concerning lay agents — similar to those that distressed the Consul, the objections of European missionaries to the emigrants in their service was based, perhaps half consciously, on their aptness in performance and, therefore, the competitive threat they presented. This attitude was to become more pronounced later, but evidences of it are apparent in the 1850's. As early as 1851, for example, Henry Townsend showed anxiety about competition from Samuel Crowther. A decade before, Townsend had been passed over in favor of Crowther to accompany the 1841 Niger Expedition.[93] When Crowther was summoned to London by Henry Venn to put the case for Admiralty intervention in Lagos, Townsend, unaware of the Secretary's plan, wrote a letter, signed by the other Europeans in Yoruba country, setting forth the undesirability of selecting an African bishop for Abeokuta.[94] Townsend's reports home contained frequent admonitions: "The Parent Committee have yet to learn a lesson or two as to the treatment of Black Young men." [95]

When T. B. Macaulay opened the Lagos Grammar School, Maser, then stationed there, wrote of him,

What a field of usefulness for him. . . . He has now 8 pupils, which is at least a beginning. But he should not call it a grammar School as he does; and Capt. Davies should not think to be "projector" of the Scheme, and both should not say that a new "Era" has begun on the Slave coast by the establishment of this Grammar school; and both together should not make up a subscription list for this School and carry it round, calling for help to get up "preliminaries as desks" etc before they ever mention it to me; and should not continue to carry it round, after I disapproved of it. My reasons for disapproving . . . were, that it was too early yet, . . . and that it was done to outdo the Finance committee, who would gladly have given the money for desks, etc, had he asked.[96]

Thus, while acknowledging the good and essential work done by African subordinates — who at this time were almost exclusively Sierra Leonians — the missionaries could not look with equanimity on the initiative and forcefulness of those who were eager to take into their own hands the work toward ideals being set forth from London headquarters.[97]

At the other end of the scale of European opinion were the traders. They had been opposed to the settlement of the Sierra Leonians in Lagos from the beginning, for they did not welcome any additional competition, let alone competition from those who had better trading contacts than they.[98] And their hostility grew as they realized that, in addition, emigrants controlled much of the middleman traffic and were powerful enough to disrupt attempts, such as Scala's in Abeokuta, to deal directly with inland traders. Nonetheless, the part played by these lesser emigrant traders in breaking bulk and amassing produce from the interior was a consideration which, in their own interest, the merchants could not overlook. Thus, toward the end of the consular period, the European traders appear to have chosen their allies without reference to color, but rather on the basis of common economic interest, and the pressure they could jointly exert. It is less than paradoxical, consequently, that those who felt they had, in some respects, most to lose from Sierra Leonian success were forced to accept the emigrants most completely and least self-consciously.

Part III

1861-1886

THE STRUGGLE FOR POWER IN THE HINTERLAND OF LAGOS COLONY

T o gain a sharper perspective on the emigrant role in the several aspects of Lagos history — trade, hinterland politics, mediation, administration, education, missions — it is necessary to project that role against the changing conditions and policies during
the remaining period of this study. African politics, the cession of
Lagos to the British Crown, policies formulated in Whitehall and
those advanced by local administrators — all affected conditions of
trade, loyalties and attitudes of the various segments of the population, and positions which the British government took. As background, let us first look at relations in the hinterland, culminating
in the Ijaye War which was going on at the time of the transfer of
Lagos in 1861 from Foreign Office to Colonial Office jurisdiction,
and then move on to the effect of the cession as seen in later developments.

POLITICS IN THE HINTERLAND

From the mid-1840's to the end of the 1850's, conditions in
Yoruba country continued almost as unsettled as during the period
just after the collapse of the Old Oyo Empire. With the victory of
Ibadan over Ilorin at Oshogbo in the early 1840's,[1] the threat of
Fulani invasion, though subtly constant, had lessened; the new
towns concentrated on internal development and consolidation
of their positions. As agreed, the *Alafin* of the new Oyo handed
over responsibility for the defense of the realm to Ibadan and
Ijaye.[2] Conflict between these two centers, each seeking to dominate the surrounding country, became inevitable; the clash,
known as the Batedo War, 1844–46, ended in a stalemate, with
mediation by the *Alafin* of Oyo who had remained neutral.[3] But
the unresolved rivalry was to erupt again less than a decade later.
In the interval, the Ibadan army occupied itself with the subjuga-

tion of the Ijesha and Ekiti peoples, whose resistance to this external rule was to assert itself in the 1880's with serious consequences for all Yoruba country and for Lagos.[4]

The Ijaye War, which began in 1859, was the first of the Yoruba conflicts directly to affect British administration in Lagos. To be sure, the consuls, like the missionaries and officers of the fleet before them, had been involved in the defense of Abeokuta against the recurrent attacks of Dahomey. But these invasions from the west were not seen to have the same consequences that turmoil throughout the hinterland had for the trade and welfare of Lagos. Because Dahomey was seen as an "external" aggressor, British aid against her was unquestioned; but in the new conflict it was impossible to intervene on either side without assuming some direct responsibility for affairs in the interior.

The causes of the war have been fully described elsewhere.[5] Here we need only recognize that the principal issue was the Oyo succession. In compliance with an unprecedented wish of the dying *Alafin*, his eldest son, Adelu, who should by tradition have died with his father, was named successor. Kurunmi, the *Are-ona-Kakanfo*, an Ijaye by birth, would not recognize the new ruler who, with the support of Ibadan which was becoming a formidable military power, then attacked Ijaye. By April, 1860, the Egba, relieved of their anxiety about a Dahomean attack that year,[6] had resolved their own factional problems and were marching to the aid of Ijaye.[7] Their immediate provocation, as reported by Townsend, was that "the Ibbadan people have kidnapped Egbas . . . and more especially they have stolen their property in coming down from Ilorin and trying to pass by Ibaddan, as Ijaye is shut in."[8] But the fundamental issue was the power of Ibadan: "the destruction of Ijaye by Ibaddan would be an evil to the country, as Ibaddan is already too strong."[9]

All the hinterland minorities, in fact, feared Ibadan hegemony. The Ijebu forgot their earlier alliances and came in on the side of the Egba and Ijaye people.[10] The country of Ijebu Remo, through which Lagos gained access to the hinterland, became a subsidiary battle ground. The question of trade routes came to the fore as Ibadan sought to protect her line of supply. Ijebu

Remo was caught between its economic ties to the north and its effective rule by Ijebu Ode.[11]

The consuls who followed each other in rapid succession from 1859 on became more and more concerned with the strife in the interior. In February, 1860, Brand was called on to help the Egba prepare for the expected Dahomean attack. A request from emigrants and missionaries in Abeokuta for arms was met at once, as similar ones had been in the past.[12] Only a plea for men from British ships was denied, for though the Consul was willing to acquiesce even in this, established policy prevailed on the grounds that orders to protect Lagos in no way sanctioned interference on behalf of towns or states "friendly" to the island.[13] The anticipated battle did not, however, materialize, and the attention of contenders and observers turned to events in Ijaye.[14]

"The effect of all this," wrote Brand in April, 1860, "is an interruption of the course of trade, and as we depend at Lagos very much upon the Yoruba country for our supplies of articles of export, that interruption is severely felt here."[15] Hoping to keep Abeokuta neutral, the Lagos traders met and arranged for a deputation, composed of two Sierra Leonians, to go to the Egba and from there to Ibadan to negotiate an end to hostilities, "to open the roads for the flow of peaceful commerce."[16] The Consul was optimistic about the mission, to be led by Lieutenant Lodder, a British naval officer:

The members of the mercantile deputation are Mr. J. M. Turner, a relative of the Bashoron or second Chief of Abbeokuta and Mr. J. R. Thomas. Both these gentlemen are Sierra Leone emigrants, natives of Yoruba, and, speaking the language of the country, they possess a great advantage of communicating directly with the Chiefs without requiring the services of an interpreter.[17]

This mission, however, was unsuccessful, as future ones were to be.[18] The delegation reported division among the Egba leaders and people, further evidence of the decentralized political organization long deplored by the missionaries in Abeokuta.[19]

In July, Hand, who had the month before taken over as acting consul after Brand's death, initiated a preventive policy which set a precedent for later action. The innovation was an embargo on the export of arms and ammunition to the hinterland. An Egba partisan,[20] Hand interpreted the conflict in the interior as a plot conceived by the Dahomeans, the Ijebu, and Kosoko to destroy the Egba and drive the English from the coast.[21] In disregard of the spirit, if not the letter, of his instructions, he was determined to influence the course of events by preventing the sale of guns and powder at Ikorodu in Ijebu Remo country, where, at a market held every five days, the Ibadan caravans bought their supplies. He persuaded Dosunmu to co-operate with him, and they stationed four men—"two Sierra Leone emigrants with Consular staff, and two King's men with Docemo's staff"—to search all canoes trading between Lagos and Ikorodu.[22]

The contenders had active supporters in Lagos. As the Rev. Maser, who was in charge of CMS work there, explained,

Mr. Hand, at the instigation of an Ultra-Egba Merchant here, did prohibit the sale of ammunition of War at Ikorodu. . . . Captain Davies [one of the most prominent emigrant traders] and all the Europeans were for strict neutrality and the order was repealed. But that Egba Merchant and Davies became now leaders between two parties the Egbas and Yorubas, or rather one was representant of the war and the other of neutrality. It came to more than disputes, and the matter is not yet settled. It is necessary that the English Consul should keep himself in a position to act at any favourable moment as a mediator. . . . It seems Ijaye (without provisions) and the Egbas, (having no open road from their encampment at Ijaye to Abeokuta) are the worse for a chance of success in the Struggle.[23]

Hand had, of course, support from the *Awujale* of Ijebu Ode on this issue. When asked by the Consul to stop disrupting the palm oil traffic, the Ijebu chief replied that his "country is in union with England, and [is in] lawful trade of palm oil for British merchants, if there will be no guns and powder to support the Ibaddans' people the peace will be established." [24]

The effect of the conflict in the interior on commerce was being increasingly felt in Lagos. The problem was not simply a matter of persuading the African rulers of the impartiality of the colony and the need to keep the trade routes open.[25] It was, in fact, just because their subjects preferred to continue their peaceful activities of farming or trading that the local chiefs in the interior took measures to "conscript" their armies by indirect methods, that is, by closing the roads "to keep the people from deserting from the camp to take up their trading occupations." [26]

In Abeokuta there were the further problems of decentralized authority and pressures from conflicting traditional interests. The consent of the *Alake* was insufficient to open roads if the *Parakoyi* (the traders' association), who felt their control of trade threatened by the expanding European and Saro operations, refused to sanction such action.[27] For a short time the consuls and European mediators relied on promises for the permanent opening of the roads.[28] Even after years of experience with the uncertain worth of such assurances, they never seemed to grasp the complex causes for breach of agreement. They lacked the knowledge of Yoruba institutions which might have enabled them to understand that hostility toward European interests was not an isolated phenomenon, or that broken promises of particular chiefs did not mean personal duplicity but rather a yielding to traditional pressures. In other words, the coastal settlement in this period hovered on the edge of a world where the pressing problems for each group were internal ones. Decisions in each were made not by a single ruler but by consensus among many interests—a political system the Europeans did not expect and did not understand.

POLITICAL EFFECTS OF THE CESSION OF LAGOS

Neither the death of the *Are* nor the fall of Ijaye itself to the Ibadan forces in March, 1862, brought peace to the interior. But events on the coast—the cession of Lagos with the changes of policy put into effect by the new government—created new attitudes in the hinterland toward the British authorities. Ten years earlier Akitoye seemed already to have grasped the implications of his acquiescence to consular jurisdiction. Dosunmu had certainly felt his meager power dwindle, and he showed no eagerness to cede his island in the summer of 1861. The evidence suggests that in Lagos the awareness of the effects of British intervention on African authority was considerably greater than it was in the hinterland up to the early 1860's.

This awareness is clear in the opposition from Lagos to the cession of the island. The impetus for the decision to make Lagos a colony came from the consular officials working through the Foreign Office. Brand wrote to Russell, in April, 1860, that such a measure would "tend to put an end to the Slave Trade, and increase the legal commerce and industrial prosperity of this line of coast to an unlimited extent"; he argued that under the consulate there was only "feeble, irregular and irresponsible jurisdiction over a variety of judicial, police, or even administrative matters." [29]

Lord John Russell had a slightly different emphasis in presenting his case to the Colonial Office. He stressed the unsatisfactory arrangement by which the British had responsibility for protecting the island without "any of the advantages of Sovereignty." [30] Within four months the matter was decided, and Russell wrote to Foote the well-known official explanation for reluctant annexation: that control of Lagos was "indispensable to the complete suppression of the Slave Trade," that it would "give great aid and support to the development of lawful commerce," and finally that it would "check the aggressive spirit of the King of Dahomey." [31]

On 6 August 1861, after a week's "persuasion" while H.M.S. *Prometheus* lay at anchor in the lagoon, Dosunmu and four of his chiefs signed the Treaty of Cession with McCoskry, the acting consul, and Commander Bedingfield.[32] The *Oba* put forward what resistance he could, and he later tried to have the new status annulled. Even after Freeman, the first governor, reported in March, 1862, that he had "terminated" to the satisfaction of Dosunmu and his chiefs "all questions arising out of the Treaty of Cession," [33] the *Oba*, his chiefs, and "certain natives" twice sent petitions pleading their case to Queen Victoria.[34] In February, 1862, it had been formally agreed that to compensate him for loss of revenue Dosunmu should receive a life pension of 1,200 bags of cowries, estimated at £1,030 annually, provided that he violated no articles of the earlier treaty.[35] When Colonel Ord visited the West African settlements in 1864 to assess their condition, the *Oba* and emigrants sent him petitions stating what they saw as the undesirable effects of creating the colony.[36]

In the hinterland, the repercussions of the cession were felt at first only among the peoples nearest to the new colony. It was not until later that Ibadan and such groups as the Ijesha and the Ekiti became aware of the new government in Lagos and how it affected them, directly or indirectly. The Ibadan leaders, however, seem to have been less apprehensive than their neighbors because the potential danger at that time threatened people who were

Ibadan's enemies. With the shift of British favor away from Abeokuta, it was, in fact, in the interest of Ibadan to support the policies and actions of the colonial administrators.

But the impact was felt quickly by the Egba, the Ijebu, and, of course, the people of Lagos itself. The cession, which stimulated the fear of British authority, was followed by ill feeling on the part of the Lagosians, culminating in an uprising led by Dosunmu in 1863.[37] News of the *Oba*'s loss of power reached Abeokuta, and this, combined with the realization of decreasing British support for Egba policies, contributed to the unco-operativeness of the authorities there. Henry Robbin, prominent emigrant trader, described the Egba feeling:

> The people of Abeokuta are very suspicious . . .; they say the object of the Governor is to extend his territory by taking Abeokuta therefore he is finding faults with them. By these mismanagement[s] of the Gov. the influence of the Missionaries are much lessened and they are not regarded with such respect as formerly, excepting by the Christian converts . . . the people in general now say that the white men are not to be trusted for they only come to take possession . . . as they did Lagos.[38]

In March, 1863, Newcastle, the Colonial Secretary, wrote to Freeman in response to criticism by a CMS delegation defending Egba interests, and affirmed that the British government had not reversed its policy toward Abeokuta.[39] Nonetheless there had been a change to what the Europeans on the coast and the Whitehall officials saw as a more objective policy, expressed more than a year earlier by Earl Russell in a communication to McCoskry, the acting governor. The Foreign Secretary wrote plainly that the British government had no favorites in the Lagos hinterland. Chiefs were judged by their acts: those who gave up the slave trade, lived "at peace with their neighbours," encouraged legitimate trade, and "developed the resources of their country" would be "considered as friends" and supported "as far as possible" by British influence. By this standard, the British had backed the Egba chiefs who "professed" to act according to it. However, if the authorities in Abeokuta were "to continue to wage wars, and refuse to listen to the advice and suggestions of the British officers," they had to understand that they would "forfeit the friendship and good will" of Whitehall. [40]

The Colonial Office, as the events of the early 1860's show, acted on this warning. Though Newcastle could truthfully deny that he advocated encouraging Dahomey against Abeokuta, he and the officials at the Colonial Office did come to feel that earlier policies had too strongly favored the interests of the Egba, whose merits had been magnified to the government in London. Frederick Elliot, assistant under-secretary at the Colonial Office, expressed this view in 1862:

> It appears very probably, that . . . Abeokuta has been petted from the mere circumstance of its having been the first to receive European Missionaries and Traders, and that for that very reason it has become aggressive, and the less deserving of the favour it has enjoyed. . . . How long ought a man to take before he believes himself a good judge of the relative merits of obscure African Tribes and Villages? . . . I feel afraid sometimes lest we should be like the Kings in a burlesque who, with comical vigour, despatch one slave with a blow, and cover the other with honours, long before they can know whether either deserves his fate.[41]

As good relations with Abeokuta disintegrated, intercessions from the Lagos government for peace, for the guarantee of open roads, or for the safety of caravans led only to agreements that were at most tentative and were quickly forgotten. The fear of domination from the coast on the one hand, and of the increasing separate threats from Ibadan and Dahomey on the other, made self-preservation the Egba's first concern. They had no particular confidence in offers of mediation from the Lagos government, in part for reasons which even antedated the cession. Thus, the angry rejection of acting governor McCoskry's offers to mediate is traceable to the enmity between him and the *Alake* during the Badagry disputes of the 1850's.[42] Neither the first mission of Captain Jones of H.M.S. *Arrogant* [43] nor the later one of Commander Bedingfield [44] had brought a more effective peace than had the unsuccessful consular ones of Lieutenant Lodder and Messrs. Turner and Thomas, and of Mr. Richards. Richards at least found the roads reopened and thought the new arrangement a permanent one. He evidently had not realized that this temporary solution was the work of the emigrant community in the Egba capital: their Abbeokutan Mercantile Association had offered to meet the duties levied for military expenses which would otherwise have been imposed on the very traders who wanted the routes cleared.[45]

Commander Bedingfield had concluded with the *Alake* and other chiefs an agreement to reinforce the one signed in 1852. In addition to agreeing to block the slave route still in use to Porto Novo via Okeodan and guaranteeing no further human sacrifices, they promised that the road between Lagos and Abeokuta should "never again be stopped on any pretext whatever, without the consent and approval of Her Majesty's Government."[46] The last clause enjoyed a short lived compliance.

The real breach between the Lagos government and the Egba came in May, 1862, with the unannounced arrival in Abeokuta of Thomas C. Taylor as British vice-consul. Lagos officials during the consular period had long thought representation in the Egba capital desirable, and McCoskry in particular had made repeated suggestions to that effect to the Foreign Office. Just after the cession, this trader and acting Governor reported the satisfactory state of the settlement but asked again for representation in Abeokuta to "look after our commercial interests" and, he hoped, to put a stop to the "war" which was said to explain the *Alake's* inaction over Egba interference with these interests.[47]

Indeed, throughout the consular period the Egba themselves would probably have welcomed such representation.[48] They wanted the aid of British officers in planning their defense against Dahomey,[49] and we may reasonably assume that they would have seen the arrival of a consul as bringing both practical advantages and prestige by lending direct British support for Egba activities.

But after the cession of Lagos the views in Abeokuta were quite different. Whatever may have been the procedural excuses for the refusal to admit Taylor,[50] the Egba reaction could be stated simply:

Their notion of a Consul is that of a person sent by an acknowledged superior Power to one in subjection. . . . England conquered Lagos and sent an Ajelle [translated as 'Consul'] there. The Consul at Lagos was, in fact, not a Consul [in the British sense] but an Ajelle; and when the English Government sends a Consul here, he is taken to be an Ajelle, and they won't have an Ajelle.[51]

So hostile were the Egba to this move from Lagos that some of them began to turn against the very man who was expending such effort to revive the "Abeokutan Policy," Henry Townsend.[52]

Anyone who was associated with the British interests — and this included the Sierra Leonian mission agents at this stage — was suspected of subversion. "So irritated are the people now," wrote Thomas King, one of the ordained Sierra Leonian missionaries, "that one can hardly pass or walk through the town without being loaded with abuses as those who are seeking to take their country from them by cunningness."[53]

In the face of this open hostility toward British intentions as the Egba interpreted them, it is hard to understand why Freeman should have been surprised at the Egba reaction. Only a month before he sent the Vice-Consul, the Governor had noted that though the Dahomean army was threatening Abeokuta, "neither the Alake nor people of Abeokuta have made any application to me for assistance; first because they think they are capable of defending themselves, and secondly because they have been persuaded to believe that if they trust too much to the English and allow them too much influence in Abeokuta the result will be a British occupation of the Country."[54]

Resentment of the new government by the Lagosians themselves and the apprehensions in the hinterland were to be fed in 1863 by measures against Epe, followed by further annexations. Just after the cession of Lagos, negotiations had begun between Kosoko and the British administration to allow the exiled ex-King and his chiefs to trade in Lagos.[55] McCoskry, then acting Governor, had no objections.[56] Tapa, the most prominent chief trading at Epe, sought and was granted permission to return to the island, although his insistence on having a similar concession for Kosoko brought tentative withdrawal of the offer.[57] But in September, 1862, Kosoko, "accompanied by his principal chiefs and several hundred people," was allowed to move back to Lagos.[58] Freeman took this step partly because he recognized Kosoko's considerable influence in the "surrounding Country," and hoped that his return and recognition of British authority would "tend greatly to bring back that confidence in the British rule which . . . the occupation of this Island has shaken so much."[59]

Still troubled by disturbances at Epe, Freeman sent a mission early in 1863 to exact an agreement. His major motive was the practical and obvious one: the need to gain acquiescence in Lagos policies from the peoples to the east in the expectation that "ere long, a passage will be open from this river by the Lagoons to Benin and the Niger." [60] The agreement with the *Possu* at Epe did not, in fact, constitute a cession of territory, for it acknowledged that the town remained under the sovereignty of the *Awujale* of Ijebu Ode, but it cleared the way for later action at Palma and Leckie. [61]

More significant was what Freeman considered a rather minor measure taken to reinforce the impression made by the shelling of Epe — the burning of Ejirin market which, "though only a few empty sheds," was, he admitted, "an important place of trade for the people of Epe." [62] The Governor seemed to have forgotten that Ejirin was also an important market for the people of Lagos and of Ijebu country. The strength of their reaction was evident when this issue claimed first place in a petition from Lagosian traders to Colonel Ord almost a year after the shelling. [63] This seemingly minor punitive measure heightened not only resentment in Lagos but intransigence in Ijebu Ode, and strengthened the alliance between the Egba and the *Awujale*, who both interpreted the action against Epe and Ejirin as foreshadowing later infringements on their own territories.

Bitterness grew further when the new acting governor, John Hawley Glover, startled by measures taken by the French at Porto Novo [64] and dissatisfied with the "pleasantly vague frontier" [65] of the colony, obtained treaties of "protection" with Addo, Okeodan, and Pocrah (Ipokia) in June, 1863, and within a month had effected the cession of Badagry. [66] In July the prominent Sierra Leonian merchant, J. P. L. Davies, wrote to Henry Venn describing the state of Lagos and giving his views on the effect of the government's policies:

We have now no trade, no food in Lagos the state of things is ... worse than ever. ... Capt. Glover ... goes up and down the river making such arrangements as he thinks will secure prosperity to Lagos. But it is a very great mistake to biass the mind of one native government against another so as to gain a point such acts only make worse war than peace. ... It has caused much grief and regret that the French have occupied Porto Novo and the Gov. is now trying to compensate for that by taking possession of several small places near Porto Novo. . . . [He] has made Mr. Tom Tickel as Vice Consul for Adokpokia without asking or consulting the Kings or Chiefs to whom these places are tributary.[67]

In September, 1863, Dosunmu, "declaring that he had never given over his Town and country to the Queen of Great Britain," started an uprising which was halted in its early stages only by the strong and immediate action of Glover.[68] The power of England, still reinforced from the sea, proved convincingly formidable, and no further incidents on the island itself were to occur.

There is strong evidence that the Africans of Lagos and the hinterland had throughout the period two major grievances — undefined boundaries and road blockades. A third, the issue of domestic slavery, dating back to the days of the consulate, now became intensified, as the distinction — an important one from the Africans' point of view — between slaves destined for the "household" and those for overseas trade was ignored in European judgments. For once Lagos was British territory, any "slave" who took refuge there became free, with no claims of rendition recognized and with only conditional compensation to his former owner. It is important to bear in mind that there was no free labor market in the West Africa of this period. In the neighboring towns, chiefs were said to fear not only loss of sovereignty if the British government extended its jurisdiction, but loss of property and "family" as well. The Sierra Leonian emigrants brought this point quite early to the attention of the people of Igbessa, whose newly elected chief had sought approval from the Lagos government. Freeman reported that

the inhabitants are beginning to show opposition to their new chief and to blame him for bringing the white man as they express it 'to give them new laws and then blow down their town as was done at Porto Novo.'
The weak point with the natives which the Sierra Leone emigrants work upon is the question of Slavery.[69]

It is difficult to tell to what extent the expression of these grievances was encouraged by the Sierra Leonians with connections in the Yoruba towns. Still more difficult is any assessment of the motives behind such prompting. In attempting such an analysis later, it will be necessary to evaluate the complaints of the Lagos administrators in the light of the policies they found they had to pursue. This much is certain — there were few clear-cut rights and wrongs on these issues, and there was considerable misunderstanding and conflict of purposes. The dilemma of the emigrant communities in Lagos Colony and beyond it, in the hinterland, was how to meet the simultaneous claims of loyalty to and identification with both the British and African authorities when the goals of the two conflicted. For in the interest of their very economic survival, let alone their cultural ties with both sides, complete consistency was virtually impossible.

CHANGING BRITISH POLICY

In 1865, the British House of Commons set up a Select Committee under the chairmanship of Sir Charles Adderley to "consider the State of the British Establishments on the Western Coast of Africa." [70] In its report the Committee gave substance to the policy of reluctant extension of responsibility which Newcastle had expressed in the preceding years.[71] Adderley and his colleagues deplored the cost in British lives and funds of putting down the slave trade with but partial success, in this case through maintaining English sovereignty at the four points along the coast.[72] After hearing evidence from London officials and some men with West African experience, the Committee set forth its conclusions that although it was not possible for the British government "to withdraw . . . wholly or immediately" from the settlements,

all further extension of territory or assumption of Government, or new treaties offering protection to native tribes, would be inexpedient; . . . the object of our policy should be to encourage in the natives the exercise of those qualities which may render it possible for us more and more to transfer to them the administration of all the Governments, with a view to our ultimate withdrawal from all.[73]

This proposal was not made with a view to granting "independence" based on a legacy of nurtured British institutions of government. Countering an earlier suggestion by Lord Grey that "the true policy is to keep constantly in sight the formation of a regular government on the European model, and the establishment of a civilised polity, taking care that each successive step

shall appear to the people themselves the natural mode of providing some want," [74] Adderley wrote, "I do not think any
guardian angel has so trained England in principles of government; and I am quite sure that no miracle can set up the European model in West Africa." [75]

In fact, he interpreted the Committee's recommendation in
these words: "We should get out of the scrape in which we have
involved ourselves, as speedily as we honourably can, leaving the
tribes in a fair way of being able to hold their own and govern
themselves, securing, of course, complete respect, on our departure, to the claims of the few merchants and agents who have
established themselves among them." [76]

The Committee itself, however, further declared, "that this
policy of non-extension admits of no exception, as regards new
settlements, but cannot amount to an absolute prohibition of
measures which, in peculiar cases, may be necessary for the more
efficient and economical administration of the new settlements
we already possess." [77] Thus, in effect, what they took away with
one hand, they gave back with the other; the administrators on
the coast were continually reminded of the strict policy, but, in
the case of Lagos, they could stretch the interpretation and still
remain within the bounds of necessity "for more efficient and
economical administration." A tug of war to define the limits of
this policy was to occupy the Lagos administrators and the Colonial
Office for the next decade.

The governors and administrators of Lagos, with the continuing
strife in the interior, and the misunderstanding and distrust of
their actions in the colony and outside it, had to deal with several
persistent problems. Foremost was the need to see that the external
slave trade was halted and to deal with the issue of domestic
salvery. Secondly, they had to assure the free flow of trade, for
they depended on successful commerce to provide funds for the
operation of the colony and its development. Another problem,
virtually insoluble, was how to bring peace in the interior
without extending colonial jurisdiction beyond the economically
unviable island or, with interpretations of suzerainty stretched
to their limit, a small, almost equally unviable strip of land
on either side of it. The officials in Lagos could scarcely do

other than press for an expansionist policy in order to meet the demands placed upon them. The extent to which they were able to make small inroads into the interior was determined, apart from the African resistance they encountered, by the degree to which they could successfully present the Colonial Office with *faits accomplis*, explained and justified by a skillful use of local information on which, compared to the officials in London, they were authorities.

Reminders from Newcastle in the early 1860's of the policy of non-expansion were evaded by the means just described. Such action was more effective before the centralization of control in Sierra Leone in 1866, in compliance with the recommendations of the 1865 Select Committee. But Freetown was a sufficient distance from Lagos so that even after 1866 with an acquiescent governor-in-chief, or one preoccupied with matters elsewhere on the coast, control was still not too rigid. Firm measures were taken only when Glover, having strained his instructions to their limits, finally met with the watchful intransigence of Pope-Hennessy, a governor-in-chief who was not acquiescent.

Still less room for maneuver was possible under the tighter reorganization in 1874 when Lagos and the Gold Coast were joined under one administration, separate from Sierra Leone and the Gambia. From the early 1870's, however, the Colonial Office viewed the problems of Lagos more sympathetically as their complexity became more evident. But not until the final return of Lagos to the status of a separate colony in 1886 were discretionary powers given to the governor as a matter of policy to solve by force, where there was African resistance, the dilemma of earlier years. For the chiefs in the hinterland it then became no longer a matter of whose advice to heed or what action to take to maintain their sovereignty.

This explains why the men in local British administration who had the greatest impact on events in the hinterland of Lagos came early in the period — Freeman and Glover — and at the end of it — Moloney. For the intervening officials between 1872 and the early 1880's, rapid replacement and decreased authority made the local formulation of a dynamic policy impossible. As a consequence, the tensions between the Africans and the Lagos government in those years lessened somewhat.

We have seen some of the steps taken by Freeman in his efforts to achieve economic stability for the new colony.[78] The more extreme measures followed logically from the initial ones. For example, the need to impose collection of customs duties in Badagry, Palma, and Leckie required him to station officials at these points,[79] and this action was followed by eventual control over the towns themselves, particularly Badagry, for it was essential to prevent the escape of produce and revenue down the lagoon system to Porto Novo and Cotonou.

John Hawley Glover, who in effect ruled the colony, except for brief intervals, from 1864 to 1872, met the same problems but in more acute form. His plans both engendered and tried to mollify the increasing antagonism of the Egba and Ijebu, against the background of Colonial Office restraint. It is beyond the scope of this study to look at the intricacies of the resulting upward spiral in which successive colonial measures of self-preservation produced in turn African counter-measures to maintain traditional autonomy. The emigrant role in these controversies will be examined later; for the present we shall only touch on a few of the larger issues.

Glover's actions differed from those of Freeman only in intensity and in the amount of experience behind them. The similarity is not surprising in view of the co-operation between the two men before the naval officer's assumption of full administrative responsibility.[80] Both thought that earlier partiality toward the Egba had been unfair; both interpreted recalcitrant behavior by the tribal groups nearest the coast as a desire to monopolize the inland trade.[81] Although Glover recognized further Egba resentment on the question of "fugitive slaves," he could not condone either their rejection of the British vice-consul or the thefts of property belonging to British traders.[82] He did not relate these actions to Egba anxieties about political self-preservation. During Glover's period of rule he amassed more and more evidence to support his hypothesis about the Egba,[83] and to attain commercial fluidity he tried to justify increasingly strong action to himself and to the Colonial Office.[84]

In Lagos itself the name of Glover was most associated with the internal development he sought to promote in the colony; only the large traders gave careful consideration to the ramifications of his "foreign policy." [85] But among the Egba his acts provoked hostile responses. They feared his road plan, not only because it might decrease their influence in the Lagos trade, but also because it would reinforce Ibadan's hegemony in Yoruba country. [86] Suspicious, they disregarded Glover's suggestions for ending punitive attacks in retaliation for the Ijaye defeat. They threatened the market town of Ikorodu, dangerously near Lagos from the government's point of view, and the steps which Glover took to secure the town from Egba domination made the rift complete. [87] Any inclination to rely on the word of the Lagos government was finally destroyed when, in the Egba view, the Governor who had sanctioned their aggression against Ikorodu then ordered their lifting the blockade within twenty-four hours. When he interpreted his ultimatum as rejected, he sent forces of the West Indian Regiments, the Hausa Police, and British naval officers to eject Abeokuta's soldiers from their camp. [88]

From this time on, Glover decided he had to bypass the Egba in his plans for the hinterland, although he still maintained that he showed no tribal partiality. He agreed to the Rev. Townsend's offer to mediate between the Lagos and Egba governments for open roads [89] but refused to correspond over grievances felt in Abeokuta, and, while he recognized the "advantages of Political and Commercial relations on a firm basis," he thought that Lagos was sufficiently supplied from the Ijebu and western lagoon trade to make feasible waiting until "the Egbas shall be prepared again to resume free intercourse with this Government." [90] In fact, at that point all Glover wanted from the Egba was peace. He would have preferred friendly relations among all the groups in the Lagos hinterland, but domestic controversies in the interior were at this time of little concern to him so long as palm oil could come down from one part or another. [91]

The report of Colonel Ord exonerated the Lieutenant Governor from charges of exceeding his instructions with regard to boundaries and of exacerbating local conflicts by showing favoritism. [92] The new centralization of authority in Sierra Leone, however, made force as the basis of any new plans impossible, and the emphasis on economy removed any hope of subsidy from the imperial treasury. Peace in the interior became the only solution, and by the time Glover went on leave in May, 1866, he could be fairly optimistic about its prospects. For the Niger was accessible by the new Ikorodu-Ibadan route, and though the Egba and Lagos governments continued suspicious of one another, the Abeokuta roads were open.

In Abeokuta in 1865, a new organization of Sierra Leonians had formed a subsidiary government of the city, with plans to work in conjunction with the traditional government. Called the Egba United Board of Management, under the leadership of a Saro named George W. Johnson, its primary aim was to handle the external relations of the Egba with Lagos in a European style. More detailed consideration will presently be given to the EUBM,[93] as the Egba United Board of Management was known in its time, and as it will henceforth be called. The important point in 1866 was that in March cordial letters had passed between Johnson and Glover with the result that, on the Lagos side, "the existing duties [of 2½ per cent] (levied for the purpose of obtaining compensation) on Goods exported to the Egba territory" ceased, and thenceforth it was declared that all persons, at their own risk, should have "*free liberty* to *pass* and *re-pass* between the Territories of Lagos and Abbeokuta." [94] The Egba had agreed reciprocally that from 9 April 1866, "the Roads for all Goods and Produce passing to and from Abbeokuta by the River Ogun and elsewhere, will be opened for all Merchants, Native-traders, and others," subject to the payment of Abeokuta export tariffs.[95]

On his return in November, 1866, Glover was made administrator of Lagos, and he continued his efforts to attain peace throughout the interior. Early in 1867, a mission of Glover's private secretary, Lieutenant J. Gerard, to end the war between Ibadan and Ijesha was not only successful, it was a vote of confidence in the administrator from the *Bashorun* of Ibadan, who withdrew his troops as they were on the verge of demolishing Ilesha, the Ijesha capital.[96] With mounting confidence, Glover stationed constables on the mainland to protect the trade routes,

and sought to negotiate a defined frontier with the Egba, following their announcement that they would set up customs houses
"below Abeokuta." [97]

According to the Egba interpretation, these actions by Glover
led directly to the *Ifole* of 13 October 1867.[98] Sometimes called
the expulsion of the missionaries from Abeokuta, this Egba uprising, which will be considered further later,[99] meant that no
Europeans, whatever their purposes, would be allowed to live in
Abeokuta or any place under her control for some years to come.
It meant that the Egba were determined that there should be no
encroachment from Lagos upon any land in the interior. It also
meant that suspicion and hostility increased on both sides.

Nonetheless, the roads into the hinterland were open, and from
1868 to 1870 the absence of noticeable conflict there made possible
growing prosperity in Lagos. By 1869 the colony was independent
of imperial financial support.[100] But though the interior wars and
the issues between African governments and that of the colony
were to abate, they were not to be resolved in this period. On his
return from leave in August, 1870, Glover faced once more the possibility of war between Ibadan and the Egba-Ijebu coalition; the
internal affairs of Abeokuta were still unsettled; [101] and these conditions were having repercussions on the Lagos trade.

THE GLOVER-HENNESSY
CONTROVERSY AND ITS REPERCUSSIONS

The administrator tried yet again to solve the road problem,
this time by insuring access to the interior by some route around
the Egba while simultaneously dealing with Abeokuta in what
he considered its own coin, that is, by blockading Egba trade outlets. To carry out this policy effectively he had to reopen the
Porto Novo question, for the port to the west was at the end of
a traditional route from Abeokuta and was still the Egba source
of arms and ammunition.[102] This was the central issue over which
Glover clashed with the new governor-in-chief, John Pope-Hennessy, who had firm ideas of policy based on the recommendations
of the 1865 Committee, and who acted, in his own view, in the
best interests of the Colonial Office and the Africans.[103]

The "Glover Controversy," which consumed considerable

paper and time both in London and on the coast, can be briefly summarized as a conflict between Glover's long formulated solution to the problems of the Lagos hinterland and that of Pope-Hennessy. Hennessy, influenced by the traders and the Egba, believed that Glover's measures had created antagonism that only a sudden reversal of policy — that is to say, compliance with the 1865 recommendations — could dispel.[104] Both officials were taken to task by the home authorities for their extreme actions. As Kimberley, the colonial secretary, wrote,

Both in my opinion are wrong. Capt. G. evidently thought that 'a man who had been 9 years on the coast' was entitled to pursue his own policy regardless of his instructions, and Mr. H. forgot that a man who has been a few weeks on the coast should act with great caution in reversing a policy being pursued by the local authorities, or rather checking and moderating it, for that rather than reversal was what was needed.[105]

Glover was saved the humiliation of recall only by applying for leave;[106] Pope-Hennessy, after a few months, was moved to a governorship in the West Indies. Both had been in some sense correct: Glover foreshadowed what would become inevitable from the British point of view; Hennessy proposed measures which were effective in the short run at best, and which could only have had lasting influence had withdrawal been the English objective, or had the situation in the interior and the relation between the colony and the hinterland not already reached an impasse.

Before Hennessy left the West Coast of Africa, he and Fowler, the new acting administrator in Lagos, made what were seen as drastic changes, reversing Glover's policies.[107] The most striking of these measures included discrediting the successful mission of Roger Goldsworthy which had brought the opening of Glover's alternative eastern trade route,[108] and increasing the powers of the *Oba* of Lagos by authorizing him to prevent the escape of domestic slaves to the island, thereby avoiding the issue of rendition.[109] The Colonial Office recognized that these actions were designed to lessen the fears of both Egba and Ijebu, but one official nonetheless wrote "pretty plainly" that "no authority should be given to [Dosunmu] . . . under any pretext, and Mr. Hennessy's policy in this respect was a grave error."[110]

As a result of the negotiations of the Sierra Leonian J. A.

Otonba Payne, the Ijebu roads were opened, at least temporarily, in October, 1872;[111] those of the Egba, whose suspicions were not allayed, remained closed. Disturbances had also broken out in Badagry—"not nearly so prosperous as it once was"—with a general refusal to pay duties and to purchase boat or liquor licenses. The acting administrator, finding the town "mutinous," abolished the licenses, though he continued the duties and was forced to leave fifty Hausa troops there temporarily to guarantee the return of peace.[112]

Gradually Fowler was, as the Colonial Office noted, "falling back upon the measures proposed by Capt. Glover," with a request for the colonial steamer to patrol the lagoon, and the suggestion to prohibit the export of goods from Lagos inland, thereby forcing the opening of the roads.[113] Kimberley commented, "Captn. G. was, I never doubted, quite right in his main views, but he went too fast. . . . We want of course free access to the interior but we cannot undertake the task of controlling all the powerful coast tribes, and if we succeeded in getting them under our control, we should immediately come into collision with tribes beyond, and so on till we come to Timbuctoo." [114]

In dealing with the problems of the West African settlements the officials in London came increasingly to appreciate the dilemma facing the administrators on the coast in the light of central policy. Knatchbull-Hugessen, parliamentary under-secretary from 1871 to 1874, who expressed the strongest views in the Colonial Office at this time for strengthening the British position in West Africa, laid out the existing contradictions:

the difficulties and troubles of our West African Settlements do not arise so much from mistakes on the part of this or that administrator as from the inherent viciousness of the system under which we find ourselves administering the governments on that coast. . . . [I]t was perfectly possible—had we chosen to do so—to have refused Docemo's cession and never to have occupied the place. Having . . . possessed ourselves of Lagos, it was perfectly possible to have seized from the weak hands of the native Kings such territory as we deemed necessary for the security of our settlement, or better still, to have accepted other cessions or bought the places desirable to hold. But we do neither one thing nor the other—to leave boundaries undefined—jurisdiction uncertain and administrators uninstructed as to either or the other, was a course which required no great faults on the part of the officer administering the government in order to produce a state of difficulty.[115]

He continued to point out the resulting confusion of the Africans who "have been left uncertain of . . . [British] intentions" toward them, and declared that this confusion blurred in African eyes the benefits to be gained from the extension of English influence. "To this state of things the report of 'Sir Charles Adderley's Committee' contributed not a little, and I am at a loss to conceive how that half-and-half policy of Great Britain — occupying territory as if she were ashamed of it and felt she had no business to be there — coaxing one day and threatening the next — can be expected to produce anything but confusion and disaster."

Concluding that since British public opinion would not consent to abandoning the posts, and that surely the objectives for which England took over Lagos originally — "to put down slavery and to extend Christian civilization" — were no less "worthy of . . . attention" than before, Hugessen saw alternative policies. One was to maintain the status quo with the clear statement, including refusal to claim disputed territory, that the British government had no intention of extending its sphere of control. Concurrently, "persuasion and conciliation" would be used to cement friendly relations between British officials and merchants and the Africans, to create a climate permitting the extension of trade.

The other possibility, which Hugessen himself preferred, would have the British government "define the boundaries . . . and let it be clearly understood that upon British territory no runaway slave law can exist." Further, in the "Protected territory" the British would not interfere with "slavery as it exists" but would "govern that territory through the Native Kings, securing their allegiance and fidelity by a moderate stipend. . . ." Similarly, stipends should be offered to the Egba and Ijebu, with payment dependent on opening the roads and continuing safety for those travelling on them. He believed that were this second course adopted, the resulting increase in the trade and revenue of "Lagos and the coast" would mean that Britain would have "eventually" no expense to bear for development there, while there would be simultaneously, "the advance of Christianity and of civilisation."

Hugessen was actually advocating implementing Glover's proposals. But he was ahead of his contemporaries at the Colonial Office in his view of policy. Though these men had stopped thinking of total British withdrawal from the West African settlements, they followed for fifteen years the first alternative that Hugessen had presented.[116] Had they sought to pursue the second, they would have needed to take stronger measures than Hugessen anticipated, for he reckoned without knowledge of the value the Africans placed on their sovereignty.

THE ECONOMY OF LAGOS AND BRITISH POLICY

By the beginning of 1873 Lagos was in serious economic straits: trade was stagnant and revenue went down steeply. The government could continue functioning only with the aid of a Treasury loan of £20,000;[117] it could not, of course, relieve the distress of the traders. Fortunately for them, trade became possible on the Ijebu and Egba roads in May and June, 1873;[118] this fact, plus the temporary assurance of the imperial loan, reduced the need for interventionist policies in the hinterland. In addition, Glover's route, which started east of Epe at Itebu and passed through Ondo country, opened,[119] though its success was later to be blocked by familiar complications.

The administrations of Lagos and the Gold Coast were merged in July, 1874, as a final measure of imperial economy and with the hope of greater efficiency. The advantage to Lagos was to be that the senior official at Accra, although still distant from the new "province," was closer than the earlier governors-in-chief in Freetown. For the following two years the Lagos hinterland was relatively undisturbed: the roads were to some degree open, however precariously, and there were no major wars. The revenue in Lagos rose; the loan from the Treasury was repaid in 1875 and 1876; and by 1877 the figures, compared with expenditures, gave satisfaction and cause for optimism to both local officials and the Colonial Office.[120] The calm was only on the surface, however, for apart from other unresolved issues, the hostilities in the interior remained. Ibadan still sought more power, and the neighboring groups still feared her hegemony and were intent on thwarting it.

In June, 1877, renewed conflict between Abeokuta and Ibadan began what the Sierra Leonian historian Samuel Johnson called "the Sixteen Years' War." [121] In fact, it was a series of wars which came to involve all Yoruba country and the Lagos government, and which, in conjunction with the impact of nearby French actions on Whitehall policy, led directly to the extension of British jurisdiction and the ultimate establishment of the Lagos Protectorate.

This is not the place for a detailed analysis of the conflicts and their development,[122] but it is necessary to mention some of the salient points (others will emerge in considering the emigrant role) and to assess the total situation facing Yoruba country and its relations with Lagos in the 1880's. The hostilities between Abeokuta and Ibadan began in 1877 over the issue of importing arms through Egba territory. The Egba had, since the Ijaye War, blockaded arms and ammunition destined for her enemy, and the Ibadan army had been forced to seek weapons from Benin.[123] However, before his death, Adelu, the *Alafin* of Oyo whose succession had caused the conflict in the 1860's, had bought gunpowder in Porto Novo, but fearing Egba confiscation of it on its way north he had it kept near the coast. In April, 1877, the *Areona-Kakanfo*, the new *de facto* ruler of Ibadan, sent an expedition to transport the supplies to Oyo. The success of the mission alarmed the still divided Egba authorities, especially when they learned that the powder was destined primarily for Ibadan. They blockaded the roads against all trade with Ibadan, and in retaliation Ibadan closed its gates.[124]

This mutual provocation, combined with the ambitions of the *Are* of Ibadan, set off further conflict, with Ibadan making raids on Egba farms.[125] In 1878, while the Ibadan forces were thus occupied in the south-west, the Ekiti, who had been under Ibadan rule since the 1850's, revolted; they persuaded the Ijesha and, more important, Ilorin to join them.[126] Early in 1879 Ijebu declared herself allied with both the Egba and the Ekiti, so that virtually all Yoruba country, plus Ilorin, was involved in the hostilities against Ibadan. Trade among the combatants was forbidden, although Lagos still managed some commercial transactions.

As if the situation were not sufficiently complicated, the Dahomeans, who had not launched a serious attack since their defeat in 1864,[127] increased their target range to include the western districts of "Yoruba proper"; they began their first battles and sieges in 1881 and continued them in spurts, destroying Okeodan in

February, 1884, and Ketu in July, 1885.[128] Their campaigns continued throughout the 1880's; the armed forces of Ibadan were in no condition to deal with them directly, and it was only their conquest by the French which put a stop to further Dahomean penetration of what was to become Nigerian territory.[129]

In addition, the Lagos government was meeting opposition on the lagoons which controlled the alternative trade route leading to Ondo.[130] Traders, some of them British subjects, were captured and their property seized.[131] Because of French pressure which threatened to cut off palm-oil supplies to the colony from its western flank, the new danger in the east took on heightened importance.[132]

Amid a barrage of suggested solutions, the Colonial Office and Ussher, the new governor in Accra, aided by Moloney in Lagos, agreed to have the colonial steamer *Gertrude* patrol the lagoons.[133] This measure was only temporarily effective, since respect for the force behind the *Gertrude* did not counter-balance the anger aroused when fugitive slaves were permitted to escape to freedom on her decks. The peoples along the eastern lagoon were feeling the effects of an expanding Lagos authority, and their reaction was different only in degree from that of their Ijebu and Egba neighbors two decades earlier. British supremacy was not to assert itself until, after the near cession of Mahin Beach to the Germans in 1885, England took the Mahin coast under protection and attached it to Lagos Colony.[134]

Meanwhile, conditions deeper in the hinterland grew steadily worse. Relations between Lagos and Abeokuta, which showed a glimmer of friendly revival in 1880 with an overture from one of the Egba factions,[135] quickly reverted to a near breakdown. J. B. Wood, the CMS missionary, wrote of scattered support in Lagos for the idea that Glover be brought out as governor of the Gold Coast.[136] Dissatisfaction with the continuing attachment of Lagos to the Gold Coast was increasingly expressed in the colony itself until the separation in 1886.[137] Griffith and Moloney worked toward settling the wars in the interior; the negotiation between Ibadan and the *Ekiti Parapo* (Ekiti confederation) produced in 1886 a "peace treaty," but it turned out to be little more than a truce.[138]

With the new central policy, Moloney had authority after 1887 to negotiate treaties with the Egba and others in the hinterland — treaties of "friendship and commerce" as before, but including now "a provision that they will not cede their territorites to any other power, or enter into any arrangement with a foreign Government except through H.M.G., or with their consent." [139] British policy was changing, but permission granted for exploratory expansion could not assure success without the threat of force behind it. [140] African rules were no more complacent about yielding their sovereignty than in the past; Moloney's efforts to sign an agreement with the Egba in 1888 were unsuccessful. [141] "Stipends to secure . . . observance of the treaties" may have been seen as an inducement in Whitehall, [142] but since the days of Dosunmu, Kosoko, and the treaty at Badagry, the hinterland chiefs had looked on the acceptance of stipends as a first step toward relinquishing power. [143]

The interior problems which had dominated the Lagos scene since the days of the consulate were not finally solved until the energetic expansionist efforts of Governor Carter in the 1890's. And even then, though in 1893 the Egba and British did sign a treaty exchanging open roads for no annexation without consent, Abeokuta managed to remain aloof until 1914. For, as David Hinderer wrote to Kimberley in 1872, "the African knows no middle course, either he must govern or be governed." [144]

EMIGRANTS IN CHANGING
TRADE RELATIONS

A^T the opening of the colonial period of Lagos history the interests represented there focused on trade. Its importance, and
the part played in it by the emigrants, must not be underestimated
even if the paucity of material available, particularly concerning
non-European enterprise, makes detailed analysis of it difficult if
not impossible. For while the role of the Sierra Leonians in the
political, administrative, and religious arenas can be extracted
both from their own accounts and from those of others, closely
kept records of commercial pursuits are fewer and, where existing,
tend to deal only with the activities of individual firms or their
agents, rather than those of the whole trading community. Nevertheless, the paramount importance of trade, despite this drawback,
can scarcely be overlooked.

There is no doubt that much of the Lagos population was engaged, to one degree or another, in trade. In 1866 the population
figures for the island itself estimated 2,540 "persons employed in
commerce" as opposed to 789 in agriculture, out of the total population of slightly over 25,000.[1] The Blue Book of 1871 records
2,871 persons in commerce; 2,165 in agriculture; 63 in "manu-
factures," in a total for "Lagos and vicinity" of about 36,000.[2] And
according to the first reasonably accurate census in 1881, 11,049
were in commerce on the island alone, with the next highest number, 5,173, "manufacturers, mechanics, artisans." It is not clear
whether or not such an estimate includes the women who have
traditionally been so important in trade in many parts of Nigeria.
The total population in 1881 was 37,452, of whom 111 were
Europeans.[3]

Thriving commerce was increasingly held essential by the Colonial Office, first because it was seen as a substitute for the slave
trade in the internal economy, and second, and of immediate

urgency, because the fiscal position of the colony depended on it. Inseparable from the problems of trade was what Governor Moloney later called the "Interior Question,"[4] the conflicts in the hinterland. Peace in the regions of production was the precondition for successful commerce, since war not only meant the blocking of trade routes but also a serious loss of manpower that could be turned to producing the coveted palm oil.

Thus, before European diplomacy came to the foreground in West-African affairs, local diplomacy was crucial. The coastal peoples and their near neighbors grew acutely aware of the meaning of the British presence. But in the deeper interior there was in the early years little more than a general uneasiness, dwarfed by traditional issues which had been causing conflict over the past decades. It is illuminating to read Samuel Johnson's discussions of the period in his *History of the Yorubas* to see just how little consideration was given by the traditional rulers to conditions in Lagos during such conflicts as the Ijaye War.[5] Johnson does not even mention the change from Foreign Office to Colonial Office jurisdiction over the island. In short, conflicts in the interior had a far greater effect on trading conditions in Lagos than did any measures of the Lagos government on the hinterland.

The interdependent issues of trade on the coast and politics in the hinterland were dominant concerns of the emigrant communities. Many Sierra Leonians were engaged in commercial pursuits of different degrees of importance. Others, working for the administration or the missions, shared the anxieties of their European counterparts. As we have seen, at the end of the consular period the emigrants' positions on specific issues correlated consistently with their varied economic interests, and neither the Sierra Leonians nor the Brazilians could be isolated as homogeneous groups with consistent "policies." The divisions among them became more clearly delineated only after 1861 when the emigrants were further affected by the complicating and steady growth of allegiances to factions in the hinterland.

In the consular decade, as in the years preceding it, the Saro showed their capacity for mediation between the Europeans on the coast and the peoples in the interior. They seemed convinced of the desirability of promoting European influence, which, at the time, had seldom come into conflict with African interests. But it was one thing to smooth the way for a mission station, or to suggest to the Egba defensive measures against Dahomey; it was to become quite another matter to promote changes which implied any actual surrender of African sovereignty. At times Saro allegiances were still determined on an economic basis, but evidence points to a heightened influence of tribal loyalties, which were called into play as the disputes in the hinterland became more virulent and drew large Yoruba factions into open conflict with one another.

Against this network of enmeshed hostilities, alliances, and policies, let us now look at the specific roles of the emigrants, first in the changing commercial climate, and then, in the next chapter, in the diplomatic negotiations between the different polities in the hinterland and the colony.

GROWTH OF TRADE FROM 1861

From 1861 on, trade in Lagos improved steadily, if slowly. The missions still encouraged production of cotton, even though the missionaries themselves did not wish to continue participating directly in the project.[6] The major exports, however, were still palm oil and palm kernels. In Geary's view, there were three factors influencing the quantity of palm exports: the price fluctuations in the European market, the amount of rainfall, and the conditions in the hinterland.[7] It is not within the scope of this study to attempt an accurate correlation on the basis of all three conditions; we know, however, that at the time of particularly severe crises in the interior — 1872, 1877, 1880 — the exports, and consequently the revenues, dropped markedly. Similarly, with the roads completely open and conditions comparatively peaceful — as from 1866 to 1871, and 1874 to 1877 — exports and revenues increased significantly. The pronounced upswing, indicating a healthy growth rather than the predictable natural increment in the colony's financial resources, did not come until after Carter's intervention in the interior in 1892.[8]

Thus the entire commercial complex rested on a bed of quicksand — perpetual uncertainty plus inadequate returns for either business expansion or programs of development supported by government. The outer structure of the community had not changed to any significant degree since the consular period, and all levels in the 1860's fastened on the difficulties in the interior as the source of their problems.

But for the emigrant and other African traders there were some factors which worked to their comparative advantage, though they were without the capital or credit on which the European merchants — especially these representing large companies with headquarters outside Africa and with factories scattered along the coast — could rely to carry them over the depressed periods in Lagos trade. Even when the roads were reported "closed," there was seldom a complete halt in the flow of produce from the interior, for the Sierra Leonians had devised means to maintain contact, either by going personally to the source of supply or working through their family ties.

These arrangements were possible for both large and "petty" traders in the emigrant group and for those other Africans in Lagos with deeper roots in the hinterland. J. P. L. Davies told of the business he carried on in Porto Novo, Lagos, and Abeokuta: "I sold cotton goods, spirits, &c. on credit and the purchaser, the trader, would take them to the markets and bring back produce and I would credit them with their value. I didn't lose much money through the traders. I know some of the producers personally. In Abeokuta native traders went themselves to the farms to collect the oil from the producers." [9]

William McCoskry, whose interpretations were not without a certain economic bias, even had a theory that the emigrants wished to prolong the war of the early 1860's in the interior, inasmuch as they gained "many advantages . . . by the present state of things; they have relations in Abbeokuta, by means of which they can carry on trade, while the Europeans carry on none." [10] There seems little question, however, that the general position of the Europeans was the more viable one. Palm oil and other products came to Lagos almost continually by the lagoons, particularly via Porto Novo in the west, though it was still more profitable for the merchants to ship their produce directly from Porto Novo where there were no export duties. But while such direct exporting increased the resources of Lagos firms with factories and agents at Porto

Novo and Whydah, it eroded the basis of the colony's revenue. Few emigrants could participate in either the direct or indirect trade along the lagoons, since their contact with the interior was usually effective only directly north of Lagos.

The fact that trade continued to be based on the credit system brought hardship to all, for when there was conflict in the hinterland none of the links in the chain was able to meet demands for repayment. But, predictably, large firms were least affected. They had legal recourse against debtors, and what was more important, they could afford to wait for the return of abundant produce. For the Africans, however, the situation reported in 1875 may be taken as typical:

Trade has suffered much from the last blockade of goods and the insecure credit system on which it has been done; almost all the Native houses of business are very largely involved in debt: Merchants and small traders suffer alike; a very considerable portion of the Town, and of it, the most important, is held in mortgage by three or four English houses, and many of the people are scarcely expected to be able to redeem their mortgages. Imprisonment for debt is large.[11]

The fate of the independent European traders was not much better; their names appeared on Lagos papers for periods of a few years and then were mentioned no more.[12] Some of the more tenacious among them turned to the more lucrative Delta area.

Although the preponderance of men and women "employed" in the colony throughout the period were engaged in "commerce," most were petty traders.[13] Only a few merchants had real wealth, and almost all of them who were not European were emigrants.[14] Despite incidences of debt and even bankruptcy among them [15] some of their names recur over as long a period as thirty years. There were at least three such men: James P. L. Davies, I. H. Willoughby, and J. W. Cole.[16]

Several other emigrants survived in commerce from the 1860's to at least the 1880's. One of these was Shitta Bey, a prominent Sierra Leonian and leader of the Saro Muslim community whose origin is often overlooked.[17] Born in Sierra Leone in 1824, he went to Badagry with his parents in 1844 and moved with his family from there to Lagos in 1852. He began trading in the colony in 1861 but concentrated his activities for some years in the Niger

Delta, working with the agent of the Glasgow firm of Miller Brothers. Once successful there, he left his brother as agent for the firm and himself traded in Lagos, though he did not center his operations there until 1885, being by then "a very wealthy merchant." [18]

Two others who sustained their importance were J. S. Leigh and Thomas G. Hoare, both of whom were established by 1864 [19] and were still influential in Lagos in 1888. [20] So was Henry Robbin, whose name, as Governor Moloney pointed out, did not appear in lists of importers because his "transactions" were local, but who, in the Governor's view, ranked as a respected "native merchant" in the 1880's. [21] There is no way of knowing how many others, prominent in trade three decades earlier, were still important but similarly did not have their signatures on petitions to the British government, or their names on lists of those dealing directly with European firms.

Some leading Sierra Leonians abandoned trade in Lagos altogether and moved to the Niger, although their interests there suffered a setback with the start of the Royal Niger Company in 1879. [22] Among these men were two of Bishop Crowther's sons, Samuel Junior, and Josiah, who had been agents for the West African Company until its amalgamation with the other British companies to form the Royal Niger Company. [23] Herbert Macaulay describes some of their activities:

my Mother's two brothers, Dr. Samuel Crowther, Junior, and Mr. Josiah Crowther arrived in their own paddle steamer ... which had come all the way from England under her own steam. ... They were trading as the firm of Crowther Brothers, flying a navy blue flag. Leaving Brass in that vessel, in June, 1881, we steamed up the River Niger, calling at Aboh, Obutshi, Onitsha, Asaba, Idah, Gbebe, Lokoja, and Eggan, 417 miles up the River where we made the longest stay and did the largest trade with the Nupe people. [24]

A few Sierra Leonians had factories in Porto Novo as well as Lagos: Thomas Welsh, John Holt's Lagos agent in 1888, wrote that, "One of J. A. Williams' people came other day and said Mr. Williams had heard I wanted to establish in Porto Novo and that he had a factory there to dispose of. ... Williams has a launch and two iron barges which carry 30 tons each, he is not using them now so it is possible one of barges might be got cheap. They were sent out 15 or 16 months ago." [25]

Although there is the occasional Gomez whose name appears in the government papers concerned with trade, no firm of emigrant Brazilians is on record as having achieved notable success. The nationality of the firm Sant Anna is unclear. Although J. A. O. Payne classified it, giving the full name as "Mansel [Manuel?] J. St. Anna," as a "Brazilian Commercial House" along with that of P. J. Gomez, and not including it in the "Portuguese" category,[26] Moloney wrote of it as a "European House" in 1888.[27] The most reasonable conjecture seems that it was a firm controlled by Brazilians from Brazil, using emigrants in Lagos and in Porto Novo as agents.[28] For the Brazilians in Lagos had one commercial outlet which was theirs alone — Brazil itself. As a scholar from Brazil wrote in the 1890's,

Our direct relations with the coast of Africa are maintained through the Nago [Brazilian name for the Yoruba]. Until not too long ago, sailing ships made the voyage to Lagos three or four times a year. In these always came Nago merchants, speaking Yoruba and English, bringing kola nuts, cowries, cult objects for gêge-yoruba [that is, Dahomean-Yoruba] worship, soap, cloths, and so on. Today communication is by English steamship, and one takes at Dakar steamers direct to Lagos.[29]

There were, certainly, occasional indications of scattered emigrant prosperity. In 1888 Welsh wrote to Holt, "Blaize seems to do a big cash trade. His house is next door. He has a landau and a pair of greys with which he drives out occasionally — footman and coachman on the box." [30] In the same year the firm of G. W. Christie and Company (J. P. L. Davies) could afford a wholesale "spirit license," as could N. T. B. Shepherd, and also B. C. Dawadu, although the other thirteen such licenses were issued to Europeans.[31]

DECLINE OF THE EMIGRANTS' COMMERCIAL POSITION

But generally the position of the emigrant merchants and traders deteriorated after the consular period. They had made few inroads as direct exporters to commission houses in England, and even those were of brief duration in the 1870's and early

1880's. In 1886 Moloney, listing the "native" importers "according to the extent of their business," stated that only Williams Brothers dealt "mostly with Liverpool," that is, directly with a commission house, "for spirits and dry goods; the others deal almost entirely with dry goods and purchase largely from wholesale houses (Lagos Warehouse Co., etc.). They import little or no liquors." Nonetheless, all those others—"R. D. Blaize, J. J. Thomas, Christie & Co., J. S. Leigh, N. T. Shepherd, J. S. Bucknor, George & Son, J. B. Williams, J. W. Cole, T. G. Hoare," in addition to Williams Brothers—wrote Moloney, "may be considered independent merchants and conduct business under their own names—same Mr. J. P. L. Davies, who travels under Messrs. Christie & Co., Davies Bros. and J. P. L. Davies." [32] Of these firms Payne listed as "Principal Commercial Houses" in Lagos in 1894, G. W. Christie & Co., James George & Son, Jacob Leigh, James W. Cole, Richard B. Blaize, James J. Thomas, and N. T. B. Shepherd; the only additional Saro name was J. A. Savage. [33]

In 1888, however, Thomas Welsh wrote to John Holt that, strangely, "all the natives have gone out of the produce trade." [34] One of the few non-emigrant African merchants, Dawadu, testified in 1898 that he had "shipped produce to England but . . . gave it up in 1887. The [produce] trade," he found in the early 1890's, did "not pay. I used to ship about 100 tons a time chiefly palm oil and kernels. I lost a little so I gave up shipping and dealt here and I gave up dealing in produce altogether in 1894." [35] The number of prominent non-European traders had increased but slightly, as we have seen, and in no way in proportion to the growth of the commercial community.

Some of the reasons for this decline in the relative importance of the emigrant traders are not difficult to discern. One was the number of European merchants, which had increased greatly since the 1860's. Another was the effect of a growing local population, augmented by newcomers from the hinterland, many of whom entered trade and thus came into active competition with the emigrants for the retail role and the position of middleman in direct contact with the merchants. Census figures, even with allowances for inaccuracy, indicate the extent to which this factor entered. The emigrant population had remained fairly stable since the consular period: according to figures collected in 1872 and transmitted to the Colonial Office in 1879, there were in the colony 1,533 "immigrants from Sierra Leone" and 1,237 from Brazil and Cuba, while the estimated total population for "Lagos and vicinity" had grown from approximately 25,000 in 1866 to 60,000 in 1872.[36] In the 1880's Brazilian immigration increased more than did that from Sierra Leone. Between Freetown and Lagos there was continued fluidity of movement, though no marked influx, while the Brazilian population had risen by 1881 to "about 2,723" and between 1882 and 1886 "there arrived by sailing vessel 412 — of these about 50 were women and 17 Children."[37]

The events to the north of Lagos also adversely affected the position of the Saro traders. Abeokuta in the mid-1860's had its own commercial struggle. Not only was there "tribal partizanship, [between] Yorubas and Egbas, [but] there . . . [had] been the White merchants against the Sierra Leone merchants, and . . . the White Chief [Glover] wishing and hoping to obtain paramount influence and command in the country."[38] A change had also come about in the policy of the European merchants, who now stressed direct contact with producers in the hinterland: "There is . . . the old African Merchant against the new . . . ; the old one says make the natives come to you the new one says let us go to the natives. The new will prevail, and every mercantile house at Lagos must have an establishment here or else become gleaner of what others have passed over only."[39]

The exclusion of Europeans from Abeokuta after 1868 ended that threat to the Sierra Leonians, who had, in any case, largely controlled the cotton production there[40] but had felt the competition over palm oil. Although non-European traders were affected by the periodic closing of the trade routes, they did manage, as we have seen, to get some produce through. Even during the unsettled days in 1870, when the authorities at Abeokuta were divided on the issue of customs collection, canoe loads of cotton were still being sent down the Ogun River.[41]

But the commercial situation in Abeokuta continued to deteriorate, as did the political. By 1885 a CMS agent there reported that,

Abeokuta is going down every year. Its trade is growing less and less; complaints are heard on every side of the general depression. Traders are leaving the town in the hope of being able to do better elsewhere. Mr. Robbin is removing to Lagos. Mr. C. B. Moore, [another Sierra Leonian] one of our most valued laymen and one of the largest traders in the town, told me ... that he is thinking of going to Lagos too, since he cannot do a profitable trade here.[42]

Contrary to McCoskry's view of emigrant complicity in the unrest of the hinterland, the Saro merchants and traders had every reason to want peace and stability in the interior on whatever terms, for neither they nor their European counterparts could foresee the results that "pacification" would bring. They did not know that, with the extension of the protectorate and the consequent liberation of domestic slaves, the shortage of labor would bring serious consequences.[43] The European merchants, with their activities concentrated at points along the lagoons, were in fact less affected by these events in the hinterland, although they had to deal with the French threat as well as disturbances at their own points of contact.

But the early years of the colony were difficult for the Europeans, as for the emigrant and other African traders. First had come the conflicts in the interior, and the Europeans continued to suspect the Egba of exacerbating them.[44] Secondly, the force of the new French competition for trade in Lagos was starting to undermine the dominant position of the Hamburg firm of O'Swald and Company, and to affect the other European concerns as well.

Even before the beginning of the decisive French action which was to come in 1865, the Hamburg firm had been dealt a blow by the return of Kosoko and Tapa to Lagos. The Germans had been concentrating on Epe and Palma and had spent considerable effort maintaining co-operation with Tapa there.[45] O'Swald's agents were convinced that the agreement about his return to Lagos had been calculated to destroy the Hamburg trade.[46] To the extent that Freeman wished at the least to make sure that customs duties did not escape through the ports at the end of the lagoon, they were undoubtedly correct.

About 1865 the French firms of Régis Aîné and Cyprien Fabre

began the struggle to capture the palm oil trade in Palma and Lagos in competition with the O'Swald agents and with each other. Their tactics, which the dismayed Germans felt would destroy the whole trade, consisted mainly in cutting the price of cowries and raising the price of palm oil by reducing the volume of the standard measure.[47] Wrote the O'Swald agent, "'One [an African] does not ask any more what price we are asking, one says instead: Do you wish to sell me the goods at this price, then I'll take it; otherwise I'll go to the next house to get it.'"[48]

Hamburg refused to enter into competition on the French terms, and as William O'Swald and Company fell into third place in oil exports, behind the two newer concerns, it decided to withdraw and concentrate on its east-coast cowrie trade. On the west coast, O'Swald's representatives sought only transactions in which credit was still unknown and cowries were accepted.[49] The firm in Lagos was taken over, as from January, 1870, by G. L. Gaiser, who had begun the first palm-kernel processing plant in Germany, and John Witt, who had been an O'Swald agent in Zanzibar.[50] German trade was to revive under these men and once again to dominate European trade in Lagos through the period under consideration here. In 1877 Witt went into partnership with another German named Büsch and their firm, with that of G. L. Gaiser, prospered.[51] They handled the largest portion of exports from Lagos Colony and its districts, to the detriment of emigrant as well as other European merchants.

Resentment of the virtual eclipse of the African — principally emigrant — merchants by the Europeans was clear in an 1881 editorial in the Lagos Times, owned and edited by Sierra Leonians. While acknowledging the benefits to the colony from the introduction of successful legitimate trade, the writer protested that, "any foreign Merchant hopes eventually to retire with all that he may have amassed to his own country . . .; his wealth remains not here, he has not adopted this as his home; his interest in the soil is simply temporary, and is measured by his success in money-making."[52] A Sierra Leonian himself, he continued to describe the effects of the European domination of the trade. The large emigrant and other African traders, with only very small capitals created by their own independent industry and thrift, and without any education other than that which the discipline of a very hard life had given them, held their way with English trading houses, and succeeded to secure for themselves decent and respectable homes, and some very appreciable measure of comfort; some of them gave their children respectable education on the Coast and in England, and visited Europe themselves. . . . It is reasonable to expect that the younger generation with opportunities and advantages greater . . . in every way, would as a rule excel their fathers; but neither here, nor at Sierra Leone do we see large native capitalists or real native wealth. Not one native here has retired from business, and not one is likely to do so in the next twenty years. Here, at present, native ownership of properties is merely nominal; for we have been credibly informed that almost all the respectable looking houses of natives, and others of an inferior style, are heavily mortgaged to a few European trading houses here and in England, and it cannot be said that this place has been famous for the redemption of its mortgages.[53]

It was not until the 1890's that the commercial balance was temporarily redressed in favor of non-European merchants. In 1898 the Commission on Trade, with two of the five commissioners — J. J. Thomas and R. B. Blaize — Sierra Leonians, reported that

some twenty years ago the trade of this Colony was practically in the hands of a few large firms, and the carrying was done entirely by sailing ships; but the spread of education, the establishment of Telegraphic and regular steamship communication with Europe and the introduction of a gold and silver currency in place of the old and cumbersome barter system have enabled many native traders of small means, who formerly dealt with the large firms, to become importers themselves and inasmuch as they are able to work on much smaller expenses than the European firms they have become formidable competitors of the latter.[54]

In the period being considered here, however, the Sierra Leonian merchants continually exerted what pressure they could in the interest of the African trading community — themselves and the non-emigrant Africans. In the colony they tried to influence structural changes in the government to improve commercial conditions. The separation of Lagos from the Gold Coast and representation on the Legislative Council of the colony were their major concerns in this respect prior to 1886.[55] But in the hinterland trade pure and simple was not their sole concern. "Interior questions," though always related to commercial conditions, were, for their own sake as well, of profound importance. From a look at emigrant involvements in these questions will emerge a more realistic picture of the different emigrant roles, and it is this problem that we will now consider.

EMIGRANTS IN THE LAGOS HINTERLAND: THE DILEMMA OF INVOLVEMENT

T HE role of the emigrants in traditional African affairs emerges from looking at its three aspects — local politics, mediation, and pressure in Lagos — in the context of each of the major trouble spots of the day: the colony itself, Abeokuta, Ijebu country, and the Ijesha-Ekiti conflict. With this examination it should be possible to assess the extent of economic as against regional loyalties, and the way the Sierra Leonians and Brazilians themselves, as well as the Africans and Europeans, viewed the emigrant position in these matters.

In Lagos itself, the play of African politics was severely limited after the cession of 1861. There could be no question of mediation between the British authorities and the powerless *Oba*: any pressure to resuscitate his position was doomed in the new political context. Opposition to the cession had been strong, both from the Lagosians and, apart from men working for the missions, from the emigrant communities. According to Henry Venn, Dosunmu had even "employed" J. P. L. Davies to intercede on his behalf with Captain Bedingfield and McCoskry,[1] but such protests were to no avail.

McCoskry, acting consul at the time of the cession, analyzed the Sierra Leonian commercial opposition purely in terms of economic self-interest: "they were indebted largely to European merchants here, and there was no means of collecting debts, and they knew that in our rule of the settlement there would be laws and a regular government."[2] The acting Consul was, of course, a "European merchant"; he made no allowances for the fact that large emigrant traders had similar troubles collecting debts owed them, and that, moreover, no machinery existed for their bringing complaints against Europeans.[3]

Protest did not end with the arrival of the first governor but persisted for several years, as we have seen, with petitions to the Colonial Office and to Queen Victoria from Dosunmu, his chiefs, and less prominent Lagosians.[4] Then came the *Oba*'s attempted revolt in October, 1863, in which, Glover was convinced, the emigrants had a hand. He wrote of "the Policy which the Ex-King had been . . . instigated to adopt by certain evil disposed persons,"[5] and his innuendo was clarified by Freeman:

[Dosunmu's] advisers are that class of Sierra Leone people whose motto is, 'Africa for the Africans,' who would rejoice to see their benefactors and supporters, the English, either swept from the Coast or subjected to the domination of the blacks, and who are instrumental in . . . opposing the views of this Government on every occasion.[6]

But the failure of the uprising and the suspension, although temporary, of the *Oba*'s pension, put an end to similar efforts until the brief promise to revive autonomy held out by Hennessy after the departure of Glover.

It is not clear what specific powers Hennessy extended to the *Oba* in his effort to regain the confidence of local rulers.[7] There was both misunderstanding and confusion surrounding the newly delegated authority. Dosunmu believed that he could now help in returning domestic slaves to the Ijebu, and dangling this bait, he sent one of his chiefs, the *Apena* of Lagos, with John A. Otonba Payne to Ijebu Ode to secure the opening of the roads.[8] But an incident, in which the return of Ijebu domestic slaves from Palma and Leckie was refused, hardened the intransigence of the *Awujale*, and the mission failed,[9] as had others from the Lagos government. Dosunmu maintained that in believing that he could guarantee rendition, he had been misled by the acting administrator, as well as by Payne, J. P. L. Davies, and an English trader named Mills.[10] The accusation was denied, the confusion clarified, and the *Oba*'s hopes were destroyed: "The Government . . . adopted at the 11th hour Captn. Glover's policy, and the king is put into his old position."[11] Not until 1919 and the "Eleko Case," which was handled by Herbert Macaulay, a grandson of Bishop Crowther, were the powers and privileges of the ruling house of Lagos again to become an issue.[12]

EMIGRANTS IN EGBA POLITICS:
G. W. JOHNSON AND THE EUBM

In Abeokuta all three aspects of the emigrant role converged. The most striking illustration was the attempt to reconstitute the local political structure through the foundation of the Egba United Board of Management (EUBM) in 1865. Where missionary persuasion had failed to centralize the government of Abeokuta within its purely traditional framework, Egba Sierra Leonians tried to reach the same end by adapting the political institutions to the model of British colonial government. The result was the organization of the EUBM primarily to deal with the British administration in Lagos in its own terms. The *Bashorun*, Shomoye, was called the "President-General"; another important traditional officer was Akodu, the *Seriki*, who became "High Sheriff"; Asalu, leader of the *Ogboni*, was also included.

The real force behind the Board, however, was its secretary — termed the *Amono Oba* — George W. Johnson. Johnson was born in Sierra Leone of Egba parents, had been to England working aboard a trading ship, and had given up his later occupation as a tailor, coming to Lagos in 1863. Shortly thereafter he decided to settle permanently in Abeokuta.[13] The EUBM was his idea, and although he was assisted by Thomas A. William as president, and J. M. Turner as treasurer, as well as by other prominent Saro, he seems to have controlled policy throughout the life of the Board. It was Johnson with whom the Lagos government was asked to deal on Egba affairs from 1865 until the early 1880's.

The EUBM had both missionary precedents and the earlier activities of the emigrants as guides in seeking to advise and control the Egba political authorities. Townsend had held the confidence of the *Alake* and the chiefs throughout the consular period and managed to ride out the threat of displacement by the younger Crowthers.[14] He had further eliminated his competition by bringing about the expulsion from Abeokuta of Samuel Crowther, Junior, over the issue of interpreting the treaty signed by the *Alake* with Martin Delaney and Robert Campbell, two Negroes who arrived in 1859 and tried to gain permission to settle American and Canadian Negroes in Abeokuta.[15]

Confidence in Townsend waned as general distrust of Europeans grew following the conversion of Lagos into a colony; moreover, suspicion of his involvement in the affair of Consul Taylor strengthened the Egba doubts.[16] Their association of the British missionaries with the unpopular policies of Glover and with Townsend's actions at Ikorodu prompted the leaders in Abeokuta to choose new advisers. Shortly after the formation of the EUBM in October, 1865, a meeting was called to which "all the Europeans, and Emigrants were specially invited."[17] There the wrath of the Egba descended upon Townsend, culminating in the advice that he return to England to "represent ... [his] case"; they then "shall hear in Africa, how far you and Governor Glover get on."[18]

Of interest for this study are other portions of the speeches made at the meeting. Addressing Townsend, John Craig, a Sierra Leonian, spoke of the responsibility the emigrant community felt for having introduced the Europeans into Egba country. He described their particular disillusionment with the policies of the British authorities. And he went on to tell how the Egba Saro saw their own role, and of the new way the missionaries were treating them:

We have always considered ourselves as Middle-Men between you and the Egbas. . . . We were thinking that our friendship together, would have remained . . . as in Shodeke's time, when the White, the Emigrants, and Native Egbas always be friends and [had] firm Unity . . . for the good of this Country. . . . We never complain until of late when to our great astonishment, as soon as Lagos was forfeited to the British Crown, then the confidence of White People, entirely removed from the Emigrants, and fixed upon all natives, so long as they are not enlightened. For we come to find, that the more a Black man is enlightened in Africa, the better his opposition, and hatred by a White man.[19]

Townsend's changing attitude toward the Sierra Leonians had thus not gone undetected for long. It helped set some leading emigrants on a course of Egba rather than European allegiance, even if some Saro — most notably Henry Robbin — from Ake, Townsend's headquarters, did not support the EUBM.[20] And although the Egba chiefs partly blame their "betrayed" trust in Europeans on the Sierra Leonians who had vouched for the British, they said they regretted having, in years past, heeded missionary advice without consulting the emigrants.[21] The EUBM came at a time when its leaders could be welcomed as new, trustworthy advisers, able to defend Egba interests against encroachments from the coast.

Townsend's opinion of the EUBM reflected his general view of unsupervised African leadership and the precariousness of his own position. As he interpreted the motives of the organizers, "some of the Sierra Leone people are jealous and ambitious of becoming chief advisers and writers of letters from the Chiefs here to Lagos. . . . The Governor has deprived these men of occupations, and they must be busy about something." [22] The missionary was, as a matter of fact, in an ambiguous position: "The Lagos Governor [and] the Home Government are representing me as a partizan of the Egbas and the people here [are] representing me as a partizan of Govr. Glover." [23]

The Lagos government was suspicious of the EUBM from the start. Glover had always had reservations about the Egba Saro, and his discovery that J. M. Turner, with whom he and Freeman had clashed in Lagos,[24] was treasurer of the Board, added to his mistrust of its leaders. Relations were strained between the two governments, particularly over Glover's prohibition of travel between Lagos and Abeokuta, the 2½ per cent duty on exports to the Egba which was intended to compensate for the robberies of the preceding years, and the arms embargo.[25]

The mediation of Blackall, the governor-in-chief from Sierra Leone, brought about in 1866 the removal of the Lagos export duty and the opening of the roads by the Egba.[26] The EUBM, unopposed by Lagos, began levying its own export duties from Abeokuta. For this method of raising revenue, Johnson had the precedent of the Abeokuta Commercial Association,[27] and he, too, was later to face obstacles raised by the *Parakoyi*.[28]

The major clash with the Lagos government came over Johnson's decision to place customs posts between Abeokuta and the colony in order to thwart customs evasion along the Ogun River. In response, Glover proposed a discussion of boundaries, which in turn led to Egba fear and hostility, the stationing of Lagos constables on the mainland, and in October, 1867, the expulsion of the Europeans from Abeokuta.[29]

The concrete actions in internal affairs taken by the EUBM after that date are difficult to ascertain; before it, though, Maser at the CMS station at Ikija wrote that, despite his sensing in the Board's actions "an antagonism against Europeans and Missionaries, . . . [he] must not be silent while they are doing good." [30] He had noted several innovations: most striking were the postal service between Abeokuta and Lagos, and the effort to improve hygienic conditions in the town.[31] He also reported the opening of a "Government School," with a teacher trained by the Wesleyan missionaries, though he was shocked that the EUBM should appear to consider, as it pointedly did, "civilisation . . . a thing by itself and able to stand without Christ." [32]

The Board even tried unsuccessfully in July, 1867, to set up a court to deal with trade disputes, possibly on the model of the emigrant court at Lagos in the consular period.[33] But the opposition of the *Parakoyi* brought the explicit declaration that "the Board neither had any nor must seek to form any court for the administration of justice." [34] Townsend, commenting on the use the EUBM made of British models for their innovations, wrote,

These Sierra Leone men are . . . forcing on civilization and English custom, teaching the people the use of writing and printing and bringing about the adoption of written laws. They are doing what we cannot for we cannot use the means they do to accomplish their purposes. I am trying to influence them; I cannot command them.[35]

G. W. Johnson and the principles of the EUBM were strongly opposed by Bishop Crowther, the most prominent of the Sierra Leonians dominated by the missions. He could not be accused, as were many of his compatriots, of ingratitude to his liberators. While he expressed a belief in the abilities of the Africans, he made it clear that in his view these capacities could be developed only under western guidance. This tenet ran directly counter to the convictions and objectives of the EUBM, as Crowther himself explained when he refused invitations in 1870 to visit Abeokuta:

There are some half-educated, unprincipled young men about the country who would have taken advantage of any seeming countenance from me or other natives of position, as if we were backing them in their short-sighted presumption when they said they were able of themselves to civilize and evangelize their own countrymen without European aid.[36]

But the EUBM, though opposed to European tutelage, never doubted the need to command European techniques in dealing with Lagos. They tried in 1868 to revise missionary education in Abeokuta so that all teaching would be done in English, foreshadowing a debate that would be taken up almost a century later. The Egba leaders, however, were suspicious of totally abandoning their own language and were persuaded to overrule Johnson; they further insisted that in the texts being used the term "Yoruba translation," be changed to "Egba translation," for "Yoruba" at that time referred to the Oyo tribal group.[37] The Board was thus not allowed to implement all the radical changes it had planned. To give another example, when denied permission to interfere in judicial procedure, they were forced to bring before an *Ogboni* court a case in which a Christian convert was charged with having assaulted G. W. Johnson.[38]

Johnson's vision that the EUBM would unite Abeokuta politically did not, however, materialize. His plan failed because of the segmentation in the traditional political system. With the death of Shomoye, the *Bashorun* and Regent, on 24 August 1868, there were two major contenders for the title of *Alake*: one, Oyekan, had the support of the EUBM and the *Seriki*; the other, Ademola, could rely on the traditional leaders of the *Ogboni* and *Parakoyi*, as well as on the conservative Christian elements of the population. There were, consequently, Sierra Leonian supporters for both candidates: "The emigrants . . . divide into two parties the Ake party and the Ogbe party. The former does not approve of what is called the Egba United Board of Management — but members of it consisted of persons of the latter party." [39]

The emigrant community in the Egba capital was, as is evident, no more unified than was its counterpart in Lagos. At least four groups can be distinguished among the Sierra Leonians of Abeokuta, though in some cases they could well have overlapped. First were the supporters of G. W. Johnson, a small number of influential men who sought to guide and control the government of the Egba. Then came two groups opposed to the EUBM: one was made up of the "pillars" of the CMS establishment and of those employed by the mission who disliked the resistance Johnson offered to Christianity in general and to European missionaries in particular; the other included some of the traders who, in not atypical fashion, opposed the imposition of export duties on their produce. A final category, with its opinion of the EUBM undefined, contained those emigrants who had been fully accepted into the Egba political structure. In 1866, for example, Townsend reported chieftaincies conferred on two Saro.[40] In 1877 a CMS agent wrote that a Sierra Leonian who had been a member of the Owu church, had "the title Oluwo . . . conferred on him being the first in the rank of the Ogboni elders of his township." [41]

The ramifications of the dispute over the succession to the *Alake*ship need not concern us here. Both sides, and an additional splinter faction as well, sought the support of the Lagos government. Finally, in 1869, Ademola, supported by the *Ogboni* chiefs and "native Christians," was recognized with the consent, however irrelevant, of Glover.[42] As an acknowledged ally of the loser, along with the *Balogun, Seriki*, and Madame Tinubu,[43] Johnson was inevitably regarded with something less than approval by the new *Alake*.

Although the *Ifole* (uprising against the Europeans) had taken place eleven months earlier, it was not until September, 1868, that the EUBM declared that, "from and after the 1st day of October, 1868 . . . no white person or persons will . . . be allowed to reside in Abbeokuta, or in any of the Territories thereof until such time, this Government [EUBM] be able to maintain due protection for all lives and properties." [44] Johnson may have delayed the ban on European residents in the hope of using the threat of it to bargain for improved relations with Lagos. But once issued the order stood, and although after 1873 European missionaries were permitted to visit their stations and agents,[45] they did not re-establish themselves there for a decade.

Yet Johnson's power was waning. This became apparent to Lagos officials through an incident in 1871. Glover, by persuading James George, who was probably trading in Abeokuta and must have belonged to an emigrant faction opposed to Johnson, to intercede with the *Seriki*, brought about the release of a Sierra Leonian — in this case referred to as a "British Subject" — who had been condemned to death.[46] The administrator used this case to open negotiations on trade questions with the Egba, and though no positive results emerged, it is to be noted that the discussions had been carried on without either approval or representation of the EUBM.[47] Nonetheless, in 1873 Johnson was still corresponding with the Lagos government over issues of roads and boundaries, and making fruitless demands for authority over Ebute Metta, just across the lagoon from Lagos.[48]

The colonial government did not need to be concerned with the EUBM for some time after May, 1874, when Johnson, having quarreled with the authorities in Abeokuta, came to Lagos.[49] The Lagos administration was, in fact, preoccupied with other parts of the hinterland, and the war which broke out in 1877, while involving the Egba, was fought to the northeast of them. The overture of friendly communication which came in August, 1880, from Ogundipe, one of the leading Egba chiefs, was a welcome surprise to the Lagos administrator, especially in view of the doubtful accomplishments of an exploratory mission the previous November.[50]

It is interesting to note that once again G. W. Johnson was in Abeokuta. Ademola, who had become *Alake* in 1869, died in 1877 and was succeeded in 1879 by Oyekan,[51] whom Johnson had supported in the earlier dispute and who, in July, 1880, recalled the EUBM secretary to resume the position of *Amono Oba*. Johnson announced that all in Lagos should "cease to look upon me as a British Subject so long as I continue in this office." [52]

No more popular with Lagos officials than he had been in the past, Johnson was again in the key advisory position, and Ogundipe insisted that any negotiations had to be carried on through him as representative of the Egba authorities. Griffith, the lieutenant governor, was determined to avoid Johnson who, in the view of the Lagos government and the Colonial Office, could not possibly be trying to improve relations.[53]

An incident in November, 1880, brought the virtual severing of communication between Lagos and Abeokuta.[54] From then on, the British officials refused to work through Johnson, and the Egba authorities refused to work without him. As a letter to the *Lagos Times* stated the Egba case,

when Mr. Hethersett [a Sierra Leonian] was . . . sent to Abeokuta [in March, 1881] for the ostensible purpose of demanding the dismissal of Mr. Johnson,

the King . . . told . . . [him] that if the Governor would request the Queen to dismiss her Secretary in obedience to (the King's) wishes and it was done, then he would remove Mr. Johnson from his post at the Governor's request.
. . .

There are German Councillors at Constantinople, French and English Commissioners in Egypt, and in nearly all of the semi-civilized countries are to be found men from the more enlightened states, who direct and control the affairs of those countries and conduct negotiations with their own and other states; yet an educated native African must not assist his less enlightened countrymen because he was personally obnoxious to a particular Governor.[55]

The arguments were, however, to no avail. The government in Lagos would not recognize Johnson, but they could not persuade the Egba authorities to reject him.

Since his return to Abeokuta in 1880, Johnson, assuming that he had new power because of his earlier support of the present *Alake*, was more determined than ever to reorganize the government there. He soon found himself in difficulties, however, over an attempt to secure the adoption of a "National Flag, for the Egba Nation — which he . . . had prepared and brought out from England." [56] His object, wrote Faulkner, the CMS missionary, "seems to be to force upon the other three Kings allegiance to the Alake. It is well there should be unity under a common head, but if the bond of unity is only from without, and not within themselves, the probability is, it cannot last long. I think the people have done right by refusing his flag and his proposals." [57]

Further controversy arose over the signing by the *Alake* of a "Memorandum," which entitled Johnson, for his services as *Amono Oba*, to receive 10 per cent of the export duties collected in Abeokuta, as well as a per diem for life of 2 heads of cowries for his "faithful services." [58] A further effort to increase the resources of the *Alake* angered "his [Johnson's] own townspeople" — the residents of the Owu quarter: in August, 1881, he "opened a new gate at which duty would be collected for the Alake, but which would be diverted from the Owu people." [59]

The details of Johnson's movements can only be pieced together, but it seems that under the pressure of the opposition aroused by these new measures and upon the death in September, 1881, of *Alake* Oyekan, he left Abeokuta for Lagos, although by 1884, with the selection of a new *Alake*, Oluwaji, he had returned once again as Egba adviser. Knapp Barrow, deputy governor in Lagos, wrote hopefully that "the power of G. W. Johnson is considerably diminished. I question very much if he is now listened to at all by the Government of Abeokuta." [60] However, a year later, in November, 1885, Johnson was still advising the new *Alake* and was working to centralize political power under him. [61] But Wood reported that both Johnson and the *Alake* were losing influence and noted that "the Ake Civil Chiefs are representatives of others, the Ogbonis, who are all over Abeokuta and are powerful: they may not consent to be placed on one side quietly. . . ." [62]

Once more Johnson moved to Lagos; though he still had the confidence of the *Alake*, he did not have the support of the Egba Saro in Lagos, on whom new demands to mediate were made by the Abeokuta leaders because of the actions of the colonial government. [63] Johnson returned briefly to Abeokuta in May, 1895, when he tried to dissuade the Egba from honoring the treaty and agreement they had signed with the Lagos government in 1893 and 1894, for he feared imminent British expansion. But his attempt was countered by a novel move from Lagos: Governor Denton went to Abeokuta himself in September, 1895, with his "principal object . . . to put a stop to the mischief [of] Mr. G. W. Johnson." He was, as he said, "entirely successful," for Johnson was expelled, and "his authority . . . broken," this time decisively. [64]

EGBA EMIGRANTS AS MEDIATORS

As mediators the Egba emigrants were in general less acceptable to the Lagos administration than were those with family ties to other groups. This was due partly to their activities in the colony itself, and even more to the interpretations the British officials made of their shifts of allegiance. In addition, after the episode with Consul Taylor in 1862, relations between the governments of Lagos and Abeokuta were so strained that friendly negotiation on any level was difficult. Later, during the 1870's when the roads were open, there were few points at issue to discuss. In 1880 when problems arose again, the Lagos authorities, as we have just seen, refused to deal with the one man the Egba chose to represent them.

There were, to be sure, occasional attempts at mediation

throughout the period. In 1862 J. P. L. Davies tried, with mission co-operation, to bring about conciliation in the Ijaye War.[65] He and the Revs. Bühler and Lamb were well received, both in Abeokuta and Ibadan, though he complained of being unable to follow up the progress made because of Glover's opposition from Lagos.[66] Freeman's and Glover's doubts about Saro impartiality precluded their using emigrants for their government missions, none of which, it may be noted, had any particular success.

In effect, it was not until 1879 that the Lagos authorities sent a Sierra Leonian emissary to Abeokuta. Before that, in February, 1872, a successful intercession was made by Bishop Crowther on his return from the Niger — his episcopal duties required a visit to the missions in Abeokuta, despite his disapproval of the EUBM. He managed then to secure a three-month "truce," whereby the Egba would do nothing to prevent the free passage of trade.[67] Crowther, in fact, was in this period the most influential Saro adviser to the administration; he was respected by the British officials and consulted by the Colonial Office.

Early in 1873 Crowther had an interview with Kimberley in London and advised him to try arranging a "general palaver" among the hinterland leaders; he said that although the most effective action against the Egba would be a blockade preventing their access to Lagos and Porto Novo, it would be preferable to try a negotiated solution.[68] But the reopening of trade removed the need for a blockade, and no general conference was held.

In November, 1879, Moloney, hoping to resume relations with Abeokuta, sent P. P. Martin, an Egba emigrant, on an exploratory mission.[69] His reception was friendly though noncommital. It is not certain whether this visit was the stimulus for the conciliatory letter from Ogundipe, which followed shortly thereafter. The government showed little understanding of the Egba frame of mind, however, by sending to Abeokuta in November, 1880, Thomas Tickel, "Government Political Agent," accompanied by Andrew Hethersett as interpreter. Whether or not lack of prior consultation led to the Egba refusal to admit them, contemporaneous Lagos opinion was correct that the choice of mediators showed that no "reference . . . [was] made to past relations with Abeokuta":[70] Tickel, who had served the government since the early

1860's, chiefly in the western districts of the colony,[71] had been influential in securing the early treaties in Badagry, Addo, and Okeodan; Hethersett, though an emigrant, was of Ibadan origin.[72]

An editorial in the *Lagos Times* commented,

we think the government would have done wisely had it taken into confidence some of the influential natives in the Settlement who, as it is natural to believe, have a more thorough knowledge of affairs in the Interior. [And] . . . a word of advice to those among the respectable natives who have the privilege of being in constant intercourse with the King and Chiefs of Abeokuta. We think it a solemn duty resting on them to use their good offices [to induce] them to bring their domestic and foreign policies into some sort of harmony with those of this government. In the event of an open conflict (which, however is improbable) between them and a civilized power like Lagos, there is not a shadow of a shade of doubt that they will come off the worst.[73]

But intercession would have had to come from a man considered "respectable" by the Egba authorities, and the pleas of Henry Robbin for Tickel's admission were to no avail.[74] Evidently Townsend's earlier view of the relative positions of Robbin and the EUBM leaders was no longer relevant, for in 1866 the missionary had written, "Robbin . . . alone has more influence here than any other Sierra Leone man he has large family connections and his general conduct wins the respect of the natives he absolutely refused to join [the EUBM]."[75] It is more than coincidence that the candidate whose succession Robbin had opposed in 1868 had just been made *Alake* and had recently recalled G. W. Johnson to Abeokuta.

In the early years of the colony the British officials had grounds to question their unity of purpose with the Egba emigrants, and each new administrator culled his first impressions of Lagos from the reports left him by his predecessor. We have seen that from the time of McCoskry, the view had gained popularity that the Sierra Leonians, and in particular those with both Egba and commercial interests, were hostile to the British government and were bent on thwarting its policies in an effort to evade paying their debts to European merchants.[76] This interpretation was applied to the Saro both in Lagos and in Abeokuta, and was the rationale used to explain not only their opposition to certain Lagos policies, but also their part in Egba pressures on the Lagos government.

Such an explanation may well have had an element of truth, though there is no conclusive evidence by which to isolate it as the determining factor; there is, in fact, no evidence apart from the statements of the administrators. No such analysis appears in missionary accounts of, for example, G. W. Johnson's actions. But if an administrator did not look for or try to understand other possible motivations, he could, given the attitudes passed on to him, find incidents to support his case. In November, 1865, for example, Glover received a memorial from five emigrant traders in Abeokuta who protested his policies, while denying participation in the dispute with Lagos.[77] The Lieutenant Governor wrote to the Colonial Office,

I have only to observe that Mr. Henry Robbin has aided, to the extent of his means, in providing supplies to the Egbas, in their prosecution of the War against Ibadan; and that not only Mr. Robbin, but the greater part of the Sierra Leone Emigrants in Lagos and Abeokuta aided the Egbas for the purpose of establishing at Ikorodu, a Sierra Leone Town, under the protection of the Egbas. ... [There] they had hoped to enjoy Independence of British law, and a full immunity of Native Customs ... and this will fully account for the Opposition which they have hitherto offered and are still offering to the Policy which this Government has, up to the present moment, successfully carried out.[78]

This statement of a projected Saro settlement at Ikorodu, apart from being unmentioned elsewhere, sounds unlikely in view of earlier emigrant reluctance to be segregated from the rest of the population.[79] It did, however, add weight to Glover's justification of his action against Ikorodu the preceding May.

In September, 1865, Glover took firm measures against the emigrants in Lagos. He tried to force "all persons, claiming to be British subjects" to take certain "oaths of allegiance" to the Lagos government; the refusal to acquiesce was punishable by imprisonment or fine.[80] As the Lieutenant Governor himself wrote in answer to the strictures of the Colonial Office, he thought his measure necessary to counteract "the usual violent opposition of the Sierra Leone Egbas" to his new compensatory duty on exports to Abeokuta.[81] Although the Colonial Office disallowed the ordinance which had given him this power, Glover attained his goal of stifling opposition by imprisoning emigrant leaders while the tax was being introduced. Glover specifically named J. P. L. Davies as one of the ringleaders who was, nevertheless, persuaded to sign the oath; another, whom Glover did not name, was actually convicted and imprisoned. The despatch reported, "The whole of the Sierra Leone Egbas, before the conviction, were fully prepared to be committed to prison in a body — but I had no intention of making martyrs." [82]

When friction developed between Glover and Pope-Hennessy, the Egba Saro supported the Governor-in-Chief. Hennessy consulted them on the measures he should take to counteract the earlier policies,[83] and it is scarcely surprising that, even after Glover's departure from Lagos, the death of Keate, who had replaced Hennessy as governor-in-chief, brought a petition from forty-five emigrants for Hennessy's return. The number of signers, all men prominent in Lagos, shows the strength of opposition to Glover, though the petition does not further illuminate the reasons for it. Some of the names, however, did belong to Egba Saro: the first signature is Davies' and is followed by such other familiar names as Thomas F. Cole, Thomas G. Hoare, J. S. Bucknor, J. S. Leigh, Charles J. George, and P. P. Martyns.[84]

One of Glover's friends in Lagos who shared the former Governor's interpretations maintained that a letter from Abeokuta in August, 1872, requesting that Glover not return to Lagos, had in fact been "concocted by the 'Egba daddies' in Lagos; and they have been very active going to Government House several times since the last mail." [85] Indeed, it is worth noting that Glover's major ally among the Sierra Leonians was I. H. Willoughby, of Ibadan origin.[86] It is possible to see the incidental nature of any Sierra Leonian cohesiveness in Willoughby's analysis of the Egba Saro in relation to Glover on the one hand and Abeokuta on the other:

Some of us, would-be-educated, would-be-finished and accomplished sons of liberated Africans, got the quiet native authorities of Abeokuta to drive away the White missionaries and merchants from that town so as to leave it in their hands; this was done: and the once pleasant, growing, rising Abeokuta, is becoming a den of all that is degrading to Xianity and civilization.[87]

The words, as will be seen later, are not from a man who so emulated Europeans that none but their ways and guidance would satisfy him.[88] But Glover's support of Ibadan had led Willoughby to oppose those who obstructed implementing the new hinterland policy, for his real fear was that the Egba would be successful in their attempt to dominate the Lagos scene.[89]

EMIGRANTS AND THE IJEBU: J. A. O. PAYNE

More of emigrant factionalism in Lagos will be seen in connection with the interior wars starting in 1877. It is necessary first, though, to consider the attempted mediation between Lagos and the Ijebu, perhaps the most openly hostile and suspicious group in the hinterland.

Almost the only link between Lagos and the Ijebu rulers was John Augustus Otonba Payne. The *Awujale*, until the mid-1880's, clung determinedly to his decision to refuse audience, let alone residence, to "foreigners."[90] Payne, however, was a son of the *Awujale*'s brother, who had been captured in war, sold as a slave, and liberated in Sierra Leone.[91] Payne reported that the sending of messages from Lagos through the Ijebu "children" had pleased the *Awujale* and other chiefs; in 1898 he told of the ties he had maintained with the Ijebu: "I am a Jebu man. I am a Prince of the country. Every week I have information concerning the country. There is no week that I have not communication with my people."[92] He was virtually the only representative of the Lagos government who could attempt negotiations with the King, despite Goldsworthy's view, expressed in 1872, that "in trying to please as he naturally would do, both the Acting Administrator and the King, he would fall between two stools."[93]

Payne's mediations began in 1871, when the closed Ijebu roads were seriously hurting the Lagos economy. His missions during the following year were frequent, but except for securing one rare and impermanent agreement, unsuccessful.[94] From the end of 1872, with the confusion and sudden temporary changes in policy that followed the departure of Glover, Payne's continued negotiations were suspected by some in Lagos on the grounds of his presumably divided loyalties. Turton, as a staunch Glover supporter, was outraged at the idea of Payne's consulting Dosunmu about his missions.[95] The *Awujale* had demanded the return of Palma and Leckie, and there were accusations that Payne had encouraged him to expect his demands to be met.[96] There were also charges that Payne had assisted in the rendition of escaping domestic slaves.[97] Payne was defended by Strahan, governor of the Gold Coast Colony, but told that in future he must take more care to avoid misunderstanding.[98] Whose interests Payne had actually considered dominant remains unclear.

In 1879, however, Moloney again sent him to the *Awujale* as part of the preliminary efforts to open good relations between Lagos and the Egba and Ijebu.[99] Discussions followed, though without particularly encouraging results. James Johnson described the Ijebu position, even toward men like Payne:

I had long heard of the stubborn dislike of my Countrymen the Jebus to the Gospel and to English customs, particularly to long trousers, shoes, and socks and to umbrellas which last I suppose only Royalty carries. . . . .Their dislike of European missionaries and suspicion of natives who had associated themselves with Europeans and who use their costumes and whom they like others are fond of designating 'White Men' are partly based upon the fears they entertain that Europeans would take away their country from them.[100]

The Lagos administration remained equally uncertain of Payne's allegiances, despite the earlier dismissal of charges against him. They were, for one thing, wary of having to deal with a potential counterpart of Abeokuta's G. W. Johnson.[101] When, in 1883, the Ijebu living in Lagos decided to send "a message of sympathy to their King" because of the *Awujale*'s departure from Ode,[102] Griffith approved sending James Johnson, but refused permission for Payne to accompany him.[103] Rowe, the governor of the Gold Coast, in approving this action wrote,

I have always understood that Mr. Payne is a British subject. He cannot, at the same time, be a subject of . . . the King of Jebu. I am of opinion if this gentleman is desirous of assuming any nationality he may imagine he may have as a subject of the King of Jebu, he is not a fitting person to hold the offices of trust which he does as a British subject in the community of Lagos. . . . so long as he holds the position which he does in Government employ . . . he should not visit Jebu on political missions except he be sent there as a messenger from the Government.[104]

It was not until Carter decided to settle Ijebu-Lagos relations in 1892 that such government missions took place. When they did, Payne was the interpreter, at the specific request of the Ijebu chiefs,[105] though we cannot know if this choice was based on trust or on caution, for a later deputation, protesting Carter's virtual conquest of Ijebu country, buttressed the arguments of its illegality by declaring that the chiefs "had never deputed Mr. Otonba Payne and Mr. Jacob Williams to act in their behalf in signing a Treaty or 'Splitting Kola Nuts.'"[106] It is worth noting, though, that whatever his diplomatic relations with the powers at Ijebu Ode, Payne's social contact with some of them continued. For in October, 1892, only months after the treaty was signed, "Prince Otonba Anobiekeh of Jebu Ode, Cousin of Mr. J. A. Otonba Payne, accompanied by Elders Kumabasi, Eki, Bajo, Debote, Odutayo, Odufala, Shibajo, Nuseive, and a retinue, in all of thirty persons, from Jebu, arrived in the Colony on a visit to Mr. Payne at Orange House, Tinubu Square." Nor was this a brief call, for entertainment continued for at least five days, including a "Musical Evening at Orange House, when the services of the Orphean Club Band were brought into requisition for the delectation of Mr. Payne's Jebu guests."[107]

EMIGRANTS AND THE WARS OF THE HINTERLAND

In the Ibadan-Ijesha-Ekiti wars, which at one time or another touched every segment of Yoruba country, the Sierra Leonians in Lagos and in the hinterland figured as advisers to the British and African governments, in exerting pressure in Lagos, and particularly as mediators. By 1882, when the British officials were seriously considering some form of peaceful intervention in the dispute, the Egba had withdrawn from the conflict in the northwest in order to concentrate on threats from Dahomey. The Ijebu, although still occupying a central position in the thinking of the colonial administration, were not direct participants either.

The emigrants in Lagos showed a greater concern in this struggle than in any of the earlier "interior questions," apart from the involvement of the Egba Saro in relations with Abeokuta. The war had been going on, punctuated periodically by major clashes, for five years; conditions in the participating towns were known to be distressing; and for the commercial interests in Lagos, the continuing conflict meant stagnation. Further, the combatants had reached a stalemate; neither victory nor withdrawal seemed likely on either side.

The Saro and Amaro were divided into factions, each supporting the Yoruba group in which its members had relatives, and
these splintered loyalties transcended all others at this stage.[108]
When the British government decided to intervene through negotiation, it was supported indirectly by those emigrants who were
concerned with trade, largely because they thought such measures
would be limited to mediation without implying expansion.

J. B. Wood, the CMS missionary, was among the first to see
the possible influence of the Lagos emigrants on the various hostile
groups in the interior:

In Lagos there are representatives of all the surrounding tribes. These men
consider themselves to be both educated and civilized. . . . They, laying claim
to the possession of greater knowledge and wider experience than their compatriots in the interior, undertake the office of counsellors of the chiefs of
their respective tribes.[109]

In 1882 David Hinderer wrote to the prominent Sierra Leonians
representing several of the major groups, urging them to use their
influence to end the war.[110] James Johnson, Henry Robbin, and
Isaac Willoughby called a meeting which decided that Dosunmu
should be sent to the *Awujale* of Ijebu Ode to ask his co-operation
in settling the conflict. Apart from the fact that the *Awujale* had
just been forced to leave his capital, there was little he could have
done, even had the mission been a success.[111] Rowe and the Colonial Office agreed that mediation by the *Oba* of Lagos, although
approved by Moloney, was likely to be neither effective nor desirable in the future.[112]

The factions in Lagos were unable to submerge regional interests and act in unity for a negotiated peace. Their preoccupations
were with their own groups. The formation in Lagos of emigrant
associations, having direct contact with the interior leaders, dated
from the consular period.[113] These organizations served the people
in the hinterland primarily as sources of military and other supplies from Lagos. Thus, in 1863, during the Ijaye War, the leaders
of the Sierra Leone Association — "which, [according to Glover] in
the days of Consul Campbell ruled both the King and Lagos" [114] —
and the African Commercial Association brought to Glover an
Egba chief who had come for help in obtaining gunpowder during

the blockade.[115] The African Commercial Association was founded

by all the different African tribes in this settlement, having for its object Peace, Unity, and Concord . . . ; to communicate to the different tribes in the interior who are their brethren, the necessity of Peace, Commerce, and Civilization, and to persuade them to give up the destructive war which is ruining the country.[116]

In October, 1865, the Yoruba National Association was formed, specifically to co-operate with the British officials in settling disputes in the hinterland, especially through offers of mediation.[117]

In the early 1880's the strongest of these associations was the "Lagos *Ekiti Parapo* Society." It was a branch of the "Ijesha Association," formed in Lagos in the 1850's by Sierra Leonian, Brazilian, and Cuban emigrants of Ijesha and Ekiti origin; they had kept in contact with their relatives by way of one or another of the roads to the interior.[118] In 1881, "with the sanction of the Elders," the second generation of these emigrants organized the *Ekiti Parapo* Society, "for doing all the needful in the interest of their Father-land"; in 1890 was to come the Atijere Utilization Company, "for developing the resources of Atijere, a place granted to the Ijeshas and Ekitis by the Kings and the Chiefs of the Mahins for carrying on Trade &c." [119]

In 1881 the Ibadan chiefs, discovering that the *Ekiti Parapo* was fighting with weapons more efficient and modern than Ibadan and her allies possessed, suspected the hand of the Lagos government, only to discover that, "the Ijeshas at Lagos formed a committee which purchases these weapons, and sent them up via Aiyesan, Itebu, to Ondo, and thence to Ilesha to assist their countrymen." [120] The Ibadan chiefs then sought redress through their own relatives in Lagos, and wrote to them accusing various Ijesha Saro of having left the colony to aid in the war. One of the accused brought libel action against I. H. Willoughby who had publicized the Ibadan letter; Willoughby was fined £50.[121] The Ijesha in Lagos continued to send supplies, while Ibadan chiefs, even after specific and urgent requests, received no concrete help from the Oyo Saro. The departure of the *Awujale* from Ijebu Ode, however, relaxed restrictions on passage through Ijebu country, and the Ibadan forces were finally able to get adequate supplies from private traders.[122]

The Ijesha emigrants continued to show their efficient organization. Maser wrote of receiving a deputation from them in Lagos — men "who were formerly in S. Leone and inhabitants of this place, but who lately left Lagos from patriotism and settled in Itebu, in order to have communication with their countrymen." [123] The Lagos *Ekiti Parapo* Society was not deterred even by the years of stalemate. When in 1886 Charles Phillips, the Saro CMS pastor from Ode Ondo, arrived at the Ekiti-Ijesha camp to negotiate a peace treaty, he found resistance there:

There is a section of . . . [Ijesha emigrants from Lagos and Abeokuta] in the camp under the leadership of one James Thompson Gureje . . . and I also found that a special messenger from the 'Lagos Ekitiparapo Society' had preceded me to the camp. He is a Brazilian Creole, a carpenter by trade; his name is Abeh. The opposition which I had from these emigrants is greater than that of the Seriki himself.[124]

Although the pressure of these men to preserve Ijesha autonomy was ultimately to no avail, they remained as advisers to the chiefs. Later envoys found them still present, with "an individual named Johnson, a bookbinder from Lagos but an Ijesha by birth, . . . [acting] as secretary to Ogedemgbe, being able to write letters for him." [125]

Having come to the view that the emigrants, acting independently and with their separate loyalties, could not or would not bring about an end to hostilities, the officials in Lagos began thinking seriously of peaceful government intervention. They had been brought a message by Samuel Johnson early in 1882 from the *Alafin* of Oyo, who asked for their mediation.[126] Griffith, not even sure of the authenticity of the request, sought the advice of several prominent emigrants; it is interesting to correlate their recommendations with the positions held by their kinsmen. For example, James Johnson, of Ijebu origin, doubted "very much . . . whether the Ijebus or the Egbas will even allow the ambassadors to go through their towns lest it be spoken of as inviting the interference of the whiteman when they are tired of war." [127] Isaac Willoughby, an "Ibadan man," stated that, "there is no great proof that the war chiefs agree with the King. . . . The right solution . . . is for the British Government to make a road to open communication between Lagos and Ibadan." [128] Although delegates were sent to begin negotiations — Simeon Kester and Oderinlo Wilson to Oyo, and Philip José Meffre and Joseph Haastrup to Ilesha — the missions were unsuccessful. [129]

When Rowe visited Lagos in May, 1883, he set out to organize systematically a properly informed mission. At the start he

consulted the three educated native gentlemen who are considered . . . best acquainted with the movements and wishes of the three most powerful factors in this feud, viz., Rev. Mr. [James] Johnson, Mr. J. H. Willoughby, and Mr. Robbin, representing respectively the Jebu, the Yoruba (or Ibadan), and the Egba . . . tribes.

These gentlemen concurred in the opinion that matters have become more complicated by the King of Jebu leaving his capital, and that any solid arrangement for peace should . . . begin by an arrangement between the Ijeshas and Ibadans, and spread from them to the other tribes who are allies and parties in the war. [130]

Within this framework, and after the Rev. J. B. Wood's failure to secure a truce in 1884 and 1885, [131] the Lagos government placed the negotiations in the hands of two Sierra Leonians in the service of the CMS: Samuel Johnson from Ibadan and Charles Phillips from Ode Ondo. [132] The intricacies of their negotiations need not detain us here. The important fact is that, by June, 1886, they had the "signatures" of all interested chiefs on a treaty of peace — the first in a succession of agreements, also obtained by these two mission agents, which linked Britain to the hinterland and were preliminary to the events of the 1890's, leading to the creation of the Lagos and subsequently the Southern Nigeria Protectorates. [133]

PERSPECTIVE ON THE EMIGRANTS:
TRADE AND AFRICAN POLITICS

That the instruments of this first conciliatory measure and of those that followed it, were Sierra Leone emigrants is important; that they were mission agents is telling as well. For as will shortly be seen, there was a split in attitude between what may be called the mission emigrants and those who were primarily in trade or connected with the diplomacy of the hinterland. We can now analyze the changing attitudes of and toward the second of these groups — the traders and those politically active in the hinterland.

The indigenous view of the emigrant communities is, as observed before, the most difficult to determine. With the establishment of the colony the hostility of the Lagosians toward the Sierra
Leonians seems to have abated, probably in part at least because
of the early warnings of the emigrant leaders against the cession
to the British. Later it was undoubtedly known that they joined
Dosunmu and the "native traders" in sending petitions to Colonel
Ord, and that they continued to show a certain respect for the
Oba by consulting him on actions they took in the interior, from
the time of the mediatory attempts of Payne to the emigrant efforts
in 1882 to work through Dosunmu in the negotiations for peace
in the hinterland.

In the interior, in contrast to Lagos, the picture is somewhat
easier to discern. The Egba were disillusioned with the Sierra
Leonians and with their arguments for the inherent value of
European ways in general, whether or not they supported specific
Lagos policies. But in the EUBM the Egba saw that a section of
the emigrant community was willing to dissociate itself from British interests. Whatever motives the Board might have had, its
members were, in the view of the chiefs, subordinating to the welfare of their countrymen what benefits they could personally derive from supporting colonial interests.

To be sure, some sections of the population in Abeokuta opposed the EUBM for economic reasons and took action against it
when Johnson and his colleagues overreached themselves in some
of their attempted innovations infringing on traditional preroga-
tives. But other parts of the segmented government retained Johnson and his associates as their spokesmen against severe external
pressure to remove them. Despite reiterated European predictions
that Johnson was becoming powerless, he was only finally expelled
from Abeokuta by means of "persuasion" from Governor Carter,
who could assert the will of the colonial government in the hinterland more firmly than his predecessors.

Egba confidence in the Saro in Abeokuta was increased through
the part others of them chose to play in such traditional institutions as the *Ogboni* Society. The fact that emigrants were seen as
eligible for such positions is also a measure of their acceptance
by the community.

In the case of the Ijebu, "distrust of all foreigners" led to a greater suspicion of anyone who might be promoting European interests than among other Yoruba sub-groups. Although restrictions were relaxed at least enough to permit discussion with such men as Payne, Blaize, and Haastrup, these men were never completely trusted, and their mediations brought permanent solutions to few problems. As an Ijebu chief who was a boy at the time of the mediations in 1892 has said, the difficulty with placing complete trust in any interpreter, even an Ijebu Saro, was that one knew what one had said to the interpreter, and could hear what the interpreter said the white man said, but one could never be sure what the white man was told or what he had in fact said.[134] There seems to be no evidence of a large settlement of returned Ijebu in their own country, partially, perhaps, because the requests for Ijebu emigrants made by the *Akarigbo* of Ijebu Remo and the *Awujale* of Ijebu Ode [135] could not be met without the guarantees which these rulers refused to give.

In fact, prominent communities of emigrants appeared only in Abeokuta, though this may be attributable to the fact that most of the "Aku" in Sierra Leone were Egba. The Saro and Amaro with whom the chiefs in Ibadan and Ilesha had contact were largely traders, or men sent from the related emigrant groups in Lagos. The Ibadan chiefs received surprisingly slight assistance from the Oyo Saro in 1883, in contrast to the aid given their enemies by relatives on the coast. The Ijesha forces were not only equipped but advised from Lagos, and they disregarded their advisers only when circumstances and external pressures became too severe to oppose British authority any further.

Thus, apart from the Ijebu, the major groups in Yoruba country during the period under consideration came to regard at least some of the emigrants as reliable spokesmen and advisers, whose primary identifications were with African interests. But it was not just a simple choice between African or European interests: the loyalty of any given emigrant was not general but particular. It was based on his "country" of origin, and if he were one whose European allegiance was secondary for him, he tended to support British policies if they coincided with the interests of his group in the interior and to oppose them when they did not. This was partially true of the Saro merchants and traders whose commercial success depended on their specific contacts in the hinterland. For in contrast to the Europeans, they did not consistently support those government measures which aimed at the opening of any access to the interior. If they had done so, there would have been no opposition in Lagos to Glover before 1872, nor would there have been the "particularism" shown over the issues of the early 1880's.

There were even exceptions to the general adherence to factional loyalties, however. Some of the emigrants favored British policies in the 1880's, though it is difficult to know if such support was in the wider cause of peace, if it coincided with trading interests, or if it had its roots in mission influence. In a letter in the *Lagos Times* in 1882, an emigrant correspondent wrote critically of the particularist attitude toward the problems of the interior:

What is the enlightened portion of our Native community doing? A word from them united I am sure would hush the tumult. . . . [But] they allow their businesses to go to wreck and themselves to perish with hunger which is now staring them daily in the face, whilst they indulge themselves in their unmeaning pride, selfish motives, and shameful and imprudent tribal jealousies, as if Yoruba, Egba, Ijebu, Ijesas &c. are not of the same immediate offspring and speaking the same Yoruba tongue at this moment.[136]

These feelings were echoed by J. A. Otonba Payne, though in a somewhat different context, upon the separation of Lagos Colony from the Gold Coast. Payne, for one, still envisaged a catalytic role for himself and his fellow emigrants:

May every true and loyal native, having the interest and progress of the country at heart, help . . . to aid the proper and responsible authorities to make Lagos the Liverpool of West Africa. All idea of self, tribal feelings, and petty jealousies must be laid aside, and being in harmony for the common good of our country, we may be able to show by the civilization and Christianity we enjoy, the blessings of peace and goodwill to our brethren in the interior, and they in turn will copy our good example.[137]

The view held by European elements in Lagos of the emigrants as intermediaries and of their position in trade had also changed over the years. The attitude of government officials after 1861 was largely conditioned by the emigrant opposition to entrenching British authority. Impatient with the undefined legal status of the Sierra Leonians who, it was claimed, came to interpret citizenship ambiguously and according to personal advantage, the administrators refused to make further allowances for emigrant interests. Not since the days of Foote in early 1861 had an official argued for action on the basis of the need to protect the liberated African community.[138]

With trade dominating the thinking of such men as Freeman and Glover, and the Sierra Leonians not only supporting factions in the interior that sought to obstruct it, but also themselves controlling a portion of this trade, policies were framed in part specifically to sidestep this emigrant influence. The Goldsworthy Mission in 1872 had been designed to place "the commercial intercourse between Lagos and the Interior on a secure and permanent basis, independent both of Egbas and Jebus and of the semi-educated Sierra Leone Egbas resident in Lagos, whose aim is to oust both the British Government and the Europeans from the Settlement; in order to obtain a monopoly of Trade and renew the traffic in Slaves." [139] Dealings with G. W. Johnson and the EUBM taxed official faith in the use of emigrants to ease conditions of trade or as political intermediaries.[140]

The European commercial community seems to have been least estranged from their emigrant associates. There was social fluidity and co-operation between the two groups when it was economically feasible, although traders' petitions did not always contain names from both. After the recreation of Lagos as a separate colony in 1886, the European merchants protested that Sierra Leonians on the Legislative Council did not represent their interests, but they were unable to change the government policy on the matter; nevertheless, no serious cleavage took place.[141] This tension, which had increased since the consular days, may have been promoted by the growth in the European merchant community and its distrust of the emigrants' increasingly apparent factional loyalties.

Finally, despite the changing views on the usefulness of the Saro for promoting British interests in Lagos and for mediating in the hinterland, not all administrators concurred in this negative evaluation. Though the judgment of Glover was accepted by those officials who, following him in rapid succession, had little time to form their own opinions, we find Moloney and Griffith in the 1880's talking of the emigrants in terms even more favorable than those expressed during the consular period. Moloney's views were shaped in part by the new role he saw for them — particularly the Brazilians — in his agricultural plans for the Colony.[142] Moreover, both officials had had more satisfactory relations with the Saro than did the earlier administrators, and they were willing to accept emigrant advice, even while recognizing its partisan framework, as useful in terms of acknowledged biases.[143] It had, in fact, become true that the context of the emigrant role had changed as the colony developed and official knowledge of the interior and its complexities increased. Administrators and traders who had the experience and insight to understand this changing role, and its effects on the leaders of the emigrant communities, were necessarily far less disappointed than those who had not.

THE EMIGRANTS UNDER
CHANGING ADMINISTRATIONS:
VOICES OF POLITICAL PROTEST

WHEN Lagos became a Crown colony in 1861, British attention turned to creating a new administration which would include a Legislative Council and a judiciary. The Sierra Leonian community watched the unfolding pattern of government with particular alertness and political awareness. The models for these institutions were British, and they logically led to ideas of representative government among the emigrants. In time, and especially after the founding of a local African press, these same models sanctioned the voicing of discontent and later the beginnings of agitation for an independent administration and preparation for eventual self-government.

Apart from mediation between Lagos and the African governments, the nature and extent of the future Sierra Leonian role in British administration had neither been explored nor delimited before the 1850's. As we have seen, recruiting emigrants during the consular period was a pragmatic solution to the immediate and ever multiplying needs of a functioning government. European mortality was still a key factor in the early 1860's, and it affected both the administrative and mission staffs.

In the case of the CMS, whose leaders had outlined much of the early emigrant role, its plans formulated in London for self-governing missions contrasted with Colonial Office policy toward African officers.[1] For, although some in England interpreted the 1865 Committee report as recommending a parallel training of Africans for government posts — and, understandably, the Sierra Leonians quickly espoused this view — Adderley himself made clear that his definition of withdrawal did not include training Africans to run a government on the British pattern.[2] Furthermore, because in England abandonment seemed less and less feasible, the Colonial Office saw no need to concern itself with such preparation during the nineteenth century.

Significantly, and ironically, these different policies produced converse attitudes toward Sierra Leonians in Lagos itself. Because it was unquestioned that the highest administrative positions would be filled by as many Europeans as the colony could finance and as could survive, the Saro were no competitive threat to government officers. Consequently, relations between the two levels of staff were more cordial, within the formal administrative framework, than they were in the missions.[3] Moreover, whereas the missionaries could work only with the consent of the local people, the government operated on a mandate of power. For this reason, the relation of the Saro to the indigenous Africans mattered more to the churches than to the administration.

However, the government had one problem the missions did not have, at least not to the same degree: that of political allegiance to British as opposed to African governments. This issue must be distinguished, on the one hand, from partisan feelings in local politics and, on the other, from defense of African cultural values. It was possible to promote the political interests of an indigenous group and at the same time to carry on Christian missionary activities. European as well as African missionaries demonstrated this fact. But it was not possible, the British officials asserted, for an African employed by the government to maintain a dual allegiance, especially when the interests were in direct opposition.

This posed a difficult problem for the administrators, partly because the legal status of the emigrants was not clearly defined. It was no longer to be an issue in the later years of the colony, since the second- or third-generation Saro and Amaro, born either in Sierra Leone or Lagos, were unquestionably British subjects. But with regard to liberated Africans who, born in the Lagos hinterland, had lived in Sierra Leone and then returned, the position was by no means effectively clarified. In a memorandum on domestic slavery, Sir George Barrow of the Colonial Office noted in 1862 that, although the Treaty of Cession in 1861 had made all inhabitants of Lagos "the Queen's *Subjects*," the declaration was "not sufficient to constitute them British Subjects." He explained further that only recently — in 1853 — had it been "discovered that the whole body of liberated Africans at Sierra Leone were not British Subjects, and an Imperial Act was required and passed to make them so, as well as all future liberated Africans to be located in the Colony." [4] But no act had specified the status of those Yoruba emigrants from Sierra Leone who had earlier returned to Lagos, nor was such an act to be passed.

By 1865 Glover had arrived at the following procedure which he considered to have been conceived during the consular period: that those Sierra Leone emigrants who were not "British born" should be considered British subjects "whilst residing within British Territory, and that on going beyond the limits of such territory, and whilst so residing, they should cease to have any claim to British protection." [5]

But more than "protection" was at stake. Though this view of legal status allowed the administrators to avoid some responsibilities and lessened their need to interfere with domestic slavery in the interior, it did diminish the assurance of emigrant loyalty when it was needed. Only the delay in communications with England had enabled Glover to enforce his "oath of allegiance" to suit his purposes in 1865.[6] The Lagos administration was never able to come to terms on this issue with George W. Johnson, or with J. M. Turner, both of whom disclaimed British jurisdiction over them once they were in Abeokuta.[7]

Within the administrative service itself, the problem arose most strikingly when mediation took place under government auspices, notably in the case of J. A. O. Payne.[8] Less directly, it called into question adherence to government policies by officials charged with executing them. In fact, however, this last question was seldom raised, and when it was, it was over support for the views or policies of a particular British administrator — such as Glover or Hennessy — rather than those of an African interest — such as Ibadan or Abeokuta; no one realized that for the emigrants there was a link between the two.

Thus, the conflict of allegiances became an issue when the actions of one administrator were reversed suddenly by another, as in the Glover-Hennessy controversy. Isaac H. Willoughby, who had been government interpreter and superintendent of police since 1862, resigned his posts after a disagreement with Hennessy

who, Willoughby maintained, refused to acknowledge his position.[9] Willoughby, an Ibadan Saro, was a strong supporter of
Glover and, understandably, of his policies to direct the commercial activity of Lagos through Ibadan.

In December, 1872, Glover wrote to the Colonial Office, protesting that the dismissal with Hennessy's approval of Emmanuel
Willoughby, an apprentice, and Thomas J. Cole, a clerk, sprang
from similar partisanship.[10] Charles B. Macaulay, who had been
Scala's agent in Abeokuta during the consular period [11] and had
been working since 1862 in the customs department in Lagos,
Palma, and Badagry, was, in August, 1872, similarly "recalled
from Badagry to Lagos and reduced both in position and salary,
with a view to ultimate disconnection with the Government," [12]
although he remained in the service until 1874. He also saw this
treatment as punishment for his association with Glover, who, he
reported, "as Special Commissioner of the Volta Expedition
against the Ashantee, hearing of the injustice with which I was
treated, sent for me." On his return to Lagos in April, 1874, Macaulay was formally notified that his services were no longer needed,
and he turned his attention to trade and to the activities of the
Wesleyan mission.[13]

The emigrants working for the Lagos government found that
their trading created another issue between them and their British
superiors. Since the establishment of the colony, the administrators had been disturbed because many of the junior officials were
engaged in trade, "directly or indirectly." [14] Unable to understand
and hence to make allowances for a traditional pattern in which
virtually everyone, and especially women, practiced one form of
commercial enterprise or another on however small a scale, the
British administrators tried to enforce rules that had been laid
down in Whitehall. Under Freeman it had been decided in 1864
that only "petty officials" would be permitted to trade,[15] but in
1870 Glover and the Colonial Office reconsidered the question.

The Governor first asked for reports from all civil servants on
their commercial activities.[16] The replies included some denials
and some disclosures of interest, though not direct participation,
in specific companies,[17] or of having a wife who traded.[18] Some men

had traded directly but agreed reluctantly to stop doing so despite the economic hardship,[19] and others wrote a straight-forward admission and firm refusal to change.[20]

Granville sent Kennedy, the governor-in-chief, instructions that clarified the earlier policy without changing it substantially:

> all Public Officers in all the West African Settlements shall be prohibited from trading, either directly, or indirectly through their wives and relatives, on pain of immediate dismissal.
>
> You will, however, except from the prohibition officials in humble position, who may still carry on petty trading on the terms sanctioned by the Duke of Newscastle in the year 1864 [that is, 'through the instrumentality of their wives and families'], but such persons should first obtain the sanction of the Administrator.[21]

These regulations, however, were often disregarded by the Lagos government because of the severe shortage of qualified staff. The need to overlook deviation from administrative dictates is seen not only with regard to the Saro, but also with a few European appointees—the case of Charles D. Turton, agent for Charles Leigh Clare, the Manchester merchant, as postmaster of Lagos in 1871 is a striking example.[22]

To enforce the regulation for the non-Europeans was, in any case, not easy, and it was in this connection that many difficulties of the Saro government servants arose. The term "indirect" was taken to mean that the families of government officials were not to trade; this ruling had serious social and economic implications, especially for the women, who by tradition had a right to their own earnings, and thus enjoyed a degree of economic independence that enhanced their own status, their children's, and their husbands' as well. More particularly, the Colonial Office did not differentiate between large-scale European trading and the way in which trade was often carried on in West African terms. For example, in 1873 the Sierra Leonian Charles Foresythe asked for a pension since, because of ill health, he was retiring as treasurer, Crown prosecutor, and clerk to the Legislative Council. He mentioned that in future he would trade instead, and the Colonial Office thereupon denied his request, despite the recommendation of the Governor, for they saw a "contradiction" in the reasons advanced for it.[23]

SIERRA LEONIANS IN A GROWING ADMINISTRATION

Both civil and judicial establishments in Lagos grew with the increasing problems and widened jurisdiction of the colony. As in the consular period, the men employed by the colonial government were primarily Sierra Leonians, as opposed to Brazilians or Lagosians, for, laborers excepted, some knowledge of English was a prerequisite for all appointments. No official interest was taken in the Brazilians until after 1887, when Governor Moloney dealt first with the question of steamboat communication between Bahia and Lagos, and then encouraged Brazilian immigration as a way of promoting agricultural development in the colony.[24]

In 1862 the governor had the assistance of a colonial secretary, a collector of customs, a colonial surveyor, a postmaster, and a harbor master.[25] There was a Liberated African Yard, designed — in contrast to the one in Freetown — to deal with former domestic slaves, although there was as yet no superintendent in charge of it. Only two of these senior officials were not Europeans and both of them were Sierra Leonians: Charles Foresythe, postmaster and clerk in the colonial secretary's office; and William James Maxwell, collector of customs, with five years' prior experience as clerk of customs in Freetown.[26] There were, however, 80 men working in the various departments; excluding the 56 laborers and the governor and 3 other Europeans, Saro held the remaining 20 posts.

The number of Europeans employed in all branches of government service, including those in Badagry, Palma, and Leckie, did not reach twenty until after the separation of the colony from the Gold Coast in 1886.[27] Before 1870 there were two or three English military officers stationed in Lagos; the number of men in the judiciary, superintending the prison, and in the medical services fluctuated between three and seven, increasing to eleven in 1886.

Posts from the clerical level to the top of the service rose from 35 in 1863 to 83 in 1882, before the Letters Patent of 1883 combined the services of Lagos and the Gold Coast. After separation this number rose again from the figure of 70 reached in 1886. The lower levels, carpenters, bricklayers, and assistant jailers, for example, were continuously enlarged and were always filled by Africans — Saro, Amaro, or Lagosian.

The rise in the percentage of Saro employed by the government was not the same at all levels. Only half a dozen emigrants held senior administrative posts. One was the above mentioned Isaac H. Willoughby, who became superintendent of police and held that post, as well as those of clerk and interpreter to the criminal court and interpreter for Glover, until his resignation in 1873. Another was Charles Foresythe, who moved from being postmaster at the beginning of the administration to become treasurer, Crown prosecutor, and clerk to the Legislative Council and to the administrator in 1871; he continued in these positions until his retirement in 1874.

Abraham C. Willoughby, a brother of Isaac H. Willoughby, moved from "subintendent" to superintendent of the Hausa Police and retained that office through the 1880's.[28] William James Maxwell continued as collector of customs from 1862 to 1868, when he was made deputy-collector under an officer of the Royal Navy, and remained in the service until 1874.[29] Charles Pike became acting treasurer and assistant collector of customs in 1876, after having been chief clerk and warehousekeeper in the customs department. He later moved into equally senior posts in the Gold Coast Colony before resuming his positions in 1885 in Lagos, where he even acted as deputy for the Governor for a short time, when Griffith was called to take charge of the Gold Coast government.[30] S. B. Williams, Consul Campbell's former interpreter, returned to the service briefly in 1864 as superintendent of works.

One distinction regarding Sierra Leonians in both the administrative and judicial services needs to be drawn. Some came for the first time to Lagos from earlier government experience in Freetown; not unlike British colonial servants, a number moved from colony to colony along the coast. Sometimes children of a recaptive and a European, rather than of liberated African parents, they considered Freetown more their home base than Lagos. Charles Foresythe, for example, returned to Sierra Leone after his retirement from Lagos service, and tried to develop Tasso Island, his birthplace near Freetown, by starting a brickworks and plantations.[31] Another, Charles Pike — son of Adolphus Pike, an English civil servant in Freetown, and a "Creole" mother — has already been mentioned as moving on from Lagos to senior posts in the

Gold Coast. Needless to say, such men had less trouble with conflicting loyalties because their ties in the Lagos hinterland were either non-existent or less central for them than for the other group in government service — the true Aku emigrants, such as J. A. Otonba Payne and I. H. Willoughby.

In the judiciary Sierra Leonians of both kinds held positions comparable to those in the civil administration. In 1862 Lagos had four courts — a police court, presided over by a stipendary magistrate; a criminal court, with "two honorary assessors . . . most respectable British merchants"; a slave court, to deal with "runaway slaves and apprentices," over which the same two assessors officiated; and a commercial tribunal, composed of three European merchants and two "Sierra Leone colored Gentlemen." [32] Shortly after the courts were constituted, each was assigned a clerk, and these clerks were all Saro. [33]

From 1862 until the unification of Lagos with the Gold Coast in 1874, there were at least eleven distinct courts which could handle cases in Lagos. [34] The four noted above, in addition to the Vice-Admiralty Court, the Court of Requests — which after 1870 superseded all earlier provision for the collection of "petty debts" — and the Divorce Court, begun in 1871, are of particular interest here because of their operation in the colony itself, and because of the men who served on them.

The Police Court was renamed the Supreme Court in February, 1864, with a chief justice substituted for a chief magistrate. But a more important change came five months later when, under the provisions for the same court, rechristened the Chief Magistrate Court, the jury system was introduced in Lagos, following the precedent in Sierra Leone. It was decided that a jury of seven men was to serve as judges of fact in criminal cases dealing with capital offenses, and that a majority of two-thirds, instead of unanimity, would determine the verdict.

This court underwent one more change before becoming finally the Supreme Court of Lagos in 1876. With the unification of the West African Settlements under Sierra Leone in 1866, it was called the Court of Civil and Criminal Justice. The jurisdiction of this court was not altered, although provision was made for a jury of up to twelve and not less than six men in all criminal, but not civil cases. The "Jury Ordinance 1870," which extended trial by jury to civil cases, set the qualifications of jurors as follows: "all resident British subjects between 21 and 60 years of age, who could speak and sufficiently understand the English language, could serve on the jury in a criminal trial. In capital cases, the verdict must be unanimous, but in all other cases, civil or criminal, majority verdict was sufficient." [35]

The problem of an unbiased jury arose continuously throughout the period dealt with in this study. Because it was difficult to secure an objective panel, the more important cases, both civil and criminal, involving prominent Lagos residents were tried either in the Gold Coast or in Sierra Leone. One notable example was the trial in 1880 at Accra of J. P. L. Davies for receiving money from his debtors after having been declared bankrupt. According to J. B. Wood, "He is removed to Accra for trial because the judge is of opinion that no matter what the evidence against him might be no jury here would venture to bring a verdict of guilty against him." [36]

All Lagos courts during this period were presided over by European officials — chief magistrates, chief justices, slave commissioners. The structure of the judicial establishment paralleled its administrative counterpart, but its subordinate positions offered greater opportunities for Saro officials. For example, in the Vice-Admiralty Court, presided over by the chief magistrate, the registrar was Walter Lewis — another with prior experience in the Freetown government [37] — from 1863 to 1872, when his position was taken over by John A. Otonba Payne. The other offices of marshal and proctor, when first filled in 1871, were held by W. J. Maxwell and Charles Foresythe, both from Sierra Leone. [38]

The Court of Requests, begun in 1870, required one "Commissioner" to sit with the police magistrate on any given case, and the original list from which such commissioners were to be drawn contained the names of Sierra Leonians Henry Robbin, J. P. L. Davies, C. J. George, T. F. Cole, and Samuel Crowther. Simpson, the acting administrator, intended "to restrict the appointment of Commissioners to Gentlemen of African birth," and though the names of all but Crowther were confirmed, [39] Glover subsequently deleted the requirement of African origin. [40]

The indispensable member of the Lagos judiciary, however, was John A. Otonba Payne. Entering government service in 1863, he became clerk and sheriff of the Court of Civil and Criminal Justice upon its establishment in 1866. Continuing in that position, he was appointed clerk to the chief magistrate as well, and was called "Clerk of Courts," in 1872, when he also became registrar of births, deaths, and marriages.[41] When the Lagos Supreme Court was recreated in 1876, he became its registrar, a post which he held for the rest of his life. He served, in fact, in positions connected with nine different courts in all,[42] and, in addition, mediated for the government and performed such services as naming the streets of Lagos in 1868.[43]

The first barrister to return to Lagos from training in England was Christopher Alexander Sapara-Williams, who qualified at the Middle Temple in 1879. He came back to Lagos only briefly in 1880, however. Setting up practice in Accra, he remained there until 1886 before again returning to Lagos.[44] The second was Nash Williams, whose arrival in Lagos was, with that of Sapara-Williams, "hail[ed] with pleasure." [45] He remained in Lagos, and while carrying on his private practice, acted at intervals as Crown prosecutor and district commissioner.[46]

When these men were absent from the colony, Payne was called upon to assume the duties they would otherwise have performed for the government. In 1881 he acted for Nash Williams as district commissioner of Lagos, an appointment that entailed being both police magistrate of the Supreme Court and coroner. Most remarkable, in view of the fact that Payne had no formal legal training, was his performance as Queen's Advocate in 1884, again in the absence of Nash Williams; Payne prosecuted for the Crown and secured a conviction in the murder case of *Regina v. Adeoshun*.[47]

The services of educated emigrants and their descendants were used by the English officials not only in administrative and judicial capacities. By the early 1880's Lagos had a small pioneer group of professionally trained Sierra Leonians. In addition to the barristers were the medical men. The first of the prominent doctors was Nathaniel Thomas King, who was "medical adviser" to the CMS and general practitioner in Lagos from the late 1870's until his death in 1884.[48] Writing of King's death, C. H. V. Gollmer, son of the early CMS missionary in Lagos, said, "he was the son of one of the Society's *excellent* native ministers (I mean — he was really a man of worth). . . . [King] was just the man suited for a Doctor, so kind and genial and delicate in his attention; the loss to Lagos cannot be estimated." [49]

Another Saro doctor was C. Jenkins Lumpkin, who was called in to certify the cause of the death of Dosunmu in 1885. [50] Because of the quality of the services of such men, it was suggested in 1885 that one of them fill the post of colonial surgeon in Lagos, but the governor of the Gold Coast opposed such a measure, [51] and an Englishman was ultimately appointed. [52] However, with the expatriate doctor's mishandling of a case in Lagos in 1888, resulting in the death of the patient, the Governor recommended giving in to popular demand and appointing at the first opportunity Dr. Obadiah Johnson, a brother of the Rev. Samuel Johnson, as assistant colonial surgeon, and this was subsequently done. [53]

All other technically skilled Saro who could be recruited were pressed into service by the administrators. In 1879 W. T. G. Lawson, a product of the CMS Grammar School in Freetown where he was reputed to have been a "brilliant mathematician" as a boy, became assistant colonial surveyor in Lagos. [54] He had worked in a builder's yard in London before qualifying there as an engineer, and had also been employed by the administration in Sierra Leone. [55] Although he had only the title of "assistant," he was in sole charge of the department from the time of his appointment until he left the service in 1886, with the exception of a few months in 1880, when a British engineer filled the senior post. [56]

Griffith wanted more men with such professional and technical training for government service. Supporting popular pressure to employ Africans in the "more important offices," just at the time the decision against a Saro colonial surgeon was taken, he wrote a testimonial to these men, based on his own experience:

I refer to the circumstances that Dr. King, a native gentleman, was employed by the Government when deprived by illness or absence of its Medical Officers; and with respect to the legal employment of natives, I was fortunate in being able for some time to avail myself of the services of Mr. Nash Williams, a native of Sierra Leone and a Barrister of the Middle Temple; whilst many of the most respectable offices have been, or are being filled by other Sierra

Leone gentlemen, as in the instance of Mr. Lawson, the Colonial Assistant Surveyor, Mr. Pike and Dr. Easmon, Mr. Willoughby and Mr. Pratt of the Constabulary, whilst Mr. Payne, a Jebu, and a most indefatigable public officer, has been for many years Registrar of the Supreme Court.[57]

Even though the number of Europeans in the highest government posts increased from the time of the separation of Lagos from the Gold Coast, offers of some senior appointments were still held out to qualified Saro. Most prominent was Henry Carr, from a Sierra Leonian family in Lagos. Educated at Fourah Bay College in Freetown, he had won from there a scholarship which enabled him to go in 1880 for further training in England, where he took an honors B.A. in mathematics and physical science at Durham University. He returned from England to be head master of the Lagos Grammar School, entered government service in 1889 as chief clerk in the Secretariat and sub-inspector of schools, and moved progressively to more senior positions.[58]

This period of African participation in the more responsible duties of government was being cited thirty years later by West Africans as the supporting evidence for a policy which, they asserted, it had been unjust to reverse; they gave as an example the practice which "at one time at Lagos gave the very important and responsible post of Collector of Customs to a Sierra Leone native, and that of Colonial or Acting Colonial Treasurer to another . . . — positions that they filled with credit to themselves and their race." [59]

EMIGRANTS AND THE FIRST LEGISLATIVE COUNCIL

With the structure of the British government serving as a model, African aspirations went beyond bureaucratic posts. Traders in particular voiced the desire for representation in making the laws which governed the colony. Sierra Leonian interest in the proceedings of the Legislative Council first became evident in 1869 with a petition to Earl Granville from seventeen emigrant "Lagos Merchants," the most prominent of whom were J. W. Cole, Thomas F. Cole, T. G. Hoare, and J. S. Leigh. They "reminded" the Secretary of State that

the Revenue of the Colony has almost doubled . . . during the last six years, and is . . . derived solely from the people. That the annual Grant in aid has been withdrawn, leaving the Colony a Selfrelying and SelfSustaining Government. That your petitioners [therefore] . . . conceive that they are now entitled to a fuller and more efficient representation of their interests in the Legislative Council . . . and that its deliberations, as in Sierra Leone, should be public.

They suggested that

considering that taxation without representation is not only opposed to the well being of the people but contrary to the Spirit of the British Constitution . . . one Merchant a Government nominee sitting at the Council is inadequate: . . . [there should be added] as many members as Your Lordship may think fit, to be elected by the people themselves.[60]

Some of the requests made in this petition coincided with Glover's views. When a similar request came to him from the Commercial Association of Lagos several months later, he agreed to increase representation, "provided that the Commercial votes do not outnumber the official ones and that the Administrator be allowed a casting vote." He made the specific point that the new representative should not be a member of the European trading community.[61]

But the Saro merchants were not to have their representation until 1872, and then were to enjoy only two years of the experience. Through the influence of Pope-Hennessy and Fowler, in 1872 the Saro, J.P.L. Davies, and George Hutchinson, an Englishman and agent for the British firm of Dunkley, became unofficial appointed members of the Council, replacing Arthur H. Porter, like Hutchinson an Englishman and agent for the British firm of Banner Brothers.[62] Minutes of the meetings of the Council from 1872 to 1874 show that the commercial representatives followed the lead of the official members.[63] The decisions of the administrators prevailed, for although Davies and Hutchinson were both suspected of partisan feelings against Glover and his policies,[64] there is no evidence of their opposing the return to Glover's measures after his departure. The Council was, however, abolished with the unification of Lagos and the Gold Coast in 1874.

The Council could not be reconstituted until the two colonies were again separated in 1886. Pressure for it was, nonetheless, heavy during the early 1880's, particularly in the Lagos press, which pointed out that the Gold Coast Council contained no representatives from its "eastern districts," apart from the administrator of Lagos. The newspapers were filled with letters and editorials commenting on this issue. One of the most forceful stated that,

the present mode of governing is a libel on the native population, and perhaps on the foreigner among us also. It proclaims that we are not capable of participating in the deliberations of the Government and assisting it. But the Government had not to inaugurate a Government on this Island. There had been a native Government whose power and influence were considerable . . . [in addition to similar governments in the interior.] What there is that disqualifies and unfits intelligent and educated natives from sitting in Council with the Queen's representatives we are at a loss to conceive. They sit at Sierra Leone and elsewhere. Why not here? [65]

EMIGRANTS AND THE LAGOS PRESS

This agitation for reconstituting the Legislative Council is only one example — and one to which we shall return — of the entry onto the Lagos scene of the press. From the disappearance in 1865 of the American Robert Campbell's *Anglo-African* after three years of appearing weekly,[66] Lagos had no newspaper until 1880. Then came, in rapid succession, three such publications, two appearing fortnightly and one monthly. All were published and printed by Sierra Leonians; all contained editorials and articles commenting on local events and policies, letters to the editors, reports of social functions, obituary notices, and advertisements by European and emigrant firms.

The first of these, the *Lagos Times and Gold Coast Colony Advertiser*, started in July, 1880, was published by R. B. Blaize, the prominent Saro trader who had been head government printer from 1871 to 1874.[67] The "Prospectus" announced that "The Journal is intended to fill up a gap long left open . . .; we doubt not that it will be hailed with pleasure by the community. . . . [I]t will have for its object the discussion of commercial, educational, and religious questions, as well as the political administration of Lagos — not excluding other sections of the Gold Coast Colony." [68]

The *Lagos Times* was joined in February, 1882, by the *Lagos Observer*, under the proprietorship of another Sierra Leonian, J. B. Benjamin, who set forth in the "Prospectus" his particular "desire . . . to repudiate the intention of opposition to any existing publication." [69] And in March, 1883, came the first issue of the *Eagle and Lagos Critic*, published and edited first monthly and then also fortnightly by Owen Emerick Macaulay, a grandson of Bishop Crowther and son of the Rev. T. B. Macaulay.[70]

The *Lagos Times* stopped publication in November, 1883,[71] but until then it presented the most direct criticism of government policies heard in Lagos, and declared itself in favor of various kinds of reform. All the newspapers tended, in fact, to concentrate on suggestions for change in Lagos policies, and to give little emphasis to rivalries among themselves, although they held divergent views on what changes were desirable. Apart from representation on the Legislative Council, and the related problem of separating Lagos from the Gold Coast, the *Lagos Times* in particular, followed by the *Lagos Observer*, gave detailed and persistent accounts of the needs, felt to be inadequately met, not only of the emigrants but of the whole African population of Lagos.

One important issue was the demand for more schools to be subsidized by the government.[72] Others centered on the relation between the trade of the colony and "Interior Questions." One focus was the position of non-European merchants in the economic structure.[73] Another was the relations between the colonial government and the Egba.[74] A third was the role of the people of Lagos in the quarrels of the hinterland. While examining this last problem the *Eagle and Lagos Critic* expressed in an editorial some of the earliest arguments for African loyalties wider than those to the Egba, Ijebu, Ibadan, or Ekiti:

First . . . [were formed] tribal associations ostensibly for the purpose of mutual support; emulation arose, jealously entered, and from them have risen the illwill and rancour which now prevails between the different sections of the same nation and we need not say between men of the same race. . . . Is there no remedy for it. . . ? Education is the only means which will relieve us of the present calamity; and education broad and correct . . . , and education which teaches every man and woman to know himself and to know herself, to be part of the same whole, to be members of the grand universe, members of the same race, of the same country and particularly of the same town.[75]

But the *Eagle* was concerned primarily with the emigrant community. Its writers saw their goal as a broad loyalty within the British framework, for their concern in the views just quoted was with the "Society of Lagos," and what they considered its deterioration since the days when John Hawley Glover, "like a true Englishman who loved Lagos with the love of a native, being convinced that his protege need[ed] the necessary foundation to enable her to rise, which is no other than a proper society; at his own expense and time and at no small personal sacrifice collected the most prominent intelligent and promising of the inhabitants and created thereby a society." [76]

While all the papers criticized the African population when they were felt not to have taken advantage of the opportunities offered them, criticism was more often aimed, especially in the *Lagos Times*, at British officials and their policies for not having given Africans sufficient opportunities. A particular object of this attack was the government service. Differential treatment of English and African civil servants, particularly through salaries and allowances, gave rise to long correspondence. The writer of a letter to the *Lagos Times* in 1882 declared,

One can hardly understand the line of policy on which the Government move. It was rumoured that an ex-Native official [I. H. Willoughby] who virtually assisted in laying the foundation of most of our Governmental Departments here, and is now a pensioner, applied some time ago to be reinstated to service, but was refused on the ground of previous resignation. Subsequently a Government Gazette announced a European pensioner [Thomas Tickel] as being appointed Political Agent and Government Interpreter. I am not aware that he actually and actively serves the Government in any wise in that capacity other than in the last Abeokuta Mission which was a failure. By virtue of that office, I think that if he is a qualified man, he should have been sent up as often as possible to negotiate and effect peace in the interior. But no, he is now also the Commissioner of the Western District, a post he had once resigned as the Native official did his.[77]

Discontent grew with the appointment of H. M. B. Griffith, the son of the lieutenant governor of the colony, as chief clerk and warehouse keeper, and the ground was laid for one of the main arguments for separating Lagos from the Gold Coast: the desire for more appointments of qualified Africans to responsible positions.[78]

The Letters Patent of 22 January 1883 which provided for even greater administrative and financial integration of Lagos and the Gold Coast,[79] gave a new impetus to the discontent shown in the newspapers and among the commercial community since 1880. Pressure had first come for the transfer of the seat of government to Lagos, in order to have representation there. It was supported by the view of independence as an ultimate goal, set forth in terms foreshadowing arguments advanced in the twentieth century. As an editorial in the *Lagos Times* stated the issue in 1881,

It is gradually becoming an anxious question with many — how long shall we be tied to leading-strings? The recommendations of the Select Committee of 1865 . . . are still a dead letter. . . .

We do not desire to be misunderstood in the remarks which we feel ourselves compelled to make upon a calm review of the situation. . . . We are not clamouring for independence, for the sufficient reason that we are *not* prepared for it; but it should always be borne in mind that the present order of things *will not* last forever. A time will come when the British Colonies on the West Coast of Africa, Lagos included, will be left to regulate their own internal and external affairs. How far, or how near the time, it is impossible to say.

Although the writer made it clear that he did not agree with those who were then suggesting "a speedy severance of our young and struggling country," he insisted that

It is time for us boldly to ask England to associate us with themselves in the matter of regulating and superintending our own affairs. What . . . could hinder the Imperial Government from nominating two or three men of intelligence and probity among us to watch over our interests; — men in whom the people have confidence, chosen, if needs be, by universal suffrage; men who, in anticipation of the exigencies of a future that must come, might begin to learn the art of governing from such a beginning? . . . If as being subordinated to the Gold Coast, Lagos cannot have an independent Council of her own . . . then we would ask that the seat of Government be transferred to this place.[80]

In April, 1883, the demand changed to separation from the Gold Coast. It was reasoned that the one-third increase in Lagos revenue over the preceding seven years was relatively small in contrast to the four-fold rise in that of the Gold Coast, and was caused by the repercussions on the Lagos economy of the conflicts in the interior. The argument continued that if a governor had been unable to solve these problems earlier, how could his deputy do so, when the seat of government was in Accra, and the primary emphasis was on problems there: "It is for the people . . . to strongly and persistently urge for a separate Government for Lagos." [81]

The mercantile community carried the agitation in petitions to the Secretary of State for Colonies. Their first memorial, signed by "T. Harding and 190 others," was received in Accra in February, 1884. It deplored the neglect of public services and development projects on the island; it demanded the draining of swamps, a bridge to the mainland and more efficient handling of shipping, customs, and the post office; it complained of inadequate educational assistance; it charged neglect of the courts and unsatisfactory discipline in the prisons. All these difficulties the petitioners attributed to the lack of a separate government in Lagos. [82]

The Deputy Governor asked the heads of departments to investigate. From their reports he concluded that the accusations had been overstated, although he recommended that when funds became available, they should be put into development of the colony. [83] In the meantime, the "African Merchants" — that is, the British merchants with commercial interests in West Africa — also petitioned the Colonial Office. Men who had connections primarily with the Gold Coast — Banner Brothers of London was the only firm prominent in Lagos trade — they argued that amalgamation had been detrimental to the interests of both colonies. [84]

The Manchester Chamber of Commerce demanded that there be separate governments and Legislative Councils with unofficial representation; they objected to the disproportionate amounts of revenue spent on the administration as compared to that paid for "educational and sanitary services." They complained that despite the increased revenue, "very little is done for the material and permanent benefit of the Colony, or for the interests of trade which contributes the revenue." The same protests were raised by the London merchants, with an additional criticism of police discipline.

Lord Derby had written to Governor Rowe in Accra, even before the Lagos petition reached London, sanctioning the expenditure of the "£30,000–40,000," which had previously been kept in reserve for "unforeseen emergencies," on public works in Lagos and the Gold Coast.[85] As for separation, he declared that sufficient time had not elapsed since the amalgamation, sanctioned only the previous year "after full consideration," to justify its reversal, and that only when the new arrangement had had sufficient trial and was then found wanting, would the question of creating separate administrations be reconsidered.[86]

A year and a half later, in May, 1885, the residents of Lagos petitioned Derby again, showing the financial ability of Lagos to support its own government. It was then that they added to their earlier demands that "the services of natives should be utilized in some of the more important offices, especially in the Medical and Law Branches, which would cause a great saving in general expenses, natives not being under the necessity of desiring a frequent leave of absence."[87]

The separation came about in 1886, largely as a result of the new positions taken by France and Germany in West Africa. In 1883 Derby had justified continuing a single government for Lagos and the Gold Coast on the grounds that, although the British government was unwilling to extend its responsibilities "unnecessarily" in West Africa, it was "fully alive" to the advantages to be gained from maintaining both "the influence which naturally belongs to them by virtue of their paramount interest" in the Gold Coast and Lagos, and "the freedom of trade and commerce" along the coast separating the two.[88]

But the actions of the French in Porto Novo between 1883 and 1886 had made that consideration irrelevant. Furthermore, the Congress of Berlin in 1885, and the subsequent British protectorate over the Oil Rivers, made placing a government in Lagos, with a view to exercising control to the east, more feasible than having Accra the administrative center. Nonetheless, the memorials from the English merchants had exerted a certain additional if not determining pressure, as undoubtedly did the agitation from Lagos.[89]

Whatever weight they may have carried in England, these local petitions and other related expressions of opinion in Lagos had an immediate effect on the policies of the newly separated colony. They clearly influenced Moloney's decision to follow the precedent of 1872–74 and include non-European unofficial members in the new Legislative Council. This was an issue which concerned neither the Colonial Office nor the merchants in England, the latter being interested only in simple representation for the trading community. In considering this demand in 1883 Derby had not objected in principle to the idea as it was carried out in Sierra Leone and the Gambia, but it is clear that he thought in terms of European members on the Council, for he wrote that it had "always been understood that there was a difficulty in obtaining the services of gentlemen who reside for a sufficiently long period on the Coast, and who would be acceptable to the rest of the mercantile community." [90]

The rejoicing in Lagos at the separation,[91] which was proclaimed on 13 February 1886, was tempered by some disappointment, reported in the press, that the demand for commercial representation on the Council had not been immediately met. Plans were already under way for selecting appointees, but the issue was not allowed to lapse in the newspapers, especially in the *Lagos Observer*, throughout June and July:

It is generally believed that upon the separation of Lagos from the Gold Coast, and her being erected into an independent colony, the causes of those multi-form and hydra-headed evils resulting in the Memorials to Lord Derby, would have been removed. But so far this theory has proved utterly false. . . . Strangely finding themselves in the exact position they had occupied and the delusion of having a share in their own government having now been swept away by the lapse of many months after the separation, it was time that the whole community should rise again, *en masse*, and re-petition for that only one privilege which could be their true safeguard.

The *Observer* editorial elaborated on the representation demanded, implying a wish to go beyond the limits of Crown Colony government, with legislative decisions transferred to the unofficial spokesmen:

We want a Legislature composed of European and Native merchants, men whose interests are thoroughly identical with the country and people, men whose 'unofficialism' would permit them to denounce openly and fearlessly those acts of misrule, abuse of power, official terrorism and those nameless annoyances to which we, at present, submit.

In the name of the whole of the Lagos Community, we ask ... how long will we tamely submit to *taxation without representation?* ... [T]here should arise from Lagos one general cry for political freedom, loud enough to reach the ears of Downing Street, if not louder still, to penetrate the Houses of Parliament.[92]

Concurrently Moloney was thinking of possible appointees. Disqualifying J. P. L. Davies, regardless of his earlier experience as the only non-European unofficial member of the earlier Council, because of bankruptcy proceedings against him a few years before,[93] the Governor made several recommendations, apparently more on the basis of position in the community in general than of extent of commercial influence. His first choice was the Rev. James Johnson of the CMS, "in justice to his abilities and interest in his race"; the second was C. J. George, a trader and "a Wesleyan, ... a J. P., one of the visiting committee of the Lagos Prison, and one of the Commissioners of the local Committee for the Colonial and Indian Exhibition." [94]

Should Johnson's "position as a clergyman ... disqualify him," Moloney expressed a preference for either Henry Robbin or I. H. Willoughby: "they are both respected and are native merchants, but, as their transactions are local, their names do not swell the list of importers." Johnson and George, with William Hammond of the Lagos Warehouse Company, were confirmed, as was their three-year tenure of office. In August, when Fred Evans was sworn in as governor, all three assumed their positions.[95]

It may be significant that George and Johnson participated in the Legislative Council debates more outspokenly than had Davies in the 1870's. Both gave arguments supporting African interests in advising on action to be taken in the hinterland, and Hammond joined George in stressing the importance of commercial factors.[96] Johnson, increasingly aware of the problems of the colony, did not confine his efforts solely to work on the Council but petitioned the Colonial Office as well, telling of the success of the peace treaties in the hinterland and requesting that action be taken against Dahomey.[97] He also urged that the liquor traffic be suppressed; that the measures used in trade be standardized; that there be increased governmental aid to the missions and to education; and that there be greater employment of Africans in government service, particularly in the legal and medical branches.

In March, 1889, Moloney received a memorial from the newly formed Lagos Chamber of Commerce, whose officers were all Europeans, although the membership was one-third emigrant.[98] The petition objected to the retention of Johnson and George on the Council, but the Governor countered that,

> the fears of the chamber of 'contemplated increases in taxation' are as imaginary as are their reflections undesirable and unsupported. . . . I still entertain the high opinion I always had of the two other unofficial members: both are highly respected in the Community and may be viewed as representatives of the Jebu [Johnson] and Egba [George] interests, on which much indeed of the commercial progress of the Colony depends. . . .
>
> I entertain . . . a feeling of just indignation of the ignorance and audacity at the representation of a Body, the members of which erroneously view themselves, instead of the consumers, as the local taxpayers.[99]

Johnson remained on the Council until 1894, and George continued through the decade.[100]

THE EMIGRANTS IN PERSPECTIVE: POLITICAL ALLEGIANCE IN THE 1880'S

After the separation of Lagos from the Gold Coast in 1886, the attention of both the local and Colonial Office officials turned to other parts of what was to become Nigeria. The hinterland of the colony was no longer seen in the earlier narrow terms of its effect upon Lagos; problems in the new Oil Rivers Protectorate and beyond it, on the Niger, received a new prominence in the Lagosian view. Two of the principal measures considered shortly after separation and affecting the colony itself, however, set forth new provisions for education,[101] and a proposal to set up a municipal government, with elected councils, to handle such matters as roads and sanitation.

This second issue aroused great controversy, for desirable as this rudimentary beginning of self-government was considered, it was to be financed through the levy of a "house-tax." The European merchants joined the almost unanimous African opinion in opposing the measure. Governor Denton received deputations, the forerunners of later protest movements in Lagos,[102] from the White Cap Chiefs, the Muslim priests, and 850 Lagosians, followed by another of 740, for whom the spokesmen were I. H. Willoughby, J. W. Cole, J. J. Thomas, I. I. I. DaCosta, J. P. Haastrup — all emigrants — and, representing the Muslim Saro traders, a man named Taba.[103] They stressed the inability of the majority of the population to pay the required tax, and Willoughby expressed regret that "neither the Aborigenes proper, nor the Sierra Leonians or Brazilians, nor the other section of Natives who might be called the working class, has any representative in the Legislative Council." [104]

In this statement Willoughby pinpointed the problem, for in favor of the plan were only the Rev. James Johnson, J. S. Bucknor, J. S. Leigh, C. S. Williams, Z. A. Williams, and J. A. Savage, all men successful in trade and prominent in mission councils, men who could well afford the tax and felt it a small sacrifice for the training it would provide.[105] The Colonial Office acknowledged with regret that the bill could not then be put into effect in the face of such general opposition.[106]

In this division of emigrant opinion we can see the beginning of a differentiation, made by both the indigenous population and the British officials, between two groups of emigrants in relation to the workings of government. There were those men who were identified as having interests corresponding to those of the British, and others who were in the vanguard of what might be characterized as proto-nationalism.

Men employed by the administration, and those chosen to sit on the Legislative Council, tended to fall into the first category. They felt under pressure to accede to the government's legislative and administrative demands. Their record in the Legislative Council and in other administrative assignments did not go unscrutinized by the Africans. John A. Otonba Payne, as an example, lost the full confidence of the Ijebu rulers and, despite continued social contact, ultimately was denied the authority to speak and negotiate for them.[107] Civil servants were particularly vulnerable to accusations from their fellow Africans, since the necessary precondition of their employment was a willingness to carry out the

government's policies. Paradoxically, it may well be that the Sierra
Leonians in government who from the British point of view were
most loyal — the "professional civil servants" from Freetown with
minimal local ties — were least disloyal from the African point of
view, since they had no specific obligations in the interior and
were, in effect, strangers.

The division appears more clearly in the press. As Coleman has
pointed out, a clear distinction was to be made in 1914 between
the "conservative, pro-government" journalism of Sir Kitoye Ajasa
and the *Nigerian Pioneer*, and the view expressed in the *Lagos
Weekly Record* by John Payne Jackson, a "race-conscious and
uncompromising nationalist." [108] We see this division in its in-
fancy in the 1880's. During its short life, the *Lagos Times and
Gold Coast Colony Advertiser* took a consistently strong position
against the government. Blaize's newspaper supported not only
such generally applauded proposals as the separation of Lagos
from the Gold Coast and educational reform; it also voiced criticism of missions to Abeokuta, of hesitation to provide greater
opportunities for qualified Africans, and it went so far as to use
the term "independence" in viewing a future condition which it
held to be inevitable. The *Lagos Observer* supported on occasion
a similar position, though there it was presented more mildly. The
Eagle and Lagos Critic expressed still more favorable opinions of
government policies, and interested itself in the formation of an
African elite emulating English patterns. [109]

The views of the *Lagos Times* of 1881 to 1883 were not taken
up again until the appearance in 1890 of the *Lagos Weekly Times*,
which later became the controversial *Lagos Weekly Record*. [110]
John Payne Jackson, [111] the founder and editor, was in 1910 to
summarize his view of the "native" press as "a needed though
feeble instrument for voicing the Native side of matters under
the aegis of an absolute system of government which is altogether
a law unto itself, and the only appeal against which for the people
is the authorities in Downing Street, and who more often than
not, take their facts and findings from the absolute authority appealed against." [112]

This division, which can better be seen as a continuum between two polar extremes of attitude, became relevant to and was conditioned by all aspects of Lagos activity. A very important segment of this activity was the missionary effort and influence. It is, therefore, necessary to turn to Christianity and the missions after 1861 to complete the examination of the forces producing this gradation.

CHRISTIANITY AND THE CHALLENGE
OF ALLEGIANCES

THE activities of the missions after 1861 continued a factor in
the affairs of the colony, even though missionary initiative,
powerful and effective in earlier decades, began to recede in the
face of new problems and new perspectives. As early as 1863,
church agents were following the penetrations of European political authority rather than leading them.[1] Years of contact in West
Africa in general, and in Yoruba country in particular, had
changed the outlook of all participants in mission activity — of
European missionaries; of African leaders; and of emigrants, who
were the men in the middle in the strict sense, caught between
criticism from both sides. For the Europeans, a consistent policy
had as yet not evolved fully. And the Africans increasingly were
looking for political and economic guidance from different
quarters and, further, were coming more and more to make their
own decisions about policy.

Progress, in strictly religious terms, was less than spectacular.
The missionaries came to acknowledge that accomplishing their
task would take longer and be harder than they had thought. It
is significant that recognition of the need to work on and through
educated Africans grew simultaneously with a reluctance to give
up control. Factionalism over policy disrupted unity of purpose
within certain denominations and created an atmosphere which
did little to enhance the appeal of Christian arguments to the
Africans.

The work of the CMS dominated the mission field in the first
fifteen years of the period between 1860 and 1890, though in the
mid-1870's the Methodists renewed their activities and were followed by increased Catholic and American Baptist efforts. The
CMS, however, carried on the most extensive program and had
the most significant connections with the emigrant communities.

It is this body, therefore, to which we will give primary attention in looking at the missionary effort bearing on the emigrants and the growth of Lagos.

Any possible clash between Townsend's emphasis on Abeokuta and Hinderer's chain plan of mission stations was irrelevant by the early 1860's, for both programs had become unfeasible. As governmental sympathies shifted away from Abeokuta, mission pressures had less and less effect on the view taken in Lagos of interior problems.[2] Again, with the consequences for the missions of the Ijaye War — principally the forced departure of the CMS and Baptist agents after the destruction of Ijaye — the links toward the Niger became precarious. As a goal Hinderer's plan could be retained, but the prospects of its being put into effect decreased as time went on.

The events of the 1860's in Abeokuta, culminating in the up-rising of 1867, necessitated a reappraisal of the position of Euro-peans in the missions, however reluctantly it might otherwise have been undertaken. Despite Townsend's increasingly suspi-cious attitude toward his rising Saro subordinates — an attitude that grew more pronounced with the consecration of Samuel Crowther as bishop in 1864, and one which with time won more and more support from his European colleagues— no alternative to emigrant control in the hinterland was possible after the ex-pulsion of the Europeans.

The British government was not alone in facing a conflict be-tween official decisions in England and the reaction of the "man on the spot," who often did what he could to sidestep them. The formulation of a central CMS policy on running missions and congregations lay in the hands of Henry Venn, who held that there was a fundamental distinction between the roles of mis-sionary and pastor, and that it was important to stress "self-government, self-support, self-extension" in the "native church."[3] With the second of these goals in mind, Venn had, from the start of CMS activity in Yoruba country, sought to provide for training Africans — that is, largely Sierra Leonians — to fill the necessary positions. From it also sprang the training schemes in England, and educational institutions in Freetown, Abeokuta, and Lagos.

Even during the consular period such men as Townsend parried these central policies with random thrusts of opposition,[4] and as time went on their criticism became more frequent and more insistent. Arguments coming from these men were not to have their full effect, however, until the end of our period, when they were advanced in a new climate of opinion, that of growing European racism. The men who so firmly disagreed with Venn's reiterated goals in the early years of the colony were eventually to accept his ideas, for the events of the 1860's and 1870's offered no alternative. But a later generation of European missionaries adopted the early attitudes of Townsend and others, and, in new circumstances, were able to force acceptance of their racial ideas, translated in hierarchical terms, though not without damaging the structure they sought to build.[5]

The early European ambivalence, seen first in Townsend, had arisen over the role of Samuel Crowther, and it was in respect to his position in the Yoruba Mission that the anomalies of the situation first became apparent. Crowther was made bishop not over only the Niger territory but over all of West Africa, with the exception, in effect, of the stations controlled by European missionaries. These remained under the jurisdiction of the Bishop of Sierra Leone. The career of Samuel Crowther, fully discussed elsewhere,[6] does not concern us here, for contrary to Venn's intention it centered on the Niger. But it is relevant in two respects.

First, for ten years following the Abeokuta *Ifole* of 1867, Crowther's authority, delimited as it was, meant that the control of the "interior" Yoruba missions was in the hands of Africans, with only nominal "supervision" from Europeans on the coast. Secondly, his high rank helped to unify the opposition of the European missionaries to the African assumption of power and to extend their arguments from Crowther to the men who followed in his path. The European reactions to the possibility of serving under Crowther were of two kinds. One, expressed by Townsend and Harrison, a medical missionary, was of extreme opposition, even to the Sierra Leonian's authority on the Niger: "This step would shut the Niger almost entirely against European Missionaries especially those raised from a humble position who feel perhaps even more acutely than the better educated the indignity of being placed in an inferior position to a black man," wrote

Harrison, exposing a familiar source of colonial conflict.[7] Townsend, referring to the Yoruba Mission, had a similar view: "I suppose you [Venn] would prefer here a mixed plan the Native Bishop and white Missionaries with him but the difficulty is to get white men to work under a native you may get some to say they will but in working they will rebel, it is too much against the grain."[8]

A second and more typical, though hardly more acquiescent, reaction was Hinderer's. He declared that pleased as he would be personally to serve under Crowther, "we are allowed to teach and preach the Gospel not because . . . [the Africans] are tired of heathenism, but because God gives us influence as Europeans among them . . .; if they hear that a black man is our master, they will question our respectability."[9]

In the years between 1861 and the crisis of 1867, the position of the missionaries in Abeokuta, their previous stronghold, had been changing. In the clashes of African diplomacy, the mission agents in the hinterland tended to espouse the political cause of the groups with whom they were working; indeed, Townsend and Hinderer came into frequent collision in their respective support of Abeokuta's and Ibadan's positions in Yoruba affairs.[10] This identification was shown most strongly by Townsend, who had sought to guide and mold the political activities of the Egba since his arrival.[11] When his advisory position was threatened by some of the leading emigrants, he had tried energetically to entrench himself more solidly.[12] But partly because he sought rapprochement between Abeokuta and Lagos, and thus appeared to the Egba to equivocate on such issues as the recognition of Consul Taylor, his attempts could not succeed. He was also handicapped by the growing strains in the relations between the colony and Abeokuta, strains which did not exist with such places farther inland as Ibadan, where Hinderer was able with less effort to retain greater confidence.

As we have seen, the *Ifole* of October, 1867, was not, as it seemed, directed expressly against the missionaries.[13] It erupted from the tensions between the Egba and the officials on the coast. Afraid and bent on self-preservation, the Egba struck out against all persons who could be identified with the new threat, against all Europeans. In one sense, however, the attack can be seen to have been aimed directly at the missionaries, both European and African. As was made clear in October, 1865, at the EUBM meeting to which Townsend and the emigrants were specifically summoned, they were to blame, however good their intentions, for the trust that had been placed in the British administrators, a trust which, in the view of Egba leaders, had been betrayed.[14]

The events of October, 1867, came as no particular surprise to the missionaries. They had observed as early as 1862 a growing resentment toward them because of their presumed support of Lagos policies.[15] In November, 1866, Maser reported,

Ogudipe, the Chief of Ikija, paid me a visit the other day. . . . Whilst he sat in the Iron Rocking-chair, I said he should send some of his children to School. He replied formerly the Egbas yielded themselves over to Whitemen, and he leaned in token of what he said comfortably back on the chair; but since the days of Ikorodu their minds as regards the Missionaries are unsettled as he was now in the chair rocking to and fro.[16]

The immediate stimulus that touched off the outbreak remains obscure. Destruction of European and mission property was indiscriminate. Only Ogundipe protected the mission premises in Ikija.[17]

The European missionaries, still reluctant to recognize that they were identified with Glover's policies, which they opposed, were forced to leave.[18] The Sierra Leonian pastors and agents remained; they and the community of Christian emigrant and non-emigrant Egba were unharmed, although further church services were forbidden. Numbers of converts did leave Abeokuta, however, fearing that general persecution would break out. Reporting on the Aroloya Church in Lagos in 1877, the Rev. Nathaniel Johnson wrote that the single benefit of the uprising had been the strengthening, by the influx of the "Christian refugees," of his congregation, which was then under the Rev. Valentine Faulkner.[19] Some of these Egba settled in Ebute Metta, some on farms in Yaba. In both places they were granted plots of land by Glover.[20]

In the confusion that followed, the three ordained Saro who had been serving in Abeokuta tried to hold their congregations together. In February, 1868, William Moore wrote,

I am (thank God) still at Oshielle and . . . not forbidden to carry on the mission work the chief and people are still very friendly to us. But we found very little satisfaction under the privilege; since the preaching of the everlasting gospel is forbidden in our capital. . . . [The] meeting which I have held with the christians of the different demoninations . . . continues to be regularly held and attended every fortnight.[21]

The European missionaries in Lagos recruited reinforcements for these men from their Saro subordinates. John F. King was one who went to Abeokuta in mid-June, 1868, and after his arrival an interview with the *Bashorun*, Ogundipe, and "Lady" Tinubu — the Madame Tinubu of consular Lagos, now prominent in trade in Abeokuta — ended with permission for him to resume services at Ake, Townsend's former station.[22] There was no further interference with mission activities in Abeokuta from then on, but Europeans were not readmitted, and complete responsibility devolved on the emigrant agents.

With Hinderer's departure from Ibadan, the concentration of all European missionaries on the coast was complete.[23] In fact, only Abeokuta and Ibadan had been affected, and Ibadan only because the Egba and Ijebu roads were closed to all Europeans, and Hinderer could not return after going on leave in 1869.[24] Ijaye had been out of the CMS picture since its destruction in 1862, and the other stations — Badagry, Otta, Igbessa — were already under African management.

Although nominal supervision over CMS work in the two inland cities was still with Townsend and Hinderer, the actual responsibility and "general superintendence" of the stations fell to William Moore in Abeokuta and Daniel Olubi in Ibadan.[25] Moore was a Sierra Leonian who had been in Abeokuta with the Yoruba Mission since 1861. Olubi was one of the two early African recruits who was not an emigrant. He was a "nephew" of the Egba chief, Ogunbonna, who had shown early kindness to the CMS agents. In 1848 Olubi was sent by his uncle as a servant to the Hinderers, then in charge of the station at Ake, and he had been especially trained by Hinderer since then.[26]

The African CMS agents continued quietly with their work. In Abeokuta Moore's fellow Sierra Leonians, William Allen, J. F.

King, and David Williams, helped him, with Samuel Cole and Samuel Doherty coming as additional catechists in the early 1870's. Olubi worked in Ibadan with Samuel Johnson, William Stephen Allen, and James Okuseinde. There was no pronounced increase or decrease in the total number of "Christians connected with the interior congregations"; nor was there any marked change when Townsend re-established himself in Abeokuta in 1875.[27]

But these facts were in themselves recommendations for the African agents. Crowther was satisfied when he stopped at the stations on his way back from the Niger in 1871.[28] Both Townsend and Hinderer praised the work done by the "native agents." By 1875, in fact, these two prominent Europeans, now convinced by the evidence that adequately trained Africans could carry on the work competently, veered to the support of increasing African responsibility within the mission. Hinderer wrote, "The past 7 years surely have sufficed to show that the native teachers of Christianity are as acceptable to people and Chiefs of this country (I speak here of heathen people, as to converts that is a matter of course) as [the] white man was some 20 years ago."[29]

Townsend had had glimpses of Saro effectiveness in Abeokuta in 1871 and 1873, before being stationed there again in 1875–76. Throughout 1870 and 1871 the emigrant agents worked for his readmission to the Egba capital. His file is filled with letters from King, Moore, Williams, and Cole to this effect. It was actually Henry Robbin, the Saro trader, who tried most vigorously to obtain the necessary permission.[30]

The Africans in charge in the interior not only met the responsibility placed on them, but showed initiative in expanding the work of the mission. For example, in 1873 Samuel Johnson went to Oyo "with a sum of money and cloth subscribed by the Ibadan Christians as a help towards the erection of a Chapel by the . . . converts" there. There he found the congregation held together by a man named John Thomas: "This man is another emigrant from Sierra Leone. He is of steady character and a leader of the small congregation there from the time of the departure of the European catechist . . . soon after the Ijaye war. . . . Thomas tried all his best to gather the Christians every Sunday at his own house to read and pray with them." It was, according to Olubi, a "great relief" to Thomas that a "native reader" was sent to take possession of the station.[31] By 1877 both Oyo and Ogbomosho had CMS stations, connected with Ibadan and supervised by Olubi.[32]

Bishop Crowther's visit early in 1871 to the inland mission stations had been arranged by the Parent Committee because of the needs of the church which could not be met by men lower in the hierarchy. The trip showed, as Ajayi points out, that Crowther's "episcopal authority was acceptable everywhere, that the Church in Yoruba which had been without episcopal visitation since 1859 needed a bishop, and that the Bishop of Sierra Leone could not conveniently fulfill the duties of the office so long as the Egba and Ijebu continued their refusal to open the roads to Europeans." [33] It was logical to extend Crowther's authority over the entire mission; indeed, such a proposal was being considered early in 1873.[34]

But policy decisions of the Parent Committee called for taking into account developments in other West-African missions, as well as those in the hinterland of Lagos.[35] The Bishop of Sierra Leone, for example, who did not support Venn's general policy of extending self-government, did not wish to remove his hand completely from the Yoruba Mission. Furthermore, his reduction of African control of the Sierra Leone missions had given rise to a movement there to found an African church, independent of European control and incorporating doctrinal and ritual variations which would make Christianity more acceptable to the local people.[36]

The Parent Committee feared a schism which would have repercussions in Lagos, for the transfer of ideas was unavoidable with continuous travel between the two colonies, mainly by Saro who had connections with one or another of the Christian churches.[37] Thus the decision was made in London to send Crowther on a visit to Sierra Leone to exert a unifying influence there. The situation in the Yoruba Mission remained unchanged until 1875. Hinderer then proposed extending Bishop Crowther's jurisdiction over the Yoruba Mission; but he excluded Egba territory, with only the explanation that it was "for reasons known to you as well as to me." [38] But Townsend pressed for vesting the authority in the Rev. James Johnson, the Ijebu Sierra Leonian who had been first a lecturer at Fourah Bay and had been in charge of St. Paul's Breadfruit Church in Lagos since 1874:

I have been considering of late the future prospects of our Mission more especially in connection with the fact that our connection with it in the ordinary course of nature cannot be long extended. . . . I feel the need of a successor in prospect. I have taken in review all of my white fellow labourers at home and here, but there is a want of tact and of practical wisdom in dealing with heathen chiefs, and also . . . with our native helpers, among them. . . . I have . . . another in view. . . . I mean the Rev. James Johnson. . . . Now to my mind it would be well to make this country, exclusive of Lagos, another Missionary Diocese and that the above named native Brother would be the best person to make its first Bishop.[39]

The Committee decided to follow Townsend's advice and planned for Johnson's consecration as Bishop of the Yoruba Mission, leaving Crowther to deal with the Niger area.[40]

GROWTH OF RIVALRY
BETWEEN EUROPEANS AND EMIGRANTS

It was inevitable, with the European missionaries still largely limited to the coast, that Lagos should be the focus of the controversy that was to follow. The Lagos congregations took a prominent part in trying to influence decisions affecting the position of Africans in the church hierarchy. In Lagos, also, the structure of a "Native Church" was being gradually built, according to directions from Salisbury Square, the London headquarters of the CMS.

In 1870 a Church Council of five laymen and five clergymen was created for this purpose. In the absence of the Bishop of Sierra Leone, Bishop Crowther was to act as chairman ex officio, and the members were to be Henry Townsend and Valentine Faulkner — the only Europeans — T. B. Macaulay, and William Morgan representing the clergy; and J. P. L. Davies, Henry Robbin, A. H. Porter, J. A. O. Payne, and J. T. N. Cole as the laymen.[41] The Council was to work with the missionaries in starting a "native pastorate," distinct from the body performing the missionary functions of the church, and to be supported by weekly class fees.[42]

The lay members of the church stressed the need to enlist the active support of the congregations in furthering this aim. Seeking to realize the proclaimed goal of self-support, several of the prominent Sierra Leonians wanted to organize a system whereby the appeal for funds for maintaining the Church schools, "as well as that for raising a Lagos Native Pastorate Fund, may be effectually and annually responded to, . . . thus [showing] . . . appreciation of the benefits of Christianity, education and civilization." But, they reported to the Parent Committee,

our movement has met with the strongest opposition on the part of your representatives in this Town: and such has been the strength of the opposition that though willing to assist in the carrying out of this scheme, the greatest number of the Church Members and Church going Community, . . . when they see that the [European] Clergy are opposed to the movement had hesitated and would not join in the movement until they are satisfied that your Committee approve and authorize the carrying out of the scheme.[43]

These men had, indeed, been amazed to find that their major opponents, Maser and Roper, had actually organized meetings of "Native School Teachers" and of their congregations at the Palm Church and Christ Church, in order to dissuade those attending from joining the movement for self-support. The European missionaries maintained that their protest was based, as had been their objections in 1859 to a fund in support of the grammar school,[44] upon their not having been consulted and notified before the organization was begun, though Maser had, in fact, been invited to the organizational meeting of the "Association to further the Interests of Christianity and Education in Lagos." [45]

The men in Salisbury Square were in a difficult position, being faced with a proposal which fitted into the theory of self-government and self-support, yet one vehemently rejected by their senior agents and countrymen. Faulkner gave them a more thoughtful view of the problem than did his other European colleagues:

The real question . . . is — Shall we take steps for breaking up such an association? — or [shall we] . . . make use of it, so long as we see no evil arising from it, as an Auxiliary of the C.M.S.?

. . . I am more in favour of using this newly formed Association. . . . The Natives are quite in favour with the Movement and could, at the Commencement, quite understand any proposed Modification on the part of the Society on behalf of whose interest they profess to be forming the Association, but they could not understand our, at once, putting a stop to it, without putting forth plain and satisfactory reasons for doing so.[46]

J. P. L. Davies, the prominent emigrant trader, wrote to the Parent Committee in October, 1873, to obtain authorization for the association, promising to dissolve it if the necessary permission were not granted.[47] He was told that the matter would receive consideration, but in August, 1874, he was still awaiting word. Despite the continued efforts of Charles Foresythe and Davies, the key men in the plan, the issue was held in abeyance until it could be revived on European initiative.

The supporters of the plan were, however, somewhat mollified by the fact that the Rev. James Johnson had been put in charge of the Breadfruit Church in Lagos, and Davies wrote that because of Johnson's appointment, "promoters of the Association" felt that no one was "more ready to recognize the worth of the African" than the Parent Committee.[48]

Johnson's appointment was made against the recommendations of the European missionaries in Lagos. Yielding to pressure from London, the local committee in Lagos had started organizing a "Native Church" and had reshuffled their resources accordingly. The "Mission Church" was to continue to be the one at Faji, with Maser as "Pastor" and T. B. Wright as "Native Pastor." At Ebute Ero, William Morgan was to remain in charge with his title changed from "Native Missionary" to "Native Pastor." At Aroloya, Nathaniel Johnson, a tutor at the Grammar School, was to be appointed catechist in charge of the station, and as a candidate for ordination would eventually become "Native Pastor" there. Similar consideration was given to the stations at Ebute Metta and Badagry.

But at the Breadfruit Church, the largest of the three Lagos churches in question, the conference of the CMS missionaries, meeting to make these changes,

thought it better to appoint the Society's Native Missionary the Rev. Saml. Pearse of Badagry who is a well known and well tried agent, intimately acquainted with the Yoruba language: rather than the Rev. J. Johnson a native Missionary of Sierra Leone, who would have to perfect himself in the native language which with the work of his Pastorate would be most difficult.[49]

The plan of the conference for the Breadfruit Church was not accepted in London, however, and Johnson took charge of the station in June, 1874. He was an Ijebu Saro and, therefore, was not unacquainted with the Yoruba language. Once appointed, he had no trouble holding services both in Yoruba and English. He reported that his sermons on Sunday mornings "are delivered first in English and then interpreted because many of the Emigrants do not understand Yoruba, and many who do cannot appreciate a Yoruba sermon . . . [but] in the Afternoon, I have a pure Yoruba service, and in the Evening a pure English one. There are therefore two Churches in one." [50]

The financial condition of the Native Pastorate was precarious, with collections taken quarterly at Sunday services of the churches. Johnson wrote that the "Association that was formed by some lay members of the Lagos Church" had suspended its activities, pending approval from London.[51] In 1875 funds became increasingly hard to obtain because of the economic effect the strife in the hinterland was having on the congregations. Johnson thought of seeking a government subsidy but feared the interdenominational rivalry that would result as it had in Sierra Leone.[52]

Finally, in March, 1876, the Bishop of Sierra Leone announced the approval of an "Auxiliary Pastorate Association," the object of which should be "to raise funds for the General purpose of the Native Pastorate, in order to supplement the ordinary Revenue of the Church Funds. . . ." [53] With a new impetus and approval from the European section of the mission, the Association was formally "introduced to the notice of the Christian Public" in August, when it began its activities, including the publication of reports.[54]

In the meantime the question of the future of the Rev. James Johnson had come to the fore. An energetic, dedicated man, Johnson had immediately set himself to improving the Breadfruit Church and the CMS stations in Lagos generally. Strict as he was, he had been unpopular at first with his congregation, although a few had been enthusiastic about him from the beginning. In August, 1874, J. P. L. Davies wrote to Hutchinson, "Mr. Johnson has begun already to improve and organize all connected with our Church and the schools and I must affirm that we have not had a Christian di[s]ciplinarian in Lagos for a long time. Mr. J. Johnson I believe is a hard worker and may the Church and your works prosper in his hands." [55] When, in February, 1877, Johnson received word to take over the missions in Abeokuta, protests about his leaving came from his congregation at the Breadfruit Church.[56]

The Parent Committee of the CMS had planned, as they wrote Crowther, to consecrate Johnson as Bishop of the Yoruba Mission.[57] But just as Hinderer, and even Townsend, came to support such a measure, opposition arose from the younger European missionaries in Lagos. Roper, who had objected to the earlier lay project to organize the Auxiliary Association,[58] was no longer in Lagos, but Faulkner, Wood, and especially Maser, were against the proposed appointment. When the alternative was put forward of sending Johnson virtually on trial to Abeokuta, the opposition did not abate, for the Europeans wanted to take charge of the former center as well. Notwithstanding Townsend's return there, it was as yet uncertain that European control of the missions would be acceptable to the Egba; in its unsettled state Abeokuta seemed a good proving ground for Johnson. If he had success there, he might be made bishop despite the objections from Lagos.[59]

In Abeokuta Johnson found a difficult situation, complicated by competition between the CMS and Wesleyan agents.[60] The CMS alone had many problems. Despite the efforts of the agents there, the stations were in financial straits, and Johnson was dismayed by the high incidence of domestic slavery, among Christians as well as non-Christians. In line with his instructions, he tried to make the churches and schools self-supporting.[61] The Church Council, which included representatives from committees Johnson had formed in each congregation, supported his plan to raise class fees, with the contributions to be assessed on a weekly basis.[62] Coming as it did with the Egba entry into the Ibadan-Ekiti war, and with trade stagnating, the plan to increase fees caused resentment in the congregations.[63]

Even more discontent arose when Johnson faced the problem of domestic slavery. Though generally pleased with Johnson's efforts at Abeokuta, the Bishop of Sierra Leone on his visit there in 1879 was perturbed by this issue.[64] The practice, which had so long distressed the missionaries, was no less deplored by Johnson, who had long since raised the issue with his clergy.[65] On receipt of the Parent Committee's minute on the subject, which stated that no agent of the Society should own a slave or hold a pawn, on pain of immediate dismissal if not cleared by 1 January 1880,[66]

Johnson, determined to enforce his instructions, called meetings of the ministers. But CMS Saro agents refused even to register the free or "slave" status of their pupils, fearing "trouble that may arise," [67] and the population of Abeokuta at large was equally adamant. Henry Robbin, an ally of Johnson, wrote that the

slave question in Abeokuta is and has always been a very strong matter so strong that I believe that the people of the country would rather go farther away into the interior with such slaves that they can take with them, than to remain in the country without them. Therefore the slave question of late has brought ministers, other Agents and people so close together that excepting there is a quiet change introduced in the Agency of the Abeokuta Church, neither you nor anyone else can get on successfully among the Agents excepting he tolerates or connives at slavery.[68]

Johnson's failure in dealing with domestic slavery, combined with continued agitation from the Europeans in Lagos, brought his replacement by Valentine Faulkner in February, 1880,[69] and his subsequent return to the Breadfruit Church.

Johnson was deeply troubled, less by his failure in Abeokuta than by the measures taken by the European missionaries to thwart his success there. He felt he had evidence of Maser's specific acts designed to arouse the agents in Abeokuta against him,[70] and he wrote that,

If Mr. Maser's policy had been to weaken my influence in the country and expose me to the malice of the people he could hardly have pursued a more effectual course. I am entitled to protection publicly from him at least as the senior official representative of the Society. I do not ask him to endorse all or anything I have done, but I have a right to ask him to uphold me before my people. . . . Placing Africans in positions of very responsible trust is only an experiment now in the mission; and it is the duty and it ought to be the pleasure of every European missionary . . . to render them every support and strengthen their hands excepting it be he has a desire and pleasure to demonstrate African incapacity for responsible trusts. . . . Why increase my difficulties or suggest them? But surely, it is nothing strange that difficulties have cropped up in Abeokuta and surely it is no offence to require people to support the Church according to their blessing or to stand up against domestic slavery in the Church of God.[71]

In spite of this defense, Johnson was seen to have failed in his test, and with his removal to Lagos went the possibility of an African bishop for the Yoruba Mission.[72] This development did not surprise the Sierra Leonian agents: "We are all persuaded that Bishop Crowther as he is the first so he will be the last negro bishop — at any rate for centuries to come." [73] But in the continuing rivalry, acknowledged by the Europeans themselves, Johnson's experience brought him the sympathy of his Lagos congregation, [74] and spread ill-feeling toward the European missionaries that was to give added impetus to the movement for separatist African churches, with its landmarks in 1891 and 1901. [75]

The CMS was not alone in having to face the problems of the changed attitudes of the European missionaries and the agitation of their African congregations for greater African responsibility, leading to self-government and self-support. At the time of the reorganization of the Methodist missions in West Africa, with Lagos becoming in 1879 a separate district attached to the Gold Coast mission, the general secretary in London was the Rev. John Kilner, a man who believed in pursuing a policy which paralleled that of Henry Venn in regard to the African church. [76]

But Kilner and his colleagues in London could not change the views of their representatives on the coast, views that were current among other European agents there. John Milum, who began the reorganization of the Yoruba mission in 1878 believed that "native" pastors "should always take a subordinate position to European agents and whilst allowed to vote on all matters pertaining to their local funds and to their own brethren, they should not be allowed (as hitherto) to vote on matters pertaining to Europeans." [77] But because he exercised discretion and tact, dissatisfaction did not burst into open conflict. [78]

His successors, though, were not so discreet, and were so strongly convinced of the superiority of their position that they went beyond the constitutional limits of their authority. A schism in the church was only narrowly averted in 1884. The issue was the summary dismissal by W. T. Coppin, who took over the chairmanship of the district from Milum, of two of the "circuit stewards" before the expiration of their terms of office. Without receiving approval from London, Coppin not only removed the men, but threatened disciplinary action against any of the missionaries who continued to deal with them. The Methodist Committee in London condemned the steps taken by the European missionaries in

Lagos and virtually apologized to the African clergy there.[79] The African agents and the congregations, both predominantly Sierra Leonian,[80] were placated, but the forceful action from London could not change attitudes which were becoming prevalent in Lagos, and which were to provoke the rift that had been temporarily averted.

ISSUES FOR THE MISSIONS: EDUCATION

The clash between the newly crystalized European attitudes and the growing aspirations in the African congregations — and, if less vehemently expressed, among the African clergy — evolved into the separatist movements of the 1890's and early 1900's. For the background to this outlet for African frustrations, it is necessary to see the parts played by the missions, missionaries, and Christian communities in education; to examine the place Christianity had come to hold through the missions in relation to traditional religion and Islam; and in this context to consider the stands taken on such issues as domestic slavery, polygamy, and the adaptation of European practices and attitudes to African patterns.

Education was a major preoccupation of all liberated Africans, as well as of many of those who had never been away from Yoruba country. It was not until 1882 that the government first considered setting up its own schools and making contributions to existing ones.[81] Until then, all schools were started on the initiative and with the support of the missions, and had remained in their hands. Thus, it was in connection with the schools that the lay members of the Christian congregations were most influential. Both the CMS and the Methodist Mission had shown early interest in primary education; in Lagos in 1862 the CMS had three such schools and the Wesleyans, one.[82] Secondary education was, however, not within easy reach. The CMS Grammar School was opened under the Rev. T. B. Macaulay in 1859, and, as we have seen, the lay members of the church rose eagerly — too eagerly in the opinion of the European missionaries — to its support.[83]

Even though the Grammar School had been placed in Lagos, the concentration of early CMS educational effort was in Abeokuta. There converts had access to the Training Institution if they sought a religious career, or the Industrial Institution if they preferred to learn about cotton growing or the trades.[84] Largely because of a conflict between the ideas of Townsend and the Rev. G. F. Bühler, the German missionary who took over the Training Institution in 1857, little was done there from the time of Bühler's death until the school was reorganized, this time in Lagos in 1872, and under even greater pressure than Townsend had exerted earlier against giving the pupils too academic a training. The missionaries on the spot were reluctant to send prospective African agents for schooling even to Sierra Leone, arguing that such education would mean greater expense for the Society and depleting the supply of assistants, who would, moreover, lose touch with local problems. The Lagos Finance Committee insisted, further, that the training of "Native Pastors" should be in Yoruba as well as English.[85]

After the Abeokuta *Ifole*, Lagos became the educational center of the CMS. The Grammar School flourished under the direction of T. B. Macaulay, and with the support of the leading members of the Sierra Leonian community. In 1867, on the initiative of J. P. L. Davies who contributed £100, a fund was started for a new building for the school.[86] Donations came primarily from emigrant traders, though the list also included several described as "pure Natives and no emigrant from Sierra Leone or anywhere else."[87] A "School Committee," composed of J. P. L. Davies, Henry Robbin, the Revs. J. B. Wood and T. B. Macaulay, was organized in 1870 to work with the new Native Pastorate toward "relieving the C.M.S. of [educational] expense."[88]

In 1870 the Grammar School had 28 pupils; in 1871, 40, with the number fluctuating between 25 and 40 until Macaulay's death of smallpox in 1878.[89] The mission decided in 1870 that the principal should have an assistant, and the Sierra Leonian and brother of Samuel Johnson, Nathaniel Johnson, who had been a schoolmaster at Ebute Ero and who was later to be put in charge of the Aroloya station, became tutor at the Grammar School.[90] It was further decided that Macaulay ought to receive a "fixed salary," to be subsidized by the mission as long as necessary, although the goal was complete self-support for the school.[91]

From 1868 on, the Wesleyan "educated people" had been agitating for a "School for the higher education of Methodist Youth in Lagos." [92] Since their individual efforts had brought no results, they held a meeting in January, 1874, during a visit of the Rev. John Milum from the Gold Coast. The lay members put not only verbal pressure on Milum, but pledged themselves to raise £500 to build the school.[93] They also petitioned the Committee in London, urging facilities for the Methodist youth so as not to oblige them to go to the CMS for "higher education," and to increase the number of potential agents.[94]

The school was opened in March, 1878, by the administrator, John Dumaresq, with Bishop Crowther and John Field of the CMS, the Revs. Milum and Coppin of the Wesleyans, and the Rev. W. W. Colley of the American Baptist Church participating.[95] Coppin was appointed principal and, except for the supervision of the CMS Grammar School, the "Europeanization" of the senior posts of Lagos Christian education was complete, for Europeans had had charge of the CMS Female Institution since its move to Lagos at the end of 1867.[96]

Several groups in Lagos thought, for different reasons, that the educational facilities there were inadequate. One was the Muslim community. Although plans had been laid by the CMS in Sierra Leone to have primary schools for Muslim children in Freetown and Lagos, such schools had not yet come into being in the late 1870's. The Rev. Henry Johnson, a Sierra Leonian newly arrived in Lagos in January, 1877, received a visit from "two Mahommedan gentlemen. . . . Born at Sierra Leone or educated in the Mission Schools, they afterwards embraced Mahommedanism whether from choice or compulsion I could not ascertain. . . . These two men expressed a desire that I would open a School for Mahommedan children. I promised to consider as I could not see my way to gratify that desire real or feigned." [97]

The Christian emigrant population thought the available educational opportunities insufficient for themselves and for the population generally. One of the first issues to which attention turned in the emigrant-produced press of the 1880's was education:

We can testify to the fact that no people, as a people, are more anxious for the advantages of a liberal education than the people of this Country. From time to time we see strenuous efforts put forth, and enormous sacrifices made by parents to secure the great boon for their children. . . . We do not require that the Government should establish for us first class Colleges, and import into them a highly educated tutorial and professional staff. . . . And we do not ask for this, not because we do not care for such provision, but because, as practical men, and not thoughtless enthusiasts, we know that we shall not have it. . . . We ask for the establishment or support of good Elementary Schools by the Government, with an efficient Inspector at their head.

This editorial, while praising the work of the mission societies, declared that the continuation and much needed expansion of the educational system were the responsibility of the government:

We are told that the sanction of the Imperial Government has been obtained for the expenditure of £16,000 to construct a Gaol! What then? Is crime considered a more respectable thing than education, insomuch that a premium must be put on it by providing for it a palatial and comfortable accommodation? . . . Let them but persist in their policy, and they will never be in want of inmates for their expensive prison.[98]

A letter signed "Africa," in the same issue of the *Lagos Times* pointed out that of Lagos' £45,000 annual revenue, only £700 was spent on education.[99]

In 1882 Governor Moloney set forth the outlines of a government school system,[100] with a general board of education appointing local boards, to deal both with schools supported entirely from public funds and "assisted" schools.[101] Five years later such a system was put into effect, and it may be noted that a minute on the explanatory despatch suggested substituting Outlines of the History and Geography of West Africa, Outlines of the History and Geography of the British Empire, and History and Geography of the British Empire, for the existing History of England to 1066, History of England from 1066 to 1660, and History of England from 1660 in Standards VII, VIII, and IX respectively.[102] In 1889 the noted Sierra Leonian, Henry Carr, was appointed to the subinspectorship of the Lagos schools.[103] In government-supported education, if not in the missions, Africans came to control the senior positions. Carr became inspector in 1892, and from then until 1918 filled senior posts in the educational structure.[104]

ISSUES FOR THE MISSIONS:
THE MUSLIM CHALLENGE

It is difficult to know the success in strictly numerical terms of the Christian missions by the 1880's. Their influence on local political affairs, especially in the early years, reached well beyond the communicants and scholars they were able to claim. But what progress did they make in gaining converts to Christianity and spreading its doctrines? For this aspect of the missionary effort influenced the attitudes and actions of those in mission work — the European and Sierra Leonian mission staff, and the emigrant and local African communicants.

At the end of 1868, John A. Otonba Payne submitted the religious statistics of Lagos, exclusive of its dependencies, based on the somewhat informal census of that year. He recorded,

14,797	Pagans
8,422	Mahomedans
2,664	Episcopalians
974	Wesleyans
290	Roman Catholics
42	Baptists
27,189	Total [105]

Ten years later the records took into account the entire colony, but the Christians were to be found almost entirely on the island itself:

Christians:		
Church of England	3,145	
Wesleyans	1,048	
Baptists	71	
Presbyterians	2	
Roman Catholics	572	
Total		4,838
Mohammedans		10,595
Pagans		44,788
Total		60,221 [106]

The increase in "Christians"—the word seems to include here everyone "connected with the congregations" [107] — was therefore not striking, especially when the natural increase in population is taken into account.[108] The CMS figures show a fair balance between the "increase" and "decrease" columns of communicants, with "enquirers" varying between 300 and 500 in the 1870's.[109]

The missionaries saw the greatest obstacle to their progress in Islam. Hinderer recognized the seriousness of the problem in the 1850's, but he could not find time to pursue his ideas of ways to deal with it.[110] In 1863 Richard Burton wrote of his "unexpected pleasure" in finding that Lagos contained "some 800 Moslems, though not yet 2000, as it is reported." [111] James Johnson wrote in 1876 that,

the population of the Station [St. Paul's, Breadfruit] and District is over 12,000 — ; that 11,000 of these are heathens and Mohamedans; that the number of professing Christians connected with the Breadfruit Church is 800 — and that of Communicants is 387. The work is both Pastoral and Missionary; . . . the one cannot be safely neglected, or worked indifferently on account of the other. The Heathenism and Mohamedanism amidst which the Church dwells have not failed to exert their influence upon her.[112]

The Lagos Native Pastorate Auxiliary drew a similar conclusion in its first report:

We are scarcely 4,000, all told of each Christian denomination; whilst they ["Heathens and Mohamedans"] are over 30,000. Protestant Christian Churches on the island are only 9, when Mohamedan Mosques are 16. Protestant Christian Schools are only 8, when Mohamedan Schools are over 30, though they are, each one, small; but Christianity has gained a footing in the soil.[113]

Thus, in the mid-1870's the CMS became acutely aware of the challenge. In Sierra Leone plans began to be laid for "qualified Native agents . . . to be set apart specifically to labour among the Moslem residents of Sierra Leone and Lagos, and the traders who periodically visit those places." [114] In 1875 the Parent Committee arranged for the Rev. Henry Johnson to spend a year studying Arabic and Hebrew in Jerusalem, for as James Johnson wrote, "An accurate Knowledge of the two languages in some of the Society's Native Missionaries is necessary for this Mission where scripture translation work is not yet complete, and there is Mohamedanism to combat." [115]

Despite the awareness of the Christian missionaries of the spread of Islam, they were unable to counteract it. James Johnson in particular understood the problem and tried to work out ways of dealing with it.

Every Mohamedan regards himself a missionary to his neighbours: he constantly manifests a strong desire for the prosperity of the religion which he

regards as his own. We want to see more of this in our Christian converts. . . .
Christians are regarded as a people separate. . . . The distance between them
and heathens is far greater than that between heathens and Mohamedans.
Often may heathens and Mohamedans be found living together in the same
house; Christians are rarely found living with either. All these contribute to
the growth and spread of Islamism. The question is, how is this religion to
be met? Would it be of any advantage to circulate Arabic scriptures? [116]

Thus the missionaries sought new means, even though they saw
that on such basic issues as domestic slavery and polygamy, both
permitted under Islam, they faced a powerful antagonist. The
Christian missionaries could not or would not adapt their own
beliefs, and where Muslims were less rigid the missionaries condemned them on moral grounds.

Perhaps the greatest disappointment to the CMS agents was the
number of Sierra Leonians who associated themselves with the
Muslim community. It has not been possible to assess their role
in West-African Islam from documentary sources, but their presence is undeniable. We have seen the growth of Islam among the
Aku in Freetown in the 1830's, as well as the participation of the
Muslim Aku in the continuing emigration to Lagos and the surrounding area.[117] These men and women undoubtedly influenced
others in Lagos. But those who had never been converted to Christianity in Sierra Leone were less a disappointment to the missionaries than were those who had once been Christians there and had
later changed their religious affiliation. One of the most prominent Muslims in Lagos was such a man — Shitta Bey.[118]

Perhaps the main reason for the slow progress of the Christian
missions in this period was the fact that, though they succeeded
with individuals, they did not effect mass conversions by securing
the support of the traditional leaders. Even in Abeokuta, where
a number of the important chiefs, from Shodeke in the early years
to Ogundipe later, showed interest and were willing to consult
and protect the missionaries,[119] the important names were not to
be found in the list of communicants.

In Lagos the ceremony founding the Native Pastorate Auxiliary Association of the CMS was counted as an important occasion, as much because of the presence of Dosunmu and some of
his chiefs as because it was a landmark in African self-support
within the church.[120] It was the first Christian service attended by

the *Oba*. A few months before it, James Johnson had visited Do-sunmu with Philippe Jose Meffre, an "Elder" of the Breadfruit Church and left discouraged.[121] Even when he learned that Dosunmu and one of his chiefs had sent several children to the CMS and the Wesleyan Mission for "instruction . . . and given a piece of land for a Church near his residence," Johnson wrote, "I do not think the Ex-King has taken this step from religious con-viction. I rather think it is from policy as he is anxious to be in good grace with the British Government and expects to have his sons to do his correspondence for him." [122]

But Johnson saw some importance in the change nonetheless, and summarized the problem the mission faced: "The step taken is fraught with importance and full of promise and hope for Lagos and the adjacent countries. The refusal of the Ex-King and his chiefs to recognize the claims of Xianity hitherto has kept many persons from us; it is the belief of many that Lagos' influence has hitherto helped to block the way to Xian Missionaries getting into some of the adjacent countries." [123]

Even apart from the key questions of domestic slavery and polygamy, Muslims showed a greater willingness to allow tradi-tional practices than did the Christians. Dosunmu's early experi-ence with Christian education was not atypical: Pope-Hennessy, on his second visit to Lagos in 1872, learned from the *Oba* that,

Some years ago he had asked the Administrator to aid him in getting his son taught English, and the Boy was accordingly sent to school. King Docemo is not a Christian; and it appears that in accordance with a custom of his re-ligion, it was his practice, on the anniversary of the death of some Relative, to proceed with his family to the house where this relative had been interred and there go through certain prayers and ceremonies. His son, who had been sent to the English School, was warned by his Teachers that this was all very sinful, and that he should assist in rooting out the heathen customs of his father. But neither the boy nor King Docemo would agree to this; and as the Teachers said their mission was to enlighten the Natives in such matters especially, no agreement as to the education of the boy could be arrived at.

Hennessy attributed to such rigidity "the fact that whilst the British Settlements exercise a certain political and commercial influence some hundreds of miles in the interior of Western Africa, their educational influence in the interior is absolutely *nil*." [124] Although he overstated his case, the administrator-in-chief had come upon one of the most important reasons for the slow progress in the acceptance of Christianity.

ISSUES FOR THE MISSIONS:
DOMESTIC SLAVERY AND POLYGAMY

The issue of domestic slavery was one on which neither the government nor the missions could compromise. Slavery, with no qualifications, had been the cause of their entry into Lagos and the hinterland, and its continuation in any guise could not be tolerated. The fact that it did continue, in a form hard to eradicate though essentially different from slavery for export, plagued the administrators and missionaries throughout the period of our study, and beyond it. It was, to the distress of the missionaries, practiced not only by non-emigrant converts but by Saro and Amaro, and even by mission agents among them — for it continued an integral and seemingly indispensable part of the changing economic system. Payne was suspected of participating in the rendition of domestic slaves in 1872; James Johnson found evidence of such slave-holding in Abeokuta in 1879; there was a case of Saro slave-holding in Onitsha in 1880, to cite a few examples.[125]

Men such as James Johnson saw the dilemma clearly. Johnson was a most dedicated Christian, and therefore, despite his understanding of the institution, he did all he could to enforce the Christian point of view when it came to a decision. The Sierra Leonian CMS agents in Abeokuta, however, felt that Johnson did not, in fact, understand, that he interpreted domestic slavery too strictly as slavery, and that he associated polygamy with it as well.[126] This position was Johnson's undoing in Abeokuta. The mission continued to devise methods for redeeming such slaves, but they did not solve the problem.[127]

In 1887 Johnson was still at work trying to find more indirect and more effective methods of displacing the system. He suggested that government subsidies for agricultural education would stimulate production for export:

All this would besides conferring a great industrial benefit upon Lagos, also help the interior countries indirectly. A widespread use of superior and effective agricultural implements could greatly tend to weaken the hold Domestic Slavery has upon these countries, as one plea upon which the problem is kept up is the need large cultivators have for labour in their fields.[128]

After seeing the economic dislocation of the late 1890's which came with freeing domestic slaves under the new British protectorate, Johnson took in 1898 a more lenient view than he had previously held:

I don't think, generally speaking, the system worked hardly on the slaves, but it is natural for every man to wish to be free. In Jebu a slave could not purchase his freedom, all the same he could attain to any rank but that of King. They were not in the habit of selling their slaves. [Now] people are altogether restless and intimidated. They live . . . in fear of people in connection with the British Government. . . . [They] want time to accustom themselves to the altered condition.129

Whereas it was impossible for any professing Christian, or indeed for anyone, to put forward a case for domestic slavery that could have the hope of outside approval, the issue of polygamy, though equally important, was of a different order. Sierra Leonians, and on occasion even British officials, pointed out to both European and African missionaries the importance of making allowances for polygamy.130 The Saro, often those among them who were the strongest supporters of the church, argued the case heatedly. As John A. Otonba Payne put it, "We are here on behalf of the heathen, for it is for us to speak on their behalf." 131

Urging the admission of polygamists to the church, H. A. Caulrick, another Sierra Leonian, systematically refuted the arguments against the practice. He denied that it had been introduced either by wars or by Islam, maintained that, rather than polygamy, it was "adultery and debauchery" that were "unnatural." And he insisted that polygamy be dissociated from domestic slavery:

Slavery is prevalent in Africa, and every educated African, especially children of emancipated negroes like myself should pray and labour for its discontinuance. But native marriage in Western Africa is contracted for and entered into with due solemnities as in other countries of kindred principles — married women (even concubines) in Western Africa or Yoruba land are fully respected according to their ranks and are not treated as slaves. — The natural industrious dispositions of especially Yoruba women are often times misunderstood by strangers and travellers for actual servitude.132

The arguments and pressures from Sierra Leonian members of the Christian congregations brought about no change in the regulations. This was one of the crucial issues which later figured in the movement for the separatist churches.

THE EMIGRANTS IN PERSPECTIVE:
VARYING RELIGIOUS VIEWS

What, then, was the emigrant position with respect to the mission structure on the one hand, and the spread of Christianity on the other? As we have seen, the attitude of the Europeans toward the Sierra Leonians underwent a change which, though it had earlier roots, became marked in the late 1860's. No longer were the emigrants regarded as ideal agents. No longer could be heard such statements as the following from Abeokuta in 1866: "We are satisfied too, that the large number of Sierra Leone people here will tell well upon the people . . ."; "Sierra Leone men are becoming men of rank and title in their own country, one was lately made the chief of his township but accepted the office on condition that no idolatrous act should be required of him." [133]

From the time of the *Ifole* in 1867, the emigrants were no longer seen as willing to follow European "guidance"; rather, there were some among them who showed inclinations and capabilities to take the advisory and controlling positions into their own hands. A number of subtly interwoven factors, of class, of status, of racial attitudes, all contributing to and deriving from the generalized attitudes of their day toward Africans, led the European agents on the West Coast to resist the policies of Henry Venn and other mission leaders like him in London.[134]

But this change in European attitude and approach, as it took shape in Lagos and the hinterland, did not mean that the missions relied less upon the emigrants throughout the mission structure. For, with expansion of the stations and continued European mortality, both school and church needs made it essential to use the services of non-Europeans. It was still necessary to have men like Charles Phillips in charge of the center at Ode Ondo, and Daniel Olubi and Samuel Johnson at Ibadan. But the positions at the top of the hierarchy were the ones in dispute. After blocking the approval of James Johnson as Bishop of the Yoruba Mission, the pressures vented their full force against the Niger appointments, culminating in the accusations against Henry Johnson and Dandeson Crowther, accusations which led to the resignation of Bishop Crowther in 1891 from the Niger Mission Finance Committee, the decline in his power, and the subsequent disappearance of Africans from the more important mission posts. [135]

The missions, however, depended on the emigrants in another respect as well. In Lagos, and in Abeokuta, Saro and Amaro were the majority of their congregations. Thus, the Record Book of Attendance upon Public Worship in the Wesleyan Methodist Churches of Lagos, 1879–85 shows that at least 95 per cent of the names — and contributions — registered were Sierra Leonian.[136] The implications of this high proportion were clearly serious when some members of the CMS and Wesleyan congregations, indignant over the actions of the Europeans in the Niger Mission, chose to secede from the parent churches. Even in this instance, however, the emigrant Christian communities did not act as a unit. The factor of stratification emerges which will later be set against the other divisions affecting emigrant action.

In general, it is clear that those Sierra Leonians who maintained a formal connection with one or another of the Christian churches came most closely to fulfill the expectations held for them before 1850. But, in the meantime, the role projected for the emigrants by European political, missionary and trading interests had changed; by 1890 the test imposed on them was that of undivided allegiance, that is, adherence to Christianity and to European policies. Yet even with the framework thus modified, the generalization still stands, though discernible shades of difference emerge. In effect, varying attitudes become distinguishable in this group: first, those of the leading members of the "native" clergy; second, the stand taken by the most prominent lay members of the churches; third, the views of those members of the congregations who had not actively entered the formal structure of the churches.

Most loyal, from the European point of view, were the African clergy, and of them, Bishop Crowther on the Niger took the position most compatible with European ideas. In the charge delivered to his clergy in 1869, he gave his answer to the question, "Are Africans yet able to regenerate Africa without foreign aid?":

Africa for the Africans, the rest of the world for the rest of mankind, indeed. If we have any regard for the elevation of Africa, or any real interest for evangelization of her children, our wisdom would be to cry to those Christian nations which have been so long labouring for our conversion, to redouble their Christian efforts.[137]

In the Yoruba Mission, James Johnson, most active of the Saro clergy there, showed more confidence in African abilities. Johnson stressed unceasingly the need to understand African attitudes, and he accordingly brought about some changes in mission procedures, such as permission for converts to retain their African names, in compliance with a Parent Committee Minute, providing "that the Missionaries of this Society in all lands be instructed not to encourage the adoption by native converts of any new names in place of the names by which they have previously been known. It is important that their identity as well as their nationality should be preserved."[138] After the Lagos Finance Committee considered the minute, Adolphus Mann, one of the senior European missionaries, complained that, "Mr. James Johnson in some cases is opposed to the English family name, even if the father bears it since some years, and also to the Bible names at Baptism. Are the Parent Committee meaning we should go to this length? . . . I trust the Committee do not fall in with the Anti English monomania or Anglophobia of the Sierra Leone Aristocracy, which of course is free from the Yoruba national law."[139]

Similarly, on the Legislative Council of the colony, Johnson urged flexibility and consideration of African interests. But when it came to a choice in a matter of belief, he showed no hesitation: he chose to remain in the church.[140] With Johnson could be listed Archdeacon Dandeson Crowther, son of Bishop Crowther; in Lagos, Samuel Pearse and Nathaniel Johnson; and such men as Samuel Johnson and Charles Phillips in the hinterland stations.

In the second group were the most active lay members of the churches, men like J. A. Otonba Payne, I. H. Willoughby, Obadiah Johnson,[141] Henry Carr, and J. P. L. Davies. These men favored reform and were particularly outspoken. We have seen their concern with the problem of polygamy. They were equally interested in questions regarding the use of African names and African dress.

The use of African names became an important issue long before the mid-twentieth century. In the 1880's it concerned a number of Sierra Leonians apart from James Johnson. John A. Payne had already begun signing himself J. A. Otonba Payne, showing the importance he placed upon his Ijebu connection. In 1883 I. H. Willoughby wrote a letter to the *Lagos Times* on the subject.[142] In 1885 G. W. Johnson proclaimed from Abeokuta that, in connection with renouncing his status as a British subject so long as he continued *Amono Oba* to the *Alake,*

both for business matters, and private and public transactions of life . . . my name has been altered from George W. Johnson to Osokele Tejumade Johnson and I am to be addressed as such from and after this date. . . . P.S. Osokele is a distinct name of the lineage of the Kings of Egba, given me by my mother . . . directly I was born — George W. Johnson is to us here, the name of a foreigner, otherwise called, 'the slave name,' when fixed on an African — which name under the circumstances of the place of my birth and Baptized, was so fixed on me by the English side of my Freedom in Sierra Leone, . . . where my Parents were both landed, as Emigrants, after being captured from slave ship.[143]

As for clothing, "The unanimous opinion of intelligent Africans is, that health in West Africa is impaired, and lives shortened by the adoption of European tastes, customs and habits, materials and forms of dress," according to Payne and his Saro friends.[144] Payne also combined traditional with English imagery in his writing: referring in 1877 to a rumor of Dahomean overtures for peace with the Egba, he wrote, "We trust that in dining with the Dahomians, the Egbas will have a long spoon with which to eat with them in the same dish; otherwise, in course of eating sweet palaver sauce, the Dahomians might throw pepper in their eyes, and while rubbing it out, or calling for cold water to wash it off, the Dahomians would take charge of them and theirs." [145]

With respect to the church, these men wanted progress within the framework of "native churches" connected to the missions. For example, J. A. O. Payne, I. H. Willoughby, and G. T. King joined James Johnson and Isaac Oluwole in complaining of the "inadequacy and inefficiency of the Educational provision which had been made for recruiting and enlarging the ranks of the Native Ministry of the Church." [146] But their ties with the mother churches were too strong to be broken suddenly; they did not join in the schism in 1891, despite the protests they had registered during the preceding years. When their indignation was at its highest over events in the Niger Mission, they exerted all possible pressure for the replacement of Crowther by another African, but even when overruled, they did not leave the church.[147]

The third segment of Christian opinion was represented by men who had been less conspicuous members of the congregations. Many of their names will not have appeared thus far in this study. As smaller traders and as less active Christians, they were in closer and more informal touch with the indigenous people than were some of the men heretofore mentioned. It was this group that insisted on self-reliance. They were not particularly concerned with interdenominational rivalry, though it must be said that none of the lay members seemed particularly preoccupied with this issue. They were interested in what Christianity could offer an African, without displacing all his earlier practices or destroying his self-esteem. Education was their paramount concern, based on an awareness that, very concretely, "knowledge was power." In this instance it was knowledge of European skills, and they were willing to support its growth from whatever source it was sponsored.[148]

This was the group that first rebelled against European domination of the missions. From St. Paul's, Breadfruit, came the nucleus which, with a portion of the former Methodist and other CMS congregations, formed the Independent Native African Church in August, 1891,[149] paralleling the creation of the Ebenezer Baptist Church from the American Baptist Mission in 1888.[150] At the first conference, held at the home of William Emanuel Cole, retired postmaster in the Lagos government service, it was resolved,

That this Meeting, in humble dependence upon Almighty God, is of opinion that Africa is to be evangelised, and that the foreign agencies at work at the present moment, taking into consideration climatic and other influences, cannot grasp the situation.
. . . that a purely Native African Church can be founded for the evangelisation and amelioration of our race, to be governed by Africans.[151]

This resolution was confirmed at a second conference, held within a few days. Seven new supporters were present, and the familiar name of George W. Johnson appears as one of them. Another is

J. P. Haastrup, a nephew of the *Owa* ("King") of Ilesha.[152] Though not present at the meetings, J. W. Cole, who had been a prominent lay member of the Wesleyan Church,[153] bought the "Old Pheonix Hall from Chief Daniel Conrad Taiwo for £150 and gave it to the church."[154] In 1894 Cole became president of the Board of the renamed United Native African Church; with him served G. A. Williams as secretary, J. O. George, H. A. Caulrick, A. L. Hethersett, "and others."[155]

The formation of this separatist church was another example, this time in the sphere of Christian activity, of the growing insistence by certain emigrants upon African direction of African affairs. And the traditional leaders, on their part, were drawing distinctions between this group and those emigrants who worked closely with the missions.[156] These leaders also seem to have perceived differences in degrees of mission adherence. Just as important mission agents were willing to mediate in the hinterland in the 1880's,[157] the combatants were willing to accept these services in the interest of achieving what they all desired then — peace. But neither European nor Sierra Leonian missionaries were any longer so effective in guiding hinterland policies as they had been in the past. The chiefs and their councillors, themselves no converts, identified Christianity with the expanding European authority and did not want further advice from mission sources. What advice they did take from Christians tended to be that of those in the third category, with views unreservedly supporting the paramountcy of African interests.

Part IV

Conclusion

CHANGING EMIGRANT ROLES
THROUGH THE NINETEENTH CENTURY

WE have projected the roles of the liberated Africans in nine-teenth-century Lagos against the many forces that shaped its political, economic, and religious institutions. Foremost among these forces were the differing attitudes and reactions of the several Yoruba groups to the impact of the British presence. These African reactions, embodied in specific steps, came in response to European activities impelled by growing humanitarian pressures; by expanding competitive trading interests; by mission philosophies as formulated in England and as implemented, often differently, on the coast; and by fluctuating Foreign Office and Colonial Office policies. All of these factors affected the changing position of the emigrants, both Sierra Leonian and Brazilian, the men and women who were later to be described as "cultural agents."[1]

No less important was the outlook of the emigrants themselves, an outlook which varied with time and particular experience, and which rested, for any one of them, on his life before slavery, on later experiences in Sierra Leone, and, after his return, on the attitudes toward him of Europeans and Africans. It is to these changing views, then — European, African, and emigrant, in that order — that we shall now turn.

CHANGING EUROPEAN VIEWS OF THE EMIGRANTS

Once the European missionaries followed the liberated Aku from Sierra Leone to Badagry and, later, reached Abeokuta, they, as well as representatives of the few British trading interests there, began to exert pressure upon the British government to intervene in Lagos. Abeokuta was seen as the first Christian stronghold in the interior, and action at Lagos was necessary both to protect evangelical work and to permit the growth of Egba power. Two central arguments were advanced for British intervention: one was the need for a tangible show of strength to support the cause of a ruler who had promised to eliminate the slave trade in Lagos; the other was the obligation, in humanitarian terms, to protect those who would spread not only the religious, but also the political and economic gospel. Although, strictly speaking, the liberated Africans were not legally British subjects, their anomalous position lent itself to the interpretation that in some sense they were, and it was argued that in this sense they were entitled to protection.

Thus the subject of the returning Aku became a means for applying persuasive pressure on the British government by interests on the coast, or by men in London representing such interests. Conviction lay behind this pressure: in the early days of European contact with Badagry and Abeokuta, it was through the agency of the liberated Africans that the British gained access to the interior, and permission to pursue their goals. Consul Beecroft and the missionaries saw the effectiveness of this intercession, and they continued to call on the emigrants to secure local African advice and support for their plans — from their entry into Abeokuta and later neighboring villages, to the building of Egba defenses against Dahomey, to obtaining the necessary acquiesence of certain factions in British intervention at Lagos.

The first negative reactions from Europeans appear in charges of Sierra Leonian "back-sliding" from Christianity, and of slave-trading or, at the least, holding of domestic slaves. Such early condemnations served inadvertently to increase pressure in England for introducing British authority.

Once that end had been achieved and Lagos was "reduced," with the consul for the Bight of Benin stationed there, the Europeans on the coast were increasingly optimistic about the prospect of emigrant activity. The Sierra Leonian agents took the missions beyond the large centers. The emigrant traders who transported goods to the interior in marketable quantities provided the European merchants in Lagos contact with the hinterland. Emigrants gave administrative aid to the consuls, advice on negotiation in the hinterland, and essential information on residual slave-trading.

The missionaries were the first Europeans to become aware of differences in the degree of commitment within the Sierra Leonian community. The initial distinction was drawn between those who were firm adherents of the church, and those who, for whatever reason, had drifted away from its influence. When consular and CMS views clashed in 1854 over the authority of different African factions in Badagry, and emigrant testimony was produced on both sides of the argument, the missionaries dismissed the opinions against them as coming from men who had strayed from the ways taught in Sierra Leone.

Toward those of the emigrants who were, in contrast, particularly zealous Christians, actively taking part in the work of the church as prominent lay members or clergy, the European missionaries showed early signs of an ambivalence that foreshadowed the later overt competition. For while plans were being made in England for more training of more liberated Africans, and such men as Henry Venn and MacGregor Laird were actively encouraging measures to implement the intermediary role, European mission agents on the coast were arguing that African activity should be restricted to executing European directives.

The change from consular to colonial status in Lagos also brought a major change of attitude in European traders and officials toward the emigrants. African opposition to the cession, combined with the failure of mediation to bring peace in the interior, led the European merchants to suggest that the Sierra Leonian traders were acting only in their own economic self-interest. Freeman and Glover, still dependent upon emigrants for their staff, began nonetheless to condemn that section of the emigrant community, largely Egba, which they felt was placing obstacles to the successful execution of changing policies.

It was, in fact, over the question of Abeokuta, and in the Egba capital itself, that the differences of attitude within the emigrant group were most clearly seen by Europeans. The missionaries faced competition for the confidence of Egba political authorities from emigrants who were themselves under mission influence. Moreover, the position of the entire Christian community as advisors was challenged by the creation of the Egba United Board of Management, led by Sierra Leonians who had dissociated themselves from the church, and who stated plainly their change of allegiance from the English to the African authorities. Administrators learned that these same men had set out to deal with the Lagos government in ways intended to follow the model of British diplomatic practice. The EUBM leaders, in denying their legal connection with England, placed themselves out of reach of retaliatory measures.

The growing influence of this group in Abeokuta, and the fact that its members came to associate missionary interests with the policies of Lagos, contributed to the *Ifole* uprising of 1867. Their moves in Abeokuta, and their intransigence to the Lagos government's overtures for diplomatic negotiation, hardened Glover's distrust of the Egba Saro, both in Lagos and the Egba capital. Similarly, the growth of the EUBM led to more than general disillusionment among the European missionaries; it convinced them that they were correct in their view that European education was inseparable from Christianity and that continued dominance of the missions by Europeans was essential.

At the same time, Glover was pressured by both Europeans and Sierra Leonians for commercial representation on the Legislative Council. His distrust of the Egba Saro made him yield only to the first group, when he reluctantly appointed a single European member in 1872. When, however, his policies, severely criticized by commercial interests for disrupting trade, were later that same year reversed by Pope-Hennessy and Fowler, the Sierra Leonians secured not only the representation they wanted, but were granted a larger voice in the workings of the colony. The European missionaries were, then, joined in their protests by the European traders, who saw no alleviation in conditions, and who opposed measures which they thought to favor the Egba and the Egba Saro.

With the departure of Glover came the coincident, though temporary, fall from favor of the secretary of the EUBM, G. W. Johnson, in Abeokuta, and a lessening of the strain between the two political centers. Each administrator in Lagos who, because of the shortage of European staff, was still dependent on emigrant resources, took on toward the Sierra Leonians the attitudes of his predecessors; Glover's influence permeated the decade, despite the frequent changes in officials and the centralization of power in the Gold Coast. A petition from the Aborigines Protection

Society, received by the Colonial Office in 1874 in connection particularly with the Gold Coast, stated that "To the Earl of Kimberley belongs the honour of having given instructions that [educated Africans] . . . should as far as possible be employed in our West African Settlements, but we believe that the rule he laid down admits of being acted upon to a much larger extent than has hitherto been the case." [2] This request, based upon support of the early goals for the Sierra Leonians, brought forth from Hugessen a memorandum, containing testimony from colonial officials on emigrant activities. A quotation from H. T. Ussher, later governor of the Gold Coast Colony, including Lagos, was an expression of views like Glover's:

A . . . movement [specifically in the Gold Coast] has been secretly at work and threatens . . . entirely to undermine British influence. A small class of discontented and unprincipled natives, principally mulattoes and semi-educated blacks (who appear to be an evil inseparable from all negro communities) is active in its endeavours to persuade the ignorant impressionable and childlike Fantees that the time has come to govern themselves and to throw off our rule, retaining us as advisers only. They cunningly and wilfully misrepresent the Parliamentary Resolutions of 1865 to these people. . . . The principles inculcated by these persons spread rapidly, and . . . are highly pernicious.[3]

The transmission of such a view, both to the Colonial Office and to succeeding officials in West Africa, helped to cast doubt on earlier confidence in the work of educated Africans who in Lagos were largely Sierra Leonians.

Even while this view was gaining currency in administrative circles on the coast in the 1870's, the mission authorities in England were still seeking to encourage training leading to the self-government and self-support of their West African missions. But the missionaries in Lagos, having already banished from their horizons the emigrants who had left the church, were dealing with the threat of competition from those who were working in the Christian context.

The *Ifole* in Abeokuta and the resulting prohibition of European travel on the roads to the interior confined the mission leaders to the coast. The older, more experienced men, such as Townsend and Hinderer who, it is true, had opposed the consecration of Bishop Crowther and had voiced doubts about the ability of Africans to manage mission activity unguided, now stated their conviction that the African agents — primarily Sierra Leonians — had proved themselves thoroughly competent in the unsupervised control of the interior stations. But by then the European mission staff consisted largely of younger men, who were soon to show united opposition to the views of Townsend and Hinderer and to orders from the London headquarters.

Efforts were made in the 1870's by this new generation, both in the CMS and the Wesleyan missions, to thwart in the first instance all projects in support of church activities not initiated by themselves. This had particular bearing on the growth of the Native Church, as it was called. They also sought to impede the advancement of senior African clergymen to responsible posts. Equally determined with regard to the missions, which were considered to some degree as separate from the parishes, they particularly rejected suggestions to place them under African authority, as was clear from their opposition to the proposed consecration of James Johnson as Bishop of the Yoruba Mission. They were similarly reluctant to give up control over mission stations in the interior, where they hoped to keep political as well as religious influence, and thus contributed to the difficulties of Johnson's "probation" in Abeokuta. They later, in the same spirit, obtained sanction for their unchallenged authority on the Niger.

Several factors gave a rationale for these attitudes of the European missionaries. For one thing, by no means all of the returned Aku had held firmly to Christian belief, the fundamentals of which they had learned in Sierra Leone. The missionaries made use of the second half of Henry Venn's advice to the first agents landing in Badagry in 1845: "the . . . Sierra Leone Christians . . . may prove such an advantage to your work as no modern Mission ever yet possessed. They may, if they backslide and relapse, prove the hindrance and ruin of your Mission." The blame for the first uprising against the Egba Christians in 1849 was placed upon the "back-sliding" Christians, and the mission agents also attributed partial incitement of the *Ifole* of 1867 to them. Participation in traditional religious practices was given as a contributory explanation of why Christianity did not advance so rapidly as they would have liked.

The fact that certain leading Saro laymen in Lagos and Abeo-kuta argued the case for polygamy, that some "communicants" and "enquirers" were known not to have rejected domestic slavery, and that even some of the non-European clergy and catechists were suspected of such practices gave added grounds for the continuing criticisms. These views were being expressed with increasing intensity to the end of the period. The Sierra Leonian role had been concretely delineated in the field of mission activity; but, as things developed, it was in this sphere that their initiative was most completely rejected.

In the 1880's Lagos officialdom began to modify views that earlier reports had implanted. As men such as Moloney and Griffith gained more extended experience on the coast, they made their own evaluation of the emigrant role. Both were aware of the divisions within the emigrant community, but since they acknowledged the need to recognize African interests, they sought to clarify these interests by consulting Sierra Leonians who were known to understand them. They thus saw again the advantages of emigrant mediation, though they took care to choose the men who were most reliable in terms of government policies.

Moloney even surpassed earlier precedents in his consultations with such men as Isaac and Abraham Willoughby, James Johnson, and Henry Robbin. Further, in his plans for the agricultural development of the colony, he encouraged more Yoruba immigration from Brazil, in the hopes of using the skills of these people to hasten economic change in the hinterland.

New attitudes toward the emigrants had also been developing among the European traders. The first suspicions had come with Sierra Leonian opposition to the cession, and with Egba emigrant activities in the interior. But the merchants and the emigrant traders largely shared the economic fortunes of the period, and that fact, combined with their commercial inter-dependence, tended to hold them together. In addition, they were after 1861 under a judicial structure which did not differentiate between them. They maintained social fluidity, and when it was to their common interest, would join in making demands.

Over the years, however, uneasiness grew among the European traders as the emigrants in the interior showed signs of political loyalties which could interfere with the smooth flow of trade. Not until the end of the 1880's is evidence of a first rupture to be discerned: only selective emigrant representation was permitted in the Lagos Chamber of Commerce, formed in 1888. More significant were European objections to Saro participation in the Legislative Council, on the grounds that the men selected did not adequately represent foreign interests.

In general, then, we can see a decreasing willingness on the part of the Europeans to let the emigrant community retain a prominent role in the affairs of the colony, and this tendency was to become more pronounced after the turn of the century. The trend may be accounted for, partly, by ideas developing in Europe as to the capabilities of Africans and, hence, their place in colonial society. In part, too, it was due to recognition of the fact that the emigrants were not unfailing supporters of European policies, customs, and interests. But these more rigid attitudes seem largely to have crystalized and gained firm hold as European involvement increased, and criticism of the emigrants grew with the determination to entrench European control in all fields of activity. Consequently, opportunities for the Saro and Amaro to fill responsible positions within the British framework were progressively reduced.

CHANGING AFRICAN VIEWS OF THE EMIGRANTS

The reactions of the local Africans to their returning compatriots equally affected the part which the emigrants could play in these events. The reception they received in early times depended upon their relation to the people they first encountered. Lagos itself was the port from which many of them had been shipped as slaves. Indigenous Lagosians were virtually unrepresented among the Sierra Leonians, and since the primary economic activity in the town was still the slave trade, the emigrants found hostility there.

In contrast, they were well received in Abeokuta, the new Egba town which had drawn together refugees from the entire countryside. There they often found not only their relatives, but also a willingness to accept newcomers in the interest of strengthening the new center against encroachments from outside. And though

Badagry, like Lagos, was a slave port, and its people did not have direct links with the newcomers, the Badagrians permitted emigrant settlement because of the relation between that town and the Egba capital to the north.

The Saro who reached Abeokuta quickly showed their command of European skills, embarking on agricultural projects and, as impressive to those watching, writing letters for the Egba to their relatives known to be in Freetown. They drew respect because of these skills, and suffered little stigma for having "been away," for everyone in Abeokuta had experienced the wars and knew the threat of capture.

There was, however, another side to the matter. The interest in the techniques the emigrants brought was joined to the hope of some local African leaders of deriving political advantage from the presence of the returning Aku. This latter consideration made possible the emigrants' introduction of British influence. By contrast, the factions in Lagos and Badagry, seeking to maintain an authority which was being challenged, by Kosoko and his allies in Badagry, for example, opposed all steps leading to British penetration. Furthermore, the emigrants themselves, apart from their British connection, aroused anxiety and even hostility in some quarters, as in Badagry where they were a growing economic threat to the local traders. Even in Abeokuta there were signs of resentment for similar reasons, to which were added hostile reactions to the growing political influence of the missionaries, culminating in the "persecution" of Egba Christians in 1849. Yet in that case, it is to be noted, the uprising was directed against non-emigrant converts, and the Sierra Leonians were not directly attacked.

During the consular period, however, the emigrants in the interior continued to be respected and were sought out for advice, even if they were not completely trusted. In Abeokuta, British policy was seen as favorable toward the Egba, and in its implementation the Saro offered a way to secure means of defense against Dahomey, thereby strengthening the position of the Egba. The Ijebu, refusing with unshakable determination to permit European penetration, nevertheless asked for the return of Ijebu Saro, presumably because of the desire for technical advancement, as well as the wish to be reunited with relatives thought to have been lost.

In Lagos, on the contrary, African feeling toward the emigrants, particularly the Sierra Leonians, increasingly deteriorated during the 1850's. They were generally associated with the virtual destruction by the British of traditional political authority, and with having been responsible for reinstating the less desirable contender for the *Oba*ship. In addition, they were in the position of primary middlemen between European merchants and the interior, and although the trading rights of Akitoye, and later Dosunmu, were recognized and even supported by the emigrants, control of trading activities was no longer in traditional hands. As a result, uprisings against the emigrants and against British influence broke out in 1854 and 1856, and their failure did not dissipate the ill feeling.

Both on the coast and in the hinterland, the emigrants were in the early days associated in African thinking primarily with the European Christian community, for the differentiations within the group had barely begun to emerge, and those that did exist appear not yet to have been recognized. The cession of Lagos, however, brought about a change in attitude everywhere. In the colony itself it heightened hostility toward the British, but it dissociated the emigrants from the "invaders" to some extent because they had opposed the change. For although the emigrants never were absorbed into the Lagosian community, partly because of lack of common origins, they came to be called on to represent the interests of the *Oba* within the framework of the *fait accompli*, to be consulted by him, as they themselves consulted and showed deference to him. In the hinterland, on the other hand, the cession increased not only distrust of the British, but also of the Sierra Leonians who were identified with them.

In Abeokuta, just as the missionaries were associated with the policies of the new colonial government, so were these policies seen to be in accord with the wishes of the Christian Saro. It was, however, at this stage that lines began to be drawn between factions of the emigrant communities. Because the political leaders in the hinterland had not been converted to Christianity, and because accepting European religion was identified with promoting

European interests, the principal differentiation was made between those of the Saro who were strong supporters of the church and those who were not.

With missionary disapproval of their converts' participation in traditional practices, those emigrants who wished to be reassimilated to their own society were forced to choose. It is not possible to determine whether the men who resumed the traditional way of life continued to use the mechanical skills and literacy they had learned in Sierra Leone. Their choice made, they were accepted as part of the indigenous communities, joining political organizations and in some cases becoming chiefs.

In Abeokuta a further distinction was drawn within the group of Saro who continued to conform to European patterns between those strongly identified with the missions, who were thought to see the introduction of Western practices as of paramount importance, and those with Christian education who wanted to apply what they had learned to strengthening the hinterland against penetration from the coast. The first group soon lost the confidence of the traditional rulers, and although they were permitted to carry on their activities, they no longer wielded political influence. The other group in Abeokuta became entangled in factional disputes. They were trusted by those whom they supported, while those they opposed resented even "loyal" interference with traditional institutions.

Increasingly, between 1860 and 1890, the Saro and Amaro of Lagos entered into the deliberations and policies of the interior. In the days of the consulate their intercessions for starting missions, for settling trade disputes, and especially for bringing aid for defense were received in a friendly manner, though even then such steps were suspect among the Ijebu. All Sierra Leonian residents of Lagos showed some identification with British policies, and this fact decreased the effectiveness of their mediations as the years passed. Measures that would have revived confidence in emigrant representations — that is, those introduced by Pope-Hennessy and Fowler in 1872 — were later reversed, causing heightened suspicion, especially among the Egba and Ijebu.

But the associations started by Saro and Amaro in Lagos to promote the interests of their kin in the interior were seen differently.

They were a source of useful advice and, more important, of tangible assistance in procuring military supplies. They were particularly respected by the Ijesha and Ekiti who, having been outside the sphere of mission penetration and government negotiation, had not witnessed emigrant conflicts of allegiances; the men who belonged to those associations were felt to have declared their loyalty, and were accordingly trusted.

Even in the case of these associations in Lagos, however, the leaders in the hinterland readily detected special pleading not completely in their interest. This shrewd appraisal of motives made it possible, for example, for the Egba leaders in 1888 to listen to the delegation of "Sons of Abeokuta" from Lagos on the subject of their signing a treaty with the French, but to reject their advice and write to G. W. Johnson in Lagos that only he was the "true Ogboni."

It is clear that just as the Europeans placed most confidence in those emigrants who supported the interests of the colony, so the African authorities trusted those who had shown primary loyalty to their groups in the hinterland. In each area in the interior the Saro and Amaro with relatives there were judged according to demonstrations of their local allegiance, rather than according to the more general positions they might take on questions arising from any conflict between African and European goals.

CHANGING EMIGRANT VIEWS OF THEMSELVES

We can now see, in answer to the first of the four questions central to this study,[4] the way in which the various sections of the emigrant community tended to view their own positions and roles. The original Sierra Leonian motives for return were diverse, and inevitably influenced their actions and reactions on arrival in Yoruba country. Their experiences in Sierra Leone were a further factor, as was their success in finding their families.

Attitudes became more and more clear as the expectations and plans of the Europeans in the colony came into conflict with those of the Africans in the hinterland, as alignments in the interior became more rigid. The landmarks in the progress of Lagos as interpreted by all sides contributed to solidifying positions. By the 1880's it is possible to discern seven more or less distinct positions shading into each other in the spectrum of roles, determined by the direction of allegiance.

The men who gave unqualified support to European policies and practices were few. Only Bishop Crowther voiced his conviction of the need to introduce and maintain European beliefs and practices unchanged, with their firm basis in Christianity; for him, Africans could take part in this process only under European guidance, unless they were thorough converts, in the most complete sense.

Following Crowther, and still closely aligned with the European position were those Sierra Leonians who had risen to relatively high places in the mission structure. In charge of parishes, these men stood firmly against such practices as polygamy and domestic slavery, although they did assert the ability and dignity of the Africans, and the admissibility of some of their practices which, though not European, did not conflict with doctrine. They felt the force of European missionary competition, yet held to their new beliefs. Men like James Johnson, faced with the local European missionaries' denial of the desirability of self-government for the churches and missions and of opportunities to able Africans like himself for advancement, nonetheless refused to leave the church, or to withdraw support from the spread of British influence. Their number included personalities such as Samuel Johnson and Charles Phillips, who were willing to mediate in the interior in order to advance their work, while knowingly or unwittingly disregarding the surrender of African sovereignty which was to result. It is quite possible that they did not expect the treaties of peace they had so important a hand in concluding to lead to annexation; perhaps, like James Johnson, they would have adamantly opposed actual penetration, while accepting the extension of mere influence. For the events of 1892, with Carter's subjugation of the Ijebu, aroused in the colony intense criticism led by Johnson, himself as we have seen of Ijebu descent but in any case always opposed to forcible annexation in the hinterland.[5] James Johnson's own words at the time best describe the anomalies of the position of this group: "Here [in Lagos], people are truly loyal British subjects; but this loyalty does not lessen or destroy their particular love for and interests in their independent countries, their original homes, the birth places of their parents or their own, and their desire to see their independence maintained. . . ." [6]

After this second group and, in fact, sharing its political views, came the emigrants who held relatively senior posts in the service of the colonial government, a few of the more prosperous merchants, and the lesser agents of the missions. The civil servants were men of moderately advanced European education, who, although not without local African allegiances, made them subsidiary in most cases to the interests of their positions, and, indeed, were under the greatest pressure to do so. With many similarities to them, yet set apart from them by being virtually outside this spectrum of allegiance, were those such as Walter Lewis or W. T. G. Lawson who may be called professional civil servants from Freetown. These men, without local connections, did not enter into affairs of the interior on any side and, keeping their base in Sierra Leone much as British officials had theirs in England, simply performed their duties in carrying out Lagos government policies.

Active members of mission congregations, those in the third group all exerted what pressure they could to persuade the Europeans that African advancement in the church structure was advisable. But they did not transfer their support to the Independent African Church, begun in 1891, even though they wanted polygamy, if not domestic slavery, accepted and understood. In strong economic positions, they favored, and could afford to support, measures to rework African patterns into a European design, and they constituted the group which, along with the professional civil servants from Freetown, most emulated European secular practices.

These men saw themselves as examples of the successful adaptation of Western ways, and expressed the hope that, as Payne wrote, "their brethren in the interior . . . [would] copy . . . [the] good example." Many of them were able to educate their children in England, and some of them went there themselves. They viewed themselves as being somewhat apart from the indigenous community, although they often, like Payne, retained ties with them, and must have provided support for such a newspaper as *The Eagle and Lagos Critic*, edited by a grandson of Bishop Crowther.

In the middle of the scale were the other large emigrant traders,

and those in the lower ranks of administration. They, too, supported Christian congregations, both CMS and Wesleyan, but they
were firmly behind all movements to strengthen the independence
of the "native churches" within the mission framework, and they
contributed, both economically and by the pressure of their opinion, to furthering that end. They maintained their contacts in the
hinterland: sometimes they sent their own deputations to try to
gain African consent to certain government proposals, but they
also belonged to the Lagos associations which, just as independently, advised and supplied particular groups in the interior in
their conflicts with each other and with the Lagos government.
These men sought representation for themselves on the Legislative Council of the colony, where they also hoped to act in the interests of their kin in the hinterland.

Although they did favor introducing some European practices
and institutions, they were unwilling to further such advances at
the price of any loss of African sovereignty. When they supported
a British policy, they did so assuming it to be in the political
interests of their particular Yoruba group. Thus, in the early
1880's, J. P. Haastrup, a "nephew" of the *Owa* of Ilesha, was recommending to his Ijesha relatives that they place complete faith
in the mediations of the Rev. Charles Phillips, assuring them that,
in his opinion, the Lagos government had no interest in their
land, but instead offered a means of obtaining independence from
the rule of Ibadan.[7] Such men, then, did not themselves act as
mediators on behalf of the British government — Haastrup only
went to arrange Phillips' later discussions — nor would they support such a proposal as the municipal reform of 1889 because of
the burden of taxation it would place upon their compatriots.

Only a few participated in the founding of the Independent
African Church in 1891, among them J. W. Cole and J. P. Haastrup. For the most part, they were unwilling to support the schism,
but they joined in the strong protest of emigrant senior civil servants and missionaries over the treatment of Sierra Leonian agents
in the Niger area in the 1890's, and they sought to have another
African succeed Crowther as Bishop of the Niger. The opposition
they met to African advancement — in administration to some degree, and more emphatically in the missions — strengthened a

growing pride in African ability. They argued the case for polygamy, for the suitability of African dress, and for the substitution
of Yoruba names for those they had been given at baptism. I. H.
Willoughby wrote to the *Lagos Times* in 1883, asking, "What
on earth have I to do with the name Willoughby, or my wife with
Puddicombe? What had my mother to do with Mary Easment?
What do these names mean? . . . It is not known, it is unmeaning-
ful what I am called by." [8]

These were the men who contributed to and controlled the
Lagos press of the 1880's, with its declarations of the inevitability
of independence. In Lagos, with English political institutions already set up, with sovereignty lost and needing to be regained
rather than maintained, their demands were vehement. They
sought rights for themselves as the representatives of African opinion and interests, and proclaimed what can be called a form of
proto-nationalism,[9] seeking self-determination and their own control of the new institutions, whose workings they alone had mastered at the time. Above all, they insisted on the ability of Africans
to govern themselves, just as they had done traditionally.

Next came the men who saw in the European influence the importance of education in its most basic, secular sense, though the
desire for Western learning was, of course, not limited to the emigrants. They sought the extension of European skills and knowledge, and were willing to support anyone who would offer it, even
if it meant belonging to more than one Christian denomination.
They were mainly small traders, men who depended on close contacts with the hinterland. They entered into the disputes of the
interior, sending supplies and advice to be used against African
factions or the Lagos government. Some of them had at one time
been in government service, usually at the lower levels. They
understood and accepted both polygamy and domestic slavery, and
they formed the core of the Independent African Church movement in 1891.

Toward the other end of the spectrum were the men, principally in Abeokuta, who acted from a sense of nationalism somewhat different from that just described among the Lagos Saro. The
dominant theme for them was reaction to the threat of English
conquest and a determination to preserve African autonomy,

while respecting traditional divisions and not necessarily seeking to create a larger unit.[10] Insisting that power should lie in African hands, they also stressed the wisdom of following certain European political and economic patterns.

Such men were George W. Johnson and his followers in the Egba United Board of Management. Their loyalties were unequivocally tied to African interests, and they sought to preserve autonomy in the interior by meeting British advances in European terms. They had been exposed to Christian doctrine, but insofar as they supported the churches at all, they favored adapting religious teaching to African patterns, and they too joined the Independent African Church. Although regarding themselves as more knowledgeable in the ways of the British than were their compatriots, their goal was their acceptance by the indigenous people, as they showed, for example, in changes of name.

While Biobaku may dismiss the EUBM as "little more than an empty bureaucracy, parading sovereign pretensions, and issuing largely idle threats," [11] the Board remains significant as the expression of a determination to protect African interests. The resistance of its members was not taking place in a traditional framework; there was the wish to introduce the new ways of the West, but selectively rather than indiscriminately. And the choice was made not because of a belief that all European ways were inherently superior but because some of them brought power to those who mastered them. It is the earliest example in Nigeria of a conscious effort, no matter how affected by a wish for personal power, by Africans to strengthen their own position by combining what they see as valuable in their own ways with what is useful in the new ones.

Finally, there were those Sierra Leonians who had been completely reabsorbed into the indigenous society, where some of them filled traditional political offices and participated fully in traditional practices. It is impossible to determine their number, for reference to them is found only in the few cases in which men had become *Ogboni* or other ranking chiefs in Abeokuta and elsewhere. But it is fairly clear that they did not differentiate between themselves and their kin, and renounced whatever European practices conflicted with what was expected of them.

One group of indeterminate size lying outside this continuum must be mentioned. These are the Muslim Saro, whose religion excluded them both from British plans and from complete absorption in traditional Yoruba society. They seem to have made for themselves a place outside of Western influence, producing only now and again a major figure in trade.

CHANGING EMIGRANT ROLES:
EXPECTATIONS AND ACTUALITIES

It is now possible to see the emigrant role, or rather, roles, in the light of the expectations and early theories about their return. Europeans tended to judge them as a unified group, meant to produce at some eventual time the "brilliant man with the skin of a negro and the mind and disposition of a well-bred European." [12] Set against this standard they were, for the most part, dismissed as simply poor imitations. Because the divisions along the spectrum were not acknowledged, even if they were perceived, the critics did not realize that such standards could at best be applied only to the first two, or at most three groups, and that, even among them, loyalty in the interior rather than incompetence could temper strict European behavior. But leaving conflict of allegiance apart as observers did, only in the cases of the first two or three groups had education been sufficient to provide for adequate acculturation to the European patterns to give such judgment any meaning at all. Even those specifically trained for their role by the churches did not undergo anything like the practice, let alone the ideal, of what the French have termed assimilation, and even that did not bring about complete renunciation of African loyalties.

Further, we have seen, in answer to the first of the four questions which we raised in the first chapter and which lie at the core of this study, that the returned liberated Africans neither saw themselves nor acted as a homogeneous group. But since they were, however incorrectly, judged as a whole, we may now view them similarly here, in order to answer concisely the second and third questions.

The second question, it will be remembered, has to do with the role of the emigrants in the British establishment of a working

Crown colony. As predicted in the 1830's, the liberated Africans came to staff the administration at a time when no alternative was possible. Through advice and mediation in the early years, they opened the way to political and commercial influence from the coast inland. Throughout the period, they conducted mediations in an attempt to make African and colonial interests coalesce. Once these interests were seen to conflict, however, many refused to champion the cause of the Lagos government, even if support of it would have been economically to their advantage. Those who continued to negotiate on behalf of the government found that their efforts did not produce African acquiesence in the measures which were formulated in Lagos without consideration for the intricacies of indigenous politics. Efforts to end hostilities in the hinterland were not successful until British policy became clearly expansionist, and the government on the coast could carry out its will with the backing of force.

The third question requires evaluating the success of the movement for African education and religious training against the catalytic goals it set itself. That the emigrants stimulated a desire on the part of the other Africans for European education is clear. But this desire was primarily for secular rather than religious training, partly because both the Africans who knew only their own culture, and the emigrants, who knew both cultures, felt the precepts of Christianity as expounded by the missionaries to be too inflexible to permit adopting the new religion without abandoning much of their traditional way of life. Any wish to strive toward such change was, moreover, not enhanced by the fact that those few who reached the levels set as a goal for them were not given the same economic and social opportunities as were Europeans.

In answer to the final question, we can now see the effect of the indigenous reaction to the emigrants upon them and their actual roles, in contrast to those expected of them. The British plans could only have been borne out had the Africans of the Lagos hinterland been as hospitable to the idea of change as the English were to the idea of changing them. On the other hand, if the indigenous population had felt no affinity for the emigrants who returned, the theory would have been negated, and isolation from the interior would have been the fate of the Saro and Amaro.

The returning Aku had in a general, or even specific sense, their origin, their language, and the customs they at one time had followed in common with the people of the interior, and, consequently, were readily able to present the new practices, beliefs, and techniques which they had learned. But it is obvious that the Saro and Amaro held the confidence of their relatives only in proportion to repeated demonstration of loyalty toward them. It is thus not surprising that many of the emigrants moved toward goals which were in conflict — occasionally in some cases, frequently in others — with what was expected of them by the Europeans, both in England and on the coast. The essential point is that they introduced European technology, institutions, and beliefs, but not without participating in transforming some of them to suit African conditions and interests, and, concomitantly, easing the adjustment of traditional ways to the innovations.

Further, the emigrants brought not only concrete European skills but also the ideas which accompanied them. For the indigenous groups, the acquisition of these skills and ideas by men and women of their own kind served, as significantly as any other factor, to dramatize the possibility of mastering in a relatively short time European knowledge and techniques.

The Sierra Leonians and Brazilians were unable to hold back the tide of European conquest. But except for the very few who unqualifiedly espoused the British cause, they sought to build a reasoned defense of African traditions, practices, and capabilities into assertions which later made their substantial contribution to the rise of modern Nigerian nationalism, with intermediaries no longer needed either to proclaim its merits or to carry out its programs.

Appendices

APPENDIX A

The sketches have been compiled from the information relevant to the lives of these men to be found in all sources I have consulted. The material comes primarily from mission and government accounts, and from Lagos newspapers, as well as from other sources cited in the text as bearing on specific individuals. C. H. Fyfe's *History of Sierra Leone* has been especially helpful for the Freetown parts of the Sierra Leonians' careers. The varying treatment of these men has resulted from the the amount of information available about them, which is necessarily uneven.

WILLIAM ALLEN: Allen was an Egba born in Yoruba country. He was captured, sold to a European slave trader, and subsequently liberated by a ship of the British fleet and settled in Sierra Leone. There he came under CMS influence, and served as a schoolmaster at Regent's Town, Gloucester, Kissey, Pademba Road, and Freetown. The same year he went to Abeokuta, where he was a schoolmaster and "assistant teacher" in the Training Institution at Ake. In 1865 he was made a deacon and moved to the Igbein station at Abeokuta, moving from there to the Igbore Hill station in 1868, after the *Ifole*. He was ordained in 1871, and died in Abeokuta on 3 April 1885.

RICHARD B. BLAIZE: Born in Sierra Leone in 1845, the son of an Egba recaptive, R. B. Blaize left Freetown in 1862 for Lagos, where he became government printer and later entered trade. He became one of the most prominent and successful merchants there, able to afford in 1900 a donation of £500 (in memory of Mary Kingsley) to the Liverpool School of Tropical Medicine. Head government printer in Lagos from 1871 to 1874, he started the *Lagos Times and Gold Coast Colony Advertiser* in 1880, and took an active part in demanding more education and representation for Africans in Lagos, as well as separation from the Gold Coast Colony. He was, with James W. Cole, James J. Thomas, and B. A. Williams, included in the otherwise all European Lagos Chamber of Commerce constituted in 1888, and, again with Thomas, he was on the 1898 Commission on Trade in Lagos. In 1904 he accompanied the *Alake* of Abeokuta on his trip to England, but died later in the year shortly after their return. The £3000 he left for free technical training of young boys in Abeokuta led to the founding, in 1908, of the Abeokuta Industrial Institute. He also kept his ties in Freetown, leaving at his death £500 to the Princess Christian Hospital there.

HENRY CARR: Carr was born in Lagos of Sierra Leonian parents in 1863. He was educated at Fourah Bay College, from which he was graduated in 1880. A scholarship from Fourah Bay enabled him to pursue his studies in England, where he attended St. Mark's College, Chelsea, and the Royal College of Science, South Kensington, London. He completed his honors B.A. in mathematics and physical science at Durham University in 1882. He returned to Lagos to become a tutor at the CMS Grammar School, and entered government service in 1889 as chief clerk in the Secretariat and sub-inspector of schools. He was appointed inspector of schools in 1892, and assistant colonial secretary for native affairs in 1900. In 1901 he again became inspector of schools, and was assistant colonial secretary in 1903. In 1906 he again took over the post of senior inspector of schools, becoming chief inspector in 1910. Between 1906 and 1918 he acted at various periods as director of education. In 1906 he took the degree of B.C.L. at Lincoln's Inn, and in the same year was made chancellor of the Diocese of Western Equatorial Africa. In 1918 he became Resident of the Colony of Nigeria.

SAMUEL COLE: Cole was born in Sierra Leone of Egba (?) parents. Liberated by the British, they returned with him to Abeokuta in 1843. He entered the service of the CMS in 1858, and worked at Ijaye, and then at Ake, Ikija, and Oshiele stations in Abeokuta, until his death in 1905. He married an Egba Christian in Abeokuta, and one of their sons, Michael Cole, also entered the service of the CMS.

SAMUEL AJAYI CROWTHER: Crowther was originally from a village called Osogun, some twenty miles north of Iseyin. In 1821, at the age of about fifteen, he was captured in an attack upon his town, sold eventually to a European slave-trader, and liberated in Sierra Leone in 1822. He was taken to England for a few months in 1826 by a CMS missionary, and returned to Freetown to become, in 1827, the first student at the Christian Institution, later to be called Fourah Bay College. In 1842 he was enrolled at the Church Missionary College at Islington, being made a deacon in June, 1843, and ordained on 1 October 1843 by the Bishop of London. In 1841 he had been selected to accompany the Niger Expedition. He was among the first CMS missionaries to come to Yoruba country in 1845, and was stationed at Badagry until 1847, when he was able to gain access to Abeokuta. He went on the Niger Expedition in 1854, returning a year later to Abeokuta and Lagos. In 1864 Crowther was consecrated Bishop of "the countries of Western Africa beyond the limits of our dominions." In the same year he was awarded an honorary D.D. by the University of Oxford. From that date on he performed his duties largely along the Niger, with visits to Yoruba country, and trips to England in 1870, 1882, and 1889. He died in Lagos on 1 December 1891, having, in addition to performing his clerical and episcopal duties, translated with the assistance of the Rev. Thomas King, part of the Bible and the Book of Common Prayer into Yoruba. He also compiled a Yoruba vocabulary, and wrote elementary books in the Nupe and Ibo languages.

SAMUEL CROWTHER, JUNIOR: The eldest son of Bishop Crowther, Samuel Crowther, Junior, was born in Freetown. He was educated in CMS Schools, and in 1841 was graduated from Fourah Bay College. He was apprenticed to a doctor in Freetown, after which he went to King's College, London, where for a time he read chemistry and anatomy as part of his medical training. On his return he went to Abeokuta, where he became a lay agent of the CMS, being placed in charge of the dispensary and cotton store in Abeokuta in 1851. He remained there until his clash with Townsend in 1861, when he moved to Lagos and was, for a year, in charge of the cotton warehouse there. He then began trading on the Niger, with his brother, Josiah Crowther.

JOSIAH CROWTHER: A son of Bishop Samuel Crowther, Josiah Crowther was born in Sierra Leone and educated there in CMS schools. He, with Henry Robbin, was chosen to go to England to the factory of Thomas Clegg, a Manchester merchant, to learn to process and pack cotton. After his training, he came to Abeokuta, where he traded and advised on the CMS cotton projects there. In 1861 he joined his brother Samuel Crowther, Junior, in trading on the Niger, and there he had connections with the West Africa Company of Manchester. He was, in the early 1870's, placed in charge of the Company's affairs, and he remained in that position until the dismissal of African staff with the amalgamation of the companies on the Niger in 1879. After that date the two Crowther brothers continued their trade independently.

JAMES PINSON LABULO DAVIES: Davies' precise origins are unclear. He refers to himself in a letter to Henry Venn, dated 9 Nov. 1861, as "a born British subject," implying that he was born of liberated African parents in Sierra Leone. It is clear that he was of Yoruba origin, though the sub-group is not stated. He entered the CMS Grammar School in Freetown in 1848 and studied there, among other subjects, "the Theory of Navigation." In 1851 he was enabled, through the pressure of Henry Venn, with his brother, Samuel, who died shortly thereafter, to receive "instruction in practical navigation and the general duties of a Sea man," on board H.M.S. *Volcano*. He came to settle permanently in Lagos in 1856, and soon became perhaps the most successful emigrant merchant, dealing in cotton and palm oil. He was a strong supporter of the CMS, behind all the movements of the period to sponsor financial aid to educational and missionary projects, donating himself £100 to the CMS Grammar School in 1867 and contributing to building a town library in 1872. In August, 1862, he married Sarah Forbes Bonetta, who had as a child been liberated from a slaver and virtually adopted by Captain Forbes of the *Bonetta*. She became a "protegee" of Queen Victoria, and the first child of the Davies', named Victoria, was the Queen's god-daughter. Davies engaged in commercial and agricultural pursuits throughout his life, managing to weather indebtedness and bankruptcy proceedings against him in 1876. Until that time he had carried on business ventures in Lagos, Abeokuta, and Porto Novo. In 1882 he began a coffee and cocoa plantation "six hours from Ebute Metta," but he shortly resumed trade in which he was as successful throughout the 1880's. He served as an unofficial member of the Lagos Legislative Council from 1872 to 1874.

CHARLES FORESYTHE: Charles Foresythe was born on Tasso Island in the Sierra Leone River. One of those who could be called professional civil servants from Freetown — referred to by an Aku emigrant in Lagos as an "alien African" — he was the son of a European army officer. In Lagos he became first postmaster and later treasurer, Crown prosecutor, and clerk to the Legislative Council. Retiring from the service in 1875, he went into private practice as a solicitor, licensed by the Supreme Court of the Gold Coast Colony until renewal of his license was denied him in 1880 over, according to some, the issue of property he held in trust for the children of J. P. L. Davies. Although the Colonial Office wrote of Foresythe's "good character whilst in public service," the officials there felt unable to interfere. But his license was renewed only a few months later, "in compliance with a petition to the judge joined by a number of influential people," including D. C. Taiwo and eleven other Lagosian traders who had enlisted Foresythe's services in the past. Retaining ties to Sierra Leone, he later made a considerable investment in his birthplace, starting plantations and a brickworks, and building a church there in line with his long standing support of the CMS in Lagos, where he had contributed financially to the Grammar School and supported other mission projects.

CHARLES JOSEPH GEORGE; JAMES GEORGE: C. J. George was the son of James George, an Egba Saro who, after commercial success in Freetown which enabled him to own considerable property there as well as ships trading along the coast, became a prominent trader in Lagos during the consular period. He subsequently established himself in Aebokuta, where, in 1871, he was able to intercede with the Egba authorities at the request of Governor Glover. In about 1880 James George took his son into partnership with him, and they resumed trade in Lagos. An active participant in Lagos affairs, and a strong supporter of the Methodist missions, C. J. George was appointed in 1886 to the Legislative Council of Lagos Colony, and he served in that capacity until his death in 1906.

JAMES H. GOODING: An Aku and a signer of the 1838 petition for government support for emigration to Badagry, Gooding became an important figure in Lagos of the 1850's and 1860's. Vice-president of the Sierra Leonian Court in 1855, he was later president of the African Commercial Association, started in Lagos in 1863, and composed of emigrants of Ibadan, Ijebu, Egba and Ijesha origins who wanted to mediate in the Ijaye War.

GEORGE W. JOHNSON: G. W. Johnson was born in Freetown of liberated African parents, and was, according to his own description, "a descendant and Prince of the tribe of the Egbas." He was educated in CMS schools, and became a tailor in Freetown. With a view to seeing the country of his parents, and with an interest in entering trade, he came to Lagos in 1863, settling finally in Abeokuta in 1865. Shortly after his arrival, he founded the Egba United Board of Management, of which he became secretary (calling himself in Yoruba, *Amono Oba*). He sought to guide the political leaders of Abeokuta in their dealings with the British government in Lagos, and remained in this position until he fell from favor over an Egba succession dispute in 1871. He went to Lagos, and from there to England, returning to Abeokuta in 1880, when he was summoned there by the new *Alake*. He renounced his British citizenship in 1880, and changed his name in 1885 to Osokele Tejumade Johnson. He left Abeokuta in the late 1880's, returning in 1895 to advise the Egba against the signing of treaties with the British. Through the influence of Governor Denton, he was expelled from Abeokuta in 1895, and he died in Lagos on 8 September 1899. In Lagos he lent his support along with others such as J. W. Cole and J. P. Haastrup to the formation of the Independent African Church. His nickname, "Reversible Johnson," was derived, according to conflicting accounts, from his early days as a tailor making mackintoshes, or alternatively, from the inconsistencies in his policies.

HENRY JOHNSON: Henry Johnson, called "Eloquent Johnson" to differentiate him from the other prominent Johnsons, was born in Hastings, Sierra Leone, the eldest son of Henry and Sarah Johnson, both liberated Africans from Yoruba country. His father was one of the two young men selected by the CMS to study at Kew Gardens, in order to determine the agricultural prospects of West Africa. The younger Henry Johnson was educated in the CMS schools and spent eight years as a tutor at the Grammar School in Freetown, before being sent, in 1865, to the Church Missionary Training College at Islington. He was made a deacon in 1866, and was ordained in 1867. In 1869 he returned to Sierra Leone and was stationed at Sherbro, where he worked on grammars of African languages and on translating the Bible into them. In 1873 he went to England for eight months before being sent to Palestine, where he was to learn Arabic so that he could work in areas under Islamic influence. He returned to England in April, 1876, and in November was sent to Lagos, where he replaced James Johnson at St. Paul's Breadfruit Church. In 1878 he was made Archdeacon of the Upper Niger, but he did not go to Lokoja until 1881. In June, 1891, he left the service of the CMS. His major work was the translation of portions of the Bible into primers and catechisms.

JAMES JOHNSON: Born in Sierra Leone of liberated Ijebu parents, James Johnson attended the CMS Grammar School in Freetown and was graduated from Fourah Bay College in 1854. He then became a catechist in the village of Kent. In 1860 he became a tutor at the Freetown Grammar School. He was made a deacon in 1863, and in 1866 was ordained. From then until he went to England in 1873 to consult about the movement to form an Independent African Church in Sierra Leone, he was stationed at Pademba Road and was a lecturer at Fourah Bay College. In 1874 he was placed in charge of St. Paul's, Breadfruit in Lagos. Considered the likely choice as Bishop of the Yoruba Mission, he was first sent to Abeokuta, in 1876, as superintendent of the Interior Yoruba Mission. In 1880 he returned to St. Paul's, Breadfruit, in Lagos, where he remained, serving on the Legislative Council of the colony from 1886 to 1894. He was known as "Holy Johnson."

NATHANIEL JOHNSON: Nathaniel Johnson was born in Hastings, Sierra Leone, the second son of Henry and Sarah Johnson, in 1843. In 1857 he left Sierra Leone with his parents, going first to Ibadan, where his father had been sent to aid the Rev. David Hinderer. Shortly after his arrival there, it was decided to send him to the CMS Training Institution in Abeokuta, where he studied under the Rev. G. F. Bühler. He remained at the school from August, 1858, to May, 1863, when he was sent as assistant schoolmaster to St. Paul's, Breadfruit, in Lagos. In 1864 he was put in charge of the day school attached to the Faji station in Lagos, and in 1868 moved to the Ebute Ero station, to revive the day school there. He assisted at the Grammar School, and with the services at Palm Church, Aroloya, being, in his own words "destined to serve in all the stations of the Society in Lagos." He became a catechist in 1873, and was ordained in 1879, when he was put in charge of Palm Church, Aroloya.

SAMUEL JOHNSON: The third son of Henry and Sarah Johnson, Samuel Johnson was born in Hastings, Sierra Leone, on 24 June 1846. He went to Lagos with his family in 1857, and from there was with them in Ibadan until the end of 1862, "being kept longer . . . than I should have been by the late unfortunate Ijaye war." In 1862 he was sent to the CMS Training Institution in Abeokuta, where he studied for three years under the Rev. G. F. Bühler. He was appointed schoolmaster in Ibadan in 1866. He remained there, superintending the schools at the Kudeti and Aremo stations until 1875, when he was "promoted a catechist." He mediated on behalf of the Lagos Government between Ibadan, and the Ijesha and Ekiti in 1885. He was made a deacon in 1886 and ordained in 1888, and sent to Oyo, where he remained until his death. His *History of the Yorubas* was completed in 1897, and the manuscripts forwarded to the CMS in London in 1899, after which, according to Obadiah Johnson, his brother, "nothing more was heard of them." Samuel Johnson died in 1901, and his brother compiled the book from his notes.

OBADIAH JOHNSON: The fourth son of Henry and Sarah Johnson, Obadiah Johnson was born in Hastings, Sierra Leone, in 1849. He attended the Grammar School in Freetown, and was graduated from Fourah Bay College in 1876. He attended King's College, London, and received his medical training at the University of Edinburgh. He was assistant colonial surgeon in Sierra Leone from 1887 to 1889, when he moved to Lagos. There he filled the post of assistant colonial surgeon until 1897. He was a member of the Legislative Council of Lagos Colony from 1901 to 1913. He was responsible for the publication in 1921 of *The History of the Yorubas*, which he rewrote from his brother's notes after the original manuscript had been lost.

NATHANIEL T. KING: A "younger son" of the Rev. Thomas King, Nathaniel King was born in Sierra Leone on 14 July 1847. He went with his parents when his father was transferred to the Yoruba mission in 1850. In 1861 he entered the CMS Training Institution in Abeokuta, and there he decided to enter the medical profession. He was sent to Sierra Leone in 1866 for further instruction, and in 1871 to England, where his medical education was subsidized by his "uncle," Henry Robbin. He became a member of the Royal College of Surgeons (M.R.C.S.) in 1875 and in 1876 returned to Lagos with two medical degrees to begin his practice, and to be medical adviser to the CMS until his death in 1884.

THOMAS KING: As a boy Thomas King was captured after a battle which destroyed his village, one of the old Egba towns, in about the year 1825. He was sold to a European slave-trader and subsequently was liberated by a ship of the British fleet, and settled in Sierra Leone. He was educated in CMS schools and was graduated from Fourah Bay Institution in 1849. He was sent to Badagry in 1850 and went from there to Abeokuta, where he was reunited with his mother. He worked in Abeokuta as a catechist, being made a deacon in 1854, and ordained in 1857. He died there on 23 October 1862, after working at the Igbein station. He worked with Samuel Crowther on translating the scriptures into Yoruba.

WILLIAM THOMAS GEORGE LAWSON: Lawson was a grandson of George A. Lawson, the "Paramount Chief of Little Popo (Anecho)," who had been educated in England before 1812, and who, according to Herbert Macaulay, "had a large family, some of whom were living as Portuguese, and some as Englishmen." One of his sons, Thomas George Lawson, was W. T. G. Lawson's father, and served as government interpreter in Sierra Leone, where he lived and his children were born. W. T. G. Lawson, the eldest son, was educated at the CMS Grammar School in Freetown, and later in England, where he qualified as a civil engineer and was an associate of the Institute of Naval Architects. In 1879 he became assistant colonial surveyor in Lagos, and in 1883 married an elder sister of Herbert Macaulay. A succession dispute in Little Popo in 1883–84 resulted in Lawson's obtaining leave from his government work, and he went there "to join the Lawson family in adjusting matters of State." His visit coincided with the arrival of Dr. Gustav Nachtigal, the German consul-general for West Africa. Opposition to Nachtigal's efforts to stake Germany's claim in Togoland resulted in W. T. G. Lawson's being taken prisoner aboard a German ship, which later called at Lagos. Through the intercession of Sir Branford Griffith, Lawson and the other prisoners were released. Lawson left the service of the Lagos government in 1886.

WALTER LEWIS: Son of Hannah Hayes (herself with an African mother and European father) but brought up in Freetown, and an English colonial secretary there, Walter Lewis was a civil servant in Lagos who had begun his career in the Sierra Leone government. Moving in 1858 to Lagos, where his wife's father, Benjamin Campbell, was consul, he became chief clerk there in 1861. Called an "alien African" — that is, non-Yoruba Sierra Leonian — in Lagos, he was at times colonial secretary there, and was registrar of the Vice-Admiralty Court from 1862 to 1872.

MATTHEW JOHN LUKE: Luke was born in Lagos, about 1845. His father was Ijesha, and had been captured as a slave, but was not sold, and, working through traditional procedures, secured his redemption. One of the earliest converts to Christianity, he sent his son to the CMS Faji Day School in Lagos. In 1861 Matthew J. Luke went to the Training Institution in Abeokuta, where he studied under the Rev. G. F. Bühler until 1865. He then taught at St. Paul's School, Breadfruit, and was subsequently "first master" at Ebute Ero School. In 1877 he was sent to Palma as a catechist, moving in 1879 to Leckie. He was made a deacon in 1886, and stationed at St. Paul's, Breadfruit, Lagos. Ordained in 1888, he took charge of the station in Ilesha.

CHARLES B. MACAULAY: Charles B. Macaulay was the youngest son of liberated African parents from Oyo. He was born in Sierra Leone in 1828, and he had two brothers, John, and Thomas Babington, later to become the CMS missionary. Charles Macaulay received his early education in the CMS schools in Freetown, and planned to enter the Colonial Surveyor's Department there to learn carpentry. It was then, however, proposed to send him to the Fourah Bay Institution, and despite his early objections — raised because he thought his father would not approve and because his elder brother, Thomas, was already there — he eventually agreed. In 1845 he and fifteen other students from Fourah Bay were selected to enter the first class of the Freetown Grammar School. In 1848 he was chosen to continue his education in England, but because he was needed to be a monitor at Fourah Bay in 1849 he did not go. In 1852 he was made a catechist at the village of Wilberforce, and from 1853 to 1856 was stationed at Bathurst. With the expectation of being made vice-consul of the British government in Abeokuta, he went there in 1857. After his arrival he became, on the recommendation of the Consul, the agent for the Sardinian trader, G. B. Scala, but after less than a year he had begun to trade on his own. In July, 1862 he entered government service in Lagos as first clerk of customs. He started the customs department in Palma in 1863, and returned to Lagos in 1864, where he was for a time postmaster and then clerk in the Colonial Secretary's Office. He was sent to Badagry in 1866 to "work the Customs and perform other official duties," and he remained there until 1873, although his salary and position had been reduced because of his ties with Glover. He began again to trade, and transferred his support from the CMS to the Methodist mission, for whom he worked thenceforth in various capacities. It is unclear whether or not he gave his support to the Independent African Church in 1891.

HERBERT MACAULAY: The son of Thomas Babington Macaulay and Abigail Crowther Macaulay, Herbert Macaulay was born in Lagos on 14 November 1864. "Within the period of the first seven years of my life, my mother . . . generally dressed me in a neat suit of purple velvet knickerbockers . . . with a purple velvet coat to match with shining silver buttons." Macaulay began his elementary education at the age of six at the Infant School of St. Paul's, Breadfruit. He then attended the Faji Day School from 1870 to 1877, when he entered the CMS Grammar School. In 1880 he went with his mother to the Niger, where they joined Samuel Crowther, Junior, and Josiah Crowther, his uncles, who were trading on the river. He returned to Lagos in 1881, and entered the government service as a clerical assistant and indexer of Crown grants at the Public Works Department. In October, 1884, he was appointed clerk of grants and draughtsman, and under the auspices of the government, he went to England in 1890 for further training. He spent three years in Plymouth as an articled pupil of the surveyor and water engineer there, and also completed a three-year course at the Royal Institute of British Architects in 1893. He also studied the violin in London. On his return to Lagos in 1893 he became surveyor of Crown grants, resigning the post to enter private practice of his profession in 1898. His political activity from then until his death on 7 May 1946 gave him his appellation, "the Father of Nigerian Nationalism."

THOMAS BABINGTON MACAULAY: Thomas Babington Macaulay was the eldest son of liberated Africans from Oyo — Ojo Oriare and Kilange — and was born in Kissey, Sierra Leone, on 17 January 1826. He received his early education in the CMS schools in Freetown, and was at the Fourah Bay Institution before being sent to the CMS Training College at Islington. On his return in 1851 he was a tutor at the Grammar School in Freetown, before taking charge of the Regent station there. In 1852 he was sent to the Yoruba Mission, where he worked at the Igbein and Owu stations in Abeokuta. After his ordination in 1854 he married Abigail Crowther, the second daughter of Samuel Crowther, and in 1859 he went to Lagos, where he founded the CMS Grammar School. He remained as principal of the school until his death, on 17 January 1878, in a smallpox epidemic. In conjunction with his teaching, he translated portions of the Bible into Yoruba.

PHILIPPE JOSE MEFFRE: An Ijesha liberated African, Meffre had for a time after his return to Yorubaland, been reabsorbed into Ijesha society. Described by a CMS missionary as once a "famous and very popular and influential priest of Ifa, the Oracle . . .," he was converted to Christianity by the CMS, and in the 1870's was an "elder" of the Breadfruit Church in Lagos and became involved in the educational questions of the 1880's in the colony. He had, in 1873, been one of those — the others being mostly Egba Saro — asking for Pope-Hennessy's return because, in part at least, of his seemingly anti-Ibadan policy. In 1882 he went with J. P. Haastrup to make preliminary arrangements in Ilesha for Phillips' later mediations.

WILLIAM MOORE: Born in Sierra Leone of liberated Egba parents, Moore received his early education at the CMS Day School in Freetown. He returned to Yoruba country as a catechist, and was in 1857 made a deacon. He was ordained in 1865, and was stationed in Abeokuta, at Oshielle and Ikija, until his death on 1 December 1893, having been in sole charge of the mission stations in Abeokuta from 1867 to 1875.

WILLIAM MORGAN: William Morgan was born in Sierra Leone, of liberated Ijesha parents. He was educated in the CMS schools there, and entered Fourah Bay Institution in 1840. He was a catechist and schoolmaster in Sierra Leone, and in 1852 was sent to the Yoruba Mission, where for two years, he was in charge of the station at Otta. He was then transferred to Ebute Ero, Lagos, being made a deacon in 1857, and ordained in 1865. He remained at Ebute Ero until his death in 1892. He translated a portion of the Old Testament into Yoruba.

JOHN T. NOTTIDGE: An Aku and one of the signers of the petition requesting government support for emigration to Badagry in 1838, Nottidge himself returned to Lagos and entered government service there; when Lagos became a colony, he became its first jailer.

JOHN AUGUSTUS OTONBA PAYNE: J. A. O. Payne was born at Kissey, Sierra Leone, on 9 August 1839. His father, an elder brother of the *Awujale* of Ijebu Ode, had been captured and sold into slavery and later liberated in Freetown. The name Payne was an anglicized version of the original Yoruba name — Adepeyin;

Otonba is a contraction of *otun oba*, meaning the senior assistant and adviser of the *Oba*. It is not known when Payne returned to Lagos, but he completed his education, begun in Freetown, at the CMS Grammar School there. He served the Lagos administration from 1863 in many and varied capacities, primarily in connection with all the courts that came into existence during his career, attaining the position of registrar of the Supreme Court in 1877, and even acting as Crown prosecutor, although he had no formal legal training. In 1874 he began publication of *Payne's Lagos and West African Diary and Almanack*, which appeared annually until 1894. He also wrote a *Table of the Principal Events in Yoruba History*, published in 1893. In 1886 he and his wife, Martha, a sister of J. P. L. Davies, left Lagos on a trip to Brazil and subsequently to England for the Colonial and Indian Exhibition. The Paynes returned to Lagos later in the year. His wife died in 1888, and in 1890 he married Maria de Rosario Joaquim, who lived only until 1891. Payne was an active supporter of the CMS, and led the agitation for an African Bishop of the Niger Mission in 1892. He was a member of numerous associations in Lagos, including the auxiliaries of the British and Foreign Bible Society, and the Anti-Slavery Society. He was also a Mason and a Forester. In 1894 he married Jessica Bruce, of a Sierra Leonian family in Accra. He died in Lagos on 1 August 1915.

SAMUEL PEARSE: Pearse was born in Sierra Leone of liberated Egba parents about the year 1830. He was educated at CMS Schools in Freetown, entering the service of the mission in 1848. In 1856 he went to Lagos as a catechist and schoolmaster, and moved to Badagry in 1859, where he stayed until 1875. He was then moved to Ebute Ero station in Lagos, and was ordained in 1880. He remained at Ebute Ero, apart from an interval in 1882, during which he took charge of the station at Bonny. He did translations of parts of the New Testament into Yoruba.

CHARLES PHILLIPS: The father of Charles Phillips, also named Charles Phillips, was born in Sierra Leone of liberated African parents. He was among the first CMS agents to return to Yoruba country, where he was a schoolmaster at Ake, Abeokuta until 1852, when he was transferred to Ijaye, where he was a catechist until his death in 1860. Charles Phillips, Junior, was admitted after his father's death to the CMS Training Institution in Abeokuta, where he studied under the Rev. G. F. Bühler until 1863. He then went as a schoolmaster to the Faji Station, Lagos, being transferred as a schoolmaster to the Breadfruit Station in 1872 and made a catechist early in 1873. He was made a deacon in 1876 and stationed at Ebute Metta. In 1877 he was sent to open the CMS station at Ode Ondo, and he was ordained in 1879. In 1885, with Samuel Johnson, he negotiated on behalf of the Lagos government to secure treaties of peace signed by the Ibadan, Ijesha, and Ekiti. In 1893, with Isaac Oluwole, he went to England, where they both were consecrated Assistant Bishops of Western Equatorial Africa and received honorary degrees of D.D. from Durham University. In November, 1893, he returned to Lagos.

CHARLES PIKE: Charles Pike was born in Sierra Leone, the son of a liberated African mother and Adolphus Pike, a retired British naval officer who became collector of customs and treasurer of Sierra Leone Colony. Charles Pike was educated at the Grammar School in Freetown and subsequently in England. He entered government service in 1869 when he was employed in the Treasury at Freetown as second clerk. In March, 1870, he was appointed chief clerk of customs in Lagos. He acted as deputy collector of customs during two intervals between 1872 and 1875, and was appointed assistant collector of customs and treasurer in 1876. In October, 1881, he became assistant colonial secretary in Lagos, and in 1883 and 1884 acted as collector of customs and treasurer of the Gold Coast Colony, thus being entitled to participate in the proceedings of the Executive and Legislative Councils. In 1885 he acted as deputy governor in Lagos, and then returned to his post as collector of customs there.

HENRY ROBBIN: Henry Robbin was born in Hastings, Sierra Leone in March, 1835, the son of liberated African parents, probably Egba. He received his early schooling there under the CMS and was selected for training in the processing of cotton in England. With Josiah Crowther he went to Thomas Clegg's factory near Manchester. He returned to Freetown early in 1856 and was sent from there to the Yoruba Mission, where he was in charge of the cotton concerns in Lagos in 1856. In 1857 he settled in Abeokuta, where he managed the CMS cotton enterprises and supervised the Industrial Institution. With the dissolution of the CMS connection with commercial cotton production, he devoted himself entirely to his own trade in Abeokuta. A strong supporter of the CMS, he interceded on behalf of the European missionaries with the authorities of Abeokuta after the *Ifole*. With the deterioration of commercial conditions in Abeokuta, Robbin went to Lagos in 1885, where he continued trading and became involved in educational questions, himself contributing to building the town library. He was consulted by the administrators there about policies towards the Egba, and was suggested by Moloney as a possible appointee to the Legislative Council when it was reconstituted in 1886. He died in Lagos on 5 March 1887.

OGUNTOLA SAPARA: The son of Ijesha liberated Africans, Oguntola Sapara was born in Sierra Leone in 1861. He received his primary education there, before being taken by his parents in 1876 to Lagos, where he studied at the CMS Grammar School. He became an apprentice in the Government Printing Department in 1879, and in 1882 began work at the Colonial Hospital as an unpaid assistant dispenser. He was appointed dispenser in 1883. From 1885 to 1887 he operated a dispensary of his own on the Gold Coast, going then to England to continue his medical studies in Edinburgh, Glasgow, and London. He became a Fellow of the Royal Institute of Public Health in 1895, and returned to Lagos, entering government service as a medical officer in 1896. He devoted his energies particularly to the alleviation and eradication of smallpox.

CHRISTOPHER ALEXANDER SAPARA-WILLIAMS: The eldest brother of Oguntola Sapara, Sapara-Williams was born in Sierra Leone on 19 July 1855, a great-grandson of Loro Agbogborigan by a daughter of the *Owa* of Ilesha. He began his primary education in Freetown, later attending the CMS Grammar School in Lagos. In 1875 he was sent for a year to Wesley College, Sheffield, and in 1876 became a student at the Inner Temple, being called to the Bar in 1879. In 1880 he returned to Lagos, the first qualified barrister. He practiced in Accra until the separation of Lagos from the Gold Coast, after which he practiced continually in Lagos.

MOHAMMED SHITTA BEY: The son of Muslim parents, liberated Africans from Yoruba country, Shitta Bey was born at Waterloo, Sierra Leone in 1824, and was baptized as a child by the CMS missionaries. In 1844 he returned with his parents to Badagry, where his father was Imam of the Muslim community there until his death in 1847. With the "reduction" of Lagos, Shitta Bey moved with his family to Lagos, where he entered trade. His commercial ventures occupied his attention outside of the colony, to which he finally returned in 1885, although he spent a part of each year there. He was prominent in the Muslim community there, and built a mosque which was completed in 1892. He is said to have been "the wealthiest and most influential among the Mohammedan traders in Lagos."

JAMES J. THOMAS: Born in Wellington, Sierra Leone of liberated African parents, probably Egba, and a printer's apprentice in his youth there, Thomas went to Lagos in 1867 as a "merchant's clerk." Later in trade on his own, he became one of Lagos' most prosperous non-European merchants himself. One of four "representative natives" in the Lagos Chamber of Commerce when constituted in 1888, he was also on the commission to investigate the state of Lagos trade, which heard testimony and reported in 1898. In 1900 he moved permanently to Freetown, where he endowed a public library and became a member of the Legislative Council in 1901.

J. M. TURNER: Turner was an Egba, captured as a boy, sold to a slave trader, and subsequently liberated at Sierra Leone. He was said to have been closely related to several prominent chiefs in Abeokuta. A signer of the 1838 petition requesting support for emigration to Badagry, he returned to Lagos himself in 1853 and soon became a prosperous trader, serving on the emigrant court during the consular period, when he also acted as surveyor of lands and lots for the *Oba*, in addition to farming his revenues. On behalf of the Lagos government he was sent to Ejirin Market to negotiate with the Ijebu, with whom he was also said to have had lineal connections. After the burning of the market he settled in Abeokuta, disclaiming British jurisdiction over him, and there he continued trading. He was an early and active member of the EUBM; after being its first treasurer, he later was given the title "Master of the Family."

JAMES WHITE: James White was born in Sierra Leone of liberated African parents from Owu. He received his early education in Freetown, where he attended both the CMS Grammar School and the Fourah Bay Institution, which he entered in 1844. He served as a schoolmaster and catechist at Waterloo and Wellington stations in Sierra Leone, and in 1850 was sent to Badagry, being placed at Otta in 1854. He was credited with preaching the first Christian sermon in Lagos in 1852, and in the early years of the consular period he acted as interpreter for Consul Campbell.

ANDREW WILHELM: Andrew Wilhelm was an Egba, whose original name was Dasalu. He was captured and sold into slavery and liberated in Sierra Leone. He came under the influence there, in the village of Hastings, of the CMS, and he was chosen to accompany Henry Townsend on his initial trip to Badagry and Abeokuta in 1842. When Townsend returned to Sierra Leone, Wilhelm remained in the Egba capital to begin work for the CMS and he acted as the major intermediary between the authorities of Abeokuta and the missionaries when they returned in 1845. According to Henry Townsend, Wilhelm was responsible for negotiating the peace between Abeokuta and Ado in August, 1853. He remained in the service of the CMS at the Ake station until his death early in 1867.

ISAAC HUMPHREY WILLOUGHBY: I. H. Willoughby was born in Bathurst, Sierra Leone, of liberated African parents related to men and women who were later found in Ibadan. He came with his parents to Badagry in 1845. There in 1852 he was a schoolmaster in the employment of the CMS. He was one of the first Sierra Leonians to enter Lagos after its "reduction." During the consular period he was a successful trader in Lagos, and following the cession he entered government service as interpreter and later superintendent of police. He worked closely with Governor Glover, after whose departure he resigned from the service and resumed trading. A contributor to the CMS Grammar School in 1867, Willoughby remained interested in education and was a member of the school board in the late 1870's. In the 1880's he was called upon to advise the government on numerous occasions, and he was considered by Moloney as a possible nominee to the reconstituted Legislative Council in 1886. On the issue of municipal government in 1889, he joined J. W. Cole, J. T. Thomas, I. I. I. Da Costa, and J. P. Haastrup as the emigrants supporting the position of the Lagos population at large. His brother, Abraham C. Willoughby, served as superintendent of the Hausa police in Lagos Colony.

APPENDIX B

*Enclosure, 15 November 1838, in Doherty to Russell, Sierra Leone,
30 November 1839. CO 267/154.*

Thomas Wills [Aku-"King"]*
John Ezzidio [Nupe]*
Emanuel Cline [Hausa]*
Thos. Pinches
James Gooding [Aku]†
John James
Christopher Taylor [Egba]
John Macaulay [Aku-"King" succeeding Will]*
John Thompson
Edward Davis
George Randle
Thomas Crook
Peter Campbell
William Sawyer
John Turner [Aku]†
John H. Atkins
John T. Nottidge [Aku]†
James Will [Aku]*
John Lewis
William Findlay
James Lewis

---

* Definitely did not return to Lagos.
† Definitely returned to Lagos.
[Tribe] where definitely known.

APPENDIX C STATISTICS OF LAGOS GRAMMAR SCHOOL, JULY, 1860

T. B. Macaulay to H. Venn, Lagos, 7 July 1860 CMS: CA 2/065

NAMES OF PUPILS	DATE OF ENTRANCE	AGE	WHERE FROM	PARENTS OR GUARDIANS	PROFESSION OF PARENT OR GUARDIAN	TRIBE	RELIGIOUS DISTINCTION
Joseph Pearse	6 June 1859	17	Lagos	George Pearse	Native trader	Egba	Christian
Dandeson Crowther	6 June 1859	16	Lagos	Samuel Crowther	Clergyman	Yoruba	Christian
Mark Willoughby	6 June 1859	16	Lagos	Isaac H. Willoughby	Merchant	Yoruba	Christian
Emanuel Wright	6 June 1859	17	Lagos	Thos. B. Wright	Scripture reader	Egba	Christian
Enos Biniditu	6 June 1859	13½	Lagos	Florence Biniditu	Trader	Egba	Non-religionist
Joaquin Abrev	13 June 1859	14	Lagos	Joaquin Abrev	Trader	Egba	Non-religionist
Aaron Pratt	20 June 1859	17	Lagos	William Pratt	Trader	Egba	Non-religionist
James Peters	8 Aug. 1859	17	Lagos	James Peters	Trader	Egba	Christian
George Hansen	12 Sept. 1859	14¾	Accra	Walter R. Hansen	Merchant	Fanti	Non-religionist
Gilbert Hansen	12 Sept. 1859	14	Accra	Walter R. Hansen	Merchant	Fanti	Non-religionist
Julius Quist	12 Sept. 1859	17	Accra	Walter R. Hansen	Merchant	Fanti	Non-religionist
David Pearse	13 Sept. 1859	14	Lagos	George Pearse	Trader	Egba	Christian
James Cole	6 Dec. 1859	16½	Lagos	James Cole	Trader	Yoruba	Christian
Samuel Roberts	2 Jan. 1860	16½	Lagos	William Campbell	Trader	Ijesa	Christian
Obadiah Campbell	2 Jan. 1860	8½	Lagos	William Campbell	Trader	Ijesa	Christian
Maximilian Faulkner	2 Jan. 1860	10½	Lagos	Charles W. Faulkner	Merchant	Egba	Christian
David Pratt	2 Jan. 1860	19	Lagos	Henry Pratt	Merchant	Yoruba	Christian
Nathaniel Shephard	4 Jan. 1860	13	Lagos	John T. Shephard	Carpenter	Ijesa	Christian
William Thompson	5 Jan. 1860	16	Lagos	John T. Nottidge	Trader	Ketu	Christian
James Wilson	9 Jan. 1860	12	Lagos	James Wilson	Trader	Owu	Christian
Charles Gabbidon	9 Jan. 1860	16	Lagos	James Gabbidon	Trader	Egba	Christian
Nathanial Joe	20 Feb. 1860	13	Lagos	Thomas Joe	Trader	Ketu	Christian
John Lawumi	12 Mar. 1860	13	Lagos	James George	Merchant	Egba	Christian
Machicha Tapa	12 Apr. 1860	13	Lagos	Otto Driedrichsen	Merchant	Dutch	Christian

APPENDIX D

REFERENCE MATTER

KEY TO ABBREVIATIONS

CHBE	*Cambridge History of the British Empire*
CMS	Church Missionary Society
CO	Colonial Office
EUBM	Egba United Board of Management
FO	Foreign Office
MMS	Methodist Missionary Society
NRO	Nigerian Record Office
PP	Parliamentary Papers
SLA	Sierra Leone Archives

NOTES

CHAPTER 1

1 Zachary Macaulay, a member of the Clapham Sect from 1789, held various positions in Sierra Leone after 1791, including that of governor from 1797 to 1799.

2 Macaulay to Castlereagh, 8 May 1807. CO 267/24. Quoted in A.P. Newton, "British Enterprise in Tropical Africa, 1783–1870," *CHBE* (Cambridge, 1940), II, 643.

3 E. Stock, *History of the Church Missionary Society*, Vols. I–III (London, 1899), I, 156.

4 Stock, *History of CMS*, I, 159.

5 Stock, *History of CMS*, I, 163. In Bickersteth's own, less explicit words, "it appears to be of the first importance, without delay to communicate that religious instruction, which, when truly received, will furnish a stimulus amply adequate to excite these poor fellow-creatures [the liberated Africans] to industry, and become the seed of every mental and moral improvement.

"Sierra Leone is, moreover, the central point, as it were, whence the blessings of religion and civilization may be diffused throughout a great part of Africa . . . ." Edward Bickersteth, "Report of Visit to the Settlements of the Church Missionary Society on the Western Coast of Africa," in the *Eleventh Report of the African Institution*, March 1817, p. 137.

6 MacCarthy to Bathurst, Sierra Leone, 21 July 1816 (Separate). CO 267/42.

7 Macgregor Laird, of a Birkenhead shipbuilding family, had been excited by the discoveries of the Lander brothers and had led an expedition to explore the Niger in 1832.

8 Macgregor Laird and R.A.K. Oldfield, *Narrative of an Expedition into The Interior of Africa*, 2 vols. (London, 1837) Oldfield's journal, II, 394–5.

9 T. F. Buxton, *The African Slave Trade and its Remedy* (2nd. ed., London, 1840), pp. 491–2.

10 This date and the following chronology of early Lagos history are the result of correlating and evaluating available and often divergent accounts, mostly of the nineteenth century but some earlier; mostly European but some African or from African informants. My analysis of them can be found in J. F. Herskovits, "Liberated Africans and the History of Lagos Colony to 1886" (D. Phil., Oxon., 1960), pp. 21ff.

11 C. A. Sapara-Williams, in "Lagos Past," a paper read by Obadiah Johnson at the Lagos Institute, 20 Nov. 1901, with discussion included, p. 31.

12 O. Johnson, "Lagos Past." This statement, heard elsewhere, is confirmed in passing by C. A. Sapara-Williams in the published discussion following Johnson's paper, though without specifying the nature of the trade.

13 Captain John Adams, *Sketches . . . during . . . voyages to Africa, between . . . 1786 and 1800* (London, n.d. [1822]), p. 80.

14 This date does not seem to be known more precisely.

15 S. O. Biobaku, *The Egba and Their Neighbours* (Oxford, 1957), pp. 10–11.

16 Although no comprehensive study of Yoruba political systems has yet appeared, a concise description of the various structures and positions, as well as a bibliography of the available literature published by 1951, appears in D. Forde, *The Yoruba-Speaking Peoples of South Western Nigeria* (London, 1951). Samuel Johnson, *History of the Yorubas, From the Earliest Times to the Beginning of the British Protectorate.* Ed., O. Johnson (London, 1921), contains considerable relevant information, and, as a guide to the titles of men who will appear in this study, we can use his description (pp. 75–77) of the system as it prevailed under Old Oyo, with the major difference that the breakup of the Empire brought decentralization of power and put greater control into the hands of the local rulers Johnson lists. "Every town, village, or hamlet is under a responsible head, either a provincial 'king' or a Bale (mayor). In every case the title is hereditary (excepting Ibadan) as such heads are invariably the founder or descendants of the founder of their town. The provincial kings are styled the lords of their town or district, and from it they take their title, e.g.: — The Onikoyi, lord of Ikoyi; Aseyin, lord of Iseyin; Alake, lord of Ake [thus the title of *Alake* in Abeokuta, where one of the quarters was Ake]; Oluwo, lord of Owu; Oluiwo, lord of Iwo; Alakija, lord of Ikija, etc. There are a few exceptions to this rule, where the first ruler had a distinctive name or title before he became head of the town or district, e.g.: — . . . Awujale of Ijebu . . . . A provincial king is, of course, higher than a Bale . . . . Smaller towns are governed by the Bale." For further information see Biobaku, *The Egba*, and "An Historical Sketch of Egba Traditional Authorities," *Africa*, XXII (1952), no. 1; and P. C. Lloyd, "The Traditional Political System of the Yoruba," *Southwestern Journal of Anthropology*, X (1954), no. 4.

17 Johnson, *History of Yorubas*, pp. 188–9. The commodities exchanged are not specified.

18 *Ibid.*, p. 207.

19 Biobaku, *The Egba*, p. 13.

20 Johnson, *History of Yorubas*, p. 210, reports this to be the first use of firearms in the area.

21 Biobaku, *The Egba*, p. 13.

22 Johnson, *History of Yorubas*, p. 225.

23 *Seriki* is a war title. According to Johnson (*History of Yorubas*, pp. 132–3), "war titles are of two grades, senior and junior," the first grade headed

by the *Balogun* or Commander-in-Chief, the second by the *Seriki*. "The term *Balogun* is contracted from Iba-li-Ogun i.e. lord of war . . . . *Seriki* is a Hausa word signifying a 'king.' He is practically like the Balogun, and is as important among the young warriors as the Balogun is among the veterans."

24 Johnson, *History of Yorubas*, p. 282.

25 J. D. Fage, *Introduction to the History of West Africa* (Cambridge, 1955), p. 103.

26 A. P. Newton, "British Enterprise in Tropical Africa, 1783–1870," *CHBE*, II, 643.

27 Fage, *History of West Africa*, pp. 101–2. These figures include slaves from south of the Cameroons.

28 C. H. Fyfe, *History of Sierra Leone* (London, 1962), p. 183, citing Liberated African Registers.

29 S. W. Koelle, *Polyglotta Africana* (London, 1854), pp. 5–6.

30 Thomas King, Journal extracts, quarter to 25 June 1850. CMS: CA 2/016.

31 See, for example, Elizabeth Donnan, *Documents Illustrative of the History of the Slave Trade to America*, Vols. 1–4 (Washington, 1930–5); Branz Mayer, *Captain Canot; or Twenty Years of an African Slaver* . . . (New York, 1854); Macgregor Laird and R. A. K. Oldfield, *Narrative of an Expedition into the Interior of Africa* . . . (London, 1837).

32 [B]eing spoken on the Pepper, Ivory, Gold, and Slave Coasts," Koelle, *Polyglotta*, p. 5.

33 According to Christopher Fyfe, "by the late 1820's most recaptives were from the Yoruba country." *History*, p. 170.

34 Buxton, *African Slave Trade*, note p. 499.

35 In fact, a possible derivation of this term is suggested in the writings of O. Dapper (1670) and John Barbot (1732), both of whom write of a "mighty" state, located between Ardrah (Porto Novo) and Benin, though not reaching to the shore. This kingdom is referred to as *Ulkami* (*Ulkuma, Alkamy*), "whence," according to Barbot, "The Adrasians get most of the slaves they sell us. . . ." John Barbot, *A Description of the Coast of North and South Guinea* ([London], 1732), p. 365. O. Dapper, *Umbständliche und Eigentliche Beschreibung von Africa und Denen Darzu Gehörigen Königreichen und Landschaften* . . . (Amsterdam, 1670), p. 485. In twentieth-century Cuba, the descendants of Yoruba are still known as *Lukumi*.

36 Doherty to G. W. Hope, London [?], 27 Oct. 1841. CO 267/166. Doherty, governor of Sierra Leone from 1837 to 1841, is objecting to describing the Aku as indigenous to Sierra Leone.

CHAPTER 2

1 There were two groups of settlers: the Nova Scotians, about 1,200 in number, were former slaves from the Thirteen Colonies who had fought on the side of the British in the American Revolution and had afterwards

fled north; the British government had arranged their emigration to Sierra Leone in 1792. The Maroons were former runaway slaves in Jamaica who, after their revolt in 1795, were deported to Nova Scotia; some 500 of them finally managed to get British permission to come to Sierra Leone in 1800.

2 Order-in-Council, 16 March 1808, quoted in J. J. Crooks, *History of Sierra Leone* (London, 1903), p. 71.

3 See C. H. Fyfe, *A History of Sierra Leone* (London, 1962), p. 114, for further information on the use of the term "recaptive."

4 MacCarthy was governor of Sierra Leone from 1814 to 1824.

5 Crooks, *History*, p. 107, citing Parliamentary Papers, nos. 352 of May 1825, and 520 of July 1825.

6 Henry Dundas Campbell was governor of Sierra Leone from 1835 to 1837.

7 "Regulations to be observed in the Treatment and Disposal of Liberated Africans when first received into the Department," encl. in Doherty to Glenelg, Sierra Leone, 24 Sept. 1838. CO 267/147.

8 W. B. Pratt [?] to Goderick, Liberated African Dept., Freetown, 15 May 1833. SLA: Liberated African Department Letter Book, Vol. V, 1831–4.

9 "Regulations to be observed in the Treatment and Disposal of Liberated Africans . . .," encl. in Doherty to Glenelg, Sierra Leone, 24 Sept. 1838. CO 267/147. This regulation had been instituted by Governor Temple in 1834 but had been replaced within a few years by the older system of permitting men to choose wives from the Yard. (Fyfe, *History*, p. 194). Nonetheless, the regulation remained part of instructions and was not officially abandoned. Like other innovations of policy in Sierra Leone, it had intermittent application.

10 "Regulations to be observed in the apprenticing of children from the Liberated African Yard," encl. in Doherty to Glenelg, Sierra Leone, 24 Sept. 1838. CO 267/147.

11 "Instructions for the Guidance of Managers . . . in the Districts or Villages," encl. in *ibid.*

12 Doherty to Glenelg, Sierra Leone, 23 Sept. 1838. CO 267/147.

13 Doherty to Russell, Sierra Leone, 3 Oct. 1840. CO 267/160.

14 The Rev. James William Barrie, testifying before the 1865 Select Committee, mentioned recognition of family and friends from before capture as a usual occurrence and suggested that, in later years at any rate, such acquaintances were settled together. *Report of the Committee on the Condition of the Settlements on the West Coast of Africa*, PP 1865. V (1), p. 283, question 7215.

15 See below, pp. 32–3.

16 Fyfe, *History*, p. 186.

17 Fyfe, *History*, pp. 202, 292–3.

18 Fyfe, *History*, p. 172.

19 Campbell to Glenelg, Sierra Leone, 5 May 1837. CO 267/140.

20 Doherty to Glenelg, Sierra Leone, 23 Sept. 1838. CO 267/147.

21 "A Picture of Sierra Leone in the Light of Christianity," *Church Missionary Intelligencer*, March 1855, pp. 60 ff.

22 J. A. O. Payne, marginal notes on *ibid*. This comment was in reference to a statement about the "unquestionable taste and talent for trade and barter" of "a great many tribes."

23 See below, p. 39.

24 Doherty to Russell, Sierra Leone, 3 Oct. 1840. CO 267/160.

25 O. Ogunsulire, *History of Fourah Bay College* (Dip. Ed., Durham Univ., n.d.), p. 3.

26 Thomas Cole to the Rev. J. Gerber, Liberated African Dept., Freetown, 11 Sept. 1830. SLA: Liberated African Department Letter Book, vol. IV, 1830–1.

27 Samuel Johnson, *History of the Yorubas, From the Earliest Times to the Beginning of the British Protectorate*. Ed., O. Johnson (London, 1921), pp. 38–9. This was confirmed in Lagos by oral evidence relating to the Muslim traders from Fulani and northern Yoruba areas.

28 M. Banton, *West African City* (London, 1957), p. 5.

29 Banton, *West African City*, p. 4. Though Savage may have been thought of as European because of his English name and his having grown up in England, his father was African. Fyfe, *History*, p. 142.

30 Pratt to Goderick, Liberated African Dept., Freetown, 15 May 1833. SLA: Liberated African Department Letter Book, Vol. V, 1831–4.

31 Doherty to Russell, Sierra Leone, 4 Dec. 1839. CO 267/154. Doherty at one point in the despatch burst out: "the people . . . not content with procuring the service and direction of the children who are confided to them . . . are in the practice of decoying others, and harbouring them in their haunts." One member of the Colonial Office, probably James Stephen, commented in the margin, "These are just the complaints the Hindoos make against our Missionaries."

32 Fyfe, *History*, p. 218.

33 Sierra Leone Colony, Blue Book, 1836. CO 272/13, p. 118. The figures are approximate.

34 Campbell to Glenelg, Sierra Leone, 5 May 1837. CO 267/140.

35 Ogunsulire, *History of Fourah Bay*, pp. 3–4.

36 Quoted in Ogunsulire, *History of Fourah Bay*, p. 5.

37 CMS *Proceedings*, 1820–1, p. 81. Quoted in Ogunsulire, *History of Fourah Bay*, p. 5.

38 James Denton, "History of Fourah Bay College," in T. J. Thompson, *The Jubilee and Centenary Volume of Fourah Bay College* (Freetown, 1930), p. 14.

39 *Ibid.*, p. 14.

40 Thompson, *Jubilee of Fourah Bay*, Appendix, "List of Students," pp. i–iii.

41 J. F. Ade Ajayi, "Christian Missions and the Making of Nigeria, 1841–1891" (Ph.D., London, 1958), p. 355.

42 Ajayi, "Christian Missions," pp. 355–7.

43 Fyfe, *History*, p. 127.

44 See E. Bickersteth to Wilhelm, London, 29 Aug. 1821. CMS: CA 1/L1.

45 Doherty to Glenelg, Sierra Leone, 23 Sept. 1838. CO 267/148.

46 Enclosure, 15 Nov. 1838, in Doherty to Russell, Sierra Leone, 30 Nov. 1839. CO 267/154.

47 There has been some question raised (see Ajayi, "Christian Missions," p. 79) as to whether any of the original petitioners regarding the emigration in 1839 is actually known to have gone to Badagry. There is definite evidence that John T. Nottidge entered the Lagos government service in 1862. With the choice of common European surnames, it is difficult to be sure of any of the others, but it is more than just possible that the signatories James Gooding and John Turner were the same men as the traders thus named in Lagos and Abeokuta in the 1850's and 1860's, especially since they are reported as "prominent." It is however, clear that some of the signatories, such as Thomas Will, John Ezzidio, Emanuel Cline, and John Macaulay, definitely did not leave Freetown for Lagos.

48 Doherty to Russell, Sierra Leone, 30 Nov. 1839. CO 267/154.

49 Minute by Vernon Smith, 18 March 1840, on *ibid.*

50 Minute by James Stephen, 18 March 1840, on *ibid.*

51 Fyfe, *History*, p. 213, citing Report from the Commissioners of the Mixed Court, Freetown, 15 Nov. 1839. FO 84/272.

52 Doherty to Maclean, Freetown, 6 Nov. 1839. SLA: Governor's Letter Book (1839–42), p. 35.

53 The reasons for this split are unclear. Doherty wrote to the Colonial Office that the twenty, fearing slave traders to the east, had asked to disembark at Accra (Doherty to Russell, Sierra Leone, 20 March 1840. CO 267/159), but he later learned that there was some doubt as to whether these same twenty had been landed at Accra with their consent (Doherty to J. W. Hanson [Commandant of British Accra], Freetown, 28 March 1840. SLA: Governor's Letter Book [1839–42], pp. 42–3).

54 Doherty to Russell, Sierra Leone, 20 March 1840. CO 267/159.

55 *Ibid.*

56 Doherty to Maclean, Freetown, 28 March 1840. SLA: Governor's Letter Book (1839–42), p. 43.

57 Doherty to Russell, Sierra Leone, 3 Oct. 1840. CO 267/160.

58 Fyfe, *History*, p. 204.

59 Doherty to Russell, Sierra Leone, 30 Nov. 1839. CO 267/154.

60 J. U. Graf, Journal, Hastings, Sierra Leone, 10 April to 25 Sept. 1843. CMS: CA 1/1015.

61 Petition, 15 Nov. 1838, encl. in Doherty to Russell, Sierra Leone, 30 Nov. 1839. CO 267/154.

62 Doherty to Russell, Sierra Leone, 3 Oct. 1840. CO 267/160.

63 Fergusson to Russell, Report on Blue Book for 1841, Sierra Leone, 30 Jan. 1842. CO 267/175. William Fergusson, himself an "Afro-West-Indian Army doctor" (to use Fyfe's description, *History*, p. 172), had been in Freetown from 1815. He was acting governor of Sierra Leone from 1841 to 1842, again in 1844, and was governor from 1844 until his death in 1846.

64 Macdonald to Stanley, Sierra Leone, 24 Nov. 1842. CO 267/176.

65 W. G. Terry (Superintendent, Liberated African Dept.) to Capt. J. Clark, Freetown, 25 April 1842. SLA: Liberated African Department Letter Book, Vol. VIII, 1842–7.

66 William Dixon ("Writer") to Henry Vincent, George Cummings, Walter Crowley, B. F. Hughes, Managers, Freetown, 20 June 1844. SLA: Liberated African Department Letter Book, Vol. VIII, 1842–7.

67 Macdonald to Stanley, Sierra Leone, 12 April 1844. CO 267/184. Macdonald was governor of Sierra Leone from 1842 to 1844.

68 Dougan to Grey, Sierra Leone, 31 July 1855. CO 267/247.

69 Fitzjames to Newcastle, Sierra Leone, 19 May 1860. CO 267/266.

70 Fergusson to Russell, Report on Blue Book for 1841, Sierra Leone, 30 Jan. 1842. CO 267/175.

CHAPTER 3

1 *Eko* is said to be the original name of the island, deriving according to some sources from its cultivation by the earliest settlers, for *eko* in Yoruba means "farm." From J. U. Egharevba, *A Short History of Benin*, (2nd ed.; Benin, 1953), p. 31, comes "war camp," the Bini meaning of *eko*, as another possibility.

2 [Henry Townsend], *Memoirs of Henry Townsend* (n.p., 1887), pp. 15–19.

3 The Rev. T. B. Freeman in his account of his first trip to Abeokuta in December 1842 wrote of an interview with the Sierra Leonians there, including their description of having been robbed in Lagos: "Out of about two hundred and sixty-five emigrants, the passengers of three vessels who landed at Lagos, it seems that not one of them escaped with any of their property, save the clothes in which they were clad. So much for liberated Africans returning to their native land, and landing among an unprincipled people on the coast, unprotected!" Journal of the trip, pp. 19–23. MMS.

4 A.K. Ajisafe, *History of Abeokuta* (n.p., 1924), p. 81.

5 Indeed, the inhabitants of Lagos had considered themselves relatively secure from slave raids, for only under the most extreme circumstances were members of one's own family sold, and one did not like to risk the revenge of a neighbor for having sold his relative. This statement is based on oral evidence collected in Lagos from various elderly persons, among others a prominent Muslim, over 80 years of age, whose father had been a slave trader there.

6 T. B. Freeman in his MS., p. 409, wrote that the Dahomean conquest

took place in 1727. See also M. J. Herskovits, *Dahomey*, 2 vols. (New York, 1938), I, 16–17.

7 A description of one of these ceremonies appears in Samuel Annear, Journal, 6 Oct. 1844. MMS.

8 P. A. Talbot, (*The Peoples of Southern Nigeria*, 4 vols. [London, 1926], I, 88) and Saburi Biobaku (*The Egba and their Neighbours, 1842–1872* [Oxford, 1957], p. 26) state that the emigrants had a letter from the Governor of Sierra Leone to the *Wawu*, recommending them to his protection. There is no trace of such a letter in the Sierra Leone records, and one wonders how Doherty would have known of the *Wawu* to write to him. A later correspondence between Governor Fergusson and "the English Governor of Badagry" does exist, however. See enclosure, Fergusson to Stanley, 28 July 1845. CO 267/187.

9 Talbot, *Southern Nigeria*, I, 88.

10 Biobaku, *The Egba*, pp. 23–4.

11 Talbot, *Southern Nigeria*, I, 130.

12 Samuel Johnson, *History of the Yorubas, From the Earliest Times to the Beginning of the British Protectorate*. Ed., O. Johnson (London, 1921), p. 256.

13 The Egba chiefs, in discussing their siege with arriving missionaries after 1845, said it was caused by attempted Ado attacks, prompted by jealousy, on returning emigrants. This explanation won the complete support and acceptance of both Methodist and CMS agents. But it seems biased in its disregard of the economic interests of the Egba. A variation told to Freeman when he first arrived — that the Ado people "had often laid violent hands on the Akus [meaning here all Egba] while travelling thro' the forest and taken them to the slave markets on the Coast. . . ." — fits more plausibly. See T. B. Freeman, Journal entry, Badagry, 6 Dec. 1842. MMS.

14 James Fergusson to the Rev. Thomas Dove, Badagry, 2 March 1841. NRO: ECC 2/1096.

15 T. B. Freeman, Journal, Jan. 1840 to Dec. 1842, especially entry for 27 Nov. 1842. MMS.

16 Shodeke to Freeman, quoted in Journal entry, 21 Oct. 1842. MMS.

17 T. B. Freeman, Journal, 16 Dec. 1842. MMS.

18 H. Townsend, Journal . . . While on a Mission of Research to Badagry and Abeokuta, 15 Nov. 1842. CMS: CA 1/0215.

19 *Ibid.*

20 H. Townsend, Journal . . . to Badagry and Abeokuta, 1 Jan. 1842. CMS: CA 1/0215.

21 *The Friend of the African*, no. 7 (Dec. 1843), pp. 105–6; S. Annear to General Secretaries, Badagry, 2 June 1844. MMS.

22 Crowther to Buxton, Sierra Leone, 14 April 1844, quoted in *The Friend of the African*, no. 14 (July 1844). Crowther also mentioned another of the ships, the *Little Grace*.

23 C. H. Fyfe, *A History of Sierra Leone* (London, 1962), p. 213.

24 See, for example, William Marsh, Journal, Badagry, 7 March 1846; 14 Aug. 1846; 2 Oct. 1846. CMS: CA 2/067.

25 Forbes to Bruce, Lagos, 9 Dec. 1851. Papers Relative to the Reduction of Lagos, PP 1852. LIV (221), p. 180.

26 C. A. Gollmer, Journal entry, Badagry, 2 Oct. 1846. CMS: CA 2/043.

27 Report of the Select Committee on British Possessions on the West Coast of Africa, PP 1842. XII (551), p. 20.

28 Doherty to G. W. Hope, London [?], 27 Oct. 1841. CO 267/166.

29 Shodeke to Macdonald, Abeokuta, 7 Jan. 1844, encl. in Fergusson to Stanley, Sierra Leone, 28 July 1845. CO 267/187.

30 Minute on Fergusson to Stanley, Sierra Leone, 28 July 1845. CO 267/187.

31 Letter from the Rev. Thomas Dove, Sierra Leone, 24 Nov. 1841, quoted in *The Friend of Africa*, no. 1 (June 1843), p. 11.

32 Crowther to Buxton, Sierra Leone, 14 April 1844, quoted in *The Friend of the African*, no. 14 (July 1844).

33 Crowther to Buxton, *Barque Adario*, at sea, 31 Dec. 1844, quoted in *The Friend of the Africans*, no. 25 (June 1845).

34 S. Annear, Journal, 21 Oct. 1844. MMS.

35 Charles A. Gollmer had been in Sierra Leone since 1841. He was from Würtemberg and had been trained at the Basel Seminary.

36 Fergusson to "English Governor of Badagry," 14 Dec. 1844; Fergusson to Shodeke, 12 Dec. 1844, encl. in Fergusson to Stanley, Sierra Leone, 28 July 1845. CO 267/187.

37 CMS Parent Committee (Henry Venn, Richard Davies, Dandeson Coates, secretaries) to Gollmer, Townsend, Crowther, 22 Oct. 1844, Instructions ... on the ... Commencement of a Mission at Abeokuta, West Africa. ... NRO: ECC 1/524.

38 *Ibid.*

39 Further Instructions.... CMS Parent Committee to Gollmer ..., 25 Nov. 1844. NRO: ECC 1/524.

40 Crowther to Buxton, Badagry, 2 July 1845, quoted in *The Friend of the Africans*, no. 29 (October 1845).

41 Gollmer was willing in this case even to consider rum. C. A. Gollmer, Journal for quarter ending 25 Nov. 1845. CMS: CA 2/043.

42 Crowther to Buxton, Badagry, 2 July 1845, quoted in *The Friend of the Africans*, no. 29 (October 1845).

43 Townsend to Coates, Badagry, 4 March 1845. CMS: CA 2/03.

44 *Ibid.*

45 Crowther to Buxton, Badagry, 2 July 1845, quoted in *The Friend of the Africans*, No. 29 (October 1845).

46 Biobaku, *The Egba*, p. 31.

47 William Savage, Yearly Reports, December 1845. NRO: ECC 2/1033. Townsend to Coates, Badagry, 27 June 1845. CMS: CA 2/03. Savage stressed that "nearly all the scholars are children who have never left

the country."; Townsend stated that at the CMS school 20 out of 26 children were from Sierra Leonian families. William Marsh reported the opening in that March of an adult school, with 40 emigrants in attendance. Journal for quarter ending 25 March 1845. CMS: CA 2/067.

48 W. Marsh, Journal for quarter ending 21 Dec. 1845. CMS: CA 2/067.

49 *Ibid.* "Of the Sierra Leone people some still persevere in the way of God, in the midst of the great temptations to which they are exposed .... One particularly, William Savage, keeps regular prayers at his house; at which time he explains the Holy Scripture, to about thirty of his relatives, in the Yoruba language.... Andrew Wilhelm generally goes among the Sierra Leone people as well as the natives on purpose to teach them."

50 Akitoye to British Subjects ..., Abeokuta, 8 Sept. 1845, encl. in S. Annear, Journal, 31 Aug. to 26 Sept. 1845. MMS.

51 To use Annear's term; Journal, November 1844. MMS.

52 Miss Tucker, *Abeokuta, or Sunrise Within the Tropics* (2nd ed.; London, 1853), p. 138.

53 One early emphatic statement of this feeling can be found in S. Annear, Journal, 21 Oct. 1844. MMS.

54 T. B. Freeman, MS., p. 414. MMS.

55 See S. Annear, Journal, December, 1844. MMS.

56 For examples see S. Annear, Journal, 21 Oct. 1844; John Martin, Journal entry, 7 July 1848; John Thomas, who in November 1847 replaced Martin, Journal, 9 Jan. 1849. MMS. Martin returned in June 1849.

57 Statement of Inquiry into a charge against Capt. W. Johnson, Badagry, 29 Sept. 1845. CMS: CA 2/05. Signed by Townsend, Gollmer, Crowther, and M. S. Parsons (Hutton's agent).

58 John Martin, Journal, 18 June 1846. MMS.

59 C. A. Gollmer, Journal, 5–7 Oct. 1850. CMS CA 2/043.

60 John Martin, Journal, 20 June 1846. MMS.

61 See John Thomas to General Secretaries, Badagry, 24 Oct. 1848, MMS, for one example. Just back from Abeokuta, he reported many cases of former Christians there with several wives.

62 Letter to T. B. Freeman, Badagry, 4 Nov. 1849, with a report from a Wesleyan convert from Abeokuta, quoted in Freeman, MS., p. 380. MMS. See also E. Bickersteth, Journal, 13–26 Oct. 1849. MMS.

63 E. Bickersteth to J. Ezzidio, Abeokuta, 7 May 1851. MMS. John Ezzidio was one of the signers of the original emigrant petition, and in 1851 was still in Freetown.

64 Fyfe, *History*, p. 292.

65 *Ogboni* is a traditional Egba political organization. See below, pp. 126–27.

CHAPTER 4

1 J. B. Wood, *Historical Notices of Lagos* (2nd ed.; Lagos, 1933), p. 28.

2 *The Travels of Richard and John Lander* (London, 1836), pp. 436 ff.

3 P. A. Talbot, *The Peoples of Southern Nigeria*, 4 vols. (London, 1926), I, 87.

4 Herbert Macaulay, Evidence (Exhibit D), Inquiry regarding the House of Docemo, 1933. NRO: CSO 33/1776. The other class of White Cap Chiefs is called *Idejo*. They hold communal title to the land and are the descendants of the sons of the *Olofin* from Iddo who originally, according to the accepted Yoruba interpretation, settled the island.

5 *Ibid.*

6 Wood, *Historical Notices*, p. 29.

7 J. B. O. Losi, *History of Lagos* (Lagos, 1914), p. 38.

8 *Ibid.*, pp. 41–42.

9 Herbert Macaulay, Evidence (exhibit D), Inquiry regarding the House of Docemo, 1933. NRO: CSO 33/1776.

10 For a discussion of this pressure, see Christopher Lloyd, *The Navy and the Slave Trade* (London, 1949), especially pp. 104–14.

11 For a thorough analysis of Venn's role in the outcome see J. F. Ade Ajayi, "Christian Missions and the Making of Nigeria, 1841–1891" (Ph. D. London, 1958), pp. 145–54.

12 S. Annear, Journal, Badagry, 1 Nov. 1844. MMS.

13 Emigrants at Badagry to S. Annear, 7 May 1845, encl. in Journal from 7 March 1845 to 7 May 1845. MMS. The petition is signed "William Sawyer, William Savage, William Johnson, Joseph Wright, John Thompson, etc. etc."

14 Townsend to Coates, Badagry, 20 Aug. 1845. CMS: CA 2/03.

15 See K. O. Diké, *Trade and Politics in the Niger Delta* (Oxford, 1956), pp. 83 ff.

16 See T. B. Freeman, Journal of voyage to Badagry and Dahomey, 1842–3, Jan. 1843. MMS.

17 Gollmer, Martin, and William Marsh accompanied Hutton and his agent, Parsons, on one of these trips. See W. Marsh, Journal, 25 Jan. 1847. CMS: CA 2/067.

18 Palmerston to Beecroft, 30 June 1849. Papers Relative to the Reduction of Lagos, PP 1852. LIV (221), pp. 1–2.

19 Missionaries at Abeokuta to Commodore Fanshaw, 7 Nov. 1850. PP 1852. LIV (221), pp. 99–101.

20 The orders were frequently repeated, with the intensity of the blockade being continually increased. The beginning of the severe pressure came after Palmerston to Lord Commissioners of the Admiralty, 27 Sept. 1851. PP 1852. LIV (221), p. 135.

21 See C. A. Gollmer, Journal for Jan. 1851. CMS: CA 2/043.

22 C. A. Gollmer, Journal, 8 May 1851. CMS: CA 2/043.

23 Palmerston to Beecroft, 25 Feb. 1850. FO 2/84.

24 S. Annear, Journal, Badagry, 21 Oct. 1844. MMS.

25 Townsend to CMS Secretaries, Exeter, 17 Oct. 1849. PP 1852. LIV (221), pp. 30–4.

26 Palmerston to Beecroft, 25 Feb. 1850. FO 2/84.

27 Beecroft to Palmerston, *Bonetta*, at Prince's Island, 22 July 1850. PP 1852. LIV (221), pp. 40–3.

28 Fanshawe to King of Dahomey, *Centaur*, at Prince's Island, 23 July 1850, and Palmerston to Beecroft, 23 Oct. 1850. *Ibid.*, pp. 77–9.

29 See C. A. Gollmer, Journal for Jan. 1851, CMS: CA 2/043, for a detailed description of these events; also Beecroft's report of his mission to Badagry and Abeokuta, 21 Feb. 1851. PP 1852. LIV (221), pp. 91 ff.

30 See above, pp. 65–6.

31 Domingo José Martinez, originally from Madeira, was based in Porto Novo, where he traded in slaves, palm oil, and rum. Thought the most evil of slave traders by the British in Badagry, his driving concern seems to have been any profitable trade. For, with his part in opening the road from Badagry to Abeokuta, he was not unaware of the missionary intention to promote legitimate trade there. And with Akitoye's increasing contact with the British, it was at least possible that alliance with him, if he succeeded in regaining Lagos, would bring Domingo profits from palm oil, not slaves.

32 S. Annear, Journal, Badagry, 7 June 1845. MMS.

33 See C. A. Gollmer, Journal for Oct. 1850, for a discussion of these developments. CMS: CA 2/043.

34 Akitoye to Beecroft, encl. in Beecroft to Palmerston, Fernando Po, 24 Feb. 1851. PP 1852. LIV (221), pp. 97–8.

35 Beecroft to Palmerston, Fernando Po, 21 Feb. 1851, no. 2. FO 84/858.

36 C. A. Gollmer, Journal, Badagry, 28 Jan. and 29 Jan. 1851. CMS: CA 2/043.

37 See above, p. 59. C. A. Gollmer, Journal, Badagry, 5–7 Oct. 1850. CMS: CA 2/043.

38 Gollmer to Straith, Badagry, 9 Feb. 1851. CMS: CA 2/043. Gollmer reported an interview between Beecroft and the Sierra Leonians on 27 January: "The first question the Consul put to them was — do you consider yourselves British subjects? Yes. Would you seek British protection suppose anyone were to injure you? Yes. Well, if you consider yourselves British subjects you must abide by British law! but many of you do not do so, only to mention one thing — some of you have bought Slaves, true you say not to sell them again, but to make them your servants — but do you know that I nor any other British subject, can not buy nor hold a Slave even as a servant. You must consider these Slaves as free people as free as yourselves."

39 See for example British residents of Badagry to Capt. Foote, 16 June 1851. PP 1852. LIV (221), pp. 125–6, and Liberated Africans to Capt. Heath, Badagry, 23 July 1851. CMS: CA 2/05.

40 Petition, British Residents in Badagry to Any of H. M.'s Officers on the West Coast of Africa, 18 Aug. 1845, encl. in S. Annear, Journal, Badagry, 20 Aug. 1845. MMS.

41 In Meade's minute on Macdonald to Grey, Sierra Leone, 3 Aug. 1850, CO 267/215, he wrote, "I scarcely see in what manner a 'Liberated African' who leaves Sierra Leone and settles in the interior is a 'British Subject.' If born in the Colony he would be so of course." The despatch contains a report from Capt. Forbes of the *Bonetta* on impending Dahomean attack upon Abeokuta, referring to it as "a wanton act of aggression upon a peaceable community of British Subjects." The debate over interpretation continued a year later, with Meade writing, "There may be a difference between an African merely 'liberated' and let loose, and a liberated African who has acquired and retains a domicile in Sierra Leone." Another opinion (Rogers?) maintained, "I have sup posed Liberated Africans became ipso facto British Subjects under the Slave Con [?] Act. How otherwise can they be bound 'apprentices' etc. – they have been always suffered to enjoy the rights and privileges of British Subjects." The question was not resolved, and it is evident that the position of liberated Africans remaining in Sierra Leone itself was not yet clear either.

42 For one example, see Townsend to CMS secretaries, Exeter, 17 Oct. 1849. PP 1852. LIV (221), p. 34. Townsend mentioned instances of the recapturing of Sierra Leonians by slave traders in Abeokuta and wrote, "it may be urged, that . . . such instances of the contempt and defeat of the benevolent intentions of the British Government afford a ground of inquiry and remonstrance, at least, with the Chiefs of Lagos."

43 Beecroft to Palmerston, Fernando Po, 21 Feb. 1851, PP 1852. LIV (221), p. 92.

44 Missionaries at Abeokuta to Commodore Fanshawe, 7 Nov. 1850. *Ibid.*, pp. 99–100.

45 See below, pp. 78, 79.

46 C. Lloyd, *The Navy and the Slave Trade*, pp. 94–95.

47 An account of Crowther's visit to Windsor appears in E. Stock, *History of the Church Missionary Society*, Vols. I–III (London, 1899), II, 111–13.

48 H. Straith to Palmerston, 20 Aug. 1851. PP 1852. LIV (221), p. 134.

49 Palmerston to S. Crowther, 18 Dec. 1851. *Ibid.*, p. 142.

50 Palmerston to Beecroft, 20 Feb. 1851, and Palmerston to Admiralty, 27 Sept. 1851. *Ibid.*, pp. 83 and 136.

51 Admiralty to Bruce, 14 Oct. 1851. *Ibid.*, p. 138.

52 See C. A. Gollmer, Journal for June-Dec. 1851. CMS: CA 2/043.

53 Admiralty to Bruce, 14 Oct. 1851. PP 1852. LIV (221), p. 138.

54 Bruce to Admiralty, 6 Dec. 1851, and enclosures. *Ibid.*, pp. 161–7. Bruce also gave the order to all of Her Majesty's Naval Forces for the total blockade of the coast, excepting Badagry, to date from 1 Jan. 1852.

55 Thomas King, Journal, 1 Oct. 1851. CMS: CA 2/061.

56 Speech, Forbes to Sierra Leonians, Abeokuta, 24 Nov. 1851, encl. in Forbes to Bruce, Abeokuta, 9 Dec. 1851. PP 1852. LIV (221), p. 182.

57 *Ibid.*, pp. 145–69.

58 Wilmot to Bruce, *Harlequin*, off Lagos, 1 Dec. 1851. *Ibid.*, p. 211.
59 See Beecroft to Palmerston, *Bloodhound*, off Lagos, 3 Jan. 1852. *Ibid.*, pp. 187–90.
60 Treaty, encl. in Beecroft to Palmerston, Lagos, 3 Jan. 1852, no. 72. FO 84/886.
61 Copies and summaries of these treaties, as well as ones with the King of Dahomey (13 Jan. 1852), the Chiefs of Porto Novo (17 Jan. 1852) and other chiefs between Lagos and the Gold Coast forts are included in Wodehouse to Campbell, 28 Feb. 1853. FO 84/920.
62 E. Hieke, *Zur Geschichte des Deutschen Handels mit Ostafrika*, 1 vol. (Hamburg, 1949), I, 119. Diederichsen's trade had previously been centered in Whydah and had been disrupted by the conflicts of the preceding months.
63 *Ibid.*, p. 120. The transfer took place early in 1853.
64 C. A. Gollmer, Journal for May–Dec. 1852. CMS: CA 2/043.
65 As Ajayi points out ("Christian Missions," p. 243) the mediation had been started by the Egba, who saw that the futile siege could continue indefinitely, and to whom the route to Badagry was less important since the opening of Lagos. See Townsend to Venn, 23 Aug. 1853. Townsend subsequently gave full credit for the successful negotiation to Andrew Wilhelm: with "his untiring and judicious efforts with the Chiefs here [Abeokuta], they were induced to further the efforts." Townsend to Venn, annual letter, Abeokuta, 1 March 1867, reporting Wilhelm's death. CMS: CA 2/085.
66 Gollmer to Venn, Lagos, 8 Sept. 1853. CMS: CA 2/043.
67 Benjamin Campbell, an early European trader in Sierra Leone who worked for the Liberated African Department in Freetown, was consul at Lagos from 1853 to 1859.
68 Gardiner to T. B. Freeman, Lagos, 9 Sept. 1853. Ghana archives: SC 4/84.
69 *Ibid.*
70 Elderly men and women in Lagos today, while agreeing that the abolition of the slave trade and the necessary installation of Akitoye may have been desirable, testify to the importance the Lagos people are said to have placed on the dominant and determined character of Kosoko, in contrast to the weak vacillation of Akitoye.
71 Gardiner to T. B. Freeman, Lagos, 9 Sept. 1853. Ghana Archives: SC 4/84.
72 C. A. Gollmer, Journal, 3 Sept. 1853. Gollmer reported that on being told of the King's death, he immediately informed Consul Campbell who "convened at once a council, consisting of three of the royal council, and three captains of war, who unanimously elected Dosumu . . . as the new King of Lagos: and he was this same afternoon installed." CMS: CA 2/043.
73 Dr. E. Irving, the CMS lay agent, who was less biased than most observers, commented, "Both the Consul and Mr. Bedingfield seem to have been much impressed with the hospitality, good intentions and general superiority of Kosoko with his Caboceers over the young King Dosumu and

his small remnant of Lagos Chiefs. In fact so much so was the case that I endeavoured to point out that this was not a point of dispute between two individuals but one of vital interest as to the final triumph in this matter of the world of Slavery or Anti-slavery, and that Kosoko was a clever and designing Savage." Irving to Venn, Lagos, 20 Jan. 1854. CMS: CA 2/052.

74 Gardiner to Hoole, Lagos, 8 March 1855. MMS.

75 Irving to Venn, Abeokuta, 1 June 1854. CMS: CA 2/052.

76 See Gollmer to Venn, Lagos, 29 July 1854. CMS: CA 2/043. See also the detailed controversy in Campbell to Irving, Lagos, 22 Aug. 1854, and Irving to Campbell, Ibadan, 9 Oct. 1854. CMS: CA 2/04. Campbell's action was rather reluctantly approved by the Foreign Office on the grounds of the "participation of Mayu in Slave trading operations of Domingo Martinez." Foreign Office to Campbell, 21 Feb. 1855. FO 84/976.

77 See correspondence in FO 84/976, 1855. The usual wider points of disagreement entered the dispute, and Gardiner of the Wesleyan Mission, as well as Sandeman and McCoskry, sided with Campbell.

78 Campbell to Clarendon, Lagos, 15 Feb. 1855, no. 3. FO 84/976. Campbell had, in addition to sending arms to Abeokuta, written to the King of Dahomey to try to prevent his attack. But he was coming to the view, undoubtedly influenced by his enmity for the missionaries working with the Egba, that the Dahomean attacks on Abeokuta were "far from entirely unprovoken," for he had lists of towns raided by the Egba both before and after the first Dahomean attack.

79 See below, pp. 105ff.

80 On 28 Sept. 1854, Campbell and Kosoko signed a "treaty," whereby Kosoko renounced the slave trade, and in exchange for this and his agreement to give up his attempts to take Lagos, he was to be the recognized authority over the port of Palma, and receive an annual subsidy from the British of 2,000 heads of cowries for the rest of his life if the agreement were not violated. Agreement with Kosoko, signed at Epe, 28 Sept. 1854, encl. in Campbell to Clarendon, Lagos, 1 Oct. 1854, no. 26. FO 84/950.

81 Thomas King to Venn, Abeokuta, 3 April 1858. CMS: CA 2/061. King said that Kosoko was bribing the Egba chiefs to support his plan to blockade Lagos from Ijebu, Abeokuta, and Otta, thus hoping to drive out the English completely. Such plans were continually being proposed and tried.

82 Campbell to Clarendon, Lagos, 1 Oct. 1856, no. 32. FO 84/1002. Campbell wrote of Kosoko's offer to aid the Dahomeans in their proposed attack on Abeokuta, in return for Dahomean aid in a plan to capture Ado and then land at Lagos.

CHAPTER 5

1 Gollmer to Venn, Lagos, 6 April 1853. CMS: CA 2/043. Petitions were sent to the consul in the hope of improving conditions on the mail boats.

One set of petitions told of "having suffered much inconveniences by the mails, more especially at the shipping and landing from and to places on the Coasts, by which many of us at times took passage up and down the roads from Sierra Leone to Lagos." Memorial to Campbell, Lagos, n.d., encl. in Campbell to Clarendon, Lagos, 24 Aug. 1854, no. 25. FO 84/950. The signatories were: W. Savage; James Gooding; Samuel B. Williams; Thomas C. Cole; Harry Pratt, X; Samuel William, X; Henry Lumbkin, X; Annie Euba; Edward Forster, X; William Johnson; Thos. Davies, X; John Moses, X; William Peters, X; J. T. Nottidge.

2 W. McCoskry, testimony, Report of the Committee on the Condition of the Settlements on the West Coast of Africa, PP 1865. V (1), p. 68, question 1458. The estimate given by Robert Campbell in 1859 is one-twentieth: 1,500 out of a total Lagos population of 30,000, *A Pilgrimage to My Motherland* (New York, 1861), p. 18. He calculated there were 5,000 emigrants from Sierra Leone, Brazil, and Cuba in Yoruba country, with concentrations in Lagos and Abeokuta. *Ibid.*, p. 73.

3 The other term by which the emigrants were called, according to S. O. Biobaku, *The Egba and Their Neighbours, 1842–1872* (Oxford, 1957), p. 52, *n.* 2, was used to refer to a Sierra Leonian who made particular efforts to approximate the behavior of the Englishman, for "oyinbo" is still used to refer to a white man. Its derivation is from a word meaning "that which has the skin peeled off."

4 See Lorenzo Turner, "African Survivals in the New World . . .," in *Africa Seen by American Negroes* ([Paris, 1958]), pp. 105 ff. In Brazil manumission was comparatively easy: a child of a slave mother and a white father became free; owners who mistreated their slaves could be forced to liberate them; on 85 — in some states 104 — days of the year slaves were allowed to earn money to buy their freedom, at a price no higher than that at which they had been purchased.

5 Campbell to Clarendon, Lagos, 28 Dec. 1853, no. 28. FO 84/886. These particular families may have been refugees from the so-called "Hausa" rebellions in Bahia in the late 1830's. According to Governor Moloney, writing in 1887, "they began first to repatriate in 1840 but in consequence of the unsettled state of the coastline, and of the notoriety of Lagos as a slave export depot, most migrated into the interior. . . . Though they did not repatriate in any number before the cession, 1862, their permanent settlement here began in a small way with the restoration in Lagos in 1847 of some sense of personal security consequent on the encouragement and confidence extended to the negroes of Brazil from a visit, under the authority of Kosoko . . . to them of Chief Tapa, alias Oshodi. . . ." Moloney to Holland, Lagos, 20 July 1887. CO 147/59.

6 A few of the New World emigrants did not retain Roman Catholicism as their European religion. Gardiner, the Methodist missionary in Lagos, wrote in 1854, "A number of Brazilians and Spanish Emigrants have joined us, and coming as they do from Catholic countries, we are all the

more astonished, and grateful to the Giver of Grace." E. A. Gardiner, Yearly report, Dec., 1854. NRO: ECC 2/1033.

7 A. B. Laotan, *The Torch Bearers or Old Brazilian Colony in Lagos* (Lagos, [1943]), p. 6. Actually "Papae and Mamae" applied to men and women who had been born in West Africa; "Yoyo and Yaya" were the names given to those born in Brazil. Gradually, though, the distinction became blurred, with "Papae and Mamae" referring to all older members of the community.

8 J. Chapman to James Beale, 22 Oct. 1855. CMS: CA 1/I, pp. 12–13.

9 Campbell to Malmesbury, Lagos, 4 Feb. 1859, no. 2. FO 2/28. Campbell was contemplating issuing the "passports" in Arabic to impress the Muslim rulers.

10 In 1855 the Wesleyan secretary wrote to T. B. Freeman at Cape Coast, "A party of Lagos people from Havana, on their return to their own country, are to sail by the Packet that conveys this letter. They are 'Emancipados,' having purchased their liberty for 13,000 dollars, and have paid 100 dollars for the passage of each adult. They are, 14 men, 12 women, and 22 children." E. Hoole to T. B. Freeman, London, 18 Aug. 1855. NRO: ECC 2/1096.

11 See "Plan of the Town of Lagos," drawn by the colonial surveyor, W. T. G. Lawson, a Sierra Leonian, pp. 90–3.

12 Laotan, *Old Brazilian Colony*, p. 6.

13 R. Burton, *Wanderings in West Africa from Liverpool to Fernando Po.* 2 vols. (London, 1863), p. 222.

14 Osborne, C. J., opinion in Att.-Gen. v. John Holt & Co., 1910. *Law Reports*, House of Lords, London, 1915.

15 It is unclear whether Wood meant indigenous people or emigrants by the term "Lagosian"; the statement quoted tends to imply the former, but he later refers to "Lagosian" clerks and ministers of religion. J. B. Wood, "On the Inhabitants of Lagos" (printed with *Historical Notices of Lagos*, [Lagos, 1933]), p. 57.

16 Gollmer to Venn, Lagos, 24 April 1852. CMS: CA 2/043.

17 Agreement with the King and Chiefs of Lagos, 28 Feb. 1852. PP 1862. LXI (339), pp. 2–4.

18 Cf. K. O. Diké, *Trade and Politics in the Niger Delta, 1830–1885* (Oxford, 1956), pp. 41–3; and C. Gertzel, "John Holt: A British Merchant in West Africa in the Era of Imperialism" (D. Phil., Oxon., 1959), p. 521.

19 See above, pp. 83–4.

20 See N. H. Stilliard, "The Rise and Development of Legitimate Trade in Palm Oil with West Africa" (M. A., Birmingham, 1938), pp. 91–2.

21 E. Hieke, *Zur Geschichte des Deutschen Handels mit Ostafrika*, 1 vol. (Hamburg, 1939), I, 174.

22 See P. T. Bauer, *West African Trade* (Cambridge, 1954), pp. 22–8, for a discussion of the importance of these functions in the West-African economic context.

23 See Evidence before the Commission on Lagos Trade, encl. in Denton to Chamberlain, Lagos, 4 June 1898. CO 147/133. See especially the testimony of Seidu Olowu and James O'Connor Williams, 6 April 1898, and Edward B. Joseph, 7 April 1898.

24 These are the names of some of the signatories to an agreement with Dosunmu, signed 10 Feb. 1859. Encl. in Lodder to Malmesbury, Lagos, 30 May 1859, no. 7. FO 2/28.

25 See below, pp. 117–18, for the encouragement of cotton production, especially by the CMS, though with Campbell's assistance. Robbin was a key figure in the CMS industrial plans.

26 Robbin to Venn, Lagos, n.d. (received, 12 Dec. 1857). CMS: CA 2/o80.

27 *Ibid.*

28 Robbin to Clegg, Abeokuta, 2 March 1858. CMS: CA 2/o80.

29 *Ibid.*

30 On the trade agreement, encl. in Lodder to Malmesbury, Lagos, 30 May 1859, no. 7, FO 2/28, there were only two Brazilian names: Francisco Gomez and Joachim D'Abreu.

31 Laotan, *Old Brazilian Colony*, p. 6.

32 See below, p. 169.

33 Hieke, *Deutschen Handels*, I, 124. See also Campbell to Clarendon, Lagos, 5 Jan. 1857, containing Report on Trade of the Bight of Benin for the year 1856. Papers Relating to the Cultivation of Cotton in West Africa, PP 1857. XXXVIII (255), p. 4.

34 Campbell to Clarendon, Lagos, 7 Dec. 1854, no. 36. FO 84/950. In fact, however, Campbell reported that "at least 80 per cent of the Tobacco and rum shipped from Bahia is consigned to, or purchased by, Domingo Martinez."

35 S. O. Biobaku, "Madame Tinubu," in K. O. Diké, ed., *Eminent Nigerians of the Nineteenth Century* (Cambridge, 1960), pp. 34–5.

36 J. B. O. Losi, *History of Lagos* (Lagos, 1914), pp. 57–8.

37 Campbell to Clarendon, Lagos, 2 Feb. 1855, no. 1. FO 84/976.

38 Campbell to Clarendon, Lagos, 12 Feb. 1855, no. 2. FO 84/976.

39 *Ibid.*

40 *Ibid.*

41 Campbell to Clarendon, Lagos, 2 June 1855, no. 8. FO 84/976.

42 Campbell to Clarendon, Lagos, 2 Aug. 1855, no. 12. FO 84/976.

43 Minutes of a meeting of the committee, 19 May 1855, encl. in *ibid.* Present were William Savage, James Gooding, Harry Pratt, J. M. Turner, J. C. Davis, J. T. Nottidge, Annie Euba, J. R. Thomas, John Thomas, John Davis, Thomas C. Cole, Thomas Davis, Thomas Gabbidon, Pedro, S. B. Williams, Samuel Williams, William Ray.

44 Campbell to Clarendon, Lagos, 29 Nov. 1856, no. 34. FO 84/1002.

45 Campbell to Clarendon, Lagos, 30 Aug. 1855, no. 15. FO 84/976.

46 *Ibid.*

47 Campbell to Clarendon, Lagos, 2 Oct. 1855, no. 22. FO 84/976. Among

the men at the meeting was "an influential man among the Sierra Leone people who had a Brig of 160 Tons now at Anchor off Lagos waiting for a cargo of Palm Oil."

48 Rules of "Abbeokutan Mercantile Association," 16 July 1860, encl. in Hand to Russell, Lagos, 13 Aug. 1860, no. 63. FO 84/1115.

49 Campbell to Clarendon, Lagos, 1 Oct. 1855, no. 21. FO 2/13.

50 McCoskry to Campbell, Lagos, 17 March 1856, encl. in Campbell to Clarendon, Lagos, 23 June 1856, no. 9. FO 2/17.

51 McCoskry to Hickley, Lagos, 18 March 1856, encl in Campbell to Clarendon, Lagos, 26 March 1856, no. 10. FO 84/1002.

52 Campbell to Hickley, Lagos, 26 March 1856. From a Badagry letter book. I am indebted to Dr. C. Gertzel for this reference.

53 Campbell to Clarendon, Lagos, 23 June 1856, no. 9. FO 2/17.

54 McCoskry's appointment as vice-consul was cancelled because of his participation in protecting Madame Tinubu. *Ibid.*

55 Hermann Grote to O'Swald and Co., Lagos, 28 Jan. 1853, quoted in Hieke, *Deutschen Handels*, I, 120. " 'The influence which the English have consists only of their cannon . . . . Here in Lagos the Hamburg flag dominates . . . . The English are bursting with envy; by legal means alone they cannot cause us damage.' " See also Campbell to Clarendon, Lagos, 27 June 1853, no. 22. FO 2/9.

56 Cowries, small shells obtainable only in the Indian Ocean, in the nineteenth century were the medium of exchange most acceptable to West Africans. In 1850 the cost of cowries in Zanzibar was between one-sixth and one-eighth their sale price in West Africa. The units of value in 1850 were the string (toka), equal to 40 shells; the gallina, equal to 200 shells; later, especially after 1860, though a string was still 40 cowries, a gallina was 10 strings, or 400 shells; the next unit was the head, containing 5 gallina or 2000 shells. The largest unit was the sack, of 12 head or 24,000 cowries. Hieke, *Deutschen Handels*, I, 73–4.

57 *Ibid.*, I, 126.

58 *Ibid.* Tapa had first enlisted Grote's aid in March 1853 to bring pressure upon Akitoye to return a wife he had "stolen" (I, 122); in 1854 and 1855 Grote gave various gifts to the trader (I, 127). The rapprochement with Kosoko had influenced the growth of the trade in Palma until in 1854 it "was near to being the second most important palm oil market in the Bight of Benin" (I, 127).

59 *Ibid.*, I, 125.

60 *Ibid.*, I, 128–9.

61 *Ibid.*, I, 131.

62 Agreement between "Docemo and Merchants and Supercargoes of the Ships in the Roads," Lagos, commencing 27 March 1854, encl. in Campbell to Clarendon, Lagos, 1 June 1854, no. 11. FO 84/950.

63 Campbell to Clarendon, Lagos, 14 May 1856, no. 15. FO 84/1002.

64 *Ibid.*

65 *Ibid.*

66 *Ibid.*

67 Encl. in Campbell to Clarendon, Lagos, 25 Sept. 1856, no. 31. FO 84/1002. The petition was signed by the following (the emigrants' names are starred): McCoskry; Sandeman; Hansen; *John Macaulay; *J. M. Turner; *Jas. P. L. Davies; *Thos. F. Cole; *Wm. Edwin Cole, X; H. Woodhead (agent for Bristol firm); A. Legresley.

68 Campbell to Clarendon, Lagos, 2 June 1857, no. 10. FO 2/20. Gregory, unable to carry on a private trade because of the bylaws of the firms with which he was connected in England, had engaged a M. Desnaux to conduct his trade in 1856; it was when this link was discovered that Gregory brought counter accusations against Williams and Scala.

69 *Ibid.*, and encl., Turner to Campbell, Lagos, 2 June 1857. Turner was subsequently appointed by Consul Foote "to visit the Market of Ejirin in order to settle disputes between Lagos people and the Jebus and thus to prevent fights and disturbances," although Foote "had no power to create any such post, that appertaining to Docemo. After the cession . . . Mr. Turner was kept on in his post and was allowed a boat and four boatmen to take him to and from the Market." Freeman to Newcastle, Lagos, 3 June 1863. CO 147/5. Turner remained at Ejirin until Freeman burned the Market. See below, p. 147.

70 Clarendon to Campbell, 22 Aug. 1857. FO 2/20. Campbell replied angrily, asking if he were expected to take the part of the British merchant in all cases.

71 Hieke, *Deutschen Handels,* I, 152. O'Swald and Company petitioned Lord Clarendon through the Resident Minister of the Hanseatic League in London.

72 *Ibid.*, p. 132.

73 Campbell to Clarendon, Lagos, 7 Feb. 1859, no. 6. FO 2/28.

74 Agreement of 10 Feb. 1859, encl. in Lodder to Malmesbury, Lagos, 30 May 1859, no. 7. FO 2/28. The signatories were as follows (the emigrants' names are starred): King Docemo; E. Dominges; Vincenzo Paggi (for Scala); *W. A. Savage; *J. M. Turner; *Jas. P. L. Davies; *James Cole, X; *Samuel Crowther [Jr.?] & Co.; *I. H. Willoughby; *Thomas F. Cole; *Samuel Williams, X; *William I. Cole, X; *Walter Lewis; Herr Grote (for Wm. O'Swald and Co.); W. McCoskry; Walter Hansen; A Legresley; E. W. Thompson; H. Horner (for John Chillingworth and Co.); *Aymez; *Emanuel Pittaluga Ezio; G. Carrena; *James Thompson; *James George, X; *Thos. C. Cole, X; *I. R. Thomas; *Francisco Gomez, X; *Joaquim D'Abreu, X.

75 Brand to Russell, Lagos, 12 Jan. 1860, no. 1. FO 2/35.

76 Minutes of Commercial Conference, Lagos, 10 Feb. 1859, encl. in *ibid.* James Cole, Peter Jones, and James Robert submitted a collective bid of 2,000 bags; G. B. Scala, who was renewing his application, put forward 1,810 bags, and I. H. Willoughby, 1,600.

77 Minutes of Commercial Conference, Lagos, 12 Jan. 1860, encl. in *ibid.* The only other bid was from W. A. Savage, 1,800 bags of cowries.

78 Freeman to Russell, Lagos, 5 March 1862, encl. in Freeman to Newcastle, Lagos, 8 March 1862. CO 147/1. See also below, pp. 142–43.

79 Freeman to Russell, Lagos, 5 March 1862, encl. in Freeman to Newcastle, Lagos, 8 March 1862. CO 147/1. McCoskry agreed to give Dosunmu 1,800 a year for the revenue "on the express condition that the contract should be for three years, for though he was expecting to lose the first year, he was convinced that the encreased Trade would enable him to make up the deficit afterwards."

80 Foote to Russell, Lagos, 9 Feb. 1861. PP 1862. LXI (147), p. 4.

81 For several contemporaneous considerations of this distinction see Robert Campbell, *A Pilgrimage to My Motherland*, pp. 64–5; and S. Johnson, *History of the Yorubas, From the Earliest Times to the Beginning of the British Protectorate*. Ed., O. Johnson (London, 1921), pp. 324–7.

82 Townsend to Venn, Abeokuta, 30 Jan. 1857. CMS: CA 2/03a.

83 See also E. A. Gardiner, Yearly Report, Lagos, Dec. 1855. NRO: ECC 2/1033. Campbell to Clarendon, Lagos, 18 Feb. 1856, no. 6. FO 84/1002.

84 Campbell to Clarendon, Lagos, 2 July 1857, no. 18. FO 84/1031. "Slaves" of S. B. Williams and John Thomas had fled to Abeokuta. The Foreign Office (Clarendon to Campbell, 21 Aug. 1857. FO 84/1031.) replied that they felt "the utmost dissatisfaction" with "the practice," and with the emigrants for indulging in it. The problem became a more difficult one for the British authorities after the establishment of the Colony, when domestic slaves from the hinterland fled into Lagos for safety. See below, p. 148.

85 See Foote to Russell, Lagos, 4 Feb. 1861, no. 5. FO 84/1141, for one example.

86 Brand to Russell, Lagos, 18 Jan. 1860, no. 2. FO 84/1115.

87 Brand to Russell, Lagos, 8 Feb. 1860, no. 6. FO 84/1115.

88 Foreign Office to Hutchinson, 19 Oct. 1856. FO 84/1001.

89 Foote to Russell, Lagos, 4 Feb. 1861, no. 5. FO 84/1141.

CHAPTER 6

1 Campbell to Clarendon, Lagos, 30 Nov. 1853, no. 12. FO 2/9.

2 *Ibid.*

3 See Campbell to E. Irving, 4 April 1855, encl. in Campbell to Clarendon, Lagos, 4 April 1855, no. 5. FO 84/976.

4 Bruce to Admiralty, *Penelope*, at Ascension, 17 Jan. 1852. PP 1852. LIV (221), p. 213.

5 Foote to Russell, Lagos, 9 Feb. 1861, no. 6. FO 84/1141. Although the sources are inconsistent in spelling the name, Pearce and Pearse in these references are the same person.

6 Russell to Foote, 23 March 1861. FO 84/1141. See also below, p. 130.

7 S. B. Williams to Campbell, Lagos, 10 Aug. 1857, encl. in Campbell to Clarendon, Lagos, 10 Aug. 1857, no. 28. FO 84/1031.

8 Willoughby to Campbell, 18 Aug. 1856, encl. in Campbell to Clarendon, Lagos, 19 Aug. 1856, no. 27. FO 84/1002.
"Hint.
"The traffic in slaves from this to Porto Novo is vigorously in persuance again.
"Which authority should cry against.
"Sir — I hope I am no intruder when I sent in this piece of information. Of the evidences above I am not to be questioned. As I am one against the horrible traffic in slaves I should not be silent and as such I sent in this Hint . . . from . . . I. H. Will O. B. Silent Observer."

9 Campbell to Clarendon, Lagos, 14 May 1856, no. 15. FO 84/1002.

10 Encl. in Campbell to Clarendon, Lagos, 25 Sept. 1856, no. 31. FO 84/1002. See above, p. 106. The signatories felt that Campbell had assumed too many powers and was persecuting them particularly, along with all "British Subjects."

11 Emigrants to Adams, Lagos, 10 Oct. 1856, encl. in Campbell to Clarendon, Lagos, 29 Nov. 1856, no. 34. FO 84/1002. Another more usual petition was enclosed as well: it too was sent to the Commodore, and it showed concern with political conditions in Lagos, possible imminent attack by Kosoko, and the interference of some of the merchants. It requested protection and was signed by Savage, Williams, Thompson, and forty-nine others.

12 Brand to Russell, Lagos, 30 Dec. 1859, no. 13. FO 84/1088. The "directors" of the Benevolent Association were: J. B. Coker, I. E. Williams, I. H. Willoughby, T. G. Hamilton, T. J. Marshall, Abr. C. Willoughby, Simeon Puddicombe. The chairman of the Road Improving Society was J. G. Hughes and the secretary, Samuel Crowther, Junior. Other members listed were: C. B. Macaulay, H. Robbin, Robt. Campbell, J. C. Dewring, Josiah Crowther, C. W. Faulkner, F. Ribeiro.

13 Hand to Russell, Lagos, 13 Aug. 1860, no. 63. FO 84/1115. See above, p. 102–03.

14 Campbell to Malmesbury, Lagos, 2 May 1858, no. 6. FO 2/24. Of the Consul's "contingent expenses" for 1857, almost one-third — £12.12.7½ — was spent on five such messengers on six missions: two to Badagry; one to Badagry and Porto Novo; two to Otta to mediate successfully between Badagry and Ado; and one to Ofin to take presents to the "king of Jaboo Ofin" who was facing threats from Ijebu Ode, to negotiate keeping open the roads between Lagos and Ibadan, and to encourage the cultivation of cotton.

15 T. Laing to Committee, Lagos, 4 Sept. 1857, and E. Bickersteth to Committee, Abeokuta, n.d., 1859. MMS.

16 Instructions, CMS Secretaries to Hinderer, 11 Jan. 1849. CMS: CA 2/11.

17 D. Hinderer, Journal, 13 Sept. to 16 Oct. 1850, conclusion.

18 Some of Townsend's objections were for personal reasons. See below, p. 132.

19 These figures are not given concisely anywhere; they are drawn from the collections of journals and correspondence of the individual missionaries. CMS: CA 2/018-098. The figures are somewhat misleading because they include all Europeans, whatever the period of their service; several, such as Dr. Van Cooten at Badagry, died after only a year on the coast. CMS: CA 2/086. The figures include lay evangelists, lay agents, and medical missionaries.

20 The information that follows comes from the personal files of each of these men; the files are in the CMS archives.

21 Campbell to the Wawu, Possu, etc., Lagos, 28 Dec. 1854. CMS: CA 2/04.

22 As Robert Campbell wrote in 1859, "The congregations of these churches [in Lagos and Abeokuta] consist principally of people from Sierra Leone. There are many native pupils who also attend the services at the churches, but the number of adult converts is small, except . . . among people from Sierra Leone." A Pilgrimage to My Motherland (New York, 1861), p. 80.

23 Encl., 1 April 1855 in Campbell to Clarendon, Lagos, 28 May 1855, no. 8. FO 84/976. The signatories were as follows (the emigrants' names are starred): Grote, Sandeman, Hansen, E. A. Gardiner, McCoskry, Thos. R. T. Tickel, Edward Lynch, T. Tickel, G. B. Scala, *Rodrigo Blaldo [?], *Antonio Martinez, *S. B. Williams, *James Gooding, *I. R. Thomas, *J. R. Nottidge, *George Lisboa, *Francisco Gomes, *Benedicto Flornicio [?], *Lizzerdo, *George Williams, A. Legresley, *J. M. Turner. Six additional names are illegible, but seem to be Brazilian.

24 Henry Venn, Instructions to Missionaries on the subject of Missions and Politics, quoted in Eugene Stock, The History of the Church Missionary Society, 3 vols. (London, 1899), II, 304.

25 S. O. Biobaku, "An Historical Sketch of Egba Traditional Authorities," Africa, XXII, no. 1 (Jan., 1952), 48.

26 When Campbell confirmed his suspicion that the stopping of trade between Abeokuta and Lagos had concerned Egba military expeditions against Dahomey (Campbell to Clarendon, 30 Aug. 1855, no. 15. FO 84/976), he protested to the Sagbua, who admitted that his authority was inadequate to end such aggressions though he disapproved of them. Campbell to Clarendon, Lagos, 9 Oct. 1855, no. 26. FO 84/976.

27 Campbell to Clarendon, Lagos, 15 Feb. 1855, no. 3. FO 84/976.

28 Gollmer to Venn, Lagos, 15 Jan. 1853. CMS: CA 2/043. See also Crowther's account of the trip, CA 2/031.

29 Stock, History of the CMS, II, 110.

30 Ibid., p. 111.

31 Irving to Venn, Ake, Abeokuta, 4 Aug. 1854. CMS: CA 2/052.

32 Robbin to Venn, Sierra Leone, 25 Feb. and 8 April, and Lagos, 9 May 1856. CMS: CA 2/080.

33 Robbin to Venn, Abeokuta, 26 May 1856. CMS: CA 2/080.

34 Ibid.

35 Robbin to Venn, Abeokuta, 2 March 1858. CMS: CA 2/o80.

36 Robbin to Venn, Lagos, 4 Nov. 1856. CMS: CA 2/o80.

37 Maser to Venn, Abeokuta, 26 Sept. 1856. CMS: CA 2/o69.

38 Townsend to Venn, Abeokuta, 26 Nov. 1857. CMS: CA 2/o3a. Campbell agreed with Townsend's explanation. See Campbell to Clarendon, Lagos, 2 June 1857, no. 10. FO 2/20.

39 Townsend to Venn, Abeokuta, 26 Nov. 1857. CMS: CA 2/o3a.

40 Campbell to Clarendon, Lagos, 16 May 1857, no. 14. FO 84/1031.

41 Campbell to Clarendon, Lagos, 12 Nov. 1857, no. 43. FO 2/20.

42 Foreign Office to Campbell, 23 Feb. 1858. FO 2/24.

43 Campbell to Clarendon, Lagos, 30 Aug. 1855, no. 15. FO 84/976.

44 Campbell to Clarendon, Lagos, 5 March 1858, no. 2. FO 2/24. "Davis" is probably J. P. L. Davies.

45 Townsend to Venn, Abeokuta, 26 Nov. 1857. CMS: CA 2/o3a. Townsend told of one of the numerous advances given to Robbin, this time £200.

46 Maser to Venn, Lagos, 6 Aug. 1858. CMS: CA 2/o68. Maser noted that "a good price was realized" for the boat — an indication of Capt. Davies' business resources.

47 Ibid., and Maser to Venn, Lagos, 10 April 1861. CMS: CA 2/o68.

48 Townsend to Holl, Abeokuta, 2 Dec. 1858. CMS: CA 2/o3a.

49 Robbin to Venn, Abeokuta, 6 July 1863. CMS: CA 2/o80.

50 T. B. Macaulay to Straith, Abeokuta, 25 Feb. 1853. CMS: CA 2/o65. T. B. Macaulay is one of the few Sierra Leonians for whom one can find detailed biographical data: he "was the eldest of three sons of OJO ORIARE of ORE AGANJU on the district of IKIRUN in the Yoruba Province of Oyo who was popularly known as Daddy Ojo at Kissy in Sierra Leone where he had been taken and liberated during the trans-Atlantic traffic in slaves, and was practising his profession as a Native Doctor which he had acquired in Yoruba Country before his capture; and his mother . . . was KILANGBE, a granddaughter of the founder of ILE-OGO in the Yoruba Province of Oyo." I. B. Thomas, Life History of Herbert Macaulay (3rd ed.; [Lagos, 1946]), p. 1.

51 Macaulay to Venn, Lagos, 28 May 1859. CMS: CA 2/o65.

52 Macaulay to Venn, Lagos, 7 July 1860. CMS: CA 2/o65. For a table giving names, ages, dates of entrance of pupils; names, "professions," tribes, and religions of guardians, see Appendix C.

53 Macaulay to Venn, Lagos, 1 July 1861. CMS: CA 2/o65.

54 Printed circular, in the file of A. Mann, Abeokuta, 9 Jan. 1860. CMS: CA 2/o66. Iwe Irohin is the Yoruba term meaning "newspaper."

55 Townsend to Venn, Abeokuta, 4 May 1860. CMS: CA 2/o85.

56 See below, pp. 137ff.

57 Gollmer to Venn, Lagos, 30 July 1852. CMS: CA 2/o43.

58 Gollmer to Venn, Lagos, 16 Nov. 1852. CMS: CA 2/o43.

59 Hinderer, Journal, Sept. 1854–March 1855. No entry date. CMS: CA 2/o49.

60 Hinderer, Journal, 26 Dec. 1854. The *Awujale's* intransigence was attributed to his alliance with Kosoko. CMS: CA 2/049.

61 Hinderer, Journal, 18 Dec. 1854. CMS: CA 2/049. Samuel Crowther on his journey up the Niger in 1854 found that similar requests were being sent to Nupe people in Sierra Leone from their relatives near the Niger. See Samuel Crowther, *Journal of an Expedition up the Niger and Tshadda Rivers . . . in 1854* (London, 1855), pp. 169–70.

62 Herbert Macaulay, typescript memoirs, "Progressive British Rule in Lagos, no. 4," p. 2.

63 *Ibid.*, p. 3.

64 King of Jebu to Hand, 19 July 1860. PP 1861. LXIV (101), p. 31.

65 E. Bickersteth to Committee, Abeokuta, 7 Oct. 1861. MMS.

66 H. Macaulay, typescript memoirs, p. 2.

67 Gollmer to Venn, Lagos, 29 June 1854. CMS: CA 2/043.

68 Campbell to Clarendon, Lagos, 17 Oct. 1855, no. 30. FO 84/976. The letter testified to the integrity of the Consul, his good intentions, and the discrepancies in the missionary case, such as the early help of the *Wawu*, not Mewu, and the fact of Mewu's not being a Badagrian. The signatories were: Wm. Savage, Jas. Gooding, S. B. Williams, Jas M. Turner, Jno. T. Nottidge, Thos. Smith, Thos. Davis, Jno. Thomas, Wm. Thomas, Jno. C. David, Thos. C. Cole, Geo. Pearce, Thos. Gabbidon, Harry Pratt, Joseph Reffell, Samuel William, Wm. Friendly, Thos. Joe, George T. Dunn, Wm. Marsh.

69 Alake to Campbell, Abeokuta, 6 Sept. 1854, encl. in Campbell to Clarendon, Lagos, 17 Oct. 1855, no. 30. FO 84/976.

70 Campbell to E. Irving, Lagos, 22 Aug. 1854. CMS: CA 2/04.

71 Gollmer to Venn, Lagos, 29 July 1854. CMS: CA 2/043.

72 See above, p. 125, and Ch. 6 *n*. 68.

73 No date, but 1854. CMS: CA 2/011. The document is signed by:

W. Savage		)
J. White		) Churchmen
W. Pratt	[in pencil on	)
I. H. Willoughby	the side is	)
L. C. Austin	written:]	Wesleyan
T. E. Williams		Wesleyan Schoolmaster
J. B. Coker		

74 Hinderer, Journal, 31 Oct. 1854. CMS: CA 2/049.

75 Biobaku, "An Historical Sketch of Egba Traditional Authorities," p. 38. The author goes on to say that, " in principle, the *Ogboni* stood between the sacred chief and his subjects, preventing the one from becoming despotic, and insuring the proper subordination of the other."

76 T. King to Straith, Abeokuta, 5 Oct. 1861. CMS: CA 2/061.

77 *Ibid.*

78 The major "inconvenience" referred to by T. King (*ibid.*), arose in accordance with the *Ogboni* custom of using "the *Oro*, an ancestral cult

organization whose symbol is the Bull-roarer, to proclaim curfews when disorders were expected, in apprehending criminals, and to execute the guilty ones in secret recesses of the *Oro* grove." (Biobaku, "Historical Sketch," p. 38). According to King, non-members of *Ogboni* were not allowed to meet the *Oro* in the streets without danger, and they were thus forced frequently into taking circuitous routes.

79 Minute, Parent Committee, 23 Nov. 1861. CMS: CA 2/L3. The Committee felt that, on the one hand, the mission should "avoid open opposition to the system" because of its traditional political role, but, on the other, *Ogboni* "is inconsistent with the principles of the Christian religion and must fall when those principles prevail in the country; it is necessary that the Native Christian Church should maintain its high position of witnessing for the truth by a broad separation from this and all other questionable 'country customs.' "

80 The negative reaction appeared occasionally in Lagos, where the shipping of slaves had actually taken place. As has been shown (see above, p. 44, and Ch. 3, *n.* 5) virtually none of the emigrants could trace lineal connections to the Lagosians.

81 For further substantiation of this point, See M. J. Herskovits, *The Myth of the Negro Past* (2nd ed.; Boston, 1958), pp. 105–9.

82 R. Campbell, *A Pilgrimage to My Motherland*, p. 30.

83 Campbell to Clarendon, Lagos, 23 June 1856, no. 9. CO 2/17. See above, p. 104.

84 Campbell to Clarendon, Lagos, 7 April 1857, no. 10. FO 84/1031.

85 *Ibid.* This statement suggests that the previous condition of slavery was a slight factor and was significant only in conjunction with the others.

86 Foote to Russell, Lagos, 8 May 1861, no. 19. FO 84/1141.

87 Straith to Koelle, 11 Feb. 1852. CMS: CA 1/I.

88 Straith to Charles Macaulay, 10 March 1855. CMS: CA 1/I.

89 Crowther to Venn, 2 Dec. 1854, quoted in preface to S. Crowther, *Journal of an Expedition up the Niger*, pp. xvi–xviii. "If this time is allowed to pass away, the generation of the liberated teachers who are immediately connected with the present generation of the natives of the interior will pass away. . . . Had not Simon Jonas been with us, who was well known to Obi and his sons, we should have had some difficulty in gaining the confidence of the people at Aboh at our ascent."

90 Laird to Clarendon, 8 Feb. 1855, quoted in *ibid.*, pp. x–xi.

91 Campbell to Clarendon, Lagos, 14 Aug. 1854, no. 23. FO 84/950.

92 In a somewhat atypical despatch he wrote to Lord Clarendon, "the services of the comparatively few of this class, trustworthy and well conducted, are duly appreciated; it is . . . very difficult indeed to obtain the services of trustworthy young men in the employment of any new branch of Commerce, such as that in Cotton, without tempting them from services in which they are already usefully employed — one great defect in the education of youth in Sierra Leone is, that the great differ-

ence between *meum* and *teum* has not been sufficiently impressed on their minds. . . ." Campbell to Clarendon, Lagos, 6 Nov. 1857, no. 2, separate. FO 2/20.

93 See J. F. Ade Ajayi, "Christian Missions and the making of Nigeria" (Ph.D., London, 1958), p. 85.

94 Townsend (and Isaac Smith, Hinderer, and Gollmer) to Straith, Abeokuta, 29 Oct. 1851. CMS: CA 2/o16. The letter makes various points to buttress its case, one of them being that the Africans would not show the same respect to another African that they gave to the European. Cf. Robert Campbell's view of this question, quoted above, p. 128.

95 Townsend to Holl, Abeokuta, 2 Dec. 1858. CMS: CA 2/o3a.

96 Maser to Venn, Lagos, 9 July 1859. CMS: CA 2/o68.

97 Cf. Straith to Charles Macaulay, p. 131 above.

98 Campbell to Clarendon, Lagos, 2 June 1857, no. 10. FO 2/20. Campbell told of the strong early opposition of Sandeman, Grote, and "the Portuguese" to Sierra Leonian landings at Lagos.

CHAPTER 7

1 S. Johnson, *History of the Yorubas, from the Earliest Times to the Beginning of the British Protectorate*, Ed., O. Johnson (London, 1921), p. 288. Johnson writes of this victory that it "saved the Yoruba country as such from total absorption by the Fulanis as a tributary state. From this time forth the power of Ilorin for an independent aggressive warfare in Yoruba land was for ever broken and the Ibadans gained the ascendancy." P. A. Talbot, *The Peoples of Southern Nigeria*, 4 vols. (London, 1926), I, 297, gives the date of this battle as "1845?"

2 See above, pp. 17–8.

3 Johnson, *History of Yorubas*, pp. 297–301.

4 See below, pp. 193ff.

5 Johnson, *History of Yorubas*, pp. 328ff.

6 See below, p. 139.

7 Johnson, *History of Yorubas*, pp. 336–7.

8 Townsend to Brand, Abeokuta, 12 March 1860. Correspondence . . . Relating to the Slave Trade from April 1 to Dec. 30, 1860, PP 1861. LXIV (101), p. 12.

9 *Ibid.*

10 Hinderer to Kimberley, 1 Nov. 1872. CO 147/26.

11 Johnson, *History of Yorubas*, p. 338.

12 Petition to Brand, Abeokuta, 19 Feb. 1860. PP 1861. LXIV (101), p. 3. The request was signed by H. Townsend, D. Hinderer, *T. King, *John G. Hughes, *C. B. Macaulay, *Samuel Crowther, Jun., *F. Riberio, *Josiah Crowther, *J. C. Dewring, *C. W. Faulkner. (The emigrants' names are starred.)

13 Bowden to Lodder, *Medusa*, Lagos, 25 Feb. 1860. PP 1861. LXIV (101), p. 6.

14 Though the Dahomeans continued annual campaigns until their decisive defeat in 1864 (see S. O. Biobaku, *The Egba, and their Neighbours, 1842–1872* [Oxford, 1957], p. 74), they ceased to be a factor in Egba foreign relations until the 1880's, when they threatened north-western Yoruba country as well.

15 Brand to Russell, Lagos, 9 April 1860. PP 1861. LXIV (101), p. 11.

16 *Ibid.*, p. 12.

17 Brand to Russell, Lagos, 16 April 1860. *Ibid.*, p. 15.

18 Townsend to Venn, Abeokuta, 4 May 1860. Townsend anticipated that despite the failure, the mission had made "an opening for future measures." CMS: CA 2/085.

19 Brand to Russell, Lagos, 8 May 1860. PP 1861. LXIV (101), pp. 19–20.

20 Hand to Russell, Lagos, 8 Aug. 1860. *Ibid.*, p. 30. Hand referred to "our enemies, the Ibaddans."

21 *Ibid.*, p. 29. There seems to be no supporting evidence for such an interpretation, though it is repeated in 1861 by Foote, citing a letter dated 3 Feb. 1861, from the *Alake* who feared "a threatened intervention of the King of Dahomey in the war now going on between the Abeokutans and the Ibadans. If the King of Dahomey should enter into the projected alliance with the Ibadans, then the destruction of Abeokuta would be certain." Foote to Russell, Lagos, 9 Feb. 1861, no. 11. FO 84/1141.

22 Hand to Russell, Lagos, 8 Aug. 1860. PP 1861. LXIV (101), p. 30.

23 Maser to Venn, Lagos, 13 Aug. 1860. CMS: CA 2/068, the "Ultra-Egba Merchant" may have been J. M. Turner.

24 King of Jebu to Hand, 19 July 1860. PP 1861. LXIV (101), p. 31.

25 Even such persuasion was not easy. As McCoskry wrote in 1861, "It seems impossible to convince the Abeokutans that we can be friends of theirs, and also of the Ibadans and other tribes, and so they obstinately refuse any interference for peace." McCoskry to Russell, Lagos, 4 Oct. 1861. PP 1862. LXI (147), p. 16.

26 Richards (a naval officer) to Hand, Lagos, 25 July 1860. PP 1861. LXIV (101), p. 31.

27 J. C. Dewring to Hand, Abeokuta, 2 Aug. 1860. Writing on behalf of the Abbeokutan Mercantile Association, Dewring told of temporarily successful efforts of his group and the *Alake* to open the roads to Lagos, despite strong opposition from the Chiefs of Igbein, the quarter housing the largest part of the Egba trading interest. PP 1861. LXIV (101), p. 32.

28 Richards to Hand, Lagos, 25 July 1860. *Ibid.*, p. 31.

29 Brand to Russell, Lagos, 9 April 1860, no. 16. FO 84/1115.

30 Memo. by Sir George Barrow, 10 July 1862, encl. in Freeman to Newcastle, Lagos, 4 June 1862. CO 147/1.

31 Russell to Foote, 22 June 1861, no. 22. FO 84/1141.

32 Treaty of Cession, Lagos, 6 Aug. 1861. Papers Relating to the Occupation of Lagos. PP 1862. LXI (339), pp. 8–9.

33 Freeman to Russell, Lagos, 8 March 1862. *Ibid.*, p. 22.

34 Petitions to Queen Victoria, Lagos, 8 Aug. 1861. *Ibid.*, pp. 9–12. The petitions were sent again on 10 Sept. 1861.

35 Additional article to the Lagos Treaty of Cession, 18 Feb. 1862. Report of the Committee on the Condition of the British Settlements on the West Coast of Africa, PP 1865. V (1), p. 421.

36 Memorials to Ord, Lagos, 27 Dec. 1863. *Report of Colonel Ord*, PP 1865. XXXVII (287), pp. 46–7; 49. Another memorial was sent from Dosunmu to British Parliament, n.d. *Ibid.*, pp. 44–5.

37 See below, p. 177.

38 Robbin to Venn, Abeokuta, 7 Feb. 1863. CMS: CA 2/o80.

39 Newcastle to Freeman, 20 March 1863. Papers Relating to the Conduct of Missionaries in Abeokuta, PP 1863. XXXVIII (45), p. 10.

40 Russell to McCoskry, 20 Aug. 1861. PP 1862. LXI (147), pp. 14–15.

41 Minute by Elliot, 12 July 1862, on Freeman to Newcastle, Lagos, 4 June 1862. CO 147/1.

42 Maser to Venn, Lagos, 10 Oct. 1861. CMS: CA 2/o68.

43 McCoskry to Russell, Lagos, 4 July 1861. PP 1862. LXI (147), p. 14.

44 Maser to Venn, Lagos, 9 Nov. 1861. CMS: CA 2/o68.

45 Brand to Townsend, Lagos, 5 June 1860. PP 1861. LXIV (101), p. 28. The Consul was appalled at the idea of a tax on the "foreign" traders "for war purposes." But he did favor "a simple tax, based on equitable principles and applicable to all, by which the Chiefs would derive a revenue increasing in amount according to the progress of agriculture and commerce in return for protection rendered." His successor, Hand, was relieved by the solution of the Abbeokutan Mercantile Association's agreement to "pay to the Authorities Fifty Bags of Cowries quarterly which they accepted"; to meet this fee they had "undertaken to impose a duty of one per cent on all produce exported . . ." from Abeokuta. Hand to Russell, Lagos, 13 Aug. 1860, no. 63, enclosing Dewring to Hand, Abeokuta, 2 Aug. 1860. FO 84/1115.

46 Agreement between Comm. N. B. Bedingfield and the Alake and Chiefs of Abeokuta, 7 Nov. 1861, encl. in McCoskry to Russell, Lagos, 10 Nov. 1861. PP 1862. LXI (147), pp. 18–19.

47 McCoskry to Russell, 3 Sept. 1861. PP 1862. LXI (147), pp. 18–19.

48 Freeman, angry at the rejection of Taylor, wrote to the *Alake*, "the Egbas have often expressed a wish either directly or indirectly, through the British residents in Abbeokuta, to have an English Consul sent to them." Freeman to Alake, Bashorun, and others, Lagos, 14 June 1862. CMS: CA 2/o7.

49 Biobaku, *The Egba*, p. 67.

50 See PP 1863. XXXVIII (61), and correspondence in CMS: CA 2/o7.

51 Townsend to Venn, Abeokuta, 2 July 1862. CMS: CA 2/o85.

52 *Ibid.* "The King begged me to send him [the Consul] away, as he was

afraid I should damage my own reputation with the people." See below, pp. 178–79.

53 King to Venn, Abeokuta, 6 June 1862. CMS: CA 2/061.

54 Freeman to Russell, Lagos, 8 April 1862, encl. in Freeman to Newcastle, Lagos, 9 April 1862. CO 174/1.

55 Bedingfield to McCoskry, *Prometheus*, Lagos, 2 Oct. 1861. PP 1862. LXI (147), pp. 16–17.

56 McCoskry to Russell, Lagos, 4 Oct. 1861. *Ibid.* For the Acting Governor's motives, see below, p. 172.

57 Docemo to Queen Victoria, Lagos, 10 Jan. 1862. PP 1862. LXI (339), pp. 19–21.

58 Freeman to Newcastle, Lagos, 6 Oct. 1862. PP 1865. V (1), p. 448.

59 Freeman to Newcastle, Lagos, 7 June 1862. CO 147/1. Freeman justified this action on the bases of "policy" and "sheer justice" — that is, Kosoko's being "rightful heir to the throne" should mean that despite the British control of Lagos and the consequent decrease in importance of being *Oba*, he should not be kept "an exile from his native land."

60 Freeman to Newcastle, Lagos, 30 March 1863. Despatches' . . . Relating to the Destruction of Epe, PP 1863. XXXVIII (117), p. 7.

61 Conditions upon which the Governor of Lagos . . . agrees to make peace with the Possoo of Epe, Epe, 26 March 1863. *Ibid.*, p. 10.

62 Freeman to Newcastle, Lagos, 26 Feb. 1863. *Ibid.*, p. 3.

63 "Natives" to Ord, Lagos, 27 Dec. 1863. PP 1865. XXXVII (287), p. 49.

64 Forced to relinquish their hold on Epe, threatened by British "infiltration," the French traders persuaded their government to arrange in March 1863 a protectorate, which was to be short-lived at this stage, over Porto Novo. Relevant correspondence is to be found in CO 147/3 and 4.

65 R. Burton, *Wanderings in West Africa from Liverpool to Fernando Po*, 2 vols. (London, 1863), II, 216.

66 These treaties are to be found in PP 1865. V (1), pp. 422–3.

67 Davies to Venn, Lagos, 6 July 1863. CMS: CA 2/033.

68 Glover to Newcastle, Lagos, 10 Oct. 1863. Glover Papers, I.

69 Freeman to Newcastle, Lagos, 10 Sept. 1862. CO 147/1. Foote had sent Commodore Edmonstone to bombard Porto Novo over the stopping of the shipment of palm oil down the creeks to Lagos, 23 April 1861. J. A. O. Payne, *Payne's Lagos and West African Almanack and Diary for 1894* (London, 1894), p. 146.

70 Report of the Select Committee, 26 June 1865. PP 1865. V (1), p. iii.

71 Newcastle had become little more than resigned to acquiring Lagos. He wrote in 1864 that he feared that "the original sin of taking possession of Lagos will . . . inevitably lead to the consequences which have followed the same policy in other places on the West Coast of Africa — intermeddling by force of arms between the neighbouring tribes. I have little hope of permanently averting this mischief, but I quite approve

of making every effort to do so." Minute by Newcastle, 17 Feb. 1864, on Freeman to Newcastle, Lagos, 9 Jan. 1864. CO 147/6.

72 C. B. Adderley, *Review of 'The Colonial Policy of Lord J. Russell's Administration,' by Earl Grey, 1853; and of Subsequent Colonial History* (London, 1869), pp. 216–18.

73 Report of the Select Committee, 26 June 1865. PP 1865. V (1), p. iii.

74 Earl Grey, *The Colonial Policy of Lord J. Russell's Administration*, II, 286, quoted in Adderley, *Review*, p. 214.

75 Adderley, *Review*, p. 214.

76 *Ibid.*

77 Report of the Select Committee, 26 June 1865. PP 1865. V (1), p. iii.

78 See above, pp. 146–47.

79 Freeman to Newcastle, Lagos, 9 June 1962. PP 1865. V (1), p. 448. The chiefs thus deprived of their revenue were each to receive, in exchange for sanctioning "export and import duties of 2 per cent," slightly over £20 per annum and "one white hat a year."

80 Freeman to Newcastle, Lagos, 10 Jan. 1864. CO 147/6.

81 Freeman was first to make both these points. The Ijaye War, he said, "was undertaken by the Egbas, professedly for the relief of the town of Ijaye, besieged by the Ibadans, but in reality to obtain a monopoly of Commerce by closing all the roads from Lagos into the Interior except by Abeokuta." Freeman to Newcastle, Lagos, 4 June 1862. CO 147/1.

82 Glover to Newcastle, Lagos, 6 Nov. 1863. CO 147/4.

83 With the death on 4 Sept. 1862, of the *Alake* of Abeokuta, Okukenu, and the ensuing regency of the *Bashorun*, Shomoye, the Egba factions became more uncontrolled; both robberies and military sallies increased. See Biobaku, *The Egba*, pp. 73ff.

84 Newcastle was not convinced. In September, 1863, he wrote, "Captain Glover's whole proceedings during his short career have very much disappointed me. His recklessness both political and financial and his disregard of all the rules and orders have exceeded anything I have ever known, even on this disorderly Coast." Minute by Newcastle, 16 Oct. 1863, Glover to Newcastle, Lagos, 10 Sept. 1863. CO 147/4.

85 See below, Chap. 7, *n*. 106.

86 Glover's road plans were to become more elaborate later, but at this stage they consisted of an alternate route from Ikorodu to Ibadan, with tolls to be paid by Ibadan and Lagos people to the *Awujale* of Ijebu Ode, through whose territory the road would pass. Glover to Russell, Lagos, 9 June 1863, encl. in Glover to Newcastle, Lagos, 10 June 1863. CO 147/3.

87 Glover had placed Ikorodu under temporary protection in 1863, a move which looked suspiciously expansionist to the Colonial Office and to the Egba and Ijebu. Trying to elicit aid from the *Awujale* of Ijebu Ode to force Abeokuta to make peace, Glover wrote that he "will never give back Ikorodu until the Egbas go home from Makun, then the Governor will

give back Ikorodu to the King of Jebu." Glover to King of Jebu, Lagos, 12 Aug. 1863. Glover Papers, I.

88 Maser, the CMS missionary then at Abeokuta, described the furious and frightened Egba reaction to the Lagos forces and rockets, and presented their point of view: "What are the sins of the Egbas, that they have been punished by the Governor with such a severe punishment? . . . They have made war originally in the best cause to help their friends . . . they could not allow their people to trade at the same time as they were wanted in the war and they therefore had to close the river. But their putting a stop to trade interfered with the newly established Colony of Lagos, . . . and therefore they were dealt with in such an exemplary manner. . . ." Maser to Venn, Abeokuta, 2 June 1865. CMS: CA 2/068. The interpretation of Glover's provocation in the preliminary maneuvers is supported by Biobaku, *The Egba*, pp. 75–6, and A. A. B. Aderibigbe, "Expansion of the Lagos Protectorate, 1863–1900" (Ph.D., London, 1959), pp. 24–5.

89 Townsend reported that in this mediation, "I was not so successful as I expected but I did what I could." Townsend to Venn, Abeokuta, 2 Oct. 1865. CMS: CA 2/085.

90 Glover to Townsend, Lagos, 27 May 1865. CMS: CA 2/04.

91 Had commerce not been open along the western lagoons, where palm-oil resources from the areas whose trade routes converged upon Porto Novo could be tapped, the economy of Lagos during these Yoruba crises would have stagnated completely.

92 Report of Colonel Ord, PP 1865. XXXVII (287), pp. 22–6.

93 See below, pp. 178ff.

94 Proclamation, J. H. Glover, Lagos, 9 March 1866. CMS: CA 2/07. For the imposition of the 2½ per cent duty and the resentment of it felt in Abeokuta, as well as the ban on the export of arms and ammunition, see below, p. 180. Glover had lifted some of the restrictions in January. He allowed "guns, power, shot and iron" to be exported from Lagos, and declared all roads from Lagos open to trade, subject still to the 2½ per cent duty until compensation had been made. "Coloured" persons could proceed to Abeokuta at their own risk, but "*no* White Person (Missionaries excepted) [would] be permitted to proceed" there until their safety was guaranteed by the Egba. Proclamation, 5 Jan. 1866, encl. in Glover to Cardwell, Lagos, 6 Jan. 1866. CO 147/11.

95 Notice, G. W. Johnson for the President General of the Egba United Board of Management, Abeokuta, 23 March 1866. CMS: CA 2/07.

96 Gerard to Glover, 31 Jan. 1867, encl. in Blackall to Carnarvon, Sierra Leone, 15 Feb. 1867. CO 147/13.

97 Notice of the EUBM, printed in *Iwe Irohin*, 1 June 1867. Egba Documents.

98 On the top of the letter, Gerard to Secretary to the Bashorun, President General, EUBM, 8 July 1867, found in the Egba Documents — the letter

proposing a treaty defining the boundary between Abeokuta and Lagos territory — is written, "*N.B.* Heathen uprising at Abeokuta in the year 1867 October is through misunderstanding between the Two Governments originated through this Despatch," and is signed "G. W. J." *Ifole* while literally "housebreaking, burglary," *A Dictionary of the Yoruba Language* (London, 1957), p. 109, here means riot, uprising.

99 See below, pp. 231–32.

100 Adderley, *Review*, p. 212.

101 See Biobaku, *The Egba*, pp. 85–7, for an analysis of the internal confusion in Abeokuta after the death of Shomoye, the *Bashorun* who had been governing as regent.

102 Aderibigbe, "Expansion," pp. 49–52, summarizes Glover's measures with regard to Porto Novo. Voluminous relevant correspondence is to be found in CO 147/21 and 23. See for example, Hennessy to Kimberley, 5 March 1872. CO 147/23.

103 See Hennessy to Kimberley, Sierra Leone, 5 March 1872; Hennessy to Kimberley, Elmina, 10 April 1872; Hennessy to Kimberley, Lagos, 29 April 1872. CO 147/23.

104 The European merchants had reversed their position on Glover's policy as relations with the hinterland deteriorated, although in 1863 they had supported his appointment as governor. See Merchants to Colonial Office, Badagry, 8 Sept. 1863, and Merchants to Colonial Office, Lagos, 9 Sept. 1863, encl. in Glover to Newcastle, 10 Sept. 1863. CO 147/4; and Hennessy to Kimberley, Gold Coast, 18 April 1872, and enclosures. CO 147/23.

105 Minute by Kimberley, 25 Feb. 1873, on Hennessy to Kimberley, Sierra Leone, 30 Dec. 1872. CO 147/24.

106 See minute by Kimberley, 14 July 1872, on Hennessy to Kimberley, Lagos, 15 June 1872. CO 147/23.

107 See Hugessen's and Kimberley's minutes on Hennessy to Kimberley, 15 Sept. 1872. CO 147/24. For a similar CMS view, see Maser to Hutchinson, Lagos, 19 June 1872. CMS: CA 2/068.

108 Fowler to Hennessy, Lagos, 6 Aug. 1872, encl. in Hennessy to Kimberley, Sierra Leone, 18 Aug. 1872, CO 147/23, and Glover to Kimberley, London, 25 Oct. 1872. CO 147/26; and Report, n.d., of A. L. Hethersett, the Sierra Leonian who accompanied Goldsworthy as interpreter, encl, in Glover to Kimberley, London, 30 Oct. 1872. CO 147/26.

109 Payne to Fowler, Jebu Ode, 14 Sept. 1872, encl. in Hennessy to Kimberley, Sierra Leone, 4 Oct. 1872. CO 147/24.

110 Minute by Hugessen, 30 March 1873, on Berkeley to Hennessy, Lagos, 4 Feb. 1873, encl. in Keate to Kimberley, Sierra Leone, 26 Feb. 1873. CO 147/27.

111 Hennessy to Kimberley, Sierra Leone, 4 Oct. 1872. CO 147/24.

112 Fowler to Hennessy, Lagos, 21 Sept. 1872, encl. in Hennessy to Kimberley, Sierra Leone, 3 Feb. 1873. CO 147/27.

113 Minute by Holland, 19 Dec. 1872, on Fowler to Hennessy, Lagos, 28 Nov. 1872. CO 147/24.

114 Minute by Kimberley, 16 Nov. 1872, on Hinderer to Kimberley, 1 Nov. 1872. CO 147/26.

115 Minute by Hugessen, 23 Feb. 1873, on Hennessy to Kimberley, Sierra Leone, 30 Dec. 1872. CO 147/24.

116 Without making a specific differentiation, the Colonial Office during the 1870's and 1880's could expand in two separate ways. One involved linking the British settlements so that the strip of coastline could be controlled, and uniform customs duties established. The other was expansion inland, with British jurisdiction extended into the hinterland. It was the first of these alternatives that Hugessen put forward: "The best thing that could happen for Lagos — and indeed for the whole of West Africa . . . [is] that the whole of the sea-board should be under British control, and that the Egbas, Jebus, and others should thus have brought to bear upon them a power and influence which would oblige them for their own sake to open up the roads into the interior, and would gradually teach them the value of well regulated trade, and imperceptibly lead them into improvement and civilisation." (Minute by Hugessen, 23 Feb. 1873, on Hennessy to Kimberley, Sierra Leone, 30 Dec. 1872. CO 147/24.) This was the kind of expansion discussed by an interdepartmental committee, composed of members of the Foreign Office, Colonial Office, and Treasury, to consider the West African Settlements in 1878. (See report of the committee, CO 267/333.) It was the kind which Hicks Beach as Colonial Secretary favored then, and which French action at Cotonou and later at Porto Novo made impossible. Expansion into the hinterland only became an issue at the end of the period treated in this study. See minutes by Herbert, 30 Oct. 1878, and Hicks Beach, 27 Nov. 1878 on Foreign Office to Colonial Office, 16 Oct. 1878, CO 147/36, and minutes by Hemming, 31 Oct. 1878, and Herbert, 31 Oct. 1878, on Foreign Office to Colonial Office, 27 Oct. 1878, CO 147/36. Herbert suggested a drastic reversal of policy and withdrawal of the establishments, favoring the French and Portuguese practice of "hoisting a flag . . . and keeping a small squadron on the coast," or at any rate, suspending thoughts of extending territory.

117 Treasury to Herbert, 13 Jan. 1873. CO 147/29.

118 The Ijebu roads opened on 12 May 1873. Berkeley to Harley, Lagos, 16 May 1873, encl. in Harley to Kimberley, Gold Coast, 24 May 1873. CO 147/27. The Egba roads opened on 12 June 1873. Harley to Kimberley, Gold Coast, 23 June 1873. CO 147/28. The Ijebu roads were not, in fact, finally opened until a year later. Shaw to Berkeley, Lagos, 6 July 1874, encl. in Berkeley to Carnarvon, Sierra Leone, 16 July 1874. CO 147/30.

119 See Fowler to Hennessy, Lagos, 10 Oct. 1872, encl. in Hennessy to Kimberley, 28 Oct. 1872. CO 147/24.

120 The figures for these years can be found in the Statistical Tables relating to the Colonial and other Possessions of the United Kingdom (CO 442).

121 Johnson, *History of Yorubas*, pp. 413ff.

122 See Aderibigbe, "Expansion," for a discussion of the intricacies of these events.

123 Johnson, *History of Yorubas*, p. 413.

124 J. Johnson to H. Wright, Abeokuta, 20 July 1877. CMS: CA 2/056; and S. Johnson, *History of Yorubas*, p. 414.

125 D. Olubi, annual letter, Ibadan, 14 Jan. 1878. CMS: CA 2/075. Olubi described the outbreak between the Egba and the Ibadan in June, 1877. He told of the roads being "closed on both sides," with the country "utterly in confusion." He and others reported these attacks as being "slave-raids." But, as Johnson said, "In the expeditions, the main object was to destroy foodstuffs, fire the barns, cut down standing corn, chop in pieces yams and other tuberous foodstuffs." Johnson, *History of Yorubas*, p. 416. No doubt captives were also desirable, for, whatever other purposes they served, they reduced the manpower of the enemy.

126 *Ibid.*, pp. 423ff.

127 Freeman to Newcastle, Lagos, 18 April 1864. CO 147/6. The Dahomean army had been decisively defeated on 15 March 1864.

128 Andrew Sanu to Finance Committee at Lagos, Lagos, 21 March 1884. CMS: G3/A2/03, no. 129 (1884); and Griffith to Stanley, Lagos, 14 Dec. 1885. CO 96/168.

129 Johnson, *History of Yorubas*, pp. 454–5.

130 Lees to Hicks Beach, Gold Coast, 2 Aug. 1878. CO 147/35.

131 Maser to Malcolm Brown, Lagos, 16 July 1878, encl. in Lees to Hicks Beach, Gold Coast, 2 Aug. 1878. CO 147/35. The Europeans could not help acknowledging that the Ijebu were justified in blocking the transport of arms and ammunition which were to be used against them and their allies.

132 Minute by Hemming, 7 Nov. 1878, on Lees to Hicks Beach, Gold Coast, 5 Oct. 1878. CO 147/36. "If we are to be cramped in our trade to the W. of Lagos by the French encroachments at Cootenoo it becomes all the more necessary to do everything in our power to foster and extend it on the eastern side."

133 Moloney to Ussher, Lagos, 19 Jan. 1880, encl. in Ussher to Hicks Beach, Gold Coast, 2 Feb. 1880. CO 147/40. Again one of Glover's earlier policies was put into use, for the *Gertrude* was performing a function similar to that of the *Eyo* in 1872 for which Hennessy had so strongly reprimanded the administrator.

134 W. Geary, *Nigeria Under British Rule* (London, 1927), p. 48, citing Hertslet's *Commercial Treaties*, XVII, 1132 and XVIII, 117.

135 Ogundipe to Griffith, Abeokuta, 30 Aug. 1880, encl. in Ussher to Kimberley, Gold Coast, 28 Sept. 1880, CO 147/42, and Griffith to Kimberley, Lagos, 23 Dec. 1880, CO 147/43. See below, p. 184.

136 Wood to Hutchinson, Lagos, 11 Dec. 1880. CMS: G3/A2/O1, no. 3 (1880).
137 See below, pp. 219ff.
138 Johnson, *History of Yorubas*, pp. 552ff.
139 Holland to Moloney, 17 Aug. 1887. CO 806/281, p. 337.
140 For a summary of the French actions which gave impetus to this change in connection with Lagos in the early 1880's, see Memo. by H. Percy Anderson, Foreign Office, 11 June 1883. Anderson recommended extending British protection not only to the west but also to the east of Lagos, over the Oil Rivers, to prevent the French from doing so. FO 803: FO Confidential Print, no. 4819, p. 10.
141 See below, p. 354, Chap. 9, *n*. 140.
142 Holland to Moloney, 17 Aug. 1887. CO 806/281, p. 337.
143 Sir Gilbert Carter in 1896 pointed out a major difficulty with the system of stipends, apart from the reluctance of the chiefs to accept them in the first place: "Individual kings and chiefs seldom rule a large territory, and still more seldom have any real authority; there is generally a power behind the king . . . which really rules, and it follows therefore that the stipend which is supposed to be given to the king, and which is seldom large, is further attenuated by being distributed among the elders, or native council." "The Colony of Lagos," *Proceedings of the Royal Colonial Institute*, XXVIII (1896–7), 275–304.
144 Hinderer to Kimberley, 1 Nov. 1872. CO 147/26.

CHAPTER 8

1 Blue Book, 1866, CO 151/4.
2 Blue Book, 1871, CO 151/9.
3 Lagos Government Gazette, 1881. CO 150/1.
4 Moloney to Stanhope, Lagos, 23 June 1886. CO 147/55. A minute discusses "what Capt. Moloney calls the 'Interior Question.'"
5 S. Johnson, *History of the Yorubas, from the Earliest Times to the Beginning of the British Protectorate*, Ed., O. Johnson (London, 1921), pp. 328–54, for example.
6 Harrison to Fenn, Abeokuta, 3 Aug. 1863. CMS: CA 2/045. See also Minutes of the Conference of the Yoruba Mission, Ikija, Abeokuta, 27 and 28 Aug. 1863, CMS: CA 2/03; and H. Robbin to Venn, Abeokuta, 6 July 1863, CMS: CA 2/080.
7 Sir W. N. M. Geary, *Nigeria Under British Rule* (London, 1927), p. 54.
8 See Statistical Tables relating to the Colonial and other Possessions of the United Kingdom (CO 442).
9 J. P. L. Davies, Testimony, 20 April 1898, before the Commission on Trade, encl. in Denton to Chamberlain, Lagos, 4 June 1898. CO 147/133.
10 William McCoskry, Testimony, 6 April 1865, before the 1865 Select Committee. PP 1865, V (1), p. 76, questions 1724–5. Asked if the conditions he described constituted a "species of monopoly," he committed himself only to the extent of saying, "It gives them a great advantage, no doubt."

11 J. Johnson to Hutchinson, Lagos, 29 April 1875. CMS: CA 2/o56.

12 For example, Meyer and Lossman; John Chillingworth and Co., a partnership between Chillingworth and a man named Horner; Southam Wick, and Co., all of whose names appear in the early 1860's but are not to be found a decade later. See petition from Merchants of Lagos to Colonial Office, encl, in Glover to Newcastle, Lagos, 9 Sept. 1863. CO 147/4. Even William McCoskry disappeared from the Lagos scene after 1865; he seems to have continued his activities in the Delta.

13 C. Gertzel, in "John Holt: A British Merchant in West Africa in the Era of Imperialism" (D.Phil., Oxon., 1959), p. 511, delineates categories of African merchants, African traders, and petty traders.

14 After the death on 2 July 1868 of Oshodi Tapa (J. A. O. Payne, *Payne's Lagos and West African Almanack and Diary for 1894* (London, 1894), p. 146), who had in any case been more prominent at Epe and Palma than he was in Lagos, there were only two non-emigrant African merchants: Taiwo and Dawadu.

15 The most notable of these cases is that of J. P. L. Davies, whose problems with bankruptcy led him to trade under different names, including Christie and Co. and Davies Brothers (Moloney to Granville, Lagos, 19 April 1886. CO 147/55), but did not put him out of business.

16 The names of these men appear on the agreement between Dosunmu and the Lagos merchants in 1859 (encl. in Lodder to Malmesbury, Lagos, 30 May 1859, no. 7. FO 2/28) and are also mentioned by Moloney as numbering among the "principal business houses" in 1888. Moloney to Knutsford, 9 Oct. 1888. CO 147/66.

17 See John B. O. Losi, *History of Lagos* (Lagos, 1914), pp. 110–12.

18 *Ibid.*, pp. 110–11.

19 Their names appear on the memorial to Colonel Ord, Lagos, 27 Dec. 1864. PP 1865. XXXVII (287), p. 47.

20 See Moloney to Knutsford, Lagos, 9 Oct. 1888. CO 147/66.

21 Moloney to Granville, Lagos, 19 April 1886. CO 147/55.

22 See Moloney to Knutsford, Lagos, 9 Oct. 1888, CO 147/66, for the influence of the fate of such traders upon commercial ventures in the Oil Rivers in the late 1880's.

23 See J. F. Ade Ajayi, "Christian Missions and the Making of Nigeria, 1841–1891" (Ph.D., London, 1958). pp. 488, 561.

24 H. Macaulay, typescript memoirs, quoting from a broadcast called "I Remember," made by him on the Lagos Rediffusion Service, 12 June 1942.

25 Thomas Welsh to John Holt, Lagos, 23 Feb. 1888. Holt Papers, Box 27, letter no. 2. I am grateful to Dr. C. Gertzel for this quotation and the reference in *n.* 30 below. Williams' first initial was "Z.," rather than "J."; his first name was Zachariah (Payne, *Almanack, 1894*, p. 44). J. P. L. Davies also traded in Porto Novo. See above, p. 166.

26 Payne, *Almanack, 1894*, p. 39.

27 Moloney to Knutsford, Lagos, 9 Oct. 1888. CO 147/66.

28 Sant Anna was registered as occupying two warehouses in Kakawa Street in 1888. The only Sierra Leonian listed was J. P. L. Davies, with a warehouse in Broad Street. *Lagos Gazette*, no. 7, 31 July 1888, p. 312. Occupiers of Warehouses under Section 20, Ordinance 10 of 1876. CO 150/8.

29 Nina Rodrigues, *Os Africanos no Brasil*, revised by Homero Pires (São Paulo, 1932), p. 160. This passage was written before Rodrigues died in 1906. He spent the years between 1890 and 1905 collecting material and writing the book.

30 Thomas Welsh to John Holt, Lagos, 23 Feb. 1888. Holt Papers, 27/2.

31 Return of Spirit Licenses, issued under Ordinance 7 of 1875. *Lagos Gazette*, no. 7, 31 July 1888, p. 319. CO 150/8. Sant Anna purchased wholesale spirit licenses for three sets of premises. The retail statistics are probably less reliable, since retail trade was more easily carried on without a license than was wholesale trade.

32 Moloney to Granville, Lagos, 19 April 1888. CO 147/55.

33 Payne, *Almanack, 1894*, p. 39.

34 Welsh to Holt, Lagos, 7 April 1888, Holt Papers, 27/2, quoted in C. Gertzel, "John Holt," p. 512.

35 Benjamin Charles Dawodu, Testimony, 7 April 1898, before Commission on Trade, encl. in Denton to Chamberlain, Lagos, 4 June 1898. CO 147/133.

36 The 1866 statistics are from the Blue Book, CO 151/4. Those of 1872 are from "Information resecting . . . Lagos," Lees to Colonial Office, 28 Feb. 1879. CO 806/130. Hennessy's guess of 6,000 Brazilians in Lagos in 1872 seems a decided over-estimate. Hennessy to Kimberley, Sierra Leone, 31 Dec. 1872. CO 267/317.

37 Moloney to Holland, Lagos, 20 July 1887. CO 147/59.

38 Townsend to Venn, Abeokuta, 2 Oct. 1865. CMS: CA 2/085.

39 *Ibid.*

40 Townsend to Venn, Abeokuta, 1 Nov. 1866. CMS: CA 2/085. "I saw Robbin's hydraulic Cotton Press at work today. He presses bales of 140 and 150 lbs. in smaller compass than by the screw presses. . . . Cotton is brought from Ibadan in seed a select few have the privilege."

41 H. Robbin to Townsend, Abeokuta, 6 June 1870. CMS: CA 2/085.

42 Wood to Lang, Abeokuta, 20 June 1885. CMS: G3/A2/03, no. 119 (1885). Moore retained his business in Abeokuta, where his interests were handled by an agent, another emigrant named Rufus Wright. Wright bought oil there for Moore from 1890 to 1894. Rufus Alexander Wright, Testimony, 4 April 1898, before Commission on Trade, encl. in Denton to Chamberlain, Lagos, 4 June 1898. CO 147/133.

43 This theme ran through the evidence before the 1898 Commission on Trade cited frequently throughout this chapter.

44 In a memorial addressed to Colonel Ord in 1864, McCoskry, then agent for the West African Co.; Henry Dunkley, agent for the London and

African Trading Co.; J. R. Leaver, agent for Banner Brothers; and Henry Horner, for John Chillingworth and Co., complained of the state of the interior, and said that they had "reason to know or fear that some at least of the Egba chiefs . . . are encouraged in their persistence in . . . [the war] by false notions, instilled in their minds by injudicious advisers here, of the advantages which they will ultimately attain by their present course of action." European merchants to Glover, Lagos, 27 Dec. 1864. PP 1865. XXXVII (287), p. 50. This is the only one of the memorials — there having been one from each of the three groups of traders — which Ord thought worthy of serious consideration. *Ibid.*, pp. 27–8.

45 See above, p. 105.

46 "The removal of Kosoko and Tapa from Epe to Lagos was in several respects a hard blow for William O'Swald and Company. When Tapa was sued in Lagos, he testified in court that he was insolvent. Kosoko, too, despite the annuity England paid him, could only repay trifling sums on his debt, which ran to more than 18,000 gallons. Philippi [O'Swald's agent] suspected the hand of the English Governor in this. 'For who else would instruct a black trader in the concept of "insolvency." ' " Hieke, *Zur Geschichte des Deutschen Handels mit Ostafrika*, 1 vol. (Hamburg, 1939), I, 117.

47 *Ibid.*, pp. 190ff.

48 *Ibid.*, p. 194.

49 *Ibid.*, p. 203.

50 *Ibid.*, p. 199.

51 E. Hieke, *G. L. Gaiser, Hamburg, Westafrika* (Hamburg, 1949), p. 38. These two firms were joined in 1877 by two more German concerns, C. G. Meyer and Company, and Escherich and Company. During the association between Witt and Gaiser, their capital had trebled. P. E. Schramm, *Deutschland und Übersee* (Braunschweig, 1950), p. 281.

52 Leader entitled "The Trade of Lagos," *Lagos Times and Gold Coast Colony Advertiser*, 27 July 1881, I, 18. The argument has not been uncommon in the twentieth century.

53 *Ibid.* The leader was advocating most immediately the standardizing of quantities of goods exchanged to avoid dishonest practices.

54 Report of the Commission on Trade, Lagos, 5 May 1898, encl. in Denton to Chamberlain, Lagos, 25 May 1898. CO 147/132. The Commission had heard testimony which showed that to complicate the situation further, "Merchants formerly sold wholesale, but now they sell retail as well and have thus become competitors with their own customers who were middlemen." John Olawunmi George, Testimony, 4 April 1898 before Commission on Trade, encl. in Denton to Chamberlain, Lagos, 4 June 1898. CO 147/33.

55 See below, pp. 214ff.

CHAPTER 9

1 Venn to Russell, 20 Sept. 1861. PP 1862. LXI (339), p. 9.
2 William McCoskry, Testimony before the Select Committee of 1865, PP 1865. V (1), p. 68, question 1543.
3 See bove, p. 106.
4 The three petitions, all dated 8 Aug. 1861, were enclosed in Venn to Russell, 20 Sept. 1861. PP 1862. LXI (339), pp. 9–14.
5 Glover to Newcastle, Lagos, 10 Oct. 1863. Glover Papers, I.
6 Freeman to Newcastle, Lagos, 31 Dec. 1863. CO 147/4.
7 Minute by Hemming, 29 Oct. 1873, on Lees to Berkeley, Lagos, 26 Sept. 1873, encl. in Berkeley to Kimberley, Sierra Leone, 10 Oct. 1873. CO 147/28. "Mr. Hennessy never took any notice of our despatches respecting the authority entrusted to Docemo, and it was only through incidental allusions that we knew anything of what was going on. It now appears that Mr. Fowler (with Mr. Hennessy's concurrence, if not his directions . . .) had given Docemo considerable power which he hastily took away, . . . but he sent us no report on the subject."
8 C. D. Turton to Glover (personal), Lagos, 26 Aug. 1872. Glover Papers, V.
9 Report (unsigned) of a meeting, Lagos, 14 Oct. 1872, with Dosunmu speaking and "all the native people (not Creoles)" present. Anti-Slavery Society Papers, MSS Brit. Emp. S–22; AntiSlavSoc. G. 119. Misc.
10 Ibid., and Turton to Clare, Lagos, 19 Nov. 1872. Anti-Slavery Society Papers, MSS Brit. Emp. S–22.
11 Turton to Clare, Lagos, 19 Nov. 1872, ibid. Because all the reports of these incidents are colored by the emotional animosity of the Glover-Hennessy controversy, it is difficult even to determine the factual outlines. Payne, of Ijebu origin, was considered an opponent of Glover's expansionist policies; thus Turton interjected frequent accusations of support of domestic slavery against Payne; similar accusations came from Samuel Crowther, Junior, who wrote to the Manchester Courier as "An Anti-Slavery Negro." See Crowther to Clare, Lagos, 1 Jan. 1873, encl. in Clare to Colonial Office, 12 Feb. 1873. CO 147/29. But Crowther was hostile to the Egba-Ijebu cause, despite his Egba origin, because of his "exile" from Abeokuta in 1862. (See below, Chap. 9, n. 15).
12 Herbert Macaulay, Justitia Fiat: The Moral Obligation of the British Government to the House of King Docemo of Lagos (n.p., 1921). See also E. A. Akintan, The Closing Scene of the Eleko Case (Lagos, [1931]).
13 G. W. Johnson, Obituary, Lagos Weekly Record, 16 Sept. 1899.
14 Townsend resented the feeling growing among the Crowthers and other emigrants that they would be more effective political advisers in Abeokuta than the leading missionary who regarded Africans as unsuited for leadership. See J. F. Ade Ajayi, "Christian Missions and the Making of Nigeria, 1841–1891" (Ph.D., London, 1958), pp. 434ff.
15 See Brand to Russell, Lagos, 10 April 1860. PP 1861. LXIV (101), p. 14.

In Abeokuta, Campbell and Delaney stayed with Samuel Crowther, Junior, who introduced them to the *Alake* and his chiefs. In November 1859 they signed a treaty, witnessed by the two Samuel Crowthers, which was intended to delimit the future development. (See Martin Delaney, *Official Report of the Niger Valley Exploring Party* [New York, 1861], pp. 35ff.) After the departure of the two "commissioners" the suspicion of the Egba authorities was aroused, largely by Townsend, and they denied ever having signed the treaty, although they admitted having granted permission for farms. Siding with the *Alake* against Samuel Crowther, Junior, in this dispute were J. M. Turner, William Cole, John Craig, David Williams (who was being trained at Townsend's request as the *Alake*'s clerk) and Andrew Wilhelm (Townsend's interpreter) among others. (Declaration by the *Alake* in the presence of witnesses, Abeokuta, 8 Feb. 1851, encl. in Foote to Russell, Lagos, 9 March 1861. PP 1862. LXI (147), p. 5) The treaty was declared void; Samuel Crowther, Junior was expelled from Abeokuta. The African Aid Society in London, with whom the commissioners had worked, was told to seek another site. Although the plan was never implemented, Robert Campbell did return to Lagos for at least a few years. He printed and edited the first Lagos newspaper, *The Anglo-African*, which contained as much news about the American Civil War as of events in West Africa.

16 See above, p. 145.

17 Minutes of a Special Meeting held on 30 Oct. 1865 in the Council Hall of Shomoye *Bashorun*, President General of the Egbas United Board of Management. CMS: CA 2/o7.

18 Address by the *Bashorun*, *ibid.*

19 Address by John Craig, " (A Sierra Leone Emigrant)," *ibid.*

20 Townsend to Venn, Abeokuta, 2 Oct. 1865. CMS: CA 2/o85. According to Townsend, their "inability to get Robbin and the others in Ake to join them was thought to come from me and so they schemed to get me out of the country." This was Townsend's explanation for the meeting of 30 Oct. 1865.

21 Address by the *Bashorun*, Minutes of a Special Meeting held on 30 Oct. 1865. . . . CMS: CA 2/o7.

22 Townsend to Venn, Abeokuta, 2 and 3 Oct. 1865. CMS: CA 2/o85.

23 Townsend to Venn, Abeokuta, 28 Nov. 1865. CMS: CA 2/o85.

24 See Freeman to Newcastle, London, 3 June 1863, CO 147/5, and Freeman to Newcastle, Lagos, 9 April 1864, CO 147/6.

25 Ordinance of 13 Sept. 1865, encl. in Glover to Cardwell, Lagos, 6 Oct. 1865. CO 147/9.

26 See above, p. 154.

27 See above, p. 102.

28 Townsend to Venn, Abeokuta, 1 Nov. 1866. CMS: CA 2/o85. "These men are introducing a fixed duty on exports . . . , they have a customs house,

give permits, printed and afterwards filled up. In doing this the greatest opposition has been met but nevertheless it stands."

29 See above, Chap. 7, *n.* 98, and Johnson to Glover, Abeokuta, 18 July 1867 and 24 Sept. 1867. Egba Documents. For the role of Sierra Leonian missionaries in Abeokuta after the *Ifole*, see below, pp. 231ff.

30 Maser to Venn, Abeokuta, 28 June 1867. CMS: CA 2/068.

31 *Ibid.*, and Wood to Venn, Abeokuta, 2 May 1867. CMS: CA 2/096.

32 Maser to Venn, Abeokuta, 31 July 1867. CMS: CA 2/068.

33 See above, pp. 100–01.

34 Wood to Venn, Abeokuta, 30 April 1866. CMS: CA 2/096.

35 Townsend to Venn, Abeokuta, 3 April 1866. CMS: CA 2/085.

36 Crowther to Hutchinson, 19 Jan. 1871. CMS: CA 3/04. Quoted in Ajayi, "Christian Missions," p. 467.

37 W. Moore to Parent Committee, Abeokuta, 28 Oct. 1868. CMS: CA 2/070. The interview with all mission representatives took place on 16 Oct. 1868.

38 *Ibid.* Moore was summoned, with the other CMS agents, to the "Kemta Ogboni's Court" on 21 Oct. 1868. Services at the Ake churches were temporarily suspended, though the other stations were allowed to continue theirs.

39 *Ibid.*

40 Townsend to Venn, Abeokuta, 1 Nov. 1866. CMS: CA 2/085.

41 William George, Journal, 11 Aug. 1877, Kemta Station, Abeokuta. CMS: CA 2/041. The emigrant, George Taylor, had "ever since neglected coming to Church."

42 A. K. Ajisafe, *History of Abeokuta* (Bungay, Suffolk, 1924), p. 137.

43 *Ibid.*

44 Proclamation, "Africa Shall Rise," George W. Johnson, "By Command of the Directors of the Board of Management," Abeokuta, 11 Sept. 1868. CMS: CA 2/07.

45 See for example, correspondence, Milum to Johnson and Johnson to Milum, Lagos and Abeokuta, November 1873. NRO: ECC 2/1035.

46 Glover to George, Lagos, 23 Feb. 1871. NRO: CSO 32/1318, p. 34. Glover was cordial in his letter: "I take the liberty of troubling you on this occasion being aware that you always interest yourself to do what you can in the cause of peace between Lagos and Abbeokuta, and the Letter [from G. W. Johnson, informing Glover of the situation] being written from your Township, I venture to ask your assistance." George may have been one of the emigrant traders in Abeokuta opposed to Johnson because of the duties he imposed on exports; never amenable to taxation, the traders as well as, later, the Egba chiefs did not like having revenue completely in the hands of the Board.

47 S. O. Biobaku, *The Egba and their Neighbours, 1842–1872* (Oxford, 1957), p. 87.

48 G. W. Johnson to W. P. Richards, Abeokuta, 20 Jan. 1873 and 5 Feb. 1873. Egba Documents.

49 G. W. Johnson to Griffith, Abeokuta, 12 Aug. 1880, encl. in Ussher to Kimberley, Gold Coast, 28 Sept. 1880. CO 147/42.

50 Ogundipe to Griffith, Abeokuta, 30 Aug. 1880, encl. in *ibid.*; see also below, p. 187.

51 Ajisafe, *History of Abeokuta*, p. 141.

52 G. W. Johnson to Griffith, Abeokuta, 12 Aug. 1880, encl. in Ussher to Kimberley, Gold Coast, 28 Sept. 1880. CO 147/42. Henry Robbin, who brought Johnson's letter announcing his resumed position in Abeokuta to the Governor, advised Griffith not to work through Johnson.

53 Griffith to Kimberley, Lagos, 23 Dec. 1880. CO 147/43. Kimberley's minute recommended continuing to refuse to give or receive communication through Johnson.

54 See below, pp. 187–88.

55 Letter signed "Lagos"—one of the Egba Saro in the colony—*Lagos Times*, 25 May 1881, I, 14.

56 V. Vaulkner to Wright, Abeokuta, 14 Aug. 1880. CMS: G3/A2/o1, no. 146 (1880).

57 *Ibid.*

58 A reference extending the provision to his heirs was crossed out. Memorandum, "Confirmed by the Alake under the National Flag Seal of the United Kingdom of the Egba Alake, Oluwo, Osele, and Agura, in the presence of the Director at Ake . . . ," 31 Jan. 1881. The witnesses were: J. O'Connor Williams, merchant; Saml. Peters, merchant; J. M. Turner, Master of family; William S. Coker, X; Prince Agbore; Prince Adesobome. Egba Documents.

59 An increase in duty paid to the *Alake* meant an increase in Johnson's revenue too, for it was with the *Alake* that the agreement had been signed. Wood to Secretaries, Lagos, 29 July 1881. CMS: G3/A2/o1, no. 83 (1881).

60 Knapp Barrow to Young, Lagos, 20 Nov. 1884. PP 1887. LX (1), p. 45.

61 Johnson's earlier proposals for reorganizing the government, signed by him on 24 Nov. 1871, were taken up and expanded in a "Programme of Steps to be taken . . . ," dated 12 Oct. 1881, and a "National Pledge for the renewal of the oath of Allegiance between the Four Kings and foremost Officers of the First and Second Division of the Standard," signed Osakele Tejumoade Johnson, 18 Sept. 1885. Egba Documents.

62 Wood to Lang, Abeokuta, 12 Nov. 1885. CMS: G3/A2/o4, no. 4 (1885).

63 Private letter (unsigned) to Johnson, Abeokuta, 16 May 1888. Over the issue of the treaty signed by the Egba with the French (see p. 354, Chap. 9, *n*. 140), the letter stated that the *Alake* and his "Friends" were contemplating sending for Johnson, "the only man who made true Ogboni, that all the rest are floating ones." Encl. in Moloney to Knutsford,

Lagos, 22 April 1888. CO 806/299. The letter continued to stress the importance of Johnson's co-operation with the Egba Saro deputation that planned to go to Abeokuta. "Unless the friends of Lagos rally round you very strongly do not come with any dependence on me; they must promise their individual support."

64 Denton to Chamberlain, Lagos, 5 Oct. 1895. CO 147/100. Johnson did not return to Abeokuta, although there was an "enquiry . . . on the 1st October 1895 . . . in regard to the expulsion," and the "Final Decision of the Directors and Committee Members of the Egba Deputation Club," 10 Feb. 1896, provided not only for his reinstatement, but also that "the agreement entered into . . . on the 31st day of January, 1881, be justly carried out by the Nation, the same having been examined and pronounced by our legal Advisers to be unquestionably binding. . . ." Egba Documents.

65 Davies to Venn, Lagos, 7 Dec. 1862. CMS: CA 2/033. The interview with the Egba chiefs had been arranged through previous communication between Davies and Henry Robbin in Abeokuta. Robbin to Davies, Abeokuta, 4 Dec. 1862. CMS: CA 2/033.

66 Davies to Venn, 8 Jan. 1863. CMS: CA 2/033.

67 Crowther to Kimberley, Abeokuta, 2 Feb. 1872. CO 147/25.

68 Minute by Kimberley, on Hennessy to Kimberley, Sierra Leone, 5 Feb. 1873. CO 147/27.

69 Moloney to Ussher, Lagos, 19 Nov. 1879, encl. in Ussher to Hicks Beach, Gold Coast, 24 Nov. 1879. CO 147/39.

70 Leader, "Failure of the Mission to Abeokuta," *Lagos Times*, 24 Nov. 1880, I, 2.

71 Tickel had, in fact, resigned shortly before as District Commissioner for the Western District. Tickel to Richmond (Acting Assistant Colonial Secretary), Badagry, 24 May 1878. Badagry Letter Book, 1877–9. NRO: BadaDis 1/695.

72 Letter, signed "Veritas," in *Lagos Times*, 24 Nov. 1880, I, 2.

73 Leader, *Lagos Times*, 24 Nov. 1880, I, 2.

74 V. Faulkner to Wood, Abeokuta, 11 Nov. 1880. CMS: G3/A2/O1, no. 175 (1880).

75 Townsend to Venn, Abeokuta, 28 Nov. 1866. CMS: CA 2/085.

76 See above, p. 176. See also Glover to Cardwell, Lagos, 7 Sept. 1865. CO 147/9, and Moloney's repetition of the view over twenty years later in Correspondence Respecting the War between Native Tribes in the Interior . . . , PP 1887. LX (1), pp. 5–6.

77 Memorial to Cardwell, Abeokuta, 3 Oct. 1865, encl. in Glover to Cardwell, Lagos, 7 Nov. 1865. CO 147/9. The signatories were F. Ribeiro, Henry Robbin, Isaac Pearse, Saml. J. Peters, Isaac Coker.

78 Glover to Cardwell, Lagos, 7 Nov. 1865. CO 147/9.

79 See above, p. 76.

80 Glover to Cardwell, Lagos, 6 Oct. 1865, enclosing Ordinance of 14 Sept. 1865. CO 147/9.

81 Glover to Cardwell, Lagos, 8 Jan. 1866. CO 147/11.

82 *Ibid.*

83 Hennessy to Kimberley, Sierra Leone, 24 June 1872. CO 147/23.

84 Memorial, Lagos, 25 March 1873, encl. in Harley to Kimberley, Sierra Leone, 8 April 1873. CO 147/27. All these names, with the possible exception of Davies', are Egba. One of the others, Phillip Jose Meffre, a Brazilian, was of Ijesha origin (See Johnson, *History of Yorubas*, p. 369).

85 C. D. Turton to Glover (personal), Lagos, 4 Sept. 1872. Glover Papers, V.

86 For Willoughby's career in the administration under Glover, see below, pp. 205–06.

87 Willoughby to Kimberley, Lagos, 30 Aug. 1872, encl. in Clare to Kimberley, 3 Oct. 1872. CO 147/25.

88 See below, p. 276.

89 Willoughby to Kimberley, Lagos, 30 Aug. 1872, encl. in Clare to Kimberley, 3 Oct. 1872. CO 147/25.

90 The Ijebu "are most conservative, and jealously guard the roads to the coast, not allowing any foreigners" — this applied to non-Ijebu traders as well as Europeans — "to trade through their country, nor, indeed, even to pass through without special permission from the Awujale." Report of Higgins and Smith, Special Commissioners . . . to the Tribes interior of Lagos, entry for 21 Aug. 1886. Further Correspondence Respecting the War . . . , PP 1887. LX (167), p. 24.

91 Payne to Glover, 27 Sept. 1871, encl. in Hennessy to Kimberley, Sierra Leone, 25 June 1872. CO 147/23.

92 J. A. O. Payne, Testimony, 4 April 1898, before the Commission on Trade, encl. in Denton to Chamberlain, Lagos, 4 June 1898. CO 147/133.

93 Goldsworthy to Kimberley, Lagos, 4 Jan. 1872. CO 147/26.

94 Payne to Fowler, Jebu Ode, 13 Sept. 1872, encl. in Hennessy to Kimberley, Sierra Leone, 4 Oct. 1872. CO 147/24. The assent of the *Awujale* was withdrawn shortly thereafter. See Payne to Fowler, 10 Oct. 1872, encl. in Hennessy to Kimberley, Sierra Leone, 28 Oct. 1872. CO 147/24.

95 Turton to Glover (personal), Lagos, 26 Aug. 1872. Glover Papers, V.

96 Shaw to Berkeley, Lagos, 6 July 1874. CO 147/30.

97 Clare to Colonial Office, 12 Feb. 1873, CO 147/29, and Turton to Glover, Lagos, 26 Aug. 1872. Glover Papers. V.

98 Strahan to Carnarvon, Lagos, 6 May 1875. CO 147/31.

99 Ussher to Hicks Beach, Gold Coast, 24 Nov. 1879. CO 147/39.

100 J. Johnson to Wright, Abeokuta, 21 June 1878. CMS: CA 2/056. Johnson had returned from a visit to Iperu in Ijebu country.

101 Rowe to Griffith, Gold Coast, 14 Feb. 1883. PP 1887. LX (1), p. 28.

102 The *Balogun* of Epe, where the King had gone, summarized the circumstances: "His Majesty's complaints are that he was requested by his

subjects to reside in his late father's house; he has done so; to drive his sons away from him, and to accept the opening of the roads to Ibadan, and these he has yielded to. Not satisfying with these, they further requested him to go and sleep — ... 'meaning that he should die.' This he will not do. ... Seeing that Epe is his country and had had a house there before, therefore he returned to his home." Agbale (*Balogun* of Epe) and Thos. W. Davis ("Secretary") to Moloney, Epe, 15 Jan. 1883. PP 1887. LX (1), p. 18.

103 Griffith to Rowe, Lagos, 31 Jan. 1883, quoted in Rowe to Griffith, Gold Coast, 14 Feb. 1883. PP 1887. LX (1), p. 28.

104 Rowe to Griffith, Gold Coast, 14 Feb. 1883, quoted in *ibid.*

105 Carter's report of the signing of the treaty with the Ijebu, 18 Jan. 1892, CO 806/357, no. 2, quoted in A. A. B. Aderibigbe, "The Expansion of the Lagos Protectorate, 1861–1900" (Ph.D., London, 1959), p. 205. "I called upon Mr. Payne and Mr. Jacob Williams, the two Jebus they had expressly asked to be present, to sign the document on their behalf, as witnessing the solemn promise their compatriots had made."

106. J. B. O. Losi, *History of Lagos* (Lagos, 1914), pp. 71–2.

107 J. A. O. Payne, *Payne's Lagos and West African Almanack and Diary for 1894* (London, 1894), p. 129.

108 Similar division had been apparent during the Ijaye War. See above, p. 140.

109 Wood to Secretaries, Lagos, 14 Dec. 1881. CMS: G3/A2/O2, no. 13 (1881).

110 Johnson, *History of Yorubas*, pp. 480–1. J. B. Wood made a similar appeal to the Lagos Egba in 1888 when there were rumors that Abeokuta might make an agreement with the French. See p. 354, Chap. 9, n. 140.

111 Johnson, *History of Yorubas*, p. 483.

112 Rowe to Derby, Gold Coast, 15 Feb. 1883. CO 96/149.

113 See above, p. 102.

114 Glover to Newcastle, Lagos, 6 Nov. 1863. CO 147/4.

115 *Ibid.*

116 *The Anglo-African*, I, 18, 3 Oct. 1863. The officers of the Association were J. H. Gooding, president; Pedro Pachico, vice-president; J. P. L. Davies, treasurer; C. W. Faulkner, T. G. Hoare, W. P. Richards, and J. S. Leigh, secretaries.

117 Glover to Cardwell, Lagos, 6 Oct. 1865. CO 147/9. The officers were James A. Cole, president, and Mahomado Alhaji, Saidu Offui (the latter two signatures are in Arabic), and Francisco Reis, vice-presidents. J. R. Thomas was "honorary secretary."

118 T. Lloyd Harrison (secretary) to H. Fox-Bourne, 27 Jan. 1892. Aborigines Protection Society Papers. Samuel Johnson wrote of a trip made by several Ijesha Amaro, including Phillip Jose Meffre, to Ilesha in 1866. Johnson, *History of Yorubas*, p. 369.

119 T. Lloyd Harrison to H. Fox-Bourne, 27 Jan. 1892. Aborigines Protection Society Papers.

120 Johnson, *History of Yorubas*, p. 460.

121 *Ibid.*, p. 490. The letter had been addressed to Willoughby, Taiwo, Sumonu Animasawun, Shitta, "and all Lagos Oyos or Yorubas." The accused included T. F. Cole and F. Astrope [Haastrop?]; "Astrope" pressed charges.

122 *Ibid.*, p. 492.

123 Maser to Lang, Lagos, 5 Jan. 1884. CMS: G3/A2/03, no. 15 (1884).

124 Charles Phillips, Report of his Second Visit to the Camps, encl. in Evans to Granville, Lagos, 24 Aug. 1886. PP 1887. LX (1), p. 134.

125 Report of Commissioners [Higgins and Smith], entry for 12 Sept. 1886. PP 1887. LX (167), p. 47.

126 Rowe to Kimberley, Gold Coast, 18 Jan. 1882. CO 147/47. Samuel Johnson, the author of *History of the Yorubas*, was then a CMS catechist in Ibadan.

127 Rowe to Kimberley, Gold Coast, 18 Jan. 1882. CO 147/47.

128 *Ibid.* In addition to these two opinions, Rowe respected those of Andrew Hethersett and of A. J. Willoughby, the brother of I. H. Willoughby.

129 Johnson, *History of Yorubas*, pp. 467–73.

130 Rowe to Derby, Lagos, 11 May 1883. PP 1887. LX (1), p. 30.

131 Wood to Lang, Lagos, 10 Dec. 1884. CMS: G3/A2/03, no. 13 (1885), and Wood to Lang, Abeokuta, 19 Aug. 1885, CMS: G3/A2/03, no. 153 (1885).

132 Moloney to Johnson, Moloney to Phillips, Lagos, 1 March 1886. LX (1), p. 55.

133 Treaty of Peace, Friendship, and Commerce between the Alafin of Oyo, the Balogun, the Maye, the Abesi, the Agbakin, the Otun Bale of Ibadan, the Owa of Ilesa, the Ore of Otun, the Ajero of Ijero, the Olajudo Obalorun, the Ajaruwa, the Arode, the Arisane, the Balogun of Ife, the Ogunsua of Modakeke, the Balogun, the Otun of Modakeke, the Awujale of Jebu, and the Balogun of Jebu, 4 April 1886. PP 1887. LX (1), pp. 116–8. Copies of this and succeeding treaties can be found in Johnson, *History of Yorubas*.

134 Personal communication.

135 See above, p. 124.

136 Letter signed "Spy," *Lagos Times*, III, 49, 8 Nov. 1882.

137 J. A. O. Payne, *Payne's Lagos and West African Almanack and Diary for 1887* (London, 1887), Preface, dated 20 Sept. 1886, p. 15.

138 Having received a letter from the *Alake* of Abeokuta, fearing Dahomean intervention on the side of Ibadan in the Ijaye War, Foote wrote that in that event "the Colony of Emigrants would be captured and sold into Slavery and all hopes of civilizing the people of the interior must be abandoned." Foote to Russell, Lagos, 8 Feb. 1861, no. 11. FO 84/1141.

139 A summary of Glover's view of the problems of the hinterland from 1867

to 1872, probably written by either Glover or Turton, undated. Glover Papers, V.

140 In 1888, when all Lagos was startled by rumors that the French had secured a treaty with Abeokuta, there was a glimmer of the old Saro intervention. At J. B. Wood's suggestion (Wood to Lang, Lagos, 23 April 1888. CMS: G3/A2/05, no. 62 [1888].) and with the Governor's sanction, Egba Saro traders — J. S. Leigh, R. B. Blaize, C. J. George, J. S. Bucknor, J. J. Thomas, J. A. Savage, J. W. Cole, Robert A. Coker — wrote a letter to the *Alake* recommending "A closer relation between Abeokuta and the British Government than hitherto existed, [expressing firm belief] . . . that if such a relationship exist no other European Power could deprive you of that independence which undoubtedly is the earnest desire of the British Government that you should maintain. . . . [T]he motive which induced us to address you on this important matter is purely patriotic, kindred with a desire to uphold the integrity of our country and race." (Lagos, 28 April 1888, encl. in Moloney to Knutsford, Lagos, 12 May 1888. CO 806/288, pp. 176–7.) A deputation composed of J. O. George, E. Wright, R. Z. Bailey, and G. A. Williams followed the letter. The Egba authorities refused to be explicit about their commitments to the French emissary, Viard, and still feared any agreement with the British. Moloney to Knutsford, Lagos, 22 May 1881 and enclosures. CO 806/299, pp. 1–3.

141 See below, p. 224.

142 See Report of a meeting with "the Brazilian and Havana repatriates," at Government House, Lagos, 6 Aug. 1890. Aborigines Protection Society Papers.

143 See for example Griffith to Derby, Gold Coast, 30 June 1885. CO 96/166; and see above, p. 197.

CHAPTER 10

1 See below, p. 229.

2 See above, p. 150.

3 See below, pp. 236ff., for the contrasting mission position.

4 Memo. by Barrow, 10 July 1862, encl. in Freeman to Newcastle, Lagos, 4 June 1862. CO 147/1. The act was passed by the British Parliament on 20 Aug. 1853. See J. J. Crooks, *A History of the Colony of Sierra Leone, West Africa* (London, 1903), p. 189.

5 Glover to Cardwell, Lagos, 7 Oct. 1865. CO 147/9.

6 See above, pp. 189–90.

7 See above, p. 184.

8 See above, pp. 191ff.

9 Willoughby to Kimberley, Lagos, 30 Aug. 1872, encl. in Clare to Kimberley, Manchester, 3 Oct. 1872. CO 147/25. Willoughby reported Hennessy's co-operation with the Egba Saro, and explained that when he had himself written to the Administrator-in-Chief putting the opposing

case, Hennessy had "publicly reprimanded" him as "too insignificant to write to him." The Colonial Office denied Willoughby's request for a pension on the grounds that he was obligated as a civil servant to continue his work despite the "coldness" of the Administrator-in-Chief.

10 Glover to Kimberley, Shrewsbury, 29 Dec. 1872. CO 147/26.

11 See above, p. 119.

12 C. B. Macaulay, account of his life, Lagos, 11 Aug. 1879. NRO: ECC 2/1039.

13 *Ibid.*

14 Glover to Kennedy, Lagos, 11 Feb. 1870, encl. in Kennedy to Granville, Sierra Leone, 21 March 1870. CO 147/17.

15 Freeman to Newcastle, Lagos, 9 Jan. 1864. CO 147/6.

16 Glover to Kennedy, Lagos, 11 Feb. 1870, encl. in Kennedy to Granville, Sierra Leone, 21 March 1870. CO 147/17.

17 Charles Foresythe to Glover, Lagos, 12 Aug. 1869, encl. in *ibid.* Foresythe was then second clerk and cashier, Secretary's Office. He admitted having an "interest" in the firm of Henry William and Company.

18 C. B. Macaulay to Glover, Badagry, 20 Aug. 1869, and Thomas Tickel to Glover, Badagry, 23 Aug. 1869, encl. in *ibid.* Both men denied their own direct connection with trade, but each wrote that his wife traded.

19 For example, I. H. Willoughby to Glover, Lagos, 13 Aug. 1869, and John A. Payne, Lagos, 12 Aug. 1869, encl. in *ibid.* Willoughby was then superintendent of police, and Payne was "Police Clerk and Registrar."

20 R. B. Blaize, then government printer, wrote, "I am directly engaged in trade . . . to meet my necessary wants." Blaize to Glover, Lagos, 10 Aug. 1869, encl. in *ibid.*

21 Granville to Kennedy, 21 April 1870. CO 147/17, enclosing copy of Newcastle to Freeman, 17 Feb. 1864.

22 See *Colonial Office List, 1872.* Turton had also been appointed to the Commission of the Peace. Clare to Kimberley, Manchester, 18 Dec. 1872. CO 147/25.

23 Foresythe to Strahan, Lagos, 22 Nov. 1873, encl. in Berkeley to Kimberley, Sierra Leone, 11 Dec. 1873. CO 147/28. Foresythe did, nonetheless, leave the service in 1875 and went into private practice as a solicitor. Foresythe to Kimberley, Lagos, 30 Nov. 1880, encl. in Griffith to Kimberley, Gold Coast, 8 Dec. 1880. CO 147/42.

24 See Report of a meeting at Government House, Lagos, 6 Aug. 1890. Aborigines Protection Society Papers.

25 Blue Book, 1862, pp. 30–2. CO 151/1.

26 C. H. Fyfe, *A History of Sierra Leone* (London, 1962), p. 318.

27 The figures which follow come from the relevant *Colonial Office Lists* and can only be used as approximate guides. In 1874 the amalgamation with the Gold Coast made the statistics unusually confused, and from 1884 to 1886 the officers of both establishments were listed together; in addition, only the highest officials were recorded.

28 The Hausa Police were known by various names — among them the "Houssa Armed Police," and "the Lagos Constabulary." Although Willoughby retained his title of Superintendent, there were four Europeans above him in rank in 1886 when the two colonies were separated.

29 The Colonial Office officials as well as modern historians had difficulty with Sierra Leonian names. In May 1866 Maxwell applied to the Colonial Office for six-months further leave with pay; he had been in England a year on leave, having had full pay for the first half, and half-pay the second. With surprise Elliot noted, "Comdr. Glover tells me that there is not the least reason for listening to Mr. Maxwell's request that the stoppage of pay may be dispensed with. He is not in ill health; he is an African who was never in England before, so that we can hardly imagine that English air is requisite for his good." Minute by Elliot on Maxwell to Cardwell, 3 May 1866. CO 147/12.

30 *The Eagle and Lagos Critic*, 9 May 1885, III, 29.

31 See above, p. 207, and Fyfe, *History*, p. 460, citing *Freetown Express* of 6 April 1883.

32 Freeman to Newcastle, Lagos, 8 March 1862. CO 147/1.

33 The clerk to the Police Court was J. R. Thomas; clerk to the Petty Debt Court, as the Commercial Tribunal was renamed, J. W. Davis; clerk to the Criminal and Slave Courts, I. H. Willoughby. *Colonial Office List, 1864*.

34 This list includes the West African Court of Appeal and the Privy Council. For it in full, see T. O. Elias, *Groundwork of Nigerian Law* (London, 1954), pp. 42ff.

35 *Ibid.*, pp. 44–5; p. 48, citing Ordinance No. 7 of 1 Dec. 1866; and p. 50, citing Ordinance No. 6 of 2 June 1870. Lists of jurors can be found in Payne's *Almanacks*.

36 Wood to Wright, Lagos, 30 July 1880. CMS: G3/A2/01, no. 136 (1880). See also Ussher to Kimberley, Lagos, 26 July 1880. CO 147/41.

37 Walter Lewis, son of Freetown's one-time colonial secretary of the same name and a woman with, herself, European father and African mother, came to Lagos from the Freetown secretariat in 1858 and became chief clerk in 1861. Fyfe, *History*, p. 318.

38 *Colonial Office List, 1872*.

39 W. H. Simpson to Robbin, Davies, George, Cole, and Crowther, Lagos, 5 Jan. 1871, and to Robbin, Davies, George, and Cole, 14 Jan. 1871. NRO: CSO 32/1318.

40 Glover to Signor Abigo and Signor Francisco Rei, Lagos, 20 Jan. 1871. NRO: CSO 32/1318.

41 Payne to Colonial Office, Lagos, 16 Aug. 1886. CO 147/57.

42 T. O. Elias, *Makers of Nigerian Law* (London, n.d., reprinted from *West Africa*, 1955–6), p. 13. The courts were the Police Court, the Chief Magistrate's Court, the Court of Civil and Criminal Justice, the Court of

Requests, the Slave Commission Court, the Petty Debt Court, the Divorce Court, the Vice-Admiralty Court, and the Supreme Court.

43 H. Macaulay, "Communications in Nigeria," 17 April 1942, typescript memoirs. "Streets were opened in . . . Lagos and Victoria Road laid out in July, 1866; but it was not until February, 1868, before names were given to eighty and three Lagos streets by Mr. John Augustus Otunba Payne. . . . The Marina was made by Mr. William McCoskry in . . . December, 1861."

44 Elias, *Makers of Nigerian Law*, p. 30.

45 Payne, eighth preface, 11 Sept. 1880, J. A. O. Payne, *Payne's Lagos and West African Almanack and Diary for 1894* (London, 1894), p. 12.

46 Elias, *Makers of Nigerian Law*, p. 31.

47 *Ibid.*, p. 16.

48 In 1878 a European agent of the CMS in Lagos wrote of his impending departure: "I might be able to hold out were it not for my wife. Her case . . . is very much worse. . . . During [the preceding three months] . . . Dr. King (a native) has been most kind and attentive. Under God we feel that Mrs. Field's life is due to him. He is a most useful man in this country, and his ability as a doctor is by no means small." Field to Wright, Lagos, 16 Jan. 1878. CMS: CA 2/038.

49 C. H. V. Gollmer to Lang, Lagos, 17 June 1884. CMS: G3/A2/03, no. 144 (1884).

50 Barrow to Derby, Lagos, 23 Feb. 1885. CO 96/166. Dosunmu died of rheumatism on 16 Feb. 1885. Lumpkin had arrived in Lagos in 1885 (Payne, *Almanack*, 1894, p. 15), and he was later considered for the post of colonial surgeon in Lagos (Evans to Holland, Lagos, 6 June 1887. CO 147/53).

51 "It is undeniable that on this Coast the generality of Europeans and officials especially, have a strong objection to being treated by negro Doctors." Young to Derby, Gold Coast, 9 March 1885. CO 96/164. Some Colonial Office officials disagreed, with Sidney Webb writing in the margin of Young's despatch, "This does not seem to be the case — everyone seems to prefer Dr. Easmon to any European doctor there." Hemming countered, "But he is the brilliant exception which proves the rule." Dr. J. F. Easmon, also a Sierra Leonian, was serving as a medical officer in the Gold Coast government.

52 Young to Derby, Gold Coast, 16 June 1885. CO 96/166.

53 Petition (signed by 35 Sierra Leonians) to Moloney, Lagos, 16 July 1888, encl. in Moloney to Knutsford, Lagos, 31 Aug. 1888; and Moloney to Knutsford, Lagos, 31 Aug. 1888. CO 147/65.

54 H. Johnson to Wright, Lagos, 17 Oct. 1879. CMS: CA 2/055.

55 Lawson to Acting Assistant Colonial Secretary, Lagos, 10 March 1884, encl. in Young to Derby, Gold Coast, 26 May 1884. PP 1884–5. LV [C.4477], p. 104.

56 Minute by Hemming on Ussher to Hicks Beach, Gold Coast, 1 May 1880. CO 147/41, and *Colonial Office Lists.*

57 Griffith to Derby, Gold Coast, 30 June 1885. CO 96/116. Griffith wrote to point out that he did support this popular demand, which had, however, already been partially met.

58 Denton to Knutsford, Lagos, 3 June 1889. CO 147/71; and *The Red Book of Nigeria* (Lagos, 1920), p. 129.

59 T. F. V. Buxton, "The Creole in West Africa," *Journal of the African Society*, XII, no. 48 (July, 1913), 388. The author quotes the information given above as coming from "one of the ablest and most enlightened Africans" he had met.

60 Petition, Merchants to Granville, Nov. 1869, encl. in E. T. Gourley, M. P., to Colonial Office, 25 July 1870. CO 147/19.

61 Glover to Kennedy, Sierra Leone, 18 March 1870. CO 147/18.

62 Hennessy to Kimberley, Sierra Leone, 28 Nov. 1872. CO 147/24. Hennessy had been unfavorably impressed by Porter when he was in Lagos; of Davies he wrote, "Captain Davies is a wealthy native — well-educated, highly intelligent, and most honorable in all his dealings. He has for many years past been in the Commission of the Peace. His wife (Mrs. Davies) is a protegee of Her Majesty. I venture to add (if I may presume to express an Opinion on such a subject in a despatch) that, as the leading people in Lagos, in all charitable undertakings and in Society, they are both worthy of the many kind favors the Queen has graciously bestowed upon them."

63 Legislative Council Minutes, 1872–4. NRO: CSO 32/1370.

64 Minute by Kimberley, 22 Dec. 1872, on Clare to Kimberley, 18 Dec. 1872. CO 147/25.

65 Leader, "View of the Year 1881," *Lagos Times*, 11 Jan. 1882, II, 29.

66 See above, pp. 346–47, Chap. 9, *n.* 15.

67 J. B. Wood wrote to the CMS Parent Committee in London announcing, "We are about to have a newspaper. It will be a boon to the place if conducted as it is perhaps possible it might be. . . . The proprietor is to be one of our people and a member of the Church Committee." Wood to Wright, Lagos, 30 July 1880. CMS: G3/A2/01, no. 136 (1880). See *Colonial Office Lists* for Blaize's positions in the government service.

68 "Prospectus," *Lagos Times*, 22 July 1880. CMS: G3/A2/01, no. 143 (1880). The subscription rate was 10/- per annum, and 250 copies of each issue were printed at the outset. See Blue Book, 1881. CO 151/19.

69 "Prospectus," *Lagos Observer*, 26 Jan. 1882. CMS: G3/A2/02, no. 43 (1882).

70 *The Eagle and Lagos Critic*, 26 May 1883, I, 3.

71 Blue Book, 1884. CO 151/22.

72 Leader, "Education in the Colony," *Lagos Times*, 26 Jan. 1881, I, 6. See below, pp. 245–46.

73 Leader, "The Trade of Lagos," *Lagos Times*, 27 July 1881, I, 18. See above, pp. 173–74.

74 Letter, signed "Lagos," to the editor of the *Lagos Times*, 25 May 1881, I, 14. See above, p. 180.

75 Leader, "The Society of Lagos," *The Eagle and Lagos Critic*, 28 July 1883, I, 5. See also, p. 200 above.

76 "The Society of Lagos," *ibid.*

77 Letter, signed "Spy," to the editor of the *Lagos Times*, 8 Nov. 1882, III, 49.

78 Leader and letters, *Lagos Times*, 23 May 1883, III, 62.

79 No copy of these Letters Patent appears in the Colonial Office papers, either for Lagos or the Gold Coast, and therefore the contents must be gathered from letter despatches. There is no mention of them in the *Colonial Office Lists*, nor by Sir Alan Burns in his *History of Nigeria*, (5th ed.; London, 1955).

80 Leader, "A Felt Want of Lagos," *Lagos Times*, 9 March 1881, I, 9.

81 Leader, "The New Letters Patent," *Lagos Times*, 11 April 1883, III, 59.

82 Memorial to Derby, n.d., received in Accra, 3 Feb. 1884, encl. in Rowe to Derby, Gold Coast, 19 Feb. 1884. CO 806/220.

83 The reports are enclosed in Young to Derby, Gold Coast, 26 May 1884. Further Correspondence Regarding the Affairs of the Gold Coast Colony, PP 1884–5. LV [C.4477]. See also Derby to Young, 23 July 1884. CO 806/220.

84 Directors of the Chamber of Commerce, Manchester, to Derby, 4 Dec. 1883, signed by Geo. Lord (President) and Thos. Browning (Secretary); and Merchants in the City of London engaged and interested in the Trade with the Gold Coast and Lagos to Derby, 7 Dec. 1883. Further Correspondence Regarding the Affairs of the Gold Coast Colony, PP 1884. LVI [C.4052], pp. 94–6.

85 Derby to Rowe, 31 Dec. 1883. PP 1884. LVI [C.4052], pp. 98–9.

86 Derby to Rowe, 31 Dec. 1883., *ibid.*, pp. 99–102. This is a second letter of the same date, transmitting the petitions from the Manchester and London merchants.

87 Memorial to Derby, Lagos, 23 May 1885, encl. in Griffith to Derby, Gold Coast, 30 June 1885. CO 96/166. The petition had 217 signatories, including a few European merchants, their prominent Sierra Leonian counterparts, the leading Sierra Leonian missionaries, newspaper editors, and numerous Sierra Leonian, Brazilian, and Lagosian traders, clerks, tailors, carpenters, and others.

88 Derby to Rowe, 31 Dec. 1883. PP 1884. LVI [C.4052], pp. 99–102.

89 "It is clear that the adoption of such a measure is much desired by the inhabitants of Lagos, and representations to the same effect have been received from persons in England interested in the Colony." Stanley to Griffith, 14 Oct. 1885. CO 96/165.

90 Derby to Rowe, 31 Dec. 1883. PP 1884. LVI [C.4052], p. 102.
91 Moloney to Granville, Lagos, 27 Feb., 1886. CO 147/54. Moloney enclosed "an address . . . received from the leading native gentlemen . . . in which they tender their grateful acknowledgements for the consideration that has been extended to them by Her Majesty's Government." The address was signed by C. J. George, Thos. Geo. Hoare, R. B. Blaize, J. J. Thomas, J. S. Leigh, J. S. Bucknor, J. W. Cole, Z. A. Williams, J. A. Savage, J. B. Benjamin, William Shitta, J. Compos, J. B. Williams, I. H. Willoughby, and W. E. Cole.
92 Leader, *Lagos Observer*, 3 July 1886, V, 11.
93 Moloney to Granville, Lagos, 19 April 1886. CO 147/55. Davies had been adjudged a bankrupt in the County Court of Lancaster in August 1876.
94 *Ibid.*
95 *The Lagos Observer*, 7 Aug. 1886, V, 13.
96 See Minutes of the Legislative Council, 1886–94, *passim*. NRO: CSO 32/1377.
97 J. Johnson to Stanhope, Lagos, 4 Jan. 1887. CO 147/62.
98 The Chamber of Commerce was constituted on 13 July 1888, and was to "consist of the representatives of all European houses existing in Lagos . . . together with four representative natives. . . ." — James W. Cole, James J. Thomas, Richard B. Blaize, and B. A. Williams (who represented Williams Brothers and Co.), Sant Anna and Company also had a member.
99 Moloney to Knutsford, Lagos, 8 March 1889. CO 147/70.
100 See *Colonial Office Lists* for the relevant years.
101 See below, p. 246.
102 See James Coleman, *Nigeria: Background to Nationalism* (Berkeley, 1958), pp. 178–82.
103 Report of the meetings with the deputations, 7 and 19 Aug. 1889, encl. in Denton to Knutsford, Lagos, 26 Aug. 1889. CO 147/71.
104 *Ibid.* Excerpts from the speeches made by the spokesmen are included in the report of the meetings.
105 J. Johnson to Knutsford, encl. in Denton to Knutsford, Lagos, 2 Oct. 1889. CO 147/72.
106 Minutes on *ibid.*
107 See above, p. 193.
108 Coleman, *Nigeria*, p. 185.
109 *The Mirror*, which appeared as a "temporary publication" in 1888, did not touch the broader political issues but gave its attention to measures of social and developmental reform in the town itself.
110 I. Coker, *Seventy Years of the Nigerian Press* ([Lagos], n.d.), p. 14.
111 Jackson was a Liberian, a close friend of Edward Blyden, and he lived in Lagos from 1890 to 1918. See Coleman, *Nigeria*, p. 183.
112 John Payne Jackson, *Lagos Weekly Record*, 19 March 1910, quoted in Coleman, *Nigeria*, p. 452, *n.* 35.

CHAPTER 11

1 CMS expansion to Okeodan came at the suggestion of Glover, after an agreement had been reached between the town and the colony. Mann began a station there in 1863 (See CMS: CA 2/066). Later Charles Phillips started a station at Ode Ondo, following the opening of the most eastern trade route from Lagos (See CMS: CA 2/078).

2 See above, pp. 143ff.

3 W. Knight, *Missionary Secretariat of Henry Venn* (1882), p. 416, quoted in J. F. Ade Ajayi, "Christian Missions and the Making of Nigeria, 1841–1891" (Ph.D., London, 1958), pp. 405–6. For a detailed discussion of this policy and of its acceptance with doctrinal variations by the other Christian denominations, see Ajayi, "Christian Missions," pp. 405ff.

4 See above, pp. 131–32.

5 See below for the resulting schisms in the church, pp. 254ff.

6 See Ajayi "Christian Missions," especially chap. 7.

7 A. Harrison to Venn, Abeokuta, 21 Nov. 1863. CMS: CA 2/045.

8 Townsend to Venn, Abeokuta, 2 Oct. 1865. CMS: CA 2/085.

9 Hinderer to Venn, Ibadan, 15 Nov. 1864. CMS: CA 2/049. Cf. Robert Campbell's analysis of the Africans' view of an African in a position of authority, above, p. 128.

10 See Townsend to Venn, Abeokuta, 4 Oct. 1860 and 29 Dec. 1864 (CMS: CA 2/085), and Hinderer to Venn, Ibadan, 11 Aug. 1868 (CMS: CA 2/049).

11 See above, pp. 115–17.

12 See above p. 178. Townsend had been influential in discrediting Samuel Crowther, Junior to the *Alake*, over the issue of the treaty with Campbell and Delaney. He had himself replaced Crowther as the *Alake*'s "Secretary," and had brought David Williams, a CMS schoolmaster, to be the clerk. See S. Crowther, Jr. to Lord Alfred Churchill, Chairman of the African Aid Society, London, 18 April 1861, encl. in Churchill to Wodehouse, 22 April 1861. PP 1862. LXI (147), pp. 6–9. Williams, with other supporters of Townsend including Andrew Wilhelm, testified to the invalidity of the treaty. See Alake to Foote, Abeokuta, 4 March 1865, encl. in Foote to Russell, 9 March 1861. PP 1862. LXI (147), p. 5.

13 See above, p. 155.

14 See above, p. 179.

15 T. King to Venn, Abeokuta, 6 June 1862. CMS: CA 2/061.

16 Maser to Venn, Abeokuta, 5 Nov. 1866. CMS: CA 2/068.

17 J. A. Maser, "The Second Persecution of the Abeokuta Mission, October 1867" (n.d., received 9 Dec. 1867). CMS: CA 2/068.

18 Townsend had been in England since the preceding April; Maser, Roper, Wood, and Faulkner joined their two European colleagues and industrial assistant in Lagos.

19 N. Johnson, annual letter, 13 Dec. 1877. CMS: CA 2/057.

20 "Almost daily some of the converts are leaving Abeokuta for Lagos and

many others are making preparations for doing the same. Most are anxious to find out whether farm land will be granted near Lagos before leaving the towns about Abeokuta. This the Govr. seems to offer them so that it will not be long before many others come down." V. Faulkner to Venn, Lagos, 3 Jan. 1868. CMS: CA 2/037. See also Crown Grants, Lands Registry, Lagos, vol. II, 25 Aug. 1866 to 8 March 1868, and Sir Mervyn L. Tew, *Report on Title to Land in Lagos* (Lagos, 1947), p. 23.

21 W. Moore to Parent Committee, Oshielle, Abeokuta, 18 Feb. 1868. CMS: CA 2/070.

22 Ogundipe had previously sanctioned the resumption of services in Ikija and had promised to protect the mission there. J. F. King, journal, 23 June 1868. CMS: CA 2/060.

23 The *Ifole* had brought no reaction in Ibadan, apart from "sorrow" among the converts. D. Olubi, Journal for the half year ending Dec. 1867. CMS: CA 2/075.

24 Hinderer had been told by the Ibadan chiefs that the events in Abeokuta would not affect his position in Ibadan (Hinderer to Lamb, Ibadan, 24 Oct. 1867. CMS: CA 2/049), and this had indeed been the case.

25 See CMS files: CA 2/070 for Moore; CA 2/075 for Olubi.

26 Olubi to Wright, Ibadan, 17 April 1876. CMS: CA 2/075.

27 See Statistics of the Yoruba Mission, 1870–1879. CMS: CA 2/013.

28 Ajayi, "Christian Missions," p. 528.

29 Hinderer to Wright, Ibadan, 18 May 1875. CMS: CA 2/049. Hinderer spent four months in Ibadan in 1875. He wrote, "upon observation the first thing that struck me was the apparent genuine esteem in which I find Olubi and the other teachers are held by both the heathen and Mahomedan Chiefs and people." Hinderer to Wright, Ibadan, 15 July 1875. CMS: CA 2/049.

30 Robbin to Townsend, Abeokuta, 6 June 1870 and 2 Jan. 1871; Townsend to Venn, Lagos, 2 Jan. 1871. CMS: CA 2/085. But when Townsend reached Abeokuta, he was denied entry (Maser to Hutchinson, Lagos, 18 May 1871, CMS: CA 2/068). He was not successful until December 1874 (Townsend to Wright, Abeokuta, 25 Dec. 1874, CMS: CA 2/085).

31 D. Olubi, journal, 16 and 24 Jan. 1873. CMS: CA 2/075.

32 J. Johnson, journal, received 19 Nov. 1877. CMS: CA 2/056.

33 Townsend to Wright, Abeokuta, 25 Nov. 1875, CMS: CA 2/085, and Ajayi, "Christian Missions," p. 529.

34 Colonial Bishoprics Council to Kimberley, 19 Feb. 1873. CO 147/29.

35 See Ajayi, "Christian Missions," pp. 529–36.

36 The most important contribution to this movement was made by Edward Blyden. See *ibid.*, p. 530.

37 How much traffic there was can be seen in the countless mentions in Payne's *Almanacks* of the arrival or return of passengers coming to Lagos from Sierra Leone.

38 Hinderer to Wright, Ibadan, 18 May 1875. CMS: CA 2/049.

39 Townsend to Wright, Abeokuta, 25 Nov. 1875. CMS: CA 2/085. Townsend added, "Bishop Crowther could not occupy it, for there are very strong prejudices against him here and his present charge is already more than enough for one man."

40 Hutchinson to Crowther, 28 Jan. 1876. CMS: CA 3/L2, quoted in Ajayi, "Christian Missions," p. 535.

41 Minutes of a Conference of the Yoruba Missionaries, Lagos, 19 Jan. 1870. CMS: CA 2/02.

42 *Ibid.*

43 This letter, transmitted to the Parent Committee by Maser, who had received it from Foresythe, was dated 15 Oct. 1873 (CMS: CA 2/011) and was signed by: Jas P. L. Davies, C. B. Macaulay, Chas. Foresythe, Thomas B. Adams, S. A. John, Saml. S. Cole, P. T. Williams, E. Wright, J. N. Doherty, John T. N. Cole, Chas. Phillips, Thomas Puddicombe, W. Morgan, Matthew J. Luke, F. H. Smith, M. L. John, Robt. A. Coker, J. A. Payne.

44 See above, p. 132.

45 The meeting was held at Foresythe's house on 3 Sept. 1873. Payne to Maser, Lagos, 1 Sept. 1873. CMS: CA 2/011.

46 Faulkner to Hutchinson, Lagos, 24 Oct. 1873. CMS: CA 2/037.

47 Davies to Wright, Lagos, 17 Oct. 1873. CMS: CA 2/033.

48 Davies to Hutchinson, Lagos, 3 Aug. 1874. CMS: CA 2/033.

49 Minutes of a Conference of the Missionaries of the CMS, Lagos, 11, 12, and 16 Feb. 1874. CMS: CA 2/02. These steps were taken in accordance with the "C.M.S. Secretaries' Plan" of 23 Dec. 1873. Payne and Foresythe were consulted as "friends" and agreed to the new arrangements, which included the decision that "the time has come for the establishment of the Native Church in Lagos. . . ."

50 J. Johnson to Hutchinson, Lagos, 27 March 1876. CMS: CA 2/056.

51 J. Johnson to Fenn, Lagos, 12 Oct. 1874. CMS: CA 2/056.

52 J. Johnson to Hutchinson, Lagos, 29 April and 6 July 1875. CMS: CA 2/056.

53 Minutes of a Combined Meeting of Clergymen and Lay Representatives of the Church in the Settlement of Lagos . . . , 10 March 1876. CMS: CA 2/012.

54 J. Johnson to Wright, Lagos, 2 Aug. 1876. CMS: CA 2/056, and *The First Report of the Lagos Native Pastorate Auxiliary Association* (Lagos, 1876). CMS: CA 2/012.

55 Davies to Hutchinson, Lagos, 3 Aug. 1874. CMS: CA 2/033.

56 J. Johnson to Wright, Lagos, 2 Aug. 1876. CMS: CA 2/056. He had received the letter of 30 June 1876, instructing him to take over the superintendence of the interior Yoruba mission.

57 See above, p. 236.

58 Davies to Hutchinson, Lagos, 1 Sept. 1873. CMS: CA 2/033.

59 As a further complication, Johnson was reluctant to leave the Breadfruit Church in the midst of his work there. But perhaps his major worry was of a situation in which "a Christian Teacher is not a member of the tribe of either of these people [Egba or Ibadan] as I am not, and [because] tribal connection, particularly with the Egbas, is a prime consideration, difficulties may sometimes be very great." J. Johnson to Wright, Lagos, 18 Jan. 1877. CA 2/o56.

60 See for example, J. Johnson to Wright, Abeokuta, 12 Nov. 1877 and 2 July 1878. CMS: CA 2/o56.

61 Circular, J. Johnson to Abeokuta missionaries, Ake, Abeokuta, 18 June 1879. CMS: CA 2/o56.

62 Class fees were to be raised from one string to seven and a half strings of cowries (about 1½ d.). Minutes of Clerical Conference, Abeokuta, 10 Oct. 1877 [? Probably 1879]. CMS: CA 2/o56.

63 J. Johnson to Wright, Abeokuta, 2 Aug. 1879. CMS: CA 2/o56. The congregations said that they could not pay more than two and a half strings, and refused to pay at all until the issue were settled. Johnson interpreted the opposition as "not of the poverty stricken" and wrote that it "amounted also to an opposition to . . . [his] own authority." Henry Robbin and the Sierra Leonian clergy still supported Johnson's plans. See Resolution passed at the Annual Meeting of the Abeokuta Church, 7 July 1879, at Ake. CMS: CA 2/o56.

64 J. Johnson to Wright, Lagos, 18 Sept. 1879. CMS: CA 2/o56.

65 Minutes of Conference of Abeokuta Ministers, Ake, Abeokuta, 7 Nov. 1877, Johnson in the chair. CMS: CA 2/o56.

66 CMS Parent Committee Minute on Domestic Slavery, 2 July 1879. NRO: ECC 1/765.

67 W. Moore, W. Allen, D. Williams, W. George, Saml. Cole to J. Johnson, Abeokuta, 28 Oct. 1879. CMS: CA 2/o56.

68 H. Robbin to J. Johnson, Abeokuta, 12 Sept. 1879. CMS: CA 2/o56. See also J. Johnson to Wright, Abeokuta, 10 and 29 Nov. 1879. CMS: CA 2/o56.

69 J. Johnson to Wright, Abeokuta, 9 Feb. 1880. CMS: CA 2/o56.

70 J. Johnson to Wright, Lagos, 18 Sept. 1879. CMS: CA 2/o56. "The people seemed to have calculated upon his sympathy: they understood his feelings very well I believe when they were here at Conference and left with the conviction in regard to which I hope I do Mr. Maser no injustice if I speak of it as a correct one, that left to him, I could not be suffered to return to Abeokuta."

71 J. Johnson to Wright, Lagos, 12 Oct. 1879. CMS: CA 2/o56.

72 As Ajayi points out ("Christian Missions," pp. 551ff.), events on the Niger contributed to discouraging further plans for making Johnson a bishop.

73 H. Johnson to Hutchinson, Lagos, 31 March 1881. CMS: G3/A2/o1, no. 21 (1881).

74 A petition signed by J. P. L. Davies, Chas. Foresythe, I. H. Willoughby,

J. A. O. Payne, Jacob Johnson, and R. B. Blaize, and sent to Wright (Lagos, 25 March 1880) protested Johnson's treatment both in Abeokuta and by the local committee in Lagos. CMS: G3/A2/O1, no. 93 (1880).

75 See below, pp. 253ff.

76 Ajayi, "Christian Missions," p. 587.

77 Milum, Notes on the Separation of the Yoruba and Popo District from the Gold Coast, quoted in *ibid.*, p. 588.

78 Not satisfied with the wage differential already existing, Milum sought to reduce the wages of African agents further, and to make them more dependent upon funds raised in their congregations. *Ibid.*, p. 589. The "Native Missionaries" — T. J. Marshall, T. E. Williams, J. B. Thomas, M. C. Hagan, W. B. George, A. E. Franklin, S. P. Johnson — did hold meetings in protest, but they threatened no extreme action. See for example, meeting held at the home of T. J. Marshall, Lagos, 5 March 1880, reported in Methodist Letter Book. NRO: ECC 2/1036.

79 Ajayi, "Christian Missions," pp. 592–7.

80 See below, pp. 244–45, and Chap. 11, *n.* 92–4.

81 Moloney to Kimberley, Lagos, 8 Sept. 1882. CO 147/51.

82 Blue Book, 1862, p. 238, CO 151/1.

83 See above, pp. 121 and 132.

84 See Minutes of a Conference of the Yoruba Mission, Ikija, Abeokuta, 27 and 28 Aug. 1863. CMS: CA 2/O2. See also H. Robbin to Venn, Abeokuta, 6 July 1863. CMS: CA 2/O80.

85 Finance Committee Minute, 1873, in Native Church Regulations, 1853–83. NRO: ECC 1/762.

86 J. P. L. Davies, promissory note, Lagos, 30 April 1867. CMS: CA 2/O33.

87 Macaulay kept a list of "further" and "major" contributors to the scheme. They included such men as Moses Johnson (£10.10), I. H. Willoughby (£10), T. F. Cole (£20), James George (£21), Charles Foresythe (£40). To Macaulay's delight the second largest contribution came from Taiwo (£50), who was, in addition to being "a pure Native Trader," a "new convert from heathenism." In the same category came Mr. Labingo (£14) and Ladeja and Fagbemi, who, with D. Williams, gave £15.15. T. B. Macaulay to Venn, 4 and 17 May 1867. CMS: CA 2/O65. Donations were also made in the early 1870's for the building of a "Town Library" in Lagos by the colonial government, itself the largest contributor to the fund (£100). After the government came the "Proceeds of an Amateur Club" (£9.8.3), gifts from J. P. L. Davies (£10), Henry Robbin (£6.6), the three Crowthers, and other prominent Sierra Leonian traders and mission agents. Five European traders joined the list with amounts up to £5.5 each. Charles Foresythe, Chief Clerk and Treasurer, Special Receipts, Lagos, 20 June 1872, encl. in Hennessy to Kimberley, 8 Feb. 1873. CO 147/26.

88 Minutes of Conference of Yoruba Mission, Lagos, 19 Jan. 1870. CMS: CA 2/O2. Bishop Crowther was to be the *ex officio* chairman.

89 Statistics of the Yoruba Mission, 1870–9. CMS: CA 2/03. T. B. Macaulay died in the smallpox epidemic in Lagos at the beginning of 1878.

90 Minutes of Conference of the Yoruba Missionaries, Lagos, 19 July 1870. CMS: CA 2/02.

91 After Macaulay's death, Isaac Oluwole came from Freetown, on 1 Sept. 1879, to succeed Macaulay permanently. (H. Johnson to Wright, Lagos, 17 Sept. 1879. CMS: CA 2/055.) In the interval Henry Johnson had acted as principal.

92 Copy of Report on the Lagos Wesleyan High School Building, Gold Coast District, Yoruba and Popo Section, Methodist Mission, 1878. CMS: CA 2/011.

93 J. B. Thomas, J. S. Leigh, W. P. Richards, T. F. Cole, J. A. Byass, C. J. George, and the Rev. W. Jones argued the case. They based the feasibility of their plan on the fact that the "Roman Catholic Mission had recently raised from the Community . . . £875 and not so many years ago the C.M. Society had raised principally from our people for their Grammar School the sum of £500."

94 Copy of Memorial to Committee, Lagos, 27 Jan. 1874. CMS: CA 2/011. The memorial was signed by 25 men, principally emigrants; in addition to the names in n. 93 were included those of J. S. Bucknor, J. W. Cole, T. G. Hoare.

95 Report of the opening of the Wesleyan High School, Lagos, 14 March 1878. CMS: CA 2/011.

96 From 1868 to 1869 it was under Edward Roper, and in 1872 it was re-opened by Adolphus Mann and his wife.

97 H. Johnson, Diary entry for 18 Jan. 1877. NRO: ECC 1/766. Henry Johnson was appointed in 1877 by the CMS to be Archdeacon of the Upper Niger Mission (Fourth preface, Payne, *Almanack, 1894*, Lagos 30 Aug. 1877, p. 9), but he spent three years in Lagos filling positions that were vacant before assuming his post.

98 Leader, "Education in the Colony," *Lagos Times*, 26 Jan. 1881, I, 6.

99 Letter, signed "Africa," *Lagos Times*, 26 Jan. 1881, I, 6.

100 The government had, in fact, made grants in aid of education regularly since 1874, giving £100 each to the CMS, Wesleyans, and Catholics. In 1872 each had received £10. At the end of 1876 the amount was increased to £200. Wood to Hutchinson, Lagos, 27 April 1881. CMS: G2/A2/01, no. 56 (1881).

101 Moloney to Kimberley, Lagos, 8 Sept. 1882. CO 147/51.

102 Moloney to Holland, Lagos, 31 Aug. 1887. CO 147/60, and minute by Wingfield.

103 Denton to Knutsford, Lagos, 3 June 1889. CO 147/71. In this despatch Denton made a suggestion which ultimately materialized: Henry Carr was to be persuaded to give up his teaching post to become both sub-inspector of schools and chief clerk in the Secretariat. He had been

senior tutor at the CMS Grammar School since 1885. See Minutes of Finance Committee, Lagos, 2 June 1885. CMS: G3/A2/03, no. 115 (1885).

104 *The Red Book of Nigeria*, p. 129.

105 Document signed by J. A. Payne, Registrar, CMS: CA 2/04. These figures and the ones which follow can be taken only with clear reservations in mind: not only were the census totals unreliable, no two sets of figures — government or mission — correlate; one can never be sure what areas are being included in them. Government sources for these mission statistics have been used to compare them with government population figures.

106 Lees to Colonial Office, Information respecting . . . Lagos, 28 Feb. 1879. CO 806/130. The CMS, which had the largest number of out-stations within the colony, counted only some 300 communicants in these stations in 1879. Statistics of the Yoruba Mission, CMS: CA 2/013.

107 According to the CMS statistics, the "number of Christians connected with the congregations" in 1879 was 3,121 for the coastal district, 2,988 for the "interior," thus making the total for the mission 6,109. Statistics of the Yoruba Mission, 1879. CMS: CA 2/013.

108 A rough idea of the growth in the general population and in the Christian population can be gained from the following comparison at ten-year intervals:

	1866–8	1876–8	1886
Population	25,000	36,000	53,500
Christians	4,000	4,800	6,700

All figures are approximate, rounded off to the nearest hundred, and are based on the sources already cited and the three relevant Lagos Blue Books, CO 151/4, 14, and 24. The ecclesiastical returns in the Blue Books of 1866 and 1876 are inadequate for comparative purposes, and therefore the statistics of "Christians" have come from the years 1868 and 1878.

109 Statistics of the Yoruba Mission, 1870–9. CMS: CA 2/013.

110 See above, p. 114.

111 R. F. Burton, *Wanderings in West Africa from Liverpool to Fernando Po*, 2 vols. (London, 1863), II, 225.

112 J. Johnson to Hutchinson, Lagos, 27 March 1876. CA 2/056.

113 First Report of Lagos Native Pastorate Auxiliary Association, 1876. CMS: CA 2/012. The Muslim schools were Koranic and did not offer the general education of the Christian schools. This accounts for the request to Henry Johnson for educational facilities under CMS auspices for Muslim children. See above, p. 245.

114 J. T. Thompson, *The Jubilee and Centenary Volume of Fourah Bay College, Freetown, Sierra Leone* (Freetown, 1930), p. 37.

115 J. Johnson to Hutchinson, Lagos, 29 April 1875. CMS: CA 2/056.

116 J. Johnson to Hutchinson, Lagos, 6 March 1876. CMS: CA 2/056.

117 See above, pp. 32–3 and 15. Throughout the nineteenth century both

Christian and Muslim Yoruba continued the movement to Lagos; in a sample of fifty Aku families currently in Freetown — Aku is used here in its twentieth-century sense, meaning Muslim Yoruba — almost every one has had someone in each generation who returned to Lagos. I am indebted to Dr. John Peterson, who has done historical research in Freetown, for this information.

118 H. Johnson, Diary entry for 22 Jan. 1877. NRO: ECC 1/766. "Mr. [James] Johnson and myself paid a visit to Shittah, one of the richest Mahommedans in Lagos. He was born at Waterloo, S. Leone, and was baptized as a child; but he is now one of the pillars of Islamism in the Island." Shitta Bey was one of the most important traders in Lagos. (See above, pp. 167–68).

119 See above, pp. 48, 50, and 232.

120 The CMS agents were delighted because "the Native Ex-King Docemu and his suite of Chiefs, all heathens, were present at the Evening service. . . . That was the first Public Christian Service the Ex-King was present at." J. Johnson to Wright, Lagos, 2 Aug. 1876. CMS: CA 2/056.

121 J. Johnson to Wright, Lagos, 2 Aug. 1876. CMS: CA 2/056. The missionaries were proud of their conversion of Meffre, an Ijesha Saro, who had once been "a famous and very popular and influential priest of Ifa, the Oracle of the whole Yoruba Country and had used to divine for Kings and Chiefs and other people of note."

122 *Ibid.*

123 J. Johnson to Wright, Lagos, 2 Aug. 1876. CMS: CA 2/056.

124 Hennessy to Kimberley, Report on the Blue Book of the West African Settlements, Sierra Leone, 31 Dec. 1872. CO 267/317.

125 See above, pp. 156, 240–41. For the Onitsha case, part of the correspondence is in Ussher to Kimberley, 8 April 1880, CO 147/40, and Ussher to Kimberley, 19 July 1880, CO 147/41.

126 William Moore even wrote an explanatory letter to Townsend, in retirement in Exeter, in the hope that the senior missionary could persuade the Parent Committee to change its policy. Townsend replied that there was nothing he could do, even if he agreed, and tried to persuade Moore to change his position. Moore to Townsend, Abeokuta, 4 Dec. 1879, and Townsend to Moore, Exeter, 26 Jan. 1880. CMS: CA 2/085.

127 See, for example, Report of the CMS Lagos Conference on the Manumission of Slaves in Abeokuta, 16–19, 22, 23, March 1880. NRO: ECC 1/765.

128 J. Johnson to Stanhope, Lagos, 4 Jan. 1887. CO 147/62.

129 Testimony of James Johnson, 14 April 1898, before the Commission on Trade, encl. in Denton to Chamberlain, Lagos, 4 June 1898. CO 147/133. J. A. O. Payne, testifying on 7 April, gave the same view, with the difference that in Ijebu country, said Payne, a "slave might redeem himself either by good conduct, or by purchase."

130 Such as Governor Dumaresq, whose "firm conviction [was] that so long

as we Missionaries make the putting away their wives the first condition of admission . . . into the Christian Church, so long will our success amongst them be nil or something not worth speaking about." H. Johnson, Diary entry for 17 Jan. 1877. NRO: ECC 1/766.

131 *Views of some Native Christians of West Africa on the Subject of Polygamy* (Lagos, 1887), p. 5. In the library of J. A. O. Payne. This issue must have been of some concern to Payne, for his library also contains a pamphlet by Thomas John Sawyerr ("Native member of the Legislative Council of Sierra Leone"), *The Sierra Leone Native Church: Two Papers read at the Church Conference held in Freetown . . . January 24, 25, 26, 1888* (Lagos, n.d.). The second paper concerned polygamy and domestic slavery, and expressed the view that there was no conflict between polygamy and Christianity.

132 H. A. Caulrick, in *Views of Some Native Christians . . . on . . . Polygamy*, pp. 12–13. Caulrick was a member of the Board of the United Native African Church in 1894. Payne, *Almanack, 1894*, p. 69.

133 Leader, *Iwe Irohin*, Abeokuta, 1 Dec. 1866, no. 70. *Iwe Irohin* reflected Henry Townsend's views.

134 Maser wrote in 1884 to the Parent Committee about their proposal "to admit natives into the Finance Committee. I was instructed by our Right Reverend Chairman [Bishop Ingham of Sierra Leone] to say that the brethren were not in favour of the measure at present. . . . Revd. James Johnson was considered too much of a partizan to work with Europeans comfortably, and a man like Revd. T. B. Wright would be no acquisition." Maser to Lang, Lagos, 17 March 1884. CMS: G3/A2/O3, no. 76 (1884).

135 For these events in the Niger Mission, see Ajayi, "Christian Missions," pp. 616–26. Bishop Crowther died in Lagos on 31 Dec. 1891 after having a stroke.

136 Record Book of Attendance . . . 1879–85. NRO: ECC 2/1101.

137 Bishop Crowther, Charge delivered to his Clergy, 1869. CMS: CA 3/04, quoted in Ajayi, "Christian Missions," p. 466.

138 Lang to Maser, 10 Aug. 1883, quoting from Parent Committee Minute in *C. M. Intelligencer*, February 1883. NRO: ECC 1/526.

139 Mann to Secretaries, Lagos, 28 Sept. 1883. CMS: G3/A2/02, no. 174 (1883).

140 See below, pp. 257–58.

141 Obadiah Johnson was a brother of Samuel Johnson, and, indeed, edited the *History of the Yorubas* after the death of the author. He served as colonial surgeon in Lagos in the early 1890's. See above, p. 213.

142 See below, p. 267.

143 Notice, Abeokuta, 1 May 1885. G. W. Johnson Papers, Egba Documents.

144 Payne and others, *Views of Some Native Christians . . . on . . . Polygamy*, p. 24.

145 Payne, Fourth preface, *Almanack, 1894*, 31 Aug. 1877, p. 9.

146 J. Johnson to Wigram, Lagos, 25 Aug. 1883. CMS: G3/A2/02, no. 152 (1883).

147 See correspondence relative to the Niger Church Bishopric Question between the Rev. (later Bishop) J. S. Hill and J. A. Otonba Payne, including a petition asking for an African to replace Bishop Crowther, dated 7 Dec. 1892, with 46 signatures, almost all of emigrants. Payne, *Almanack, 1894,* pp. 134–6.

148 T. F. Cole, among others, had contributed to both the CMS Grammar School and the Wesleyan High School. C. B. Macaulay had worked for the CMS before entering the service of the Wesleyans. In his will William Reffle, a Methodist supporter, provided for £1 apiece annually for the CMS and Wesleyan missions for educational purposes (Will of William Reffle, 1872. NRO: ECC 2/1100). J. S. Bucknor, another prominent trader, had both agitated for the Wesleyan High School in 1874 (see p. 336, Chap. 11, *n.* 94) and been on the sub-committee of the CMS building committee in 1880, working to finish the new CMS Collegiate Institute (Sub-committee to Finance Committee, Lagos, 20 Nov. 1880. CMS: G3/A2/01, no. 178 [1880]). In 1881 he was serving on Methodist committee (see below, Chap. 11, *n.* 152).

149 Herbert Macaulay, typescript memoirs, "Missionary Work in Nigeria," dated 16 Sept. 1941.

150 The break came over actions similar to those of the CMS and Methodists in the early 1880's — in this case, the summary dismissal of the Rev. Moses Ladejo Stone, the African pastor of the church, without consulting the congregation. Ajayi, "Christian Missions," p. 613.

151 Herbert Macaulay, typescript memoirs, "Missionary Work in Nigeria," dated 16 Sept. 1941. The conference took place on 14 Aug. 1891, and present were John O. George, N. T. Nelson, J. A. Thompson, George A. Williams, David A. Glouster, John B. Kenny, R. Chase Leigh, Rev. C. W. Cole, W. E. Cole, and the Governor.

152 *Ibid.* The second conference was held on 17 Aug. 1891. The other new supporters were W. N. Macaulay, Z. C. Roberts, C. D. [B.?] Macaulay, D. A. Jones, and E. O. Williams.

153 J. W. Cole, a leading Saro trader, had been an active supporter of the Wesleyan missions since the 1870's. See Miscellaneous Correspondence, Methodist. NRO: ECC 2/1096. He had, with C. J. George, J. S. Leigh, J. J. Thomas, J. L. Baptist, C. B. Macaulay and J. S. Bucknor, been on the short lived Methodist "Committee of Special Business" in 1881. NRO: ECC 2/1041.

154 Herbert Macaulay, typescript memoirs, "Missionary Work in Nigeria," dated 16 Sept. 1941. It is not clear whether Taiwo, the "pure Native Trader" the CMS were so pleased to have converted (see p. 365, Chap. 11, *n.* 87), supported the new church or not. The building was renamed Jehovah Shalom on 10 Sept. 1891.

155 Payne, *Almanack, 1894,* p. 69.

156 The evaluation was clear in the case of the EUBM and the mission Saro. It also emerged among the Ijesha and Ekiti in the 1880's. For further discussion of this point, see below, pp. 268ff.

157 Samuel Johnson and Charles Phillips; see above, p. 197.

CHAPTER 12

1 K. Little, "The Significance of the West African Creole for Africanist and Afro-American Studies," *African Affairs*, XLIX, no. 197 (October, 1950). Little writes, "the term 'cultural agent' is more meaningful . . . than 'cultural intermediary', because it implies what 'intermediary' does not — the possibility of personal interpretation of what is offered or conveyed." Although the Europeans who viewed the Sierra Leonian roles did not envisage "personal interpretation," it was particularly important because of the partial acculturation of the emigrants.

2 Aborigines Protection Society to Carnarvon, 18 June 1874. CO 96/113.

3 Memo. by Hugessen, 20 June 1874. CO 96/113.

4 See above, pp. 22–3.

5 See A. A. B. Aderibigbe, "The Expansion of the Lagos Protectorate, 1861–1900" (Ph.D., London, 1959), pp. 226ff.

6 J. Johnson, in CO 806/357, p. 131, quoted in *ibid.*, p. 231.

7 J. P. Haastrup to "King Owa of Ilesa," Lagos, 7 June 1886, encl. in Haastrup to Moloney, Lagos, 23 July 1886. PP 1887. LX (1), pp. 112–3.

8 Letter to the editor, *Lagos Times*, 13 June 1883, III, 63.

9 There are, of course, some difficulties in using the term nationalism outside the context of a national unit. The "proto-nationalism" here is one early reaction to European domination, which, however, includes the adoption of some western political ideas and institutions in its demands.

10 For the uses of the term "nationalism" in the modern Nigerian context, see J. S. Coleman, *Nigeria. Background to Nationalism* (Berkeley, 1958), pp. 425–6.

11 S. O. Biobaku, *The Egba and Their Neighbours, 1842–1872* (Oxford, 1957), p. 79.

12 H. H. Johnston, "British West Africa and the Trade of the Interior," *Proceedings of the Royal Colonial Institute*, XX (1888–9), 97.

BIBLIOGRAPHY

MANUSCRIPT SOURCES

I. PRIVATE PAPERS

CARR, HENRY. University Library, Ibadan.
These papers contain diaries and small treatises on various philosophical issues.

GLOVER, JOHN HAWLEY. Royal Commonwealth Society Library, London.
Glover's papers are not catalogued but are divided into groups, of which six have pertained to this study, and have, for purposes here, been referred to as Glover, I–VI:

I. Letters, 1861–9. These are primarily copies of Glover's official correspondence, and his communications with indigenous authorities.

II. Miscellaneous official correspondence, 1870.

III. Records of some proceedings of the Lagos Vice-Admiralty Court, 1867.

IV. Correspondence with G. W. Johnson and the *Alake* of Abeokuta, 1871.

V. Personal correspondence, letters received by Glover from Charles D. Turton, Clare's agent in Lagos, 1872.

VI. An analysis, undated, of issues concerning the Colony and the hinterland in 1867.

JOHNSON, G. W. University Library, Ibadan.
Johnson's papers, bought from him by the *Alake* of Abeokuta toward the end of Johnson's life, are part of a collection called "Egba Documents, 1865–1934." They are uncatalogued, but they contain:

1. Letter book, from 1865, with communications between the Lagos Government and the EUBM. This book also contains the oath of allegiance to the EUBM put forward in 1883.

2. Copies of EUBM correspondence, 1867.

3. Correspondence between G. W. Johnson and J. H. Glover in Lagos, and between Johnson and J. Fitzgerald, editor of the *African Times*, in London, 1868–72.

4. Papers on "the misunderstanding between Lagos and Abeokuta," 1872–3.

5. Proposal for the reorganization of the Egba Government, passed by the EUBM on 24 Nov. 1871.

6. Correspondence between Johnson and Lagos officials, 1872–3.

7. Memorandum, signed by *Alake* Oyekon, 31 Jan. 1881, entitling G. W. Johnson to 10 per cent of customs duties collected in Abeokuta.

8. Program of steps to be taken for the reorganization of the Egba Government, 12 Oct. 1881.

9. Correspondence relevant to the investigation of Johnson's expulsion from Abeokuta, 1895.

10. Some personal correspondence: letters from W. Moore to Johnson, and from Johnson's brother in Freetown.

MACAULAY, HERBERT. University Library, Ibadan.

The papers preserved in this collection are primarily relevant to the twentieth-century activities of Macaulay. Macaulay's unpublished memoirs, in typescript, have also been made available by Dr. T. O. Elias.

PAYNE, JOHN A. OTONBA. Orange House, Tinubu Square, Lagos.

Some letters from Payne's contemporaries, such as Victoria Davies, R. B. Blaize, Henry Johnson, remain in his home in Lagos. But more valuable is his collection of books and periodicals, which contain his annotations.

II. PUBLIC RECORD OFFICE, LONDON

CO 96: Gold Coast, Original Correspondence, 1874–86.
CO 147: Lagos, Original Correspondence, 1861–98.
CO 150: Lagos, Government Gazettes, 1881–90.
CO 151: Lagos, Blue Books, 1862–90.
CO 267: Sierra Leone, Original Correspondence, 1833–74.
CO 272: Sierra Leone, Blue Books, 1835–45.
CO 442: Statistical Tables, Colonial, 1860–90.
CO 806: Africa, Confidential Prints, 1876–93.
FO 2: Consular Correspondence, 1849–63.
FO 84: Slave Trade, Consular Correspondence, West Africa, 1849–72.
FO 403: Africa and Slave Trade, Confidential Prints.

III. CHURCH MISSIONARY SOCIETY, LONDON

CA 1/L: West African Mission (Sierra Leone), Letter books from Home Secretaries to Missionaries, 1820–54 and 1865–83.

CA 1/0215: Letters and papers of Henry Townsend, including Journal . . . while on Mission of Research to Badagry and Abeokuta, 1842–3.

CA 2/L: Yoruba Mission, Letter books from Home Secretaries to Missionaries, 1844–80.

CA 2/01–017: Minutes and correspondence of official bodies of the Yoruba Mission, 1844–80.

CA 2/018–098: Letters and papers of individual missionaries, to 1879.

After 1880 correspondence was no longer separated into files of individual missionaries and was instead arranged chronologically:

G3/A2: Yoruba Mission, correspondence from missionaries, 1880–92.

IV. METHODIST MISSIONARY SOCIETY, LONDON

Correspondence from missionaries on West Coast of Africa, Boxes 1, 2–4, 1877–1902.

Also typescript of untitled book, completed about 1885, by Thomas Birch

Freeman, on his travels in West Africa. The section on Abeokuta was written about 1860.

V. NIGERIAN RECORD OFFICE, IBADAN

The relevant papers in the Nigeria archives are divided into five classifications. The government despatches, largely duplicates of correspondence to be found at the Public Record Office in London, bear the serial prefix "CSO" (Chief Secretary's Office). The records of the missionary societies are separated into those of the CMS ("ECC 1") and those of the Methodist Missionary Society ("ECC 2"). The official papers from Badagry are catalogued as "BadaDis," and the letter and minute books from Badagry and Leckie are in a series entitled "LagLand."

Detailed citations to some of the documents used in this study appear in the notes.

VI. LANDS OFFICE, LAGOS

Crown Grants, from 12 June 1863 to the present. Vols. I–XV are relevant.
Deeds of Conveyance, Mortagage, etc., from February 1862 to the present. The first series, vols. I–XXXV, are relevant.

VII. GHANA NATIONAL ARCHIVES, ACCRA

SC 4/33–154. T. B. Freeman papers, especially SC 4/82–6, containing correspondence in 1853 between E. A. Gardiner in Lagos and Freeman in the Gold Coast.

VIII. SIERRA LEONE ARCHIVES, FREETOWN

The papers in the Sierra Leone archives have been classified but not catalogued.
Statement of Disposal (of Liberated Africans), 1821–33.
Liberated African Department Letter Books, vols. I–VIII, 1820–47.
Registers of Liberated Africans, vols. I–XV, 1808–48.

IX. ABORIGINES PROTECTION SOCIETY PAPERS AND ANTI-SLAVERY SOCIETY PAPERS, RHODES HOUSE LIBRARY, OXFORD

MSS. Brit. Emp. S–22. The pertinent papers are in section G, 1–35: nineteenth-century documents concerned with Africa.

Published Primary Sources

I. PARLIAMENTARY PAPERS

Parliamentary Papers, from 1842 to 1895, are referred to as PP, with the volume number and the printed page number following.

II. OTHER OFFICIAL PUBLICATIONS AND DOCUMENTS.

Colonial Office Lists. London, 1861–1890.

Donnan, Elizabeth. *Documents Illustrative of the History of the Slave Trade to America.* 4 vols. (Publn. no. 409) Washington, D.C., Carnegie Institution, 1930–5.
Nigeria Law Reports, vol. I, 1881–1911.

III. NEWSPAPERS

The Anglo-African, Lagos, 1863–5, vols. I–III.
The Eagle and Lagos Critic, Lagos, 1883–8, vols. I–VI.
The Friend of Africa (continued as *The Friend of the African; The Friend of the Africans*), London, 1841–3, vols. I–III.
Iwe Irohin, Abeokuta, 1860–7.
The Lagos Observer, Lagos, 1882–8, vols. I–VII.
The Lagos Times and Gold Coast Colony Advertiser, Lagos, 1880–3, vols. I–III.
The Mirror, Lagos, 1887–8, vol. I.

PUBLISHED SECONDARY SOURCES

Abraham, R. C. *Dictionary of Modern Yoruba.* London, University of London Press, Ltd., 1958.
Adams, John. *Sketches taken during Ten Voyages to Africa, between the years 1786 and 1800; including observations on the country between Cape Palmas and the River Congo; and cursory remarks on the physical and moral character of the inhabitants; with an Appendix, containing an account of the European trade with the West Coast of Africa.* London, Hurst, Robinson, and Co., n.d.
Adderley, Sir C. B. *Review of "The Colonial Policy of Lord J. Russell's Administration," by Earl Grey, 1853; and of Subsequent Colonial History.* London, Edward Stanford, 1869.
Ajayi, J. F. A. "Henry Venn and the Policy of Development," *Journal of the Historical Society of Nigeria*, I, 4 (Dec., 1959).
Ajisafe, Ajayi Kolawole. *History of Abeokuta.* Bungay, Suffolk, Richard Clay and Son, Ltd., 1924.
Akintan, E. A. *The Closing Scene of the Eleko Case and the Return of Prince Eshugbayi Eleko.* Lagos, Tika-Tore Press, n.d.
Alldridge, Thomas J. *A Transformed Colony. Sierra Leone as it was and as it is.* London, Seeley and Co., 1910.
Banton, Michael. *West African City: A Study of Tribal Life in Freetown.* London, Oxford Univ. Press, 1957.
Barbot, John. *A Description of the Coasts of North and South-Guinea . . . .* [London], 1732.
Bascom, William R. "Les Premiers Fondements Historiques de l'Urbanisme Yoruba." *Présence Africaine*, XXIII, n.s. (Dec., 1958–Jan., 1959).
———. "The Principle of Seniority in the Social Structure of the Yoruba." *American Anthropologist*, XLIV 1 (Jan.–March, 1942).

Bascom, William R. "Social Status, Wealth and Individual Difference among the Yoruba." *American Anthropologist*, LIII, 4 (Oct.–Dec., 1951).

————. *The Sociological Role of the Yoruba Cult Group.* Memoir Series of the American Anthropological Association, no. 63, *American Anthropologist*, XLVI, n.s., no. 1, part 2 (Jan., 1944).

————. "Urbanization among the Yoruba." *The American Journal of Sociology*, LX, 5 (March, 1955).

Bauer, P. T. *West African Trade, A Study of Competition, Oligopoly and Monopoly in a Changing Economy.* Cambridge, Cambridge Univ. Press, 1954.

Biobaku, Saburi O. *The Egba and their Neighbours, 1842–1872.* Oxford, Clarendon Press, 1957.

————. "An Historical Sketch of Egba Traditional Authorities." *Africa*, XXII, 1 (January, 1952).

————. *Lugard Lectures, 1955.* [Lagos], Federal Information Service, [1955].

Blyden, E. W. *African Life and Customs.* London, Phillips, 1908.

————. *Christianity, Islam, and the Negro Race.* London, W. B. Whittingham and Co., 1889.

————. *West Africa Before Europe, and other addresses, delivered in England in 1900 and 1903 . . . .* London, Phillips, 1905.

Bosman, William (Dutch chief factor at Elmina). *A New and Accurate Description of the Coast of Guinea, Divided into the Gold, the Slave, and the Ivory Coasts . . . .* London, 1705. In John Pinkerton. *A General Collection of the Best and Most Interesting Voyages and Travels in all Parts of the World.* Vol. XVI. London, Longman, Hurst, Rees, Orme, and Brown, 1814.

Bowen, T. J. *Adventures and Missionary Labors in Several Countries in the Interior of Africa, from 1849 to 1856.* New York, Sheldon, Blakeman and Company, 1857.

————. *Grammar and Dictionary of the Yoruba Language, with an Introductory Description of the Country and People of Yoruba.* New York, Smithsonian Institution, 1858.

Buell, Raymond Leslie. *The Native Problem in Africa.* New York, The Macmillan Company, 1928.

Burns, A. C. *History of Nigeria.* 5th ed., rev. London, George Allen & Unwin, Ltd., 1955.

Burton, Richard F., *Abeokuta and the Camaroons Mountains. An Exploration.* 2 vols. London, Tinsley Brothers, 1863.

————. *A Mission to Gelele, King of Dahomey.* 2nd ed., 2 vols. London, Tinsley Brothers, 1864.

————. *Wanderings in West Africa from Liverpool to Fernando Po.* 2 vols. London, Tinsley Bros., 1863.

Butt-Thompson, Frederick W. *The First Generation of Sierra Leonians.* Freetown, Government Printer, 1952.

————. *Sierra Leone in History and Tradition.* London, H. F. & G. Witherby, 1926.

Buxton, Thomas Fowell. *The African Slave Trade and its Remedy.* 2nd ed London, John Murray, 1840.

————. *Memoirs of Sir Thomas Fowell Buxton.* Ed. by Charles Buxton London, J. M. Dent and Sons, n.d.

Buxton, T. F. V., "The Creole in West Africa," *Journal of the African Society*, XII, 48 (July 1, 1913).

Cambridge History of the British Empire. Vol. II. *The Growth of the New Empire.* Ed. by J. Holland Rose, A. P. Newton, E. A. Benians. Cambridge, Cambridge Univ. Press, 1940.

————. vol. III. *The Empire — Commonwealth, 1870–1919.* Ed. by E. A. Benians, James Butler, C. E. Carrington. Cambridge, Cambridge Univ. Press, 1959.

Campbell, Robert, *A Pilgrimage to my Motherland: An Account of a Journey among the Egbas and Yorubas of Central Africa, in 1859–60.* New York, Thomas Hamilton, 1861.

Carter, Sir Gilbert. "The Colony of Lagos." *Proceedings of the Royal Colonial Institute*, XXVIII (1896–7).

Clarke, John. *Specimens of Dialects: Short Vocabularies of Languages: and Notes of Countries and Customs in Africa.* Berwick-upon-Tweed, Daniel Cameron, 1848.

Claude, George. *The Rise of British West Africa.* London, Houlston & Sons, 1904.

Coker, Increase. *Seventy Years of the Nigerian Press.* [Lagos], *Lagos Daily Times*, n.d.

Cole, William. *Life in the Niger, or the Journal of an African Trader.* London, Saunders, Otley and Co., 1862.

Coleman, James S. *Nigeria. Background to Nationalism.* Berkeley, Univ. of Calif. Press, 1958.

Coupland, R. *The British Anti-Slavery Movement.* London, Thornton Butterworth, Ltd., 1933.

Crocker, W. R. *Nigeria. A Critique of British Colonial Administration.* London, George Allen & Unwin, Ltd., 1936.

Crooks, Major J. J. *A History of the Colony of Sierra Leone, West Africa.* London, Simpkin, Marshall, Hamilton, Kent & Co., Ltd., 1903.

Crowther, Rev. Samuel. *Journal of an Expedition up the Niger and Tshadda Rivers, Undertaken by MacGregor Laird, Esq., in Connection with the British Government, in 1854.* London, Church Missionary House, 1855.

Crowther, Samuel, and the Rev. James Frederick Schön. *Journals of the Rev. James Frederick Schön and Mr. Samuel Crowther, who, with the Sanction of Her Majesty's Government, accompanied the Expedition up the Niger in 1841, in behalf of the Church Missionary Society.* London, Hotchard and Son, 1842.

Cruikshank, Brodie. *Eighteen Years on the Gold Coast of Africa.* London, Hurst and Blackett, 1853.

Dalzel, Archibald. *A History of Dahomy, an Inland Kingdom of Africa; compiled from authentic memoirs, with introduction and notes.* London, T. Spilsbury & Son, 1793.

Dapper, O. *Umbständliche und Eigentliche Beschreibung von Africa, und Denen Darzu Gehörigen Königreichen und Landschaften* . . . Amsterdam, Jacob von Meurs, 1670.

Davies, K. G. *The Royal African Company.* London, Longmans, Green & Co., 1957.

Delany, M. R. *Official Report of the Niger Valley Exploring Party.* New York, Thomas Hamilton, 1861.

Destruction of Lagos, The. 2nd ed. London, James Ridgeway, 1852.

Dictionary of the Yoruba Language, A. 2nd ed. London, Oxford Univ. Press, 1937.

Diké, K. O. (ed.). *Eminent Nigerians.* Cambridge, Cambridge Univ. Press, 1960.

————. *Trade and Politics in the Niger Delta, 1830-1885. An Introduction to the Economic and Political History of Nigeria.* Oxford, Clarendon Press, 1956.

Duncan, John. *Travels in Western Africa, in 1845 and 1846, comprising a journey from Whydah, through the Kingdom of Dahomey, to Adofoodia, in the interior.* 2 vols. London, Richard Bentley, 1847.

Egharevba, Jacob U. *A Short History of Benin.* 2nd ed., rev. and enlarged. Benin, Privately Published, 1953.

Elias, T. Olawale. *Groundwork of Nigerian Law.* London, Routledge & Kegan Paul Ltd., 1954.

————. "Makers of Nigerian Law," reprinted from *West Africa* (Nov. 19, 1955–July 7, 1956). London, Hazell Watson & Viney, Ltd., n.d.

Ellis, A. B. *The Yoruba-Speaking Peoples of the Slave Coast of West Africa. Their Religion, Manners, Customs, Laws, Language, etc.* London, Chapman and Hall, Ltd., 1894.

Fage, J. D. *An Atlas of African History.* [London], Edward Arnold, Ltd., 1958.

————. *An Introduction to the History of West Africa.* Cambridge, Cambridge Univ. Press, 1955.

Falconbridge, Alexander. *An Account of the Slave Trade on the Coast of Africa.* London, J. Phillips, 1788.

Fergusson, William. *A Letter to Thomas Fowell Buxton . . . on the Character of the Liberated Africans at Sierra Leone, and on the Cultivation of Cotton in that Colony and its Vicinity.* London, printed for private circulation by Green and Co., 1839.

Flint, John E. *Sir George Goldie and the Making of Nigeria.* London, Oxford Univ. Press, 1960.

Forde, Daryll. *The Yoruba-Speaking Peoples of South-Western Nigeria.* London, International African Institute, 1951.

Fox, William. *A Brief History of the Wesleyan Missions on the Western Coast of Africa: including Biographical Sketches of all the missionaries who have died in that important field of labour. With some account of the European settlements, and of the slave trade.* London, Aylott and Jones, 1851.

Freyre, Gilberto. *The Masters and the Slaves.* Translated from the Portuguese by Samuel Putnam. New York, Alfred A. Knopf, 1946.

Fyfe, C. H. "European and Creole Influence in the Hinterland of Sierra Leone before 1896." *Sierra Leone Studies,* N.S., no. 6 (June, 1956).

————. *A History of Sierra Leone.* [London], Oxford Univ. Press, 1962.

Geary, Sir William Nevill M. *Nigeria under British Rule.* London, Methuen & Co. Ltd., 1927.

Glover, Lady [Elizabeth]. *Life of Sir John Hawley Glover.* Ed. by Sir Richard Temple. London, Smith, Elder, and Co., 1897.

Goddard, T. N. *The Handbook of Sierra Leone.* London, Grant Richards, 1925.

Greenberg, Joseph H. *Studies in African Linguistic Classification.* New Haven, Compass Publishing Company, 1955.

Groves, C. P. *The Planting of Christianity in Africa.* 4 vols. London, Lutterworth Press, 1948–54.

Hair, P. E. N. "An Analysis of the Register of Fourah Bay College, 1827–1950," *Sierra Leone Studies,* N.S., no. 7 (Dec., 1956).

Hancock, W. K. *Survey of British Commonwealth Affairs.* 2 vols. Vol. II, part 2. *Problems of Economic Policy. 1918–1939.* London, Oxford Univ. Press, 1942.

Hargreaves, J. D. *A Life of Sir Samuel Lewis.* London, Oxford Univ. Press, 1958.

Herskovits, Melville J. *Dahomey: An Ancient West African Kingdom.* 2 vols. New York, J. J. Augustin, 1938.

————. *The Myth of the Negro Past.* 2nd ed. Boston, Beacon Press, 1958.

Hertslet, Sir Edward. *The Map of Africa by Treaty.* London, H.M.S.O., 1894.

Hieke, Ernst. *G. L. Gaiser, Hamburg, West Afrika.* Hamburg, Hoffman und Campe Verlag, 1949.

————. *Zur Geschichte des Deutschen Handels mit Ostafrika.* Vol. I. *Wm. O'Swald & Co., 1831–1870.* 1 vol. Christians, Hamburg, 1939.

Hinderer, Anna. *Seventeen Years in the Yoruba Country.* London, The Religious Tract Society, 1872.

Hoare, Prince. *Memoirs of Granville Sharp, Esq. composed from his own Manuscripts, and other authentic documents in the possession of his family and of the African Institution.* London, Henry Colburn & Co., 1820.

Hogben, S. J. *The Muhammadan Emirates of Nigeria.* London, Oxford Univ. Press, 1930.

[Holt, John]. *The Diary of John Holt with the Voyage of the "Maria."* Ed. by Cecil R. Holt. Liverpool, Henry Young & Sons, Ltd., 1948.

Hutchinson, Thomas J. *Impressions of Western Africa with remarks on the diseases of the climate and a report on the peculiarities of trade up the* *rivers in the Bight of Biafra.* London, Longman, Brown, Green, Longman & Roberts, 1858.

Hutchinson, Thomas J. *Ten Years Wandering Among the Ethiopians.* London, Hurst and Blackett, 1861.

Ingham, the Rt. Rev. E. G. *Sierra Leone After a Hundred Years.* London, Seeley & Co., Ltd., 1894.

Johnson, Hon. Dr. O. "Lagos Past." Duplication of a paper read before the Lagos Institute, 20 Nov. 1901.

Johnson, Samuel. *History of the Yorubas, from the Earliest Times to the Beginning of the British Protectorate.* Ed. by O. Johnson. London, George Routledge & Sons, Ltd., 1921.

Johnston, H. H. "British West Africa and the Trade of the Interior." *Proceedings of the Royal Colonial Institute,* XX (1888–89).

Kidder, Rev. D. P. and the Rev. J. C. Fletcher. *Brazil and the Brazilians, portrayed in historical and descriptive sketches.* Philadelphia, Childs & Peterson, 1857.

Kingsley, Mary. *West African Studies.* London, MacMillan & Co., 1899.

Koelle, S. W. *Polyglotta Africana; or a Comparative Vocabulary of nearly three hundred words and phrases, in more than one hundred distinct African languages.* London, Church Missionary House, Salisbury Square, 1854.

Kuczynski, R. R. *Demographic Survey of the British Colonial Empire.* 3 vols. Vol. I. *West Africa.* London, Oxford Univ. Press, 1948.

———. *Colonial Population.* London, Oxford Univ. Press, 1937.

Laird, MacGregor and R. A. K. Oldfield. *Narrative of an Expedition into the Interior of Africa, by the River Niger, in the steam-vessels Quorra and Alburkah, in 1832, 1833, and 1834.* 2 vols. London, Richard Bentley, 1837.

Laotan, A. B. *The Torch Bearers or Old Brazilian Colony in Lagos.* Lagos, Ife-Olu Printing Works, [1943].

Leroy-Beaulieu, Paul. *De La Colonisation Chez Les Peuples Modernes.* 5th ed. Paris, Guillaumin et Cie., 1902.

Lewis, Roy. *Sierra Leone, A Modern Portrait.* London, H.M.S.O., 1954.

Little, K. L. *The Mende of Sierra Leone.* London, Routledge & Kegan Paul, 1951.

———. "The Significance of the West African Creole for Africanist and Afro-American Studies." *African Affairs,* XLIX, 197 (Oct., 1950).

Lloyd, Christopher. *The Navy and the Slave Trade. The Supression of the African Slave Trade in the Nineteenth Century.* London, Longmans, Green and Co., 1949.

Lloyd, P. C. "The Traditional Political System of the Yoruba." *Southwestern Journal of Anthropology,* X, 4 (Winter, 1954).

———. *Yoruba Land Law.* London, Oxford Univ. Press, 1962.

Losi, John B. *History of Lagos.* Lagos, Tika-Tore Printing Works, 1914.

Lukach, Harry Charles. *A Bibliography of Sierra Leone, with an introductory essay on the origin, character, and peoples of the Colony.* Oxford, Clarendon Press, 1910.

Macaulay, Herbert. *Justitia Fiat: The Moral Obligation of the British Government to the House of King Docemo of Lagos. An Open Letter.* n.p., 1921.

Mathieson, W. L. *Great Britain and the Slave Trade, 1839–1865.* London, Longmans, Green and Co., 1929.

Mayer, Brantz. *Captain Canot; or Twenty Years of an African Slaver. Being an account of his career and adventures on the coast, in the interior, on shipboard, and in the West Indies. Written out and edited from the Captain's Journals, Memoranda and Conversations.* New York, D. Appleton and Company, 1854.

Nigeria Handbook, Containing Statistical and General Information Respecting the Colony and Protectorate, The. 11th ed. London, West Africa Publicity, Ltd., 1936.

Ordinances and Orders and Rules Thereunder, in Force in the Colony of Lagos on April 30th, 1901: With an Appendix Containing the Letters Patent Constituting the Colony, and the Instructions Accompanying them; Various Acts of Parliament; Orders of the Queen in Council; Treaties and Proclamations. 2 vols. Comp. by Edwin Arney Speed. London, Stevens and Sons, Limited, 1902.

Page, Jesse. *Samuel Crowther, The Slave Boy of the Niger.* London, Pickering and Inglis, n.d.

Parrinder, Geoffrey. *Religion in an African City.* London, Oxford Univ. Press, 1953.

————. *The Story of Ketu, An Ancient Yoruba Kingdom.* Ibadan, Ibadan University Press, 1956.

————. *West African Religion. Illustrated from the Beliefs and Practices of the Yoruba, Ewe, Akan, and Kindred Peoples.* London, the Epworth Press, 1949.

[Payne, J. A. O.]. *Payne's Lagos and West African Almanack and Diary for 1887.* London, T. G. Johnson, 1887.

————. *Payne's Lagos and West African Almanack and Diary for 1894.* London, J. S. Phillips, 1894.

Perham, Margery. *Native Administration in Nigeria.* London, Oxford Univ. Press, 1937.

Pierson, Donald. *Negroes in Brazil, A Study of Race Contact at Bahia.* Chicago, Univ. of Chicago Press, 1942.

Ramos, Arthur. *The Negro in Brazil.* Translated from the Portuguese by Richard Pattee. Washington, The Associated Publishers Inc., 1939.

Rankin, F. Harrison. *The White Man's Grave: A Visit to Sierra Leone, in 1834.* 2 vols. London, Richard Bentley, 1836.

Red Book of West Africa, The. London, W. H. & L. Collingridge, 1920.

Ribeiro, René. *Cultos Afrobrasileiros do Recife: un Estudo de Adjustamento Social.* [Recife, Brazil], Boletim do Instituto Joaquim Nabuco, 1952.

Rodrigues, Nina. *Os Africanos no Brasil*. Rev. by Homero Pires. São Paulo, Bibliotheca Pedagogica Brasileira (Serie 5, vol. 9), 1932.

Ryder, A. F. C. "The Re-establishment of Portuguese Factories on the Costa da Mina to the Mid Eighteenth Century." *Journal of the Historical Society of Nigeria*, I, 3 (Dec., 1958).

Sawyerr, Thomas John. *The Sierra Leone Native Church: 2 Papers read at the Church Conference held in Freetown, Sierra Leone . . . January, 24–6, 1888*. Lagos, T. A. King & Company, n.d.

Schramm, Percy Ernst. *Deutschland und Übersee*. Braunschweig, Georg Westermann Verlag, 1950.

Simpson, S. Rowton. *A Report on the Registration of Title to Land in the Federal Territory of Lagos*. Lagos, Federal Government Printer, 1957.

Snelgrave, Captain William. *A New Account of Some Parts of Guinea, and the Slave-Trade . . . .* London, James, John and Paul Knapton, 1734.

Stock, Eugene. *The History of the Church Missionary Society, its Environment, its Men, and its work*. 3 vols. London, Church Missionary Society, 1899.

Stone, Rev. R. H. *In Afric's Forest and Jungle, or Six Years Among the Yorubans*. New York, Fleming H. Revell Company, 1899.

Talbot, P. Amaury. *The Peoples of Southern Nigeria*. 4 vols. London: Humphrey Milford, 1926.

Tardits, Claude. *Porto-Novo, Les Nouvelles Générations Africaines Entre Leurs Traditions et L'Occident*. Paris, Mouton & Co., 1958.

Tew, Sir Mervyn L. *Report on Title to Land in Lagos. Together with the Report of a Committee set up to advise the Governor in regard thereto, and Draft Legislation to give effect to certain Recommendations contained therein, 1939*. Lagos, Government Printer, 1947.

Thomas, Isaac B. *Life History of Herbert Macaulay*, 3rd ed. [Lagos, 1946].

Thompson, T. J. *The Jubilee and Centenary Volume of Fourah Bay College, Freetown, Sierra Leone*. Freetown, The Elsiemay Printing Works, 1930.

Townsend, Henry [?]. *Memoirs of Henry Townsend*. n.p., 1887.

Travels of Richard and John Lander, into the Interior of Africa, for the Discovery of the Course of the River Niger, from unpublished documents in in the possession of the late Captn. John William Barber Fullerton employed in the African Service, The. 2 vols. Comp. by Robert Huish. London, J. Saunders, 1835–6.

Tucker, Miss [Sarah]. *Abbeokuta; or Sunrise Within the Tropics: An Outline of the Origin and Progress of the Yoruba Mission*. 2nd ed. London, James Nisbet and Co., 1853.

Turner, Lorenzo D. "African Survivals in the New World with Special Emphasis on the Arts." *Africa from the Point of View of American Negro Scholars*. [Paris], *Présence Africaine*, [1959].

———. "Some Contacts of Brazilian Ex-Slaves with Nigeria, West Africa." *Journal of Negro History*, XXVII, 1 (Jan., 1942).

Verger, Pierre. "Influence du Bresil au Golfe du Benin," *Les Afro-Americains.* Memoir no. 27. Dakar, IFAN, 1953.

————. *Notes sur le Culte des Orisa et Vodu a Bahia . . . au Bresil et a l'Ancienne Côte des Esclaves en Afrique.* Memoir no. 51. Dakar, IFAN, 1957.

Views of Some Native Christians of West Africa, on the Subject of Polygamy, etc. Lagos, General Printing Press, December, 1887.

Walker, Rev. Samuel Abraham. *Missions in Western Africa, among the Soosoos, Bulloms, &c. . . .* Dublin, William Curry, Jun. and Company, 1845.

Whitford, J., *Trading Life in West and Central Africa.* Liverpool, The "Porcupine" Office, 1877.

Wood, Rev. J. Buckley. *Historical Notices of Lagos, West Africa, and on the inhabitants of Lagos: their character, pursuits, and languages.* 2nd ed. Lagos, Church Missionary Society, 1933.

UNPUBLISHED THESES

Aderibigbe, A. A. B. "The Expansion of the Lagos Protectorate, 1861–1900." Ph.D., London, 1959.

Ajayi, J. F. Ade. "Christian Missions and the making of Nigeria, 1841–1891." Ph.D., London, 1958.

Gertzel, Cherry J. "Imperial Policy towards the British Settlements in West Africa, 1860–1875. B.Litt., Oxon., 1953.

————. "John Holt: A British Merchant in West Africa in the Era of Imperialism." D. Phil., Oxon., 1959.

Lloyd, P. C. "Local Government in Yoruba Towns. An Analysis of the roles of the Obas, Chiefs, and the elected councillors." D. Phil., Oxon., 1958.

Madden, A. F. "The Attitude of the Evangelicals to the Empire and Imperial Problems, 1820–1850." D. Phil., Oxon., 1950.

Ogunsulire, Omotayo. "The History of Fourah Bay College and its Influence in West Africa from the Foundation to the Elliot Commission, 1943." Dip. Ed., Durham University, n.d.

Stilliard, N. H. "The Rise and Development of Legitimate Trade in Palm Oil with West Africa." M.A., Birmingham, 1938.

INDEX

The names of Sierra Leonians and Brazilians are in SMALL CAPITALS.

Abbeokutan Mercantile Association. *See* Associations, Sierra Leonian

Abeokuta: founding of, 17; emigrants in, 48, 78, 79, 116, 178–86; hostility toward missions, 59; and Dahomey, 72, 321*n78*; agreements with British, 80, 145, 162; *Alake* of, 118, 119, 125, 126, 144, 145, 178, 182, 183, 184, 185, 186, 188, 334, 347, 354; traditional authority in, 140–41; conflict with Ibadan, 159–60; trade of, 171–72. *See also* Egba; *Ifole*; *Ogboni*; *Parakoyi*

Aborigines Protection Society, 264–65

ABREV, JOAQUIN. *See* D'ABREU, JOACHIM

Adams, Capt. John: quoted, 14; cited, 308

ADAMS, THOMAS B.: and CMS school fund, 363*n43*

Adderley, Sir Charles B.: 149, 150, 203; cited, 337, 339

Adele (*Oba* of Lagos), 64

Ademola (*Alake* of Abeokuta), 182, 183

Aderibigbe, A.A.B.: cited, 338, 339, 341, 352, 371

Ado (Addo): treaty of with British, 147

African Commercial Association. *See* Associations, Sierra Leonian

Agreements: trade, with Akitoye, 94; trade, with Dosunmu, 107; British and Abeokuta, 145; British and Epe, 147; signers of, Brazilians on trade, 324*n30*; merchants and Dosunmu, 326*n74*. *See also* Treaties

Ajasa, Sir Kitoye, 226

Ajayi, J. F. A.: quoted, 235; cited, 312, 317, 320, 333, 343, 346, 361, 362, 363, 364, 365, 369

Ajisafe, A. K.: cited, 313, 348, 349

Akintan, E. A.: cited, 346

Akitoye (*Oba* of Lagos): and *Oba*ship, 44–45, 66; position of in Badagry, 73–74; view of British aid, 73–74; signs treaty with British, 79; returns to Lagos, 80; death of, 82; mentioned, 141, 270

Akitoye-Kosoko conflict. *See* Lagos, politics of

Aku: derivation of, 309*n35*. *See also* Sierra Leonians

Alake of Abeokuta. See Abeokuta, *Alake* of

ALLEN, WILLIAM: biographical sketch of, 283; in Abeokuta for CMS, 233

ALLEN, WILLIAM STEPHEN: in Ibadan for CMS, 234

Amaro: meaning of, 87. *See also* Brazilians

Anglo-African, The (newspaper), 216, 347*n15*

Annear, Samuel (Methodist missionary), 53, 69, 75

Apprenticeship system, Sierra Leone, 26

Arakanga War, 46

Associations, Sierra Leonian: Abbeokutan Mercantile, 102–03, 113, 144–45, 334*n27*, 335*n45*; Abbeokuta Road Improving Society, 113, 328*n12*; Young Men's Benevolent, 113, 328*n12*; Abeokuta Commercial, 180, 194–95; 352 *n116*; Sierra Leone, 194; Yoruba National, 195, 352*n117*; Atijere Utilization Company, 195; Ijesha, 195; Lagos *Ekiti Parapo* Society, 195, 196; To further interests of Christianity and Education in Lagos (CMS), 237, 239; Auxiliary Pastorate (CMS), 239; Lagos Native Pastorate Auxiliary (CMS), 248

AUSTIN, L. S.: signs testimonial to Gollmer, 331*n73*

Awujale of Ijebu Ode. *See* Ijebu Ode, *Awujale* of

DATE DUE			
MAY 0 2 2005			